Presidential Lightning Rods

STUDIES IN GOVERNMENT AND PUBLIC POLICY

Presidential Lightning Rods
The Politics of Blame Avoidance

Richard J. Ellis

University Press of Kansas

To the memory of
Aaron Wildavsky

E

/ ?6. /

E 46

/ 994

© 1994 by the University Press of Kansas
All rights reserved

Published by the University Press of Kansas (Lawrence, Kansas 66049), which was organized by the Kansas Board of Regents and is operated and funded by Emporia State University, Fort Hays State University, Kansas State University, Pittsburg State University, the University of Kansas, and Wichita State University

Library of Congress Cataloging-in-Publication Data

Ellis, Richard (Richard J.)
    Presidential lightning rods : the politics of blame avoidance /
Richard J. Ellis.
    p.   cm.
    Includes index.
    ISBN 0-7006-0636-X
    1. Presidents—United States—History—20th century.
2. Responsibility—Political aspects—United States—History—20th
century.   3. Political ethics—United States—History—20th century.
4. Blame—Political aspects—United States—History—20th century.
5. Cabinet officers—United States—History—20th century.
6. Presidents—United States—Staff—History—20th century.
7. United States—Politics and government—1945-1989.   I. Title.
E176.1.E46   1994
973'.099—dc20   94-12007

British Library Cataloguing in Publication Data is available.
Printed in the United States of America
10 9 8 7 6 5 4 3 2 1

The paper used in this publication meets the minimum requirements of the American National Standard for Permanence of Paper for Printed Library Materials Z39.48-1984.

Contents

Acknowledgments

This book has been a number of years in the making, and my debts are many. It started off life as a dissertation at the University of California Berkeley. All the members of my committee, Aaron Wildavsky, Arnold Meltsner, Nelson Polsby, and Michael Rogin, were encouraging at a stage when it would have been easy to be dismissive. The Institute of Government Studies at Berkeley helped me greatly at this early stage with both an office and funds for the acquisition of data from the Roper Center.

My greatest debt is to Aaron Wildavsky, who continuously prodded me to turn the dissertation into a book when I wanted nothing so much as to bury it as an unsightly reminder of youthful indiscretion. Aaron's unshakable conviction that lightning rods were a wonderful subject sustained me through several periods of self-doubt. He also played a particularly important role in persuading me to add a chapter on chiefs of staff as well as in feeding me a steady stream of relevant news clippings.

Willamette University, where I have spent the last three years, has provided me with a wonderfully supportive environment in which to carry on this as well as other work. Although ostensibly not a research institution, or so others tell me, the Willamette community has provided almost everything I could ask for in terms of financial and emotional support. I am particularly thankful to Willamette's Dean of Liberal Arts, Julie Carson, who has been unflagging in her encouragement and help. I am also grateful for a summer grant funded by Willamette University's Atkinson program that facilitated the completion of this book. Among the Willamette students who have ably assisted me on this project are Ryan Petersen, Julian Snow, Duane Bales, Karen Filipovich, Nicole Hendricks, Lisa Johnson, Steve Kirk, Erik Kupka, Lani Parr, and Julie Webster.

This book owes a tremendous amount to the two reviewers for the University Press of Kansas, John Burke and Joseph Pika, whose critical yet supportive comments pushed me to revise and to explain at a point when I would have much preferred to leave bad enough alone. The shape (and size) of the conclusion, in particular, owes a great deal to their counsel. Chapters 5 and 7 also are much stronger for their advice and criticism. Also of help to me was the judicious hand of the press's director, Fred Woodward.

I am also grateful to those who provided me with important data along the way, including George Edwards, Robert Lichter, Stephen Bennett, and Patricia Luevano of the Center for Political Studies. Sarah Norman of the Miller Publishing Company kindly provided opinion polls relating to the secretaries of agriculture. Most valuable of all was the assistance of John Benson and Lois E. Timms-Ferrara of the Roper Center, who conducted much of the statistical analysis reported in this book.

A number of scholars were kind enough to take time to respond to my inquiries—among these were Bruce Buchanan, Richard Fenno, Stephen Hess, Glenn Parker, Michael Robinson, Richard Rose, James Rosenau, Stephen Wayne, and James Sterling Young. I also benefited from communication with Herbert Brownell, Orval Faubus, and Sierra Club president Phillip Berry. Suggestions along the way by Richard Neustadt and Paul Peterson helped alert me to deficiencies or ambiguities in the argument that I have tried to remedy.

The staff at the Eisenhower Library was enormously helpful in assisting me to make good use of my all-too-short time there. I also received prompt and helpful assistance from the University of Virginia Library.

Finally, I would like to single out for thanks Fred Greenstein. I am indebted to Professor Greenstein not only for his interest and helpful advice in the later stages of this project but also for having written the book that provided so much of the inspiration for this one. *The Hidden-Hand Presidency,* in my view, is not only the best book on the Eisenhower presidency but is perhaps the most significant work on any presidency. If I have fallen well short of such an exacting model of scholarship, that model nonetheless deserves a large amount of credit for whatever virtues this book may possess.

1

The Lore of Lightning Rods

Criticism, Harry Truman once said, "is something [a president] gets every day, just like breakfast."[1] Few people, if any, who have occupied that high office would disagree with Truman's judgment (although not all would be as sanguine about receiving their daily diet). Given that it is criticism rather than deference that usually goes with the office, some commentators have suggested that it behooves a president to position members of his administration on the front lines to absorb blame for unpopular policies.[2] Presidential advisers might thereby function as "lightning rods," deflecting criticism away from the president and onto themselves.

The idea, and practice, of advisers serving as lightning rods is probably as old as governing itself. In *The Prince,* Machiavelli taught "that princes must delegate distasteful tasks to others; pleasant ones they should keep for themselves."[3] Francis Bacon observed that one of the uses that kings make of their advisers is "to interpose them between themselves and the envy or malice of their people; for kings cannot err; that must be discharged upon the shoulders of their ministers; and those who are nearest unto them must be content to bear the greatest load."[4]

Presidents, it hardly needs noting, are not kings. One essential difference is that to directly criticize a king (or sultan or czar or emperor or dictator) can land one in jail or worse, whereas criticizing a modern American president is more likely to land one on the front page or television news. The greater the social and political sanctions against criticizing the ruler, the greater the incentive to denounce advisers for leading the ruler astray rather than directly attacking the ruler. Because the sanctions against criticizing an American president are so radically different from those that have existed during most of the rest of world history, I have resisted the temptation to survey lightning rods of past historical eras. My analysis is instead confined to modern American presidents, although some of my conclusions may have wider applicability.

THE CONTRADICTORY CERTAINTIES OF PRESIDENTIAL LORE

Some fifty years ago Pendleton Herring in his seminal, if seldom read, *Presidential Leadership* stated the lightning rod hypothesis in the context of the American presidency. To be effective, Herring argued, a president "must be guarded from the frictions that his administration creates." By becoming too closely identified with "policies or actions which the voters may decide to repudiate, he runs the constant danger of becoming discredited before his term of office has expired." A president can deflect blame, Herring reasoned, by acting "as a generalissimo who devolves upon his generals the responsibility for the attainment of particular objectives. If they fail they can be disgraced and removed; or kicked upstairs to posts of less crucial importance." As an example, Herring pointed to the "notable procession of scapegoats" who "retreated from office [during the New Deal] under a weight of popular disapproval," while President Roosevelt remained popular.[5]

This argument seems plausible enough. But so too does the opposite case, argued by Harold Laski in his classic *The American Presidency,* published in the same year (1940) as Herring's treatise. An American president, Laski maintains, cannot deflect blame onto subordinates. A president's position as head of the executive branch, Laski insists, "makes him a target to be attacked by every person or interest at all critical of his purposes. He is there, in all cases, to be blamed; and there is no one, in any real sense, who can help to bear the burden of the blame." In contrast to England, where

we blame an anonymous entity 'the Government' if things go wrong, . . . in the United States it is the president who is blamed. A decision of the Supreme Court is regarded as adverse to *his* policy; a defeat in Congress is a blow to *his* prestige; the mid-term congressional elections affect *his* policy, for good or ill. No one thinks of them in terms of their effect upon his cabinet.

Laski takes the argument a step further by suggesting that those presidents who do not defer to subordinates will be more popular than those who do. "A masterful man in the White House," Laski suggests, will "be more to the liking of the multitude than one who is thought to be swayed by his colleagues. . . . The mere fact that the president insists upon being the center of the stage continuously strengthens his position." Like Herring, Laski points to the example of Franklin Roosevelt to support his proposition.[6] Who is right, and how would we decide? Are cabinet members, as Laski argues, of no help in protecting a president? Or can they, as Herring suggests, prevent him from being beaten down by daily political struggles? Is the White House, as Patrick Anderson has asserted, "so constructed that credit flows upward and blame downward,"[7] or is it the case, as Lord James Bryce insisted, that a president "cannot avoid responsibility by alleging the advice of his ministers, for he need not follow it, and they are bound to obey him or retire?"[8] Is it true, as Arthur Krock would have it, that "subordinates are always available in profusion to take the gaff, or, without diminishing [the president], the credit,"[9] or is John Ehrlichman correct in holding that "if a Secretary makes political waves it's his President who gets wet?"[10] Which if any of these contradictory propositions (one is tempted to say proverbs) are correct?

Such contradictory claims are characteristic of much of the literature on the presidency. Propositions about the presidency are too often put forth as if they were self-evident truths rather than hypotheses needing to be investigated. Unsubstantiated assertions, such as those enumerated above, are often repeated in textbooks, but rarely is an attempt made to demonstrate the validity of the claim (or even to show how the claim might in principle be validated). As a result, little work on the presidency is cumulative in character.

Instead, judgments about the presidency often swing in reaction to the travails or triumphs of the latest president. Harry Truman showed that the office ennobled the man; Lyndon Johnson showed that the office corrupted the man. Richard Nixon demonstrated that a president should not have a chief of staff blocking access to the president; Gerald Ford demonstrated that a president needs a chief of staff restricting access to the president. Jimmy Carter proved that presidents need to focus on the big picture, delegating the rest to subordinates; Ronald Reagan proved that presidents could not afford to become too detached from the details of day-to-day policy making. Franklin Roosevelt established that the public loved a political master in the White House; Dwight Eisenhower established that the public loved a detached, apolitical leader in the White House.

Surveying the state of the field, Fred Greenstein has recently written that it is "more appropriate to speak of lore than of laws in discussing the conduct of the presidency."[11] With so few presidents and so many variables, laws may be more than we can hope for, but perhaps we can still aspire to something better than the current presidential lore. My aim is to improve upon existing lore by treating the competing claims made by Laski, Bryce, Herring, Patrick Anderson, and others as rival hypotheses to be tested. These contradictory assertions can be reconciled by specifying *conditions* under which a president can deflect blame onto subordinates.

The task of stating such conditions is complicated by the lack of agreement among observers about which presidential advisers have served as lightning rods and which as liabilities.[12] A first step in evaluating the competing hypotheses is to distinguish an adviser who deflects blame away from a president (and thus acts as a lightning rod) from one who attracts blame toward a president (and thus serves as a liability).

Before proceeding with this line of inquiry, however, I want to address the peculiar neglect that students of the presidency have shown toward the question of the effect that advisers (whether cabinet members, staff, or vice presidents) have on a president's public (mass or elite) support. Although one can cull a collection of suggestive, if contradictory, sentences and even paragraphs, nowhere has the subject been given sustained, let alone rigorous, analysis.[13]

BETWEEN POLITICAL BEHAVIOR AND PUBLIC ADMINISTRATION

The topic of presidential lightning rods has been a casualty of the division within political science between public administration, which considers its proper domain of inquiry to be modes of executive decision making, management techniques, leadership styles, and the like, and political behavior, which concerns itself largely with statistical analyses of mass political attitudes and behavior. Models of presidential popularity have thus remained the province of those versed in mass political attitudes, while the study of presidential leadership styles has been left almost entirely to those with a public administration bent.

The lightning rod concept is premised on the assumption that the behavior of leaders affects how the public perceives and attributes responsibility. This possibility has been largely ignored by students of presidential popularity, who have instead focused on the impact of war, inflation, unemployment, and other real world events on the public's evaluation of presidential performance.[14] Largely missing from the debate over the relative influence of these factors on presidential popularity is an appreciation that what cannot be explained by events may be at least as important as what can. The lightning rod hypothesis suggests that where there is only a loose fit between events and popularity, one might profitably look to leadership style for an explanation.

This neglect of the role of presidential behavior by students of presidential popularity is particularly surprising in view of the conclusion reached by John Mueller in his pioneering essay, "Presidential Popularity from Truman to Johnson." Mueller's work is usually remembered, and rightly so, for introducing such variables as the "coalition of minorities," "economic slump," "war," and "rally around the flag." Largely forgotten, however, is Mueller's conclusion that any "analysis of Presidential popularity cannot rely entirely on [these] . . . variables . . . , but must also incorporate parameters designed to allow for the special character of each administration." Mueller found that a high degree of fit could be achieved only "by allowing the special character of each Presidential administration to be expressed in the equation."[15] Mueller's model thus not only left plenty of scope for presidential behavior, it *required* that presidential behavior be incorporated.

Rather than explore what it is that more popular presidents do to maintain their popularity, the dominant tendency among researchers in this field has been to try to improve the fit between events and popularity by turning to more refined statistical techniques. This research has shown Mueller's findings to be marred by statistical errors and, building upon his edifice, has constructed superior models of the effect of events on popularity.[16] But as Richard Brody, a leading student of the determinants of presidential support, has recently pointed out, "In no study—no matter how sophisticated the econometrics employed—is the link of the economy to evaluations of the president at a level of strength which would justify the conclusion: 'Now we have the explanation, we need pursue the question no further.' "[17]

Existing models of presidential popularity are particularly poor in accounting for Dwight Eisenhower's pattern of public support. "Only for Eisenhower," Samuel Kernell finds, does his "equation fail to explain a substantial share of fluctuation in his public support." A one-percentage-point increase in prices, for instance, lowered Eisenhower's popularity by one percentage point, while reducing Lyndon Johnson's by more than four points.[18] Similarly, Charles Ostrom and Dennis Simon find that "the economic problems of the late 1950s . . . cost President Eisenhower significantly fewer points . . . than the penalty imposed on President Nixon for similar conditions in the 1970s."[19] Because Eisenhower's popularity was not a hostage to events (or time), I have chosen to pay particularly close attention to his presidency in evaluating the lightning rod hypothesis.

Faced with an incomplete fit between real world events and presidential popularity (not to mention the statistical problems presented by time-series analysis),[20] a number of researchers have turned their attention to the individual perceptions that mediate between real world events and evaluations of presidential performance.[21] The attribution of blame, these scholars have shown, is not a reflexive response to objective events. Rather, blame is assigned by filtering events through a perceptual screen. This research marks an important step away from "the assumption of automatic political blame"[22] that has informed so much of the research on presidential popularity.

Recognizing the contingency of blame compels one to look not only at how followers attribute responsibility but also at the "blame games"[23] played by politicians that are geared to altering the perceptions of followers. The use of advisers as lightning rods is only one of a number of blame-avoidance strategies a president can pursue.[24] Where the opposition party controls one or both houses of Congress, for example, presidents may try to deflect blame onto the legislative branch. Or, particularly at the outset of a term, a president might blame the previous incumbent for negative outcomes. My contention is that our understanding of the dynamics of presidential popularity can be enhanced by analyzing the process through which presidents attempt to shift blame onto others.

If the study of presidential popularity has been hampered by a neglect of how presidential behavior mediates between events and the perceptions of followers, the study of presidential subordinates has suffered from slighting advisers' interaction with the public. Members of the president's cabinet, when studied at all, are conventionally viewed as either advisers to the president or administrators of public policy. The first Hoover Commission report, for instance, observed that departmental heads have a "dual function . . . as advisers to the President, and administrators of the departments."[25] Similarly, Leonard White writes of heads of departments as occupying the "dual position" of adviser and administrator.[26]

For those interested in the cabinet member as adviser (or president as decision maker), the relevant topics include the extent to which a cabinet member has direct access to the president and whether the department head's advice is proffered in a formal or informal setting. Such scholars commonly contrast a "formalistic" or "bureaucratic" decision-making style, in which advice is funneled up through a formal hierarchy, with a "collegial" or "competitive" model of organization, in which advisers at every level have direct access to the president.[27] These alternative advisory structures are compared for the range of options and quality of information with which the president is presented.

Students concerned with cabinet members as implementors (or saboteurs) of presidential policy are interested in the degree of congruence between the policies of the president and those pursued by a cabinet member. A standard question is whether members of the cabinet, because of the "many masters" they must serve—Congress, interest groups, the department itself—are "a President's natural enemies."[28] Such scholars pay particular attention to the strategies a president may pursue to secure compliance from the department head.[29]

Understanding a cabinet member's contribution to the formulation and execution of public policy is, of course, essential to a study of presidential-cabinet relations. But cabinet members, indeed all presidential advisers and assistants, can also be usefully studied from the perspective of how they contribute to, or detract from, a president's public standing inside and outside of Washington. The adviser as lightning rod—defined as a relationship in which an unpopular adviser deflects criticism away from the president—is only one of at least four possible forms that the relationship between president, adviser, and the public may assume. The other three forms are a popular adviser bolstering a president's popularity (the adviser as asset); a popular adviser detracting from a president's popularity (the adviser as upstager); and an unpopular adviser diminishing a president's popularity (the adviser as liability).

FOUR HYPOTHESIZED RELATIONSHIPS

In his classic book *The President's Cabinet,* Richard Fenno hypothesizes that a prominent cabinet member adds prestige to an administration, thus boosting support for the president. Those few cabinet members who achieve prominence, Fenno argues, "add to the public confidence and public prestige which are the fundamental underpinnings of the President's success as Chief Representative of the Nation." It is unlikely, Fenno continues, "that a Cabinet member could achieve national standing without its redounding to the net credit of the President."[30] This positive-sum conception of the relationship between president and adviser treats the well-regarded adviser as an asset to the president.

An adviser's favorable reputation, however, may not necessarily bolster a president's popularity. An alternative possibility is that the favorable reputation of an adviser may be gained at the expense of the president. Many in the Johnson White House felt that Press Secretary Bill Moyers had this sort of negative-sum relationship with President Johnson. As one staffer put it: "Moyers became the White Hat and Johnson was the Black Hat. If anything good happened in the government, it was Moyers. If anything bad happened, it was Johnson."[31] Jim Baker's relationship with George Bush was sometimes seen in a similar negative-sum light: "If Baker is the great poohbah and savior," comments Lynn Nofziger, "it makes George Bush look weak."[32] The relationship between Gerald Ford and Henry Kissinger, examined in Chapter 5, provides an additional illustration of an admired adviser upstaging the president.

A third type of interaction between adviser and president is, at first glance, somewhat difficult to distinguish from the lightning rod relationship. Here the adviser attracts criticism but, rather than deflecting blame away from the president, generates dissatisfaction with the president. Reagan's interior secretary James Watt, I argue in Chapter 3, is an archetypal example of this type of adviser who so angers critics that he becomes a liability to the president.

The distinction between a liability and a lightning rod is sometimes mud-died in everyday discourse by using the term "lightning rod" to indicate the attraction of controversy, shorn of its connotation of deflecting criticism. For examples, a journalist reports, "It is understandable that the White House had no desire to send an Administration bill to Congress to become the lightning rod for environmentalists' ire."[33] At times, the term "lightning rod" seems to become virtually a synonym for liability, as, for instance, in the remark that "everyone realized that the Democrats would be unable to attack the beloved President directly, yet the combative Nixon remained a lightning rod for controversy; would it not be better to choose someone else to serve as Ike's running mate?"[34] Reagan's first press secretary, Larry Speakes, appears to use the term in a similar fashion when he writes, "We certainly had our share of lightning rods, like Watt, who drew constant fire from the environmentalists; Ray Donovan who could never establish rap-port with the labor unions; and Ted Bell over at Education. All three were decent gentlemen who were unsuited for their posts."[35] Equally confusing is the usage of the term adopted by a conservative activist who, before the 1992 New Hampshire primary, explained that "if [Pat] Buchanan runs, then [John] Sununu is a lightning rod." Because "people [Sununu] antagonized . . . might be drawn to Buchanan," Bush needed to jettison his lightning rod and "be standing there by himself" come February.[36]

In this book, I use the term "lightning rod" to designate not merely the attraction of criticism but the deflection of criticism away from someone or something. The term "liability" is reserved for those individuals whose actions not only engender criticism of themselves but of others. Whether an adviser is a lightning rod thus depends not only on the volume or intensity of criticism aimed at an adviser, but also on the effect that criticism has on support for the president.

PITFALLS OF A METAPHOR

To identify an adviser as a "lightning rod" is to engage in the use of meta-phor. A metaphor, as defined in Webster's dictionary, is "a figure of speech containing an implied comparison, in which a word or phrase ordinarily and primarily used of one thing is applied to another." Metaphor enables us to move from the familiar to the unknown. Yet there is always the danger that a metaphor may conceal as much or more than it illuminates.[37] More precisely, the peril of taking a metaphor literally is that one confuses attributes of the analogy with attributes of reality.

To begin with, presidential advisers are not inanimate objects. They have agendas, ambitions, and aspirations that may or may not coincide with the president's. The metaphor leads one to assume that an adviser is providing political cover for a president, but it may well be that the adviser is pursuing a policy about which the president cares little or perhaps even disagrees with. One needs therefore always to ask whether the adviser is taking the heat while pursuing the president's or his own agenda.

Just as likening advisers to lightning rods may lead one to overlook the strategic calculations of the adviser, so it may result in neglecting the strategic interests of presidential adversaries, particularly members of Congress. The metaphor presumes that the president has positioned his adviser in such a way that the adviser rather than the president absorbs the criticism. Neglected is the possibility that it is the strategic calculations of the president's political opponents that explain why the adviser rather than the president is criticized.

The costs to a congressman of attacking an unpopular president are lower than those of criticizing a popular president. As one pundit, writing about President Eisenhower, put it, "In politics, you can't kick a man when he's up."[38] The obverse is also true. As Lyndon Johnson explained, "If some folks think a fellow is winged or crippled, they pile into him. . . . If you've got an enemy, it gives him a lot of hope."[39] The thesis that it is the opposition's strategic interests, rather than a president's behavior, that accounts for the lightning rod phenomenon is advanced by a former member of the Eisenhower administration, who suggests: "I think whether he [Eisenhower] had delegated or not . . . it was simpler not to attack him. This made the next line fair game, and the next line was Cabinet members."[40]

We need therefore to distinguish the "strong" lightning rod hypothesis—people attack an adviser because they believe that person is corrupting a president's good intentions—from a "weak" version of the lightning rod hypothesis—opponents, for tactical reasons of their own, criticize the adviser rather than the president. Examples of the weak lightning rod hypothesis include the assertion by a GOP pollster that Vice President George Bush "is a lightning rod for all those constituencies angry at Ronald Reagan," or journalist Robert Donovan's suggestion that Sherman Adams "has been a whipping-boy for extreme right-wing Republicans who dislike the direction in which Eisenhower is taking the party but who have found it safer to hit Adams with blows intended for the President."[41] The weaker version submits that the lightning rod phenomenon is not only, as the metaphor implies, something constructed and manipulated by the president, but is also manipulated by an opposition trying to influence the policies of a popular president, the unintended consequence of which is to help sustain a president's popularity.

When we refer to an individual as a "lightning rod," there is a further presumption that the individual was placed there by the president with malice aforethought. The danger again is that the metaphor leads us to assume what needs to be demonstrated. A president's intentions (like those of his opponents) must remain an empirical question. It cannot be presumed that the president is cognizant of the lightning rod phenomenon in making appointments or organizing his government. It may be, for instance, that a president chooses cabinet members with the aim of increasing the administration's prestige (the adviser as asset), with the unintended consequence of providing highly visible members who can function as lightning rods.

Finally, literal adherence to the metaphor may obscure the costs attached to using advisers as lightning rods. Even when an adviser is pursuing policies the president approves of, one must still ask whether a president's public detachment from a policy entails a sacrifice in the president's effectiveness. To what extent does the president have to put himself in the line of fire to persuade others to go along with the administration's plans? Chapter 7 addresses questions about the limits of a lightning rod strategy through an examination of the relationship between President Eisenhower and Attorney General Herbert Brownell during the battle over civil rights legislation.

PUBLIC VISIBILITY OF PRESIDENTIAL ADVISERS

Unknowns cannot function as lightning rods. If people don't know who a president's advisers are they can hardly blame those advisers for policies gone awry. How publicly visible, then, are a president's cabinet and staff? The only systematic treatment of this subject, Fenno's *The President's Cabinet,* comes to the conclusion that "the activities of Cabinet members simply do not get reported in the public press."[42] If Fenno is right, then there might seem to be little point in pursuing the lightning rod hypothesis any further.

Fenno's evidence for this contention comes from the *New York Times Index* from 1912 to 1932. During Woodrow Wilson's administration, for instance, Fenno finds that the secretaries of agriculture, interior, commerce, and labor got their names in the *Times* an average of no more than once a week. With the exception of a single year, the same was true for the postmaster general. Their appearances on the front page were even rarer, ranging from a low of about once a year for the secretary of agriculture to a high of almost ten times a year for the attorney general. The same held true for the Republican administrations of Warren Harding, Calvin Coolidge, and Herbert Hoover. Two-thirds of Hoover's cabinet, for example, averaged less than one appearance a week in the *Times* and less than one appearance a month on the front page.[43]

The pattern of news coverage that characterized the cabinets of Wilson, Harding, Coolidge, and Hoover, however, seems to be substantially lower than the coverage of "modern"—i.e., post–Franklin Roosevelt—presidents. Whereas Fenno reports that for the "outer cabinet" posts of agriculture, interior, commerce, labor, and postmaster general the norm was less than one

TABLE 1.1.   Average yearly number of front-page mentions of department heads in the *New York Times*.

	Wilson 1912–1920	Harding/ Coolidge 1921–1928	Hoover 1929–1932	FDR 1933–1940
Agriculture	1.4	3.3	7.0	10.6
Interior	4.1	3.4	1.8	14.8
Postmaster General	6.9	4.9	2.8	33.8
Labor	6.1	5.6	6.0	10.8
Commerce	2.3	31.6	9.3	12.1
Total	4.2	9.8	5.4	16.4

Sources: The Wilson through Hoover averages are computed from data presented in Richard F. Fenno, Jr., *The President's Cabinet* (Cambridge, Mass.: Harvard University Press, 1959), 165–66, with the exception of the number for the secretary of commerce under Harding and Coolidge, data for which are not presented in Fenno. The latter figure and the FDR averages have been computed by the author from the *New York Times Index*.

mention a week in the *Times*, the evidence for Franklin Roosevelt's first two terms is startlingly different.[44] No secretary of any of these departments averaged less than one mention a week during the first eight years of the Roosevelt administration. Indeed, only in one year (1938) did a department head (Labor Secretary Frances Perkins) average less than one mention a week. The least prominent of the six posts (commerce and agriculture) averaged close to two mentions a week, and the most prominent post (postmaster general) averaged five mentions a week. The other two (interior and labor) averaged between two and two-and-a-half mentions a year.[45] As Table 1.1 shows, front-page stories reveal a similar contrast in coverage. The cabinet heads during the Roosevelt presidency received something in the order of a threefold increase over the coverage of cabinet heads during the preceding presidencies. Most telling of all, of the "outer cabinet" heads who served between 1912 and 1932 only Secretary of Commerce Herbert Hoover (1921–1928) received more coverage than the least visible of FDR's cabinet heads.

In any event, the validity of the lightning rod hypothesis depends not on the average visibility of administration officials but rather on the visibility of a few extraordinary officials. During Roosevelt's first term, for instance, Postmaster General James Farley got his name in the *New York Times* an average of 355 times a year, or almost once a day, and received a front-page mention almost once a week. During the first year of the Eisenhower administration, to take another example, Secretary of Agriculture Ezra Taft Benson appeared in the *New York Times* 274 times, an average of more than five times a week. In marked contrast to President Wilson's secretary of agriculture, who appeared on the front page eleven times in eight years, or the secre-

TABLE 1.2.   Top ten administration officials and members of Congress in television coverage.

	1989	1990	Two-Year Total
J. Baker	322	503	825
Cheney	148	217	365
Quayle	119	117	236
Fitzwater	85	94	179
Sununu	53	102	155
Thornburgh	100	48	148
Bennett	88	50	138
B. Bush	70	45	115
Scowcroft	52	56	108
Darman	34	66	100
Administration Total			2,369
R. Dole	89	143	232
Mitchell	80	122	202
Nunn	103	63	166
Foley	78	84	162
J. Wright	149	4	153
Gingrich	42	59	101
Kennedy	37	59	96
Glenn	44	46	90
Gephardt	32	55	87
Rostenkowski	27	47	74
Congressional Total			1,363

Source: Calculated as the total number of entries in the Vanderbilt Television News Index and Abstracts.

tary of agriculture during the Harding-Coolidge period, who was front-page news twenty-six times in eight years, Benson appeared in a front-page story thirty-five times in his first year alone.[46]

Relative to members of Congress, moreover, top cabinet members and other high administration officials do very well in terms of media coverage. During President George Bush's first two years in office, as Table 1.2 indicates, no senator or representative received nearly as much television coverage as Secretary of State Jim Baker or Defense Secretary Dick Cheney. And the top ten administration officials easily outdistanced the top ten senators or representatives in terms of television news coverage. Indeed the ten most visible administration officials received close to twice as much coverage as the ten most visible senators and representatives.[47]

Just because newspapers or even television news report the activities of administration officials does not, of course, mean that the public knows who these people are.[48] Indeed, one might object to the lightning rod hypothesis, in so far as it pertains to the mass public, on the grounds that it re-

TABLE 1.3. Public awareness of administration officials (in percentages).

	Feb. 1953	Nov. 1953	July 1954	July 1955	Sep. 1956	Jan. 1957
Wilson	91	81	84	83	85	85
Dulles	84	85	92	92	93	96
Durkin	66					
Brownell	51	72	76	68	67	68
Dodge	47	41				
Benson		79	79	72	83	81
Mitchell		47	48	48	53	54
Humphrey			51	55	56	66
Weeks			35	35	41	39
Summerfield			51	52	52	59
McKay			32	32		
Hobby			57	78		
Stassen				71	88	81
Seaton					30	29
Folsom					37	39
No Opinion	5	5	3	3	2	1

Source: Opinion Research Corporation; data provided by Roper Center. The question was, Which of these members of the present administration have you heard or read about?

quires an unrealistic degree of political knowledge on the part of the general public and thus ignores decades of public opinion research demonstrating minimal public awareness of the political realm. As Richard Neustadt warns, "One never should underestimate the public's power to ignore, to acquiesce, and to forget, especially when the proceedings seem incalculable or remote from private life."[49] Any thesis that requires most people, most of the time, to be informed and concerned about politics is unlikely to be valid.

Equally vital, though, is the need to differentiate "the" public. As Neustadt himself recognizes, " 'the' presidential public is actually an aggregate of publics as diverse and overlapping as the claims Americans and allied peoples press on Washington."[50] In thinking about lightning rods, it is essential to be clear about which of these diverse publics one has in mind. To function as a lightning rod, an administration official must be known to the subpopulation that is antagonized by an administration policy. The relevant population for evaluating whether a secretary of agriculture has served as a presidential lightning rod, for instance, is probably the subpopulation of farmers rather than the population as a whole.

Just as one cannot reduce the public to an undifferentiated, and largely apathetic, ill-informed mass, one cannot regard all administration officials other than the president as equally unknown to the public. As suggested earlier, press coverage of administration officials varies dramatically, and as a result so too does public awareness of administration officials. In Eisenhower's administration, for instance, anywhere from 80 to 95 percent of the public ordinarily claimed to have heard or read about Secretary of State John Foster Dulles, Secretary of Agriculture Ezra Taft Benson, and Secretary of Defense Charles Wilson. In a totally different category, as Table 1.3 shows, were the likes of Interior Secretary Douglas McKay or Commerce Secretary Sinclair Weeks. Only about a third of the population even claimed to have heard of either of these two cabinet secretaries. In evaluating the validity of the lightning rod thesis, at least at the mass public level, we need not concern ourselves with how little is known of the least prominent officials but instead should focus on those extraordinary few who are highly visible and well known.

In the next two chapters, I examine two of the most prominent and controversial cabinet members in recent history—Reagan's first secretary of the interior, James Watt, and Eisenhower's secretary of agriculture, Ezra Taft Benson. In comparing the tenures of these two men, I show how one might distinguish a presidential lightning rod from a liability, and I identify some of the conditions necessary for an adviser to deflect blame away from the president.

2

Ike's Lightning Rod:
Secretary of Agriculture
Ezra Taft Benson

Any exploration of the lightning rod phenomenon must begin with the presidency of Dwight D. Eisenhower. No modern president has maintained such high levels of popularity for so long, and no modern president has so successfully insulated himself from bad news and controversy.[1] In a tremendously influential book, *The Hidden-Hand Presidency: Eisenhower as Leader,* political scientist Fred Greenstein argues that Eisenhower's success in insulating himself from the day-to-day controversies of his administration was a direct result of his "hidden-hand" leadership style, which kept "the controversial political side of the presidential role largely covert" and accented his role as "an uncontroversial head of state."[2] A key component of Eisenhower's hidden-hand style, as described by Greenstein, was his use of advisers as lightning rods to take the heat on controversial policies.[3]

That President Eisenhower thought in terms of lightning rods and the deflection of blame onto subordinates is suggested by the much-quoted recollection of Press Secretary James Hagerty. According to Hagerty: "President Eisenhower would say, 'Do it this way.' I would say, 'If I go to that press conference and say what you want me to say, I would get hell.' With that he would smile, get up and walk around the desk, pat me on the back and say, 'My boy, better you than me.' "[4] In a similar vein, Attorney General Herbert Brownell recalls Eisenhower telling him in their first official meeting: "It's your responsibility, you know, as well as your authority. Now if anything goes wrong, you know who's going to get it, don't you."[5] And Emmet Hughes, a speech writer for President Eisenhower, recounts a conversation late in 1957 in which Eisenhower defended keeping John Foster Dulles as secretary of state: "People just don't like the personality of Foster's, while they do like me. . . . I know what they say about Foster—dull, duller, Dulles—and all that. But the Democrats love to hit him rather than me."[6]

The crux of Eisenhower's leadership strategy was to allow trusted cabinet members significant autonomy in formulating and administering policy. By delegating the authority to make decisions, Eisenhower hoped also to delegate responsibility for the results of those decisions, thereby allowing him to maintain a noncontroversial or nonpolitical public profile. That Eisenhower understood this connection is clear from his underlining of a passage in Arthur Krock's memoirs critical of President Lyndon Johnson's leadership style. Krock wrote (and Eisenhower underlined): "Johnson, as much as any president in our history, has closely identified himself and his office with the disasters, foreign and domestic, economic and social, into which the United States has become more and more deeply involved in his time. . . . [A] source of this close identification with all acts, policies and thorny situations is a passion to control every function of government, though subordinates are always available in profusion to take the gaff."[7]

Foremost among the Eisenhower administration lightning rods Greenstein identifies is Secretary of Agriculture Ezra Taft Benson.[8] "Farmers who rankled at the moves toward decreasing subsidization of agriculture," Greenstein suggests, "blamed the zealous Mormon elder, Ezra Taft Benson . . . not Eisenhower."[9] The claim is suggestive, even plausible, but Greenstein provides no evidence to support it. That Benson was the target of heated criticism by farmers is beyond doubt to anyone familiar with the period, but that Benson deflected blame away Eisenhower is far from self-evident. Indeed the conventional wisdom among press and politicians during the 1950s was that Benson was a damaging *liability* for President Eisenhower. Farmbelt congressmen complained constantly that Benson undermined farmers' confidence in Eisenhower.[10] Many on the White House staff shared this view of Benson as a political liability,[11] and it was frequently repeated by journalists and academics. Writing in the closing years of the Eisenhower administration, Richard Fenno, to take one prominent example, asserted that "more than any other member of the Eisenhower Cabinet, [Benson] has been a political liability."[12]

How might one mediate between these rival claims? How is one to determine whether Benson was a liability or a lightning rod? The question is important for how one judges the quality of Eisenhower's leadership. If Benson was a liability, Eisenhower's decision to retain Benson throughout his two terms seems to indicate incredible political naiveté if not obtuseness. If Benson was a lightning rod, that same decision seems to be evidence of devilish cleverness. In answering the question of whether Benson served as a lightning rod, this chapter (1) examines available survey evidence of farmers' opinions in the 1950s, (2) compares these survey results with farm surveys taken in later administrations, (3) investigates elites' reaction to Benson's tenure, and (4) looks at Eisenhower and Benson's behind-the-scenes relationship. The aim of this intensive examination of the Eisenhower-Benson relationship is both to judge the validity and utility of the lightning rod construct and to gauge the effectiveness of Eisenhower's leadership.

EISENHOWER, BENSON, AND THE FARMERS

When Eisenhower entered the presidency, he inherited an agricultural system that established price supports at 90 percent of parity (a government-set "fair" price) for six basic crops: wheat, corn, cotton, tobacco, peanuts, and rice. Established during World War II to boost food production, price supports quickly became seen as the farmers' due. As the supply of crops increased (a result of technological innovations as well as government subsidies), the price of crops fell. The further prices fell, the more crops government had to buy at 90 percent of the parity price. For the government, declining prices meant storing immense surpluses that were difficult to unload without further depressing agricultural prices (by 1954 the government had enough wheat and cotton and other crops to supply the market for a full year);[13] for taxpayers it meant increasing subsidies for farmers; and for farmers declining prices meant economic hardship.

Eisenhower's long-term objective was to restore a free market in farm products; his short-term goal was more modest—to reduce price supports by instituting a flexible system of payments ranging from 75 percent to 90 percent of the parity price. But even such modest reforms brought howls of protest from farm-state congressmen and important agricultural groups. Agricultural interests' unhappiness over the specific reforms proposed by the Eisenhower administration was exacerbated by the prolonged downturn in farm prices. In contrast to the national economy as a whole, which was relatively favorable for Eisenhower most of the time, the farm economy remained a trouble spot throughout the 1950s.

Given the state of the agricultural economy and the administration's chosen course it is not surprising that Secretary Benson would be, as Chief of Staff Sherman Adams described him, "the most unpopular and the most harshly criticized figure in the Cabinet."[14] What is surprising is that by and large President Eisenhower remained remarkably popular among farmers. Surveys of farmers conducted during the 1950s strongly support Greenstein's contention that Benson's unpopularity among farmers did not translate into disapproval of Eisenhower. A substantial proportion of farmers, these polls show, simultaneously liked Ike and disapproved of the performance of Secretary Benson.

A Gallup poll taken at the outset of 1958, for instance, found that two-thirds of farmers approved of Eisenhower, while slightly less than 30 percent approved of Benson. Among those farmers who held an opinion about both Benson and Eisenhower (three-fourths of the sample), moreover, more than two in five combined disapproval of Benson with approval of Eisenhower.[15] A similar discrepancy between attitudes toward Eisenhower and attitudes toward Benson shows up in surveys of farmers at the state level.

A particularly rich source of farmers' opinions during the Eisenhower years are the surveys of Iowa farmers conducted by *Wallace's Farmer,* which periodically asked farmers to evaluate the performance of President Eisenhower and Secretary Benson on a scale of "good," "fair," or "poor."[16] In none of these polls did more than 14 percent of Iowa farmers judge Eisenhower's performance as poor, while, in contrast, no more than 15 percent ever rated Benson's performance as good.

In the fall of 1953, 88 percent of Iowa farmers judged the president's performance as either good or fair, while only 8 percent gave the president a poor rating. In contrast, 33 percent believed the secretary was doing a poor job.[17] By the end of 1954, only 3 percent of Iowa farmers judged Eisenhower to be doing a poor job, compared with 28 percent who believed Benson's performance was poor. Close to 60 percent rated Eisenhower's performance good, while only 15 percent were willing to give the same grade to the secretary of agriculture.[18]

Although discontent among Iowa farmers increased as farm prices fell, the disparity between attitudes toward Eisenhower and Benson remained large. In the summer of 1957, for instance, 55 percent believed the secretary was doing a poor job, while only 14 percent rendered the same judgment about the president. More than 80 percent believed the president was doing either a good or fair job, while only one-third of the sample would say the same about Benson. A poll conducted the following summer revealed almost precisely the same pattern of support.[19]

Another survey, conducted less than a month before the 1958 midterm elections, found that only 8 percent of Iowa farmers believed Eisenhower was doing a poor job, compared with 44 percent who disapproved of Benson's performance. Fifty-five percent believed the president was doing a good job, and only 13 percent gave the secretary of agriculture the same high mark. Moreover, of the 88 percent who had an opinion about both Eisenhower and Benson, two-thirds gave Eisenhower a higher rating than they gave Benson, one-third judged the performances of Eisenhower and Benson the same, and less than 1 percent viewed Benson more positively than Eisenhower.[20]

These surveys suggest that Benson's popularity among farmers was highly susceptible to changes in the farm situation. This connection did not go unnoticed by Benson, who lamented "the discouraging correlation between the level of farm prices and my level of popularity."[21] When prices fell, elite demands for Benson's resignation increased and his popularity among farmers fell. What is remarkable is that Eisenhower's popularity among farmers remained relatively impervious to changes in Benson's popularity or drops in prices.

Eisenhower's relative insulation from farmers' distress is particularly evident in a special survey of midwestern farm households conducted by Gallup in the spring of 1956, which found that although 76 percent believed farmers were *worse* off than they had been a few years ago, 62 percent still expressed *approval* of Eisenhower's performance. The widespread perception that the farmers' situation had deteriorated during Eisenhower's first term was evidently blamed on Benson, who received only a 32 percent approval rating.[22]

These surveys tend to belie one farmer's confident report that "those that had a good year are still all for Ike, and those who didn't ain't."[23] Instead what they show is that although attitudes toward Benson were closely tied to the state of the farm economy, attitudes toward Eisenhower were relatively independent of conditions on the farm.

BLOCK, BERGLAND, AND BUTZ

The extraordinary nature of the Eisenhower-Benson pattern can be more fully appreciated by contrasting it with farmers' attitudes toward the recent administrations of Ronald Reagan, Jimmy Carter, and Gerald Ford. Surveys of farm opinion taken during these three presidencies suggest that, by and large, farmers tend not to distinguish much between the secretary of agriculture and the president.[24]

Among Iowa farmers, for instance, the popularity of President Reagan and Secretary of Agriculture John Block closely coincided. Throughout the first term, both Reagan and Block were approved of by a modest majority of Iowa farmers. At no point was the percentage of farmers who disapproved of the two men more than three percentage points apart.[25] In the opening year of the second term, as discontent rose sharply, Iowa farmers soured on *both* Block and Reagan. By January 1986, 61 percent of farmers disapproved of Block's performance and 56 percent disapproved of Reagan's.[26]

In Illinois, Block's home state, both Block and Reagan were well liked during the first term, but to the extent that there was a discrepancy in attitudes toward the two, Block tended to be *less* unpopular than Reagan. On average, about 5 or 6 percent more Illinois farmers disapproved of Reagan than disapproved of Block.[27] Indiana farmers showed a similar tendency during the first term to evaluate both Block and Reagan positively, with Reagan's unpopularity running, on average, a few points lower than Block's.

Neither Carter nor his secretary of agriculture, Bob Bergland, were very popular among farmers, but to the extent that a divergence of opinion existed, Bergland tended to be less unpopular than his beleaguered chief.

Among Iowa farmers, for instance, Carter's disapproval rating averaged about 47 percent, almost 7 percent higher than disapproval of Bergland.[28] Similarly, averaging the results from Illinois polls shows that slightly more than half of Illinois farmers expressed disapproval of Carter, while Bergland's unpopularity was roughly 5 percentage points lower. Among Indiana farmers, the average disapproval rating of Carter was 47 percent, and for Bergland 40 percent.[29]

In the case of Gerald Ford and his secretary of agriculture, Earl Butz, surveys again suggest a tight coupling of farmer attitudes toward the president and secretary of agriculture, with a slight tendency toward greater disapproval of the president than the secretary. Averaging the four Illinois polls taken in 1975 and 1976 reveals that virtually the same number of Illinois farmers disapproved of Butz (27 percent) as disapproved of Ford (28 percent).[30] Indiana farmers tended to express slightly higher levels of dissatisfaction with Ford's performance (32 percent), while only 26 percent said they disapproved of Butz.

In comparing the attitudes of farmers toward the Reagan, Carter, and Ford administrations with those toward the Eisenhower presidency, the most striking feature is the extent to which farmers' evaluations of the president and the agriculture secretary are joined in the case of these other three presidents and divorced in the case of Eisenhower. There was sometimes as much as a 40 (and never less than 20) percent difference between disapproval of Benson and disapproval of Eisenhower. In contrast, Reagan, Carter, and Ford rarely had disapproval ratings that were more than five or six percentage points lower than the secretary's and, more often than not, the president's disapproval rating was actually higher than that of the secretary's.

BLAMING BENSON FIRST

Farmers did not connect Eisenhower with Benson in large part because elites either did not perceive or were reluctant, for strategic reasons of their own, to make such a connection. The message farmers consistently received from opinion leaders was that it was Benson, and not Eisenhower, who was responsible for declining farm prices and the reduction of price supports.

In the halls of Congress, Benson was routinely blamed for any number of maladies that afflicted the farmer, while Eisenhower usually went unmentioned or was absolved from blame.[31] Typical in this respect was a Senate resolution submitted by Texas Democrat Ralph Yarborough, which stated that it was the sense of the Senate that the secretary of agriculture should be fired because his "oppressive policies . . . have failed." The sixteen-point resolution asserted, among other things, that "Mr. Ezra Taft Benson has depressed the prices received by farmers, . . . stirred up economic civil war between producer groups of different farm commodities, . . . [and] tried to eliminate the small family-type farm in America."[32] This indictment was characteristic of anti-Benson sentiment in that it (1) blamed Benson for falling farm prices, (2) portrayed Benson as a heartless enemy of the family farmer, (3) identified the administration's farm policies as Benson's policies, and (4) made no mention of President Eisenhower.

Although few believed, as one congressman did, that Benson was "evil personified,"[33] many were convinced that the secretary was unsympathetic to the small farmer's plight. Benson's public image as a heartless ideologue, who lacked sympathy for small farmers, can be seen in Missouri Senator Thomas Hennings's complaint that "no relief, or even sincere sympathy, can be expected from the Department of Agriculture by farmers who face drought disaster,"[34] as well as in Montana Democrat James Murray's plaint that "Secretary Benson's administration of farm programs has been uniformly callous and heartless."[35] In the words of South Dakota Republican Francis Case, "The great difficulty which Mr. Benson has had all along has been to persuade the farmers that he has been on their side."[36]

Many critics found it only a short step from the view that Benson didn't care about declining prices to the view that the secretary's policies were actually designed to bring about lower prices. Senator Hubert Humphrey, for instance, argued that it was "Benson's deliberate objective . . . to force farm prices down." Benson, Humphrey concluded, had "not merely mismanaged our Nation's farm programs; he has deliberately wrecked them."[37] Others accused Benson of pursuing policies that were aimed at "driving the farmer off the land,"[38] while still others attacked him for being "dedicated to the creation of a scarcity of food."[39]

Listening to some congressmen, one could come away with the impression that it was Benson's administration. The maverick senator from Oregon, Wayne Morse, declared that "more than a million farmers have left the farms since Benson came into power in 1953, and under his policies American agriculture will continue to be depressed." The time has come, Morse concluded, to "repudiate the Benson program."[40] When Eisenhower's name was drawn into the debate, usually because of some presidential action such as a veto, his decisions were often attributed to the "bad advice" of Secretary Benson. For instance, after Eisenhower vetoed the "freeze bill" (so called because it would have frozen all price supports for the coming year at 1957 levels), William Proxmire told his colleagues that he was sure that "the motives of the President are excellent. I have always assumed this to be true. . . . He is, of course, interested in the welfare of farmers. But the President of the United States . . . is ill-advised."[41] Yarborough concurred with this view, recalling that he had "served under the President in the European theatre during the war. I admire him as a great leader, and also personally. . . . If he knew what was going on at the economic front, we would have had his signature of approval instead of his veto."[42]

Even Hubert Humphrey, one of the most vocal and partisan critics of administration farm policy, for the first few years blamed Benson and not Eisenhower for administration decisions.[43] After the reduction of price supports for dairy products from 90 percent to 75 percent of parity, for instance, Humphrey called upon the president, "who is a good man, a considerate man, to reconsider the action which has been taken by his Secretary." Prefacing his remarks with the observation that "the people of my state . . . have high regard and true affection for the President," Humphrey pleaded that "if my voice could reach the White House this afternoon . . . I would ask him [Eisenhower] not to permit one of his agents, one of his department heads, to disavow a pledge which the President made to the people of my state and to the people of the Nation."[44]

The heavily Democratic National Farmers Union, although not above taking swipes at Eisenhower, reserved the great preponderance of its considerable venom for Benson, whom they vilified as "the chief advocate of the farmer's oppressors, . . . the major instrument in the efforts to destroy the farmers' programs, [and] . . . the chief prophet of the ideology which has been constructed to rationalize the oppression and doom of independent family-scale agriculture." In contrast, "President Eisenhower's role in the farm situation is primarily innocent," suggested the editor of the Farmers Union's *Washington Newsletter*. "Ike neither knows nor cares much about what is going on in agriculture."[45]

The belief that Eisenhower was not paying much attention to what Benson was doing is evident in a cable the newly elected Senator Proxmire sent to President Eisenhower. Proxmire called on Eisenhower "to take immediate action to replace Ezra Taft Benson as secretary of agriculture. *Secretary Benson's unwise and unsound policies* have brought many American farm families close to ruin."[46] How was this belief that Benson rather than Eisenhower was responsible for the administration's farm policies sustained? The answer lies in Eisenhower's capacity to be different things to different people as well as in his willingness to delegate authority.

THE IMPORTANCE OF BEING AMBIGUOUS

To sustain a successful lightning rod a president must keep his intentions ambiguous, thereby allowing opponents to believe that if the president paid closer attention he might behave differently than the overly zealous aide. Eisenhower succeeded in keeping his intentions ambiguous enough for farmers to feel that, despite Benson's policies, the president was on their side.

Eisenhower projected an image to farmers that was sharply at variance with the image projected by Benson. While Benson went around the country preaching the virtues of self-reliance and free markets and his unalterable opposition to programs that foster dependence on government, Eisenhower's public statements on agriculture tended to "muddle through." Consider, for instance, the contrast between the president's first annual message to Congress, which promised that "the Secretary of Agriculture and his associates will . . . execute the present act faithfully and thereby seek to mitigate the consequences of the downturn in farm income,"[47] and Benson's "General Statement on Agricultural Policy," issued only a few days later at his first press conference. In a sweeping statement of first principles, Benson declared:

> Too many Americans are calling on Washington to do for them what they should be willing to do for themselves. . . . It is doubtful if any man can be politically free who depends upon the state for sustenance. A completely planned and subsidized economy weakens initiative, discourages industry, destroys character and demoralizes the people. . . . The principles of economic freedom are applicable to farm problems. . . . Farmers should not be placed in a position of working for government bounty rather than producing for a free market.[48]

Eisenhower's public statements on agriculture avoided the doctrinaire attacks on the dangers of government intervention in the marketplace that characterized many of Benson's speeches. Typical in this respect was Eisenhower's first agricultural address, which came in October 1953 at the annual convention of the Future Farmers of America. In the speech, Eisenhower stressed his affinity with, and sympathy for, the small family farmer. He reminded his audience of young farmers that he "worked on the farm during my boyhood in Abilene, some 160 miles west of here," "grew up among farmers," and currently owned a farm in Pennsylvania. The president stressed that he understood and was "deeply concerned" with the problems facing farm people who had been hurt by the "economic grinding machine" of declining prices and rising costs. Eisenhower talked up the invaluable role the federal government was playing in helping cattle farmers of the Southwest survive the drought and assured his audience that "the federal government is continuing, and will continue as long as necessary, to assist in meeting the misfortunes of our people, in the drought areas." The president artfully fuzzed over the "extremely complex" question of price supports by vowing that his administration would propose no program "that fails to provide solidly for the national interest by continuing prosperity in American agriculture." "All of us know," he concluded reassuringly, "that the price support principle must be a part of any future farm program."[49]

This speech might lead one to conclude that Eisenhower disagreed with the free-market message his secretary of agriculture was spreading to farm groups across the country. But that conclusion would be erroneous. Indeed, in the early stages of the formulation of this very speech, Eisenhower had rebuked Republican National Chairman Leonard Hall, telling him, "I don't believe for a minute the farmer wants the government to be his boss."[50] In his memoirs, Eisenhower unambiguously endorsed "the fight to free the farmers and make the agricultural industry more responsive to the competitive market."[51]

Although Eisenhower and Benson were in agreement about the need to get government out of agriculture, Eisenhower was attuned to the need to devise policies that would allow the president to appear as a defender of the small farmer. Meeting with Benson, during the president's convalescence at Fitzsimmons Hospital in the fall of 1955, Eisenhower insisted on the need to show that "we are sympathetically concerned with the [farm] situation."[52] This desire to project his sympathy for the plight of the small family farm led Eisenhower to champion the Soil Bank program.[53]

In meetings with farm leaders and farm-belt congressmen, Eisenhower succeeded in conveying an impression of compassion and sympathy that contrasted with the heartless, close-minded image projected by Benson. Minnesota Republican Senator Edward Thye, for instance, tells of meeting with Benson to protest the secretary's decision to lower dairy price supports and finding that Benson "paid no attention" to his pleas. In contrast to Benson, who "you could sense . . . wasn't sympathetic to your views," Thye recalls that "once you reached the President, and he became aware that you may be right and his administrators wrong, he was as positive as, you might say, a rocket on the target."[54]

A similar tale is related by the master of the National Grange, Herschel D. Newsom. "I knew darn well," Newsom reports, "that basically, philosophically, he [Eisenhower] wanted to do what the Grange wanted to do." Eisenhower fed this impression, telling Newsom after one meeting: "Well, frankly Herschel, I think I find no disagreement with your philosophy and it sounds to me as though the Grange has worked out some mechanics pretty well. Now you go talk to Ezra." The obstacle, in Newsom's view, was that Benson was stubbornly committed to a rigid, free-market ideology, and Eisenhower, because of his "military philosophy," was unwilling to go over the head of his political lieutenants.[55]

Another Benson critic and Eisenhower admirer, North Dakota Senator Milton Young, recalled a debate over wheat price supports, in which he and other farm-state congressmen were pushing for full parity while Secretary Benson urged low price supports. Eisenhower, Young reported, "finally settled it himself by setting it at $2 a bushel." To Young, this scene showed that on farm policy Eisenhower was not "nearly as conservative as secretary Benson" and that in contrast to Benson, whom Young described as "stubborn," "immovable as a rock," and "irritating," Eisenhower was "tolerant" and "considerate."[56] By casting himself as the compassionate conciliator and Benson as the heartless ideologue, Eisenhower was able to shift criticism onto Benson while still pursuing his goal of reducing price-support payments for farmers.

In meetings with congressional leaders, Eisenhower let Benson defend the administration's position. On one such occasion, House Minority Leader Joe Martin and ranking Republican of the House Agricultural Committee William Hill came to the White House to press for a softening of the administration's position on reducing price supports for dairy products. According to Benson, after Martin and Hill made their appeal, "the President looked at me and again, for the umpteenth time, I had to say no."[57] By deferring to Benson's "expert" judgment, Eisenhower shifted congressional resentment onto the secretary.

Periodically, however, Eisenhower found it necessary to defend his secretary of agriculture publicly in order to maintain Benson's effectiveness. Defending a subordinate in the face of demands for that individual's resignation threatens to undermine the lightning rod relationship by making it more difficult for others to believe that significant policy differences exist between the leader and adviser. If a president is to sustain the adviser as lightning rod, he must defend the adviser in a way that leads critics to believe that the decision to retain the adviser is based on grounds other than agreement on policy.

This is precisely what Eisenhower tried to do. He defended Benson without identifying himself with Benson's policy positions. Typical were Eisenhower's comments at a 1958 news conference, in which the president defended Benson on the grounds that "when we find a man of this dedication, this kind of courage, this kind of intellectual and personal honesty, we should say to ourselves, 'We just don't believe that America has come to the point where it wants to dispense with the services of that kind of a person.'"[58] An even more masterful combination of firmly defending Benson's character while still distancing himself from Benson's policies can be seen in Eisenhower's response to Minnesota Senator Edward Thye's call for Benson's dismissal. Eisenhower wrote:

Naturally I am not unaware of your strong feelings in this matter; yet it seems to me that upon reflection you will concede to Mr. Benson not merely the right but more importantly the obligation vigorously to set forth the programs and concepts which, *in his best judgment,* are essential to the well being of our farm people. It is my opinion that if he failed to do so, he would be derelict in his responsibility, and though so doing may understandably create some difficulties, I hardly see how he could effectively carry out his responsibilities in any other manner.[59]

Judging by the explanations that key figures, including Thye, later gave for the president's decision to retain Benson, it would appear that Eisenhower was successful in defending Benson in a way that allowed him to maintain a sense of distance between himself and Benson's farm policies. Some years after the end of the Eisenhower administration, Thye was asked during an interview why he thought the president resisted calls from congressmen and farm leaders to fire Benson. Thye responded by telling the interviewer that he believed that Eisenhower thought: "I've delegated you as Secretary of Agriculture. It's your responsibility to administer that office, and I'm not going to interfere with you." This attitude, Thye reasoned, was probably leftover from Ike's military training.[60]

Even more revealing is the explanation that North Dakota Senator Milton Young, one of Benson's most vocal congressional critics, gave in answer to the same question. Young attributed the decision to retain Benson to Eisenhower's "lack of experience in political life." As a result, Young explained, Eisenhower was not "as familiar as most Presidents are with . . . the problems that arise from having Cabinet officials who have a different political philosophy than you have." Furthermore, Young suggested that Eisenhower was "a very tolerant, kindly, considerate person, [not] . . . the kind that would . . . fire someone . . . if he disagreed with him."[61] Thus despite publicly supporting Benson, Eisenhower persuaded key elites that Benson and Eisenhower disagreed on farm policy.

THE STRUGGLE OVER PRESIDENTIAL INVOLVEMENT

Although Benson was relatively successful at deflecting blame away from the president, uncritical acceptance of the lightning rod metaphor can obscure important questions about Eisenhower's strategy and Benson's role. Cabinet members are not inert objects, as the lightning rod metaphor implies, but strategic actors with objectives of their own. They may welcome the autonomy that delegation brings and willingly absorb the blame for unpopular policies, but they may also periodically require a president's public backing if they are to achieve their policy objectives. The president's need to distance himself from day-to-day controversies can thus conflict with the cabinet member's need to draw the president into the political fray.

Eisenhower was quite content for Benson to be "on the front lines, taking the blows,"[62] but Benson was not always so content to have Eisenhower maintain his distance from policy disputes. In his memoirs, Benson notes that from the outset "it was evident that the President expected to choose his men, give them sufficient authority, and let them work out proposed solutions to their problems which he could either approve or reject." While conceding this to be "good executive procedure," Benson believed that "in the case of agriculture the strength of the opposition and its readiness to do battle indicated that we needed the support of a President who himself had strong policy convictions. . . . Even the President's sympathetic understanding would not be enough; we had to have *fighting support*" (emphasis in original). If opponents succeeded in portraying the president and himself as divided, Benson realized that "our farm proposals would die of political malnutrition."[63]

Benson was consequently engaged in a continuous tug-of-war with members of the White House staff, who wanted to keep a safe distance between the president and Benson, over the public visibility of the president.[64] Typical of such wrangling was the struggle over the form in which the 1954 agricultural message should be delivered to Congress. The administration's proposal to abandon the fixed price supports established during World War II in favor of flexible supports was bound to create intense opposition. Desiring to maximize the distance between the president and controversy, some members of the White House staff wanted to have the department send up an agricultural message, accompanied only by a covering letter from the president. Benson insisted that the president should send the agricultural message, believing it was essential that we "get it across to Congress and the country that this wasn't a Benson recommendation, but an Eisenhower program." Benson explained to the president that "this message must be yours with no attachments. There should be one program—the administration's program, with no Benson plan." Eisenhower eventually relented and decided to do it Benson's way.[65]

Although the agricultural message was sent to Capitol Hill over the president's signature, Eisenhower managed to maintain some public distance from the program by having Benson hold a press conference immediately afterward to explain the proposals. The following day, the *New York Times* carried the text of the message accompanied by a picture not of the president but of Secretary Benson defending the message at the news conference.[66] Benson's public profile was further heightened by an extensive speaking tour he undertook to sell the administration's farm program.[67] With Benson having "carried the ball on farm policy,"[68] it is hardly surprising that friends and foes alike commonly referred to the administration's program as "Secretary Benson's farm program."

Although wary about drawing too close to Benson's agricultural policies,[69] Eisenhower also recognized that if he wanted to achieve his objective of reducing federal government involvement in agriculture he would periodically have to weigh in on the side of his farm program. Although Eisenhower carefully meted out his public involvement, he occasionally did assent to Benson's requests for public presidential backing. When things looked bleak for the administration's 1954 farm program, for example, Eisenhower consented to go on television to make a public appeal for the administration's bill.[70]

Without the president's public support for the 1954 program, it would undoubtedly, as Benson foresaw, have gone down to defeat. At the same time, more overt activity on the part of Eisenhower also opened him up to criticism from the opposition. The trade-off between policy objectives and personal popularity can be seen in congressional reaction to the president's vetoes of agricultural legislation.

AVOIDING THE VETO

In general, Eisenhower used the veto relatively sparingly (at least before 1958), particularly considering that for six years of his eight-year tenure both houses of Congress were controlled by the opposition party.[71] His reluctance to exercise the veto power was consistent with a leadership strategy aimed at keeping the president off the firing line. A veto threatens to undermine a lightning rod strategy by placing the president prominently and unambiguously on the front lines.[72]

Eisenhower's first veto of agricultural legislation did not occur until the spring of 1956. The Democrats, with at least one eye on the upcoming presidential election, had attached more than one hundred amendments to the administration's farm bill, many of which demanded a rigid 90 percent parity.[73] Eisenhower followed the advice of Secretary Benson and vetoed a bill that the president considered "less a piece of farm legislation than a private relief bill for politicians."[74]

Congressional Democrats immediately jumped on the president's veto as evidence that it was Eisenhower, and not just Benson, who was responsible for the administration's farm policy. Oklahoma Senator Robert Kerr, in typically extravagant language, declared:

No longer can any outraged American say that Eisenhower is not to blame for the farm policy of this administration. . . . Mr. Benson has a great many skirts, . . . but Ike can no longer hide behind them. The mask of hypocrisy has been stripped, and now he must stand forth in the full glitter of the shining truth that he is the implementor and architect of this farm policy. The nails that have been driven into the farmer's hands, the cross upon which he is being crucified, may have been furnished by Benson, but the hammer that drove those nails into the farmer's hands was wielded by the hand of Eisenhower. The hand that placed the crown of thorns upon the farmer's head was the hand of Eisenhower.[75]

Senator Allen Ellender, a Democrat from Louisiana, hammered away, although in a more restrained manner, at the same theme: "Heretofore Secretary of Agriculture Benson has been blamed for the present depressed plight of our agriculture, but now the farmers of the country will blame the President. They have no other alternative."[76] Hubert Humphrey, too, believed the veto exposed the reality that "it is Mr. Eisenhower's farm program, not poor Benson's. It is Mr. Eisenhower who is responsible."[77] South Carolina Senator Olin Johnston also felt himself "dutybound to take the President of the United States to task for his veto." He denounced Eisenhower for having "completely broken his word and faith with the farmers of the Nation." Eisenhower, Johnston concluded, had become "totally infected with the disease of the Republican Party that has plagued the little people of this country since the first Republican drew breath."[78]

Democratic efforts to pin the blame on Eisenhower failed, however, because Eisenhower, in a nationally televised address, took advantage of his above-politics image to persuade farmers that the blame lay with Congress for passing a "bad bill" that he had "no choice" but to veto.[79] His success in defining the bill as a political "hodge-podge" that was bad for the country was revealed by a subsequent Gallup poll of midwestern farmers, which showed that fewer than three in ten respondents disapproved of the president's veto.[80] Although Eisenhower had come through the incident relatively unscathed, the veto had left him more exposed to personal criticism than he preferred.[81]

Two years later, when Benson again recommended a presidential veto, this time of the "freeze bill," Eisenhower expressed exasperation with his secretary. Although Eisenhower decided to back Benson's decision, he was clearly upset that Benson was forcing him back onto an exposed stage. To White House aides, Eisenhower complained that he was "unhappy and irritated" about the position Benson had placed him in, and he told them that he "hated to veto the bill" because "his action would be taken as 'kicking the farmer in the teeth.' "[82] When Benson sent a letter to the president setting out the reasons why the legislation should be rejected,[83] Eisenhower sent back a testy reply reminding Benson that "there is little need for you to enumerate again all of the advantages both of us believe should result from our present farm program. I am not only familiar with these but have time and time again supported them publicly." Eisenhower went on to give Benson a lengthy lecture on politics, recalling the aphorisms: "Never lose the good in seeking too long for the best," or as some say it "The best is always the enemy of the good." "In future," Eisenhower advised, "we should avoid advanced positions of inflexibility. We must have some room for maneuver, or we shall suffer for it."[84]

LIGHTNING RODS HAVE PREFERENCES TOO

The preceding exchange, and others like it,[85] suggest that although Eisenhower and Benson were in agreement on the general direction of farm policy, Benson was not simply doing Eisenhower's bidding. If it was true, as Eisenhower told Benson, that "you and I rarely, if ever, had any difference of conviction as to the basic principles we should follow in our attempt to establish the proper relationship between the government and agriculture,"[86] it was also true that the two often had significantly different views about the pace of change.

The difference between the president and secretary manifested itself immediately after Eisenhower's election in a debate over whether price supports should be maintained at their current level until the current law expired in 1954, or whether flexible supports should instead be instituted immediately. Believing that his campaign pledge obligated him to maintain price supports for at least a year, Eisenhower refused to follow Benson's recommendation that fixed price supports be abandoned right away.[87] The same conflict over the pace of change was evident in a dispute in the summer of 1954 concerning the appropriate level for wheat price supports. At a meeting with legislative leaders, Benson suggested that

the impact [of a drop to 75 percent] would be softened by virtue of the fact that the price for wheat is now at 82 percent of parity rather than the theoretical 90 percent and that the drop to 75 percent would thus be limited to merely 7 percent. The President refused to accept that reasoning and called attention to the important psychological factor involved in dropping the formula's upper level from 90 percent to 75 percent.[88]

In both of these cases Eisenhower overruled Benson. But at other times, Benson's preference for more rapid change won out, as, for instance, when he decided at the outset of 1954 to reduce dairy price supports from 90 percent to 75 percent. This action, although consistent with Eisenhower's general position of reducing price supports, moved more precipitously than Eisenhower thought wise. In a private letter to his long-time friend Swede Hazlett, Eisenhower confessed that "I personally think that the Secretary of Agriculture made a mistake in failing to take smaller bites." [89]

Other elites sensed this difference between Eisenhower's emphasis on gradual reductions in price supports and Benson's preference for more sweeping changes. August Andresen, a Republican congressman from Minnesota, wrote to Eisenhower that he believed "the recent action of Secretary Benson to lower the support price on dairy products from 90 percent to 75 percent . . . was a terrible mistake. It was anticipated," Andresen continued, "that the Secretary of Agriculture would follow your suggestion by making a gradual reduction in the support price rather than to go the full limit allowed by law."[90] In a similar vein, Herschel Newsom, master of the National Grange, praised Eisenhower's call for gradual reduction of price supports, adding that "I have not seen recognition by the Department of Agriculture of the President's own emphasis on gradualism."[91]

Benson served as a target of criticism, then, because there *were* genuine differences of opinion between the president and the secretary of agriculture. The elite perception that Eisenhower was more disposed to "go slow" than Benson was grounded in reality. This important kernel of truth sustained the lightning rod by making it plausible for elites to blame Benson while appealing to Eisenhower to rein in his secretary.

EISENHOWER AND BLAME AVOIDANCE

Eisenhower's political sagacity did not lie solely, or even mainly, in his recognition that advisers could serve as lightning rods. Few are the presidents who have been unaware of the utility of deflecting blame onto subordinates. Rather, what distinguishes Eisenhower from other presidents is that his behavior made it possible for his subordinates to become plausible lightning rods.

Critically important to Eisenhower's ability to insulate himself from Benson's actions was the president's willingness to delegate significant decision-making authority to department heads.[92] Although Eisenhower played the pivotal role in shaping the administration's commitment to reducing price supports, the all-important details of this general policy (how fast, how far, which crops, and so on) were largely left to Benson. Like most department secretaries, Benson ran into conflict with White House staff members who felt his decisions did not conform with the president's policy. In his memoirs, Sherman Adams reported that Benson, "enveloped in a kind of celestial optimism, . . . convinced that his big decisions were right," would often carry out his plans without getting White House clearance.[93] Others (voicing the usual staff complaint about departmental sabotage) accused Benson of actively undermining presidential decisions.[94]

What differentiated Eisenhower from President Nixon or President Johnson was that he did not react to such reports of departmental subversion by drawing decision making into the White House. There are, of course, costs attached to this strategy: granting cabinet members autonomy means that public policy may not always develop in precisely the direction the president prefers.[95] But Eisenhower reaped advantages also. Allowing subordinates to exercise significant discretion made it plausible (rather than seeming disingenuous) to blame a cabinet member for a controversial policy, a claim I attempt to bolster in Chapter 4, which compares Eisenhower's use of Vice President Richard Nixon with Lyndon Johnson's use of Vice President Hubert Humphrey.

No less important in making Benson a successful lightning rod was Eisenhower's capacity to cloak his underlying intentions and principles in ambiguity, thus allowing those on different sides of an issue to read into Eisenhower's political views their own political preferences. Eisenhower's studied ambiguity allowed Secretary Benson and his allies to come away convinced that Eisenhower was a fervent believer in applying free-market principles to agriculture.[96] At the same time, supporters of continued high price supports, like Senators Edward Thye and Milton Young, continued to believe that Eisenhower was sympathetic to their viewpoint that government had an important role to play in helping farmers. Both sides thus believed that were the president to become more involved he would side with them.

The importance of this ambiguity in sustaining a lightning rod can be better appreciated by contrasting Benson's eight-year tenure as secretary of agriculture with James Watt's two-and-a-half years as secretary of interior under President Ronald Reagan. Watt's viability as a lightning rod, the subsequent chapter argues, was severely handicapped by the ideological clarity of Reagan's environmental vision.

3

Reagan's Liability:
Secretary of Interior James Watt

Lightning rods figured prominently in the strategic thinking of top officials in the Reagan White House. Reagan aides were determined to avoid what they perceived to be the prior administration's error of overexposing the president. "One of the most destructive aspects of the Carter administration," observed David Gergen, Reagan's first director of communications, "was that they continually let him go out there and be the point man, on everything!"[1] Unlike Carter, Reagan would delegate authority and responsibility to subordinates. As one presidential aide told a *New York Times* reporter: "The President feels that he ought not to be answering questions about the B-1 bomber or anything else that specific. . . . His job is to announce broad policy. Let Cap Weinberger take the heat on the B-1 or let Ted Bell take the heat for cuts in school aid. We believe in the delegation of authority."[2] "It is terribly important," Gergen explains, "that the President not be out on the line every day, particularly on bad news. . . . You only have one four-star general in battle, but you've got a lot of lieutenants who can give blood. And if the going is getting hot and heavy, it is far better to have your lieutenants take the wounds than your general." This meant that "on the budget issue, we intentionally put [David] Stockman out front" and "on environmental issues, as controversial as [James] Watt was, it was better to have Watt out talking about environmental issues than the President."[3]

White House staff took care to have bad news or unpopular policies announced at departments. Press Secretary Larry Speakes explained ("mostly tongue-in-cheek" he insisted later): "What's good news, we announce at the White House; bad news comes from Interior or Education."[4] James Baker, Reagan's first chief of staff, made sure that proposed Social Security reforms in the spring of 1981 were announced by Health and Human Services Secretary Richard Schweiker rather than by the White House, and, as negative congressional reaction mounted, White House staff began referring to the package on background as "Schweiker's Folly."[5] Baker's successor, Don Regan, told Secretary of Agriculture John Block that it was the department's job to get the farm credit story out to the press. "We were keeping the President away from it," Regan later explained, because it was "a no-win situation in which the President can be damaged because there literally is no way to help these farmers."[6] When Watt resigned in the spring of 1983, Reagan's staff canceled a scheduled environmental address "because it would shift the attention to the President" and opted instead for a low-key appearance at the swearing-in ceremony of Watt's successor, William P. Clark. "The idea," explained a presidential aide, "was, 'Get it over there [in the Interior Department].' When we have something developed that we can go out and talk about in a positive way, then bring it back to the White House."[7]

The administration's lightning rod strategy was facilitated by Reagan's detached leadership style. Avoiding blame on a policy gone awry was bound to be easier for a president who was widely reported to be inattentive to and uninformed about the details of policy. Claims of noninvolvement that would have seemed disingenuous if not dishonest coming from a Carter or a Johnson were believable coming from Reagan. Of course, the style itself invited criticism from those who felt this degree of detachment to be unbecoming a president of the United States. As was the case with Eisenhower, Reagan absorbed a steady stream of elite criticism disparaging him for being a caretaker president who simply ratified decisions reached by his advisers.[8] When these criticisms reached a crescendo, as in the case of Reagan being allowed to "sleep through" the 1981 downing of two Libyan fighter planes, White House staff vigorously worked to dispel the public image of Reagan as disengaged by emphasizing the president's involvement in the decision-making process.[9]

For the most part, however (at least before the Iran-contra scandal), Reagan and his aides generally seemed comfortable with the image of a relatively detached president, willing to sacrifice credit on some issues if it meant avoiding blame on most issues.[10] Reagan and his aides made a conscious effort not to have Reagan equated with everything that occurred in the government. "The President does not strictly speaking 'run the Government,' " one aide told a *New York Times* reporter. "He makes the key decisions, but the Government is 'run' in the department and agencies."[11] As Reagan himself, in a 1986 interview with *Fortune* magazine, explained his leadership philosophy, "I believe that you surround yourself with the best people you can find, delegate authority, and don't interfere as long as the policy you've decided upon is being carried out."[12]

In several respects, Reagan's public persona closely resembled Eisenhower's.[13] Both were widely viewed as passive executives, detached from the specifics of policy, affable but not particularly bright, and even somewhat befuddled. But in at least one critical respect Reagan and Eisenhower's public images and leadership styles were decisively different. Reagan came to office with a well-defined policy agenda and a past history of ideological commitment.[14] Eisenhower had never even voted before 1952, and his policy message often lacked definition. Few could have doubts about where Reagan stood on the issues that were dear to his heart; few ever did figure out exactly what Eisenhower or "modern" republicanism stood for.

One should be careful not to exaggerate Reagan's ideological clarity of purpose.[15] For one thing, as Bert Rockman points out, that clarity was "often . . . greater in rhetoric than in operations."[16] If the broad direction was clear, Reagan rarely offered much in the way of specific guidance about the policy implications of these general objectives.[17] Moreover, clarity of purpose was not characteristic of every policy area nor was it a constant throughout Reagan's tenure. In marked contrast to the clear policy agenda of the 1980 campaign, for instance, Reagan's 1984 reelection campaign was notably vague on specific issues.[18] And when it came to foreign policy, particularly in the second term, Reagan's position was often difficult to pin down. Did "letting Reagan be Reagan" mean following the path of confrontation with "the evil empire" or did it mean pursuing nuclear arms control? His cold warrior instincts coexisted with his desire to be remembered by history as a man of peace.[19] This lack of clarity, as Jane Mayer and Doyle McManus report, meant that "Schultz, Weinberger, Casey, and McFarlane all interpreted the president's will according to their own, often conflicting inclinations. Each insisted that he alone knew the true mind and meaning of the president; each insisted he was doing what the president truly wanted."[20] In domestic policy, however, particularly during the first term, Reagan's position was rarely ambiguous, even when his directives were framed broadly.

Reagan's well-defined agenda had its benefits. Because Reagan had made it clear to others where he stood on such issues as taxation and national defense, he was able to plausibly (even if incorrectly[21]) claim a mandate and push Congress to enact sweeping tax cuts and defense increases. But there was a downside to having a "clear and polarizing agenda that let everyone in government know what the broad objectives of the Reagan administration were."[22] Where Reagan's position was popular, as with taxes, clarity served him well. But in other areas where his position was unpopular, as with the environment or funding for the Nicaraguan contras, clarity often left Reagan exposed to criticism despite his detached governing style.

This chapter is a case study of how clarity of purpose can undermine a president's attempt to distance himself from policy conflict and thus thwart the attempt to deflect blame onto subordinates. The particular vehicle chosen for analyzing this phenomenon is the tenure of Reagan's first secretary of the interior, James Watt. Because Reagan unambiguously signaled to attentive elites that he favored economic growth over environmental protection, development over conservation, it was difficult for Watt (or Environmental Protection Agency [EPA] director Anne Gorsuch Burford) to provide effective cover for Reagan. Having a clearly defined ideology and agenda thus worked to undercut Watt's viability as a lightning rod.[23]

LIGHTNING ROD OR LIABILITY?

Was Watt a lightning rod or a liability? Proponents can be found on both sides of the question. Watt often referred to himself as a presidential lightning rod,[24] and his claim has been repeated by a number of commentators, among them Laurence Barrett and Hedrick Smith.[25] No evidence, however, is marshaled to support the contention. Others have argued the opposite thesis that Watt was a liability to President Reagan, bringing criticism to the president,[26] but again it is usually presented as a self-evident fact rather than a proposition needing to be established.

One of the aims in this chapter is to show that evidence can be brought to bear on these competing claims. In the case of Watt, the answer depends on the time period under investigation. During the first year of his tenure there is support for Watt's view of himself as a presidential lightning rod. Beginning in 1982, however, Watt afforded Reagan little, if any, protection from critics of the administration's environmental and public land policies, and by the third year of the Reagan presidency, Watt's high-voltage politics was unmistakably burning the president. In contrast to Secretary Benson, who served to deflect criticism away from Eisenhower throughout his eight-year tenure, Watt quickly became a liability for the president.

"THE SINS OF WATT"

During the summer of 1981, it was standard fare among political pundits and strategists to refer to Watt as a lightning rod for the president. Writing in August 1981, Kenneth Walsh of the *Denver Post*, for example, argued that Watt "is the lightning rod for the president's philosophy on natural resources, energy and the environment." Reagan, Walsh pointed out, "can look down from his lofty perch at the White House and watch Watt doing the dirty work for him."[27] A California Republican strategist agreed that Watt was serving Reagan as a lightning rod. "Watt's critics aren't striking at Reagan himself, are they?" he asked rhetorically.[28]

These claims accurately reflected the reality that during the first year, by and large, critics of the administration's environmental policies targeted Watt, not Reagan.[29] Typical in this respect was a much publicized speech delivered on May 2, 1981, by Nathaniel Reed, a Republican and former assistant secretary of interior under Presidents Nixon and Ford. Reed told his Sierra Club audience that "my quarrel is not with Ronald Reagan. I think he will be a good President and a notable environmentalist." Rather the source of the problem was James Watt and other appointees who "have broken faith with the Republican Party and betrayed their President." Pointing to the "significant environmental progress . . . California made . . . under the leadership of Governor Ronald Reagan," Reed suggested that Watt's reckless approach was at variance with "the environmental philosophy and the record of his President," which he characterized as "very good." Even "the Watt budget," Reed maintained, was "an aberration from . . . the true Reagan philosophy." Having reached the conclusion that Watt was "utterly lacking in the vision and judgment necessary to continue as Secretary of the Interior," Reed closed by reaffirming his belief that not only was "President Reagan . . . a good man . . . who knows and cares for the outdoors," but "that when he has fully recuperated [from the assassination attempt], he will steer the natural-resource policies of his Administration back in the direction of the great Republican leaders of the last two centuries."[30]

Even among those less sympathetic to Reagan, Watt was the primary target. California Senator Alan Cranston, for instance, called for Watt's resignation on the grounds that "his policies are reckless and irresponsible [and] a radical reversal of a long-standing bipartisan California tradition of love and respect for the land that includes probably as many Republicans as Democrats—in some cases even Ronald Reagan."[31]

The entire "dump Watt" movement, which was sponsored by the leading environmental organizations and climaxed during the late summer of 1981, focused almost exclusively on what the movement termed the "sins of Watt."[32] The Sierra Club opened the campaign against Watt in April by accusing him of "sabotaging conservation goals supported by a vast majority of the American people."[33] Environmental policies of the administration were commonly referred to as "Watt's policies." The president of the Wilderness Society, for example, called "Mr. Watt's policies . . . the gravest threat to the integrity of the national park system in its entire history."[34]

This separation that environmental and political elites drew between Watt and Reagan was reflected in public opinion polls taken during 1981. A CBS/ New York Times poll, conducted during September 1981, for instance, found that half the respondents believed they could "trust President Reagan to make the right kind of decision about the environment," while only a third did not.[35] Gallup polls conducted in June and October found more people approving of Reagan's handling of the environment than disapproving.[36] On the basis of a California Field poll conducted in August 1981, Mervin Field concluded that "President Reagan's popularity does not seem to be adversely affected by Watt's poor image. The public seems to separate the very favorable view it has of the president from that of the secretary of the interior."[37]

"RONALD REAGAN IS THE REAL JAMES WATT"

This separation between Watt and Reagan did not persist, however, much beyond the first year. Criticism of Watt increasingly became coupled with criticism of the president. Environmentalists came to see Reagan and Watt as a team bent on squandering the nation's natural resources.[38]

After the "dump Watt" movement of the summer of 1981 failed to produce Watt's dismissal, the notion that Watt was being flogged for what were in fact Reagan's policies became a recurrent theme in environmental circles, starting first with the more radical groups such as Friends of the Earth and then rippling out to more mainstream conservation groups, such as the Audubon Society and the National Wildlife Federation. A letter to the editor published in the October 1981 issue of the Friends of the Earth publication, *Not Man Apart,* strenuously objected to "the environmental movement's attacks on James Watt," who was only the president's "front man." The letter stressed that it was "a fundamental error" to blame Watt for what were after all "Mr. Reagan's policies." In closing, the letter called for environmentalists to "shift our fire from Mr. Watt and focus our efforts on Mr. Reagan and his administration."[39] This view was echoed by another reader who believed that "Watt is the symptom, Reagan is the disease."[40]

After a year of limiting themselves to criticizing Watt, Friends of the Earth launched a direct assault upon Ronald Reagan with a full-page advertisement in the *New York Times,* charging that "Mr. Reagan is the real James Watt." The advertisement scored Reagan for failing to make additions to the endangered species list, blocking additions to the national park system, and encouraging more oil drilling, logging, and strip mining. President Reagan, the ad continued, "is taking apart nearly every institution that protects planetary and human life. His actions and rhetoric are consistent: Destructive, disdainful and uncomprehending of environmental values."[41]

This shift in focus from Watt to Reagan was dramatized by the decision to rename the "Watt Watch" column in *Not Man Apart* "Administration Watching." The sacrifice in alliteration was necessary, the editors felt, because although Watt is "the most colorful of the Washington wrecking crew, he is by no means the only one." Accompanying the new monthly column was a telling picture of Ronald Reagan revealing himself behind a mask of James Watt.[42] Similarly, the Sierra Club announced in early 1982 that the campaign against Watt was being broadened into a "war on WATTism—the whole panoply of anticonservation policies of the Reagan administration."[43]

The changing focus among environmental groups can also be seen in the contrast between *The Watt Book,* published in August 1981 by the Wilderness Society at the height of the dump Watt movement, and an "indictment" released in March 1982 by ten leading environmental groups—including the Wilderness Society, Friends of the Earth, National Audubon Society, and the Sierra Club[44]—entitled *Ronald Reagan and the American Environment.* While the former publication had stressed Watt's betrayal of a bipartisan tradition of environmental protection, the latter never mentioned Watt and instead pinned the blame squarely on the president's shoulders. "President Reagan," the 1982 book begins, "has broken faith with the American people on environmental protection." Rather than calling for Watt's resignation, as *The Watt Book* had done, *Ronald Reagan and the American Environment* demanded that "President Reagan be called to task."[45]

Representatives of the ten environmental organizations that produced the 1982 report subsequently held a joint press conference in San Francisco, in which they sharply criticized Reagan for what they characterized as his "war on the environment." William Turnage, executive director of the Wilderness Society, blamed Reagan for the "incredible pattern of destruction of environmental programs" that amounted to a "counterrevolution." A representative of the Natural Resources Defense Council echoed Turnage's view, explaining that the decision to "indict" the president was made on the basis of "an across-the-board pattern of lawlessness and heedlessness with regard to the nation's natural resources." Repeating the charge made earlier by the Friends of the Earth, Turnage declared that "Ronald Reagan is the real James Watt."[46]

This anti-Reagan message was repeated by Russell Peterson, president of the Audubon Society, a former Republican governor of Delaware, and chair of the Council on Environmental Quality under Presidents Nixon and Ford. Writing in the *New York Times Magazine,* Peterson attacked Reagan personally for having "repudiated what I hold to be a Republican tradition of conservation and protection of natural resources that goes back to Theodore Roosevelt." "No other President in my experience," Peterson continued, "has seemed to be less caring about the need to protect the nation's natural beauty and natural resources." Peterson recounted the environmental movement's realization that Watt was "no maverick Cabinet officer whose zealous policies might embarrass the President," but rather "was doing exactly what he had been hired to do," which was prosecute "the President's war against environmental protection."[47]

Further evidence of this change in attitudes exists in the very different reactions that accompanied the 1981 scheme to increase oil drilling off the coast of California and Watt's announcement in August 1982 of the intention to sell off 35 million acres of "surplus" public lands to private companies. The former plan was widely portrayed as a product of Watt's "anti-environmental extremism," while the latter initiative was attributed directly to the Reagan White House, even though Watt, and not the White House, announced the plan.[48]

By 1983, the tendency among environmentalists to blame both Watt and Reagan was even more pronounced. When Watt announced a coal-leasing plan in the summer of 1983, for instance, the Sierra Club immediately went after Reagan in an article entitled "Coal Leasing: More Reagan Giveaways."[49] In the minds of environmentalists, Reagan was so closely identified with the cause of privatization that they saw Watt's role as little more than announcing the president's policy.

Another full page advertisement taken out by Friends of the Earth, this time in early 1983, showed just how intimately connected Reagan and Watt had become in the minds of the group's leaders. Under pictures of the president and the secretary, the ad declared:

> After two years, it's clear that Ronald Reagan and James Watt do not believe in preserving publicly owned land for the future. They have made unconscionable "sweetheart" leases to oil, mining and timber companies within your national forests and wilderness. They have refused to add to the national parks. . . . Reagan and Watt have shown virtually religious devotion to converting public land to private use. . . . Their minds are set in concrete and their hearts are cold to the natural world. To them, the only values in nature are commercial ones.[50]

More moderate voices followed in stressing the consistency between Watt's statements and actions and Reagan's preferences. John Seiberling (D-Ohio), chair of the House Interior subcommittee on public lands, concluded that "it begins to appear that Mr. Crowell and Mr. Watt are not acting on their own but are part of an Administration-wide broadside assault on the nation's wilderness heritage."[51] In the summer of 1981, former President Jimmy Carter had publicly criticized "the misguided and radical new policies of the Department of Interior" without ever mentioning Reagan by name, but two years later he lambasted Reagan personally for "a deliberate across-the-board abandonment of United States leadership on environmental issues."[52]

Editorials in the *Los Angeles Times,* which had begun by reserving criticism for Watt, eventually felt forced to conclude that the "only . . . reason why President Reagan would continue to tolerate Watt in his cabinet" is that "he must agree with Watt's policies." The *Times* described "Watt's, and Reagan's, policies" as "totally unacceptable to a majority of Americans." Watt, the *Times* concluded, was only "the whipping boy for the wrongful conservation policies of the Reagan Administration."[53]

The reaction among environmentalists to Watt's resignation in the fall of 1983 provides additional evidence that Watt had long since ceased to function as a lightning rod. Watt's departure, according to Sierra Club president Denny Shaffer, meant "the insults to the nation's intelligence will end, but not the assaults on the environment." Liz Railbeck, legislative analyst for Friends of the Earth, acknowledged that "we are delighted to see Watt go" but quickly added that "we feel Ronald Reagan has the responsibility for three years of environmental wreckage. You don't change Ronald Reagan by getting rid of James Watt. The mouth is gone, but the policies are apt to be the same." These sentiments were echoed by Rafe Pomerance, president of Friends of the Earth, who stated that "Ronald Reagan bears the responsibility for nearly three years of mounting environmental wreckage left by James Watt. The general in charge of *Ronald Reagan's war on the environment* may be gone but the Commander-in-Chief and just about all the officers remain." Marion Edney, head of the League of Conservation Voters, agreed that Watt's resignation "doesn't change the fact that Ronald Reagan remains personally responsible for the actions of his agents." Democratic party national chair Charles Manat reminded people that "James Watt has been speaking for Ronald Reagan. . . . The President has been letting Watt be Reagan."[54] Believing that Watt was only executing the Reagan agenda, Democratic elites and environmental activists did not view Watt's departure as likely to result in policy changes.

The elite view stressing the similarity between Watt and Reagan trickled down to the mass public. Increasingly the public connected Reagan personally with antienvironmental positions. In contrast to the Gallup polls taken in June and October of 1981, which had shown slim pluralities approving of Reagan's handling of the environment, surveys conducted by Gallup in 1982 and 1983 found increasing disapproval of Reagan's handling of environmental issues. Whereas in June 1981, 39 percent had approved of Reagan's handling of the environment and 33 percent disapproved, by the following June the numbers had reversed, with 35 percent approving of Reagan's performance and 41 percent disapproving. By the following April, the public perception of Reagan's performance had slipped even further, with only 33 percent approving and 49 percent disapproving.[55] Only after the firing of Watt did a plurality again express approval of Reagan's handling of environmental issues.[56]

Even more telling was a *Washington Post*/ABC News poll, conducted in February 1983, which found that by a two to one margin (54 to 27 percent) the public believed Reagan "cares more about protecting the firms that are violating antipollution laws than he cares about enforcing those laws."[57] Virtually the same percentage (60 percent) of the public answered the same way when asked the identical question about Anne Gorsuch Burford, suggesting that Reagan's public image on environmental matters was not much different from that of his environmental advisers.

THE COSTS OF IDEOLOGICAL CLARITY

If Eisenhower's behavior encouraged the impression that the president was following the judgment of his secretary, Reagan's behavior often fostered the opposite belief that Watt was following the ideological dictates of the president. In contrast to Eisenhower's studied ambiguity, Reagan did little to cultivate an image on environmental issues that was distinct from Watt's.[58] If President Reagan's EPA director, Anne Gorsuch Burford, could reach the conclusion that the president "doesn't care about the environment,"[59] then it is hardly surprising that others less sympathetic to Reagan arrived at the same conclusion.

One of the most important factors working to undercut Watt's status as a lightning rod was the Reagan administration's highly ideological pattern of appointments to key environmental posts.[60] Because a president's appointments are carefully scrutinized by elites as indicators of a president's intentions, they play an important role in sustaining a lightning rod. For environmentalists, Watt was only "the largest sparkler in this diadem of Republican rhinestones," which included Anne Gorsuch Burford as head of the EPA; John Crowell, an outspoken critic of restrictions limiting timber cutting in national forests, as the man in charge of the United States Forest Service at the Department of Agriculture; Robert Burford, a leader of the Sagebrush Rebellion, as Bureau of Land Management chief; and James Harris, who as an Indiana state senator had argued that the federal law to control strip mining was unconstitutional, as head of the Office of Surface Mining.[61] By filling so many top positions with people perceived as antienvironment (and by centralizing appointments in the White House), Reagan telegraphed his intentions to environmentalists and thereby undermined Watt's utility as a lightning rod.

During Watt's tenure, Reagan made only occasional, half-hearted efforts to persuade environmentalists of his good intentions, with little success.[62] Toward the beginning of 1982, Ed Meese and other White House aides met with three prominent environmental leaders—Russell Peterson of the National Audubon Society, Jay Hair of the National Wildlife Federation, and J. Michael McCloskey of the Sierra Club—to persuade them that Reagan was a "good environmentalist." Instead, Peterson reported, the meeting served only to provide "confirmation of the complete disrespect on the part of the President and his team for what . . . the conservation and environmental movement stand for." "To describe President Reagan as a good environmentalist, as Meese did," Peterson said later, "is a claim that would never meet the truth-in-advertising standards."[63]

In July 1983, President Reagan tried to reach out to the environmental community by meeting with the famous photographer and naturalist Ansel Adams. According to Adams, Reagan told him that "we are not so far apart as you think we are. I've always been an environmentalist." Adams remained unconvinced, however, telling the press afterward that the president had a "totally different concept of the world and it is very hard to break through."[64] The effort was too little, too late.

Reagan's campaign statements made it even more difficult to persuade environmentalists that his intentions toward them were ambivalent, let alone benevolent. During the 1980 campaign, Reagan had publicly identified himself with the Sagebrush Rebellion—"count me in," he told a Utah audience.[65] His assertions during the campaign that air pollution in the United States had been "substantially controlled" and that nature rather than industry was the chief cause of air pollution helped to sow distrust toward Reagan among those attentive to environmental issues.[66]

Reagan's vigorous public defenses of Watt further eroded the ambiguity of his position. Here it might be objected that Reagan was behaving no differently than President Eisenhower, who also forcefully defended his secretary of agriculture against critics. The difference is that Eisenhower defended Benson without attacking his opponents, and often without even siding with Benson's policy positions. Reagan, in contrast, joined Watt in attacking the secretary's critics. In August 1981, for instance, as anti-Watt sentiment was reaching a peak, Reagan not only pledged his "full support" for Watt, but expressed his opinion that Watt was correct that "we have been victimized by some individuals that I refer to as environmental extremists."[67] By accepting Watt's definition of his opposition as "extremists," Reagan hardened environmental attitudes toward himself. The more closely Reagan identified himself with Watt the more difficult it became for critics to follow Nathaniel Reed's lead of defending the president while attacking Watt's policy.

A notable exception to Reagan's pattern of identifying himself with Watt in opposition to "environmental extremists" came in the March 23, 1983, press conference announcing William Ruckelshaus's appointment as head of the EPA. In this conference, Reagan tried to stake out a middle position between the "zealots on both sides." Some people, Reagan acknowledged, "won't be satisfied unless they can pave over the entire countryside."[68] The conciliatory rhetoric, as well as the act of selecting the highly respected Ruckelshaus, made Reagan seem more sympathetic to the environment than his secretary of interior and thus might have been a first step in making Watt a more plausible lightning rod.

This press conference, however, remained an isolated incident and never became part of a consistent strategy for distancing himself from Watt. Indeed only ten days earlier, Reagan had encouraged direct attacks upon his person by attacking, in words reminiscent of Watt, his opponents' motives. "The lobbyists for the environmental interests," Reagan suggested at a March 12 press conference, "feel that they have to keep their constituents stirred up or they might not have jobs anymore." Those who attacked Anne Gorsuch Burford, Reagan continued, were not concerned about the environment or wrongdoing, but rather were motivated by opposition to the administration and its policies.[69] In an interview at the end of the month, a week after announcing the Ruckelshaus appointment, Reagan repeated his belief that "professional" environmentalists who criticized Watt weren't interested in solving problems, only in making sure "their careers will go on."[70]

Reagan's behavior contrasts strikingly with that of Eisenhower who, as Fred Greenstein has pointed out, studiously avoided calling into question opponents' motivations.[71] A key ingredient in getting others to believe that his intentions were good, Eisenhower reasoned, was to resist the temptation to call into question the intentions of those with whom he disagreed.

The lesson of Reagan's experience in the environmental arena is that a willingness to delegate, although probably a necessary condition, is not sufficient for a presidential lightning rod to work successfully. If distance from day-to-day operations tended to protect Reagan, his ideological orientation, as read by others through campaign statements, appointments, and attacks on the environmentalists, kept him more closely identified with policy than his hands-off management strategy might have suggested. Reagan's words and actions created a sense that, as a writer for *Audubon* put it, "if Jim Watt did not exist, Ronald Reagan would have had to invent him. Watt is everything Reagan wanted at Interior."[72] In sum, Reagan was too closely connected ideologically with the schemes that Watt and Burford were carrying out, such as privatization and deregulation, to allow him to maintain the same degree of separation between the policy and the person that Eisenhower achieved in the area of agriculture.

A SELF-INFLICTED LIGHTNING STORM

Although Watt's failure as a lightning rod was importantly connected to President Reagan's leadership style, Watt's own actions also contributed to that failure. In the first place, Watt himself furthered the impression of a close link between Watt and Reagan. When faced with criticism, Watt frequently stressed his ideological affinity with Reagan. The president and he, Watt insisted, were "soul mates" on environmental issues.[73] In an early interview with *Public Opinion,* Watt suggested that "no other Secretary of the Interior, in recent times at least, has had a President who understands my department like Ronald Reagan does. . . . When I said, 'I want to do this, I want to do that,' he replied, 'Sic 'em.'"[74] Watt's repeated insistence on portraying himself as a presidential lightning rod,[75] ironically, undermined his ability to function as a lightning rod, for, as Fred Greenstein comments, "an aide viewed as a lightning rod . . . will not keep bolts from striking the president."[76]

Watt's failure to function as a successful lightning rod was also due to his penchant for controversial public gaffes on matters totally unrelated to environmental policy. Too often the creation of controversy is taken as a sufficient indicator of the existence of a lightning rod effect. But Watt resembled less a lightning rod than a storm creator, as his one-liners—from his comments about the Beach Boys, to his letter to Moshe Arens, to his joke about the coal lease advisory commission as including "a black, a woman, two Jews, and a cripple"—sent the White House scrambling for cover. A presidential aide deserves the appellation "lightning rod" only for absorbing heat in the pursuit of a president's objectives or for absorbing blame for negative outcomes, not for generating gratuitous controversy.

To be sure, many of the policies Watt pursued were bound to generate controversy. No interior secretary could aggressively promote oil drilling off the coast of California, accelerate the leasing of western public lands for coal mining, and attempt to open up national wilderness areas to mineral exploration, and hope to avoid becoming embroiled in controversy.[77] Interviewed in 1990, Reagan indicated that Watt had done what Reagan wanted done. "I appointed him," Reagan explained, "with the understanding that he was going to do those things that he and I had talked about. . . . And he knew when he took the job that he would turn enough people off that pretty soon he would lose any effectiveness that he had if he did the things that we wanted done. . . . And I have to say, if you look back and analyze point by point the things that were done, he was darn good."[78]

Even viewed solely from the perspective of Reagan's own strategic and programmatic interests, Watt's tenure was far from the success Reagan claims. As Paul Portney points out in a review of the Reagan administration's environmental record during the first term, although many of the administration's public land and water resource policies were "inherently controversial," "they became more so because of Secretary Watt."[79] Much of the criticism of Watt, Portney argues, stemmed as much from style as from substance, particularly from Watt's unwillingness to consult with state government officials and congressional committees or subcommittees and their staffs.[80]

To be sure, style is not so easily separated from substance. It is difficult to be inclusive and cooperative while pursuing policies that radically break with existing expectations and constituencies. The style—confrontation and exclusion—stems from the substance—radical change in the direction of public policy. But in refusing to permit political realities to shape strategic calculations, Watt squandered opportunities to restore the balance between commercial versus natural uses of public lands that the Reagan administration believed had been lost in the preceding decade. Watt expected to be able to trade on Reagan's support; he failed to understand that success depended in large part on building support so that the president could then afford to back his preferences.[81]

Portney identifies a number of areas where it would have been possible for a more politically skillful secretary to enact significant changes in directions consistent with the Reagan administration's basic philosophy. There was, for instance, "a large measure of expert consensus" on reducing federal spending in areas such as federal water projects. There was also substantial support for increased leasing of energy resources on public lands; indeed the Carter administration had already pledged to increase such leasing in a second term. In addition, a number of long-time observers of public land management had concluded that some federal lands were too difficult to manage and not worth the trouble; support also existed for selling or exchanging certain lands to local or state governments. Moreover, even some of those sympathetic to the environmental movement felt that the multiple-use mandate had been supplanted by "the ideological fantasy that the only decent and harmonious natural relationships were nonconsuming ones."[82] Had Watt's definition of his policy goals combined judgments about what is desirable with estimates about what is possible, he might have been able to advance significantly the Reagan agenda.[83]

Instead, Watt's attempt to radically recast governmental policy created so much controversy that relatively little change actually occurred, a fact celebrated by liberals and lamented by conservatives but agreed upon by both.[84] Writing toward the close of Reagan's first term, one expert concluded that despite the liability that environmental and natural resource policy had become for Reagan, "less happened, for good *and* for ill, than either the administration promised or the public believes." "In spite of the administration's intention to greatly increase public land sales," for instance, "such transactions have been no greater than in previous administrations because of adverse public and congressional reaction." "In spite of all the *Sturm und Drang*, . . . no truly fundamental change" took place at the Interior Department.[85]

Such an outcome was not preordained by the nature of contemporary public opinion on the environment. Public support for the environment is widespread, but the issue is not highly salient for most people most of the time. Although during the 1980s a substantial majority of Americans, for instance, agreed that environmental protection standards "cannot be too high" and believed environmental improvements must be made "regardless of cost," only a small fraction named the environment as one of the most important problems facing the country.[86] In such situations where public opinion is characterized by a "permissive consensus," Riley Dunlap explains, the government ordinarily "has considerable flexibility in pursuing the goal and is not carefully monitored by the public." Only if administration policy becomes "obviously out of tune with the public consensus" does the administration risk incurring substantial political costs.[87] By violating that zone of indifference, Watt helped to create a backlash against the administration's policies and to discredit antienvironmental positions in a way that continues to hamper the Republican party.[88]

SEDUCTION BY METAPHOR

It is one thing to shoulder the blame for a controversial policy; it is quite another to push an agenda so recklessly that one discredits a president's policy objectives. One of the great dangers of the lightning rod metaphor is that its uncritical use can lull cabinet members into a false sense of usefulness. To claim lightning rod status is to suggest that the criticism one is receiving is a sign that one is serving the president well. Little wonder then that Watt rushed to endorse the description of himself as a lightning rod for it allowed him to wear controversy as a badge of honor. But the label begs some tough questions.

To say, as David Gergen does, that "on environmental issues, as controversial as Watt was, it was better to have Watt out talking about environmental issues than the President" sidesteps the question of whether Reagan would have been better served by another interior secretary (a la Donald Hodell) who would pursue the same basic policies in a less confrontational and controversial manner.[89] Even if criticisms of Watt had been completely insulated from perceptions of the president (which, we have seen, they were not), we would still need to ask about the effect that Watt's actions had on the administration's ability to achieve its policy objectives. The danger of the lightning rod metaphor is that it tempts us to avoid asking this all-important question.

The answer in Watt's case is clear enough. As Paul Portney, among others, has pointed out, Watt's "style created a backlash that came to stand in the way of achieving his substantive objectives."[90] In the face of mounting criticism, the Reagan administration had to retreat from many of its policy objectives. Not only did public support for environmental positions and groups increase in the wake of Watt's tenure,[91] but sensible antienvironmental positions became tarnished with the brush of antienvironmental extremism. To have Watt out front on environmental issues did not so much deflect blame away from the president as to caricature antienvironmentalism in such a way as to make it easier for environmentalists to mobilize support and to thwart administration objectives. To speak of Watt as a lightning rod is thus not only to misstate Watt's effect on public support for Ronald Reagan but, more important, to lose sight of Watt's monumental failure as a public manager and political strategist.

LESSONS FROM THE BUSH PRESIDENCY

In a recent paper, political scientists Michael Kraft and Norman Vig ask, "Why So Little Applause for the Bush Environmental Record?"[92] As they surveyed the Bush environmental record toward the end of the summer of 1990, they found a president who had attempted to strike a judicious balance between decisions that supported environmental values and decisions that gave priority to economic development. Despite Bush's substantial environmental achievements and his markedly better environmental record than Reagan's,[93] Kraft and Vig found that "Bush gets surprisingly little credit from the environmental community or from the public at large." The environmental community focused on those decisions that favored economic development and gave the president little credit for those decisions that came down on the side of environmental values.[94] Just a few months before the president would sign the Clean Air Act in November 1990, for instance, a Sierra Club official could blast Bush for his "shameful lack of leadership on the global environment."[95] Toward the end of his term, as the debate about the president's role at the Earth Summit in Rio de Janeiro reached its peak, criticism of Bush among environmentalists reached a crescendo. Many environmentalists had come to believe that "Mr. Bush is no environmentalist." A few even insisted that he would go "down in history, second only to Ronald Reagan, as America's anti-environmental President."[96]

The rising tide of negative elite evaluations trickled down to the mass public. Although the American public rated Bush better on the environment than it had Reagan, it still did not view Bush's environmental performance particularly positively.[97] Even when Bush's overall approval scores were high, 62 percent of the public said that Bush had "mostly just talked about" protecting the environment rather than having "really made progress."[98] By the summer of 1992, only 31 percent approved of Bush's handling of the environment.[99] Cued by elite interpretations, the public came to see the gap between Bush's rhetoric and his administration's actions not as a sign that the president was well intentioned but rather that he was insincere.

Kraft and Vig attribute Bush's failure to get credit for the environmental achievements of his administration in part to poor salesmanship on the part of the Bush White House. But Kraft and Vig also argue that a large part of the answer lies in the "demanding and highly critical environmental community."[100] Bush's failure as a leader, in other words, cannot be explained without looking at his would-be followers. Why were these followers so unwilling to accept the mixed record of the Bush administration? Why were they so unforgiving of the president when the administration leaned in the direction of economic growth? And why were they so unappreciative of the president when the administration leaned in an environmental direction?

Before explaining Bush's failure, though, it is worth recalling the good will initially shown toward Bush in the environmental community and the words and deeds through which Bush earned that good will. Bush self-consciously set out to differentiate himself from the more divisive, partisan politics of Reagan, not only in the area of the environment but also in such areas as civil rights and education.[101] The "kinder, gentler" phrase was meant to convey Bush's intention to govern by inclusion and conciliation rather than through polarization and confrontation.[102]

Throughout the first year or so of the administration, Bush appeared to be quite successful in persuading environmentalists that his heart was with them even when his policies always weren't. After meeting with president-elect Bush, Jay Hair, president of the National Wildlife Federation, told reporters that he found the difference between Mr. Bush and President Reagan's "ideological shrillness and lack of commitment to good stewardship of the land" to be like "night and day."[103] Shortly into the new administration, journalist Jack Germond commented that he thought "Bush's heart is in the right place on environmental questions. His record is not up to this point, but I think it is too soon to tell."[104]

Bush's appointments, particularly the selection of William Reilly as head of the EPA but also the choice of Michael Deland as head of Council on Environmental Quality (CEQ) and Robert Grady as associate director of the Office of Management and Budget (OMB) for natural resources, energy, and science, helped to signal the president's sympathy for environmental positions.[105] The appointment of Reilly gave Bush something Reagan never had in his first two and a half years: a prominent administration official with credibility in the environmental community who could try, as one official close to Mr. Reilly put it, "to reassure his friends that he believes that the President has his heart in the right place."[106] When the White House weakened a wetlands agreement to take into account objections raised by Alaskan officials and development interests, for instance, Reilly explained to a reporter that "the President's commitment to no net loss of wetlands is one he believes in quite strongly."[107]

The portrayal of Bush as a president with environmental instincts opened the way for advisers to play the role of lightning rod when administration policy did not match presidential rhetoric. Several people within the administration played this role but none so visibly or with such gusto as Chief of Staff John Sununu.[108] As early as February 1990, leaders of eight national environmental groups wrote to Bush to complain that "the direct, personal involvement of your chief of staff [is] reversing your pledges [and] driving a wedge between you and conservationists."[109] "You have articulated laudable goals," the signers continued, "but it appears your chief of staff is not committed to meeting them." Sununu was identified as the "nation's chief environmental foe" and as "the new James Watt."[110] Sununu's "idea of open space," joked one critic, "was a K Mart parking lot." Sununu was charged with "isolating President Bush from other world leaders on environmental issues." A *New York Times* editorial scored Sununu for an "impatience with environmentalists [that] stops just short of contempt."[111] Columnist Tom Wicker excoriated Sununu, "the White House chief of everything," for his "myopic approach to energy," and columnist Leslie Gelb held Sununu responsible for Jim Baker's and William Reilly's unwillingness to speak their minds in public and to the president.[112]

Sununu attracted perhaps the most intensive criticism for his role in the dispute over global warming. The press carried the story of an arrogant chief of staff high handedly overriding the considered opinion of not only the relevant experts within the administration but within the entire scientific community.[113] Sununu's skepticism of the models upon which predictions of greenhouse warming are based was genuine; what was misleading was the implication that Sununu was a rogue elephant. In fact Sununu expressed the misgivings of important elements within the Republican party who feared that warnings of "global warming" and impending doom were being used by environmentalists to justify government regulation of private enterprise. Because the debate over global warming has critically important consequences for how we choose to organize our social lives—if nature is resilient, individuals should be left to their own devices; if nature is fragile, individuals should be regulated in the name of the collective good—it is understandable that the controversy is politically charged.[114] It is also understandable that a president who conceives of himself as an environmentalist and wants others to do so would give Sununu running room on an issue that is central to the Republican party's self-definition and yet also has proven troublesome for Republicans who have not yet figured out how to package this skepticism without seeming to be indifferent to "the fate of the earth."

The environmentalists' view of Bush as a president whose good intentions were being thwarted and diverted by scheming aides was genuine. It was not just dissembling designed to avoid antagonizing a popular president. Even relatively dispassionate observers, like Kraft and Vig, for instance, felt that "Bush's advisers may be pulling him back from his political instinct to support environmental efforts."[115] Kraft and Vig's harshest condemnation is reserved for Sununu. The chief of staff, they argue, "has clearly exerted personal influence on climate change policy that goes . . . beyond his own technical competence. He has imposed his own judgment against others' on scientific issues in a manner that reflects his biases and values."[116]

This sense that Bush, unlike his immediate predecessor, possessed environmental instincts is what enabled Sununu to be an effective lightning rod. Many environmentalists seemed to believe that if only Bush had another chief of staff or if only Bush would involve himself more directly in environmental policy making, administration policy with respect to climate change or wetlands preservation or clean air would look very different.[117] Sununu was well cast as an environmental bogeyman for not only did he exercise considerable power but he also harbored a well-advertised distrust of the scientific evidence that provided the basis for many environmental proposals.[118]

Ultimately, though, Sununu's role as an environmental lightning rod broke down, and environmentalists increasingly aimed their pointed barbs directly at the president. Environmentalists became less and less willing to view Bush's intentions in a charitable light. As the attacks became more vehement and more personal, administration officials publicly expressed "a growing frustration here that we never get credit for anything."[119] In the spring of 1990, press reports emerged that Bush "privately has seethed at the criticism from [environmental] activists, angry that they keep demanding more when he believes he has offered them much."[120] The simmering feud erupted in public in the summer of 1990, with headlines proclaiming, "Bush, Environmentalists End Relationship in a Huff."[121] Environmentalists criticized Bush for bad faith, broken promises, and empty rhetoric. Many in the Bush administration, meanwhile, wrote environmentalists off as implacable critics who could not be pleased. As one Bush aide expressed it, "If we are going to get beat up, why bother?"[122]

Why did the environmental community give Bush so little credit and so much blame? Why were they so hypercritical of an administration that had done so much better than its predecessor? Robert Grady of the OMB offers an organizational explanation. In order to maintain and expand their memberships, Grady argues, environmental groups must continually press for more.[123] If the groups praise the administration, members may feel that there is a less pressing need to contribute to the group. If things are going well on the environmental front, contributors may decide that perhaps scarce resources would be better spent in some other area. To combat this threat to organizational maintenance, these organizations keep up a steady drumbeat of criticism and demands. There is truth to this analysis, but there must be more to the story. After all, many voluntary groups share this same basic incentive structure yet not all are as harshly critical of existing policies and authority or as apocalyptic about the future as are environmentalists.

An additional part of the story is provided by focusing on the egalitarian, antiauthority ethos of many environmental advocates.[124] Many such advocates are openly hostile to the political and economic system and are not particularly interested in letting the president, or any other established leaders, off the hook.[125] Lightning rods presuppose followers who want to believe in leaders. In the absence of such a belief, blame avoidance is not a viable strategy. But this explanation by itself is also insufficient. Many environmentalists are Republicans. The leaders of organizations like the National Wildlife Federation and even the Sierra Club are very much part of the establishment and regularly engage in the necessary bargains and compromises of politics.[126]

Bush's failure to continue to deflect blame in the area of environmental policy is more deeply rooted still. It is a failure that is grounded in a growing ideological divide between political elites on environmental questions that made it virtually impossible for Bush to chart a middle course.[127] The gap between movement conservatives and business interests on the one hand and environmentalists on the other was simply too great. Passage of the Clean Air Act seemed to belie this divide but the division quickly reasserted itself in the intense debate over how to enforce the law. One senior administration official confided, "At the heart of this debate [are] really . . . different world view[s] inside this administration." The opposing sides tried to iron out their differences in a series of contentious sessions, but "the conclusion was the sides were so far apart that Bush would have to make the choice."[128] Similarly, Bush found it virtually impossible to adopt and hold a middle ground in the controversies swirling around the Earth Summit. Bush's "split-the-difference" or "find-a-balance" pattern of decision making ultimately proved ill suited to a political environment in which the competing sides were so far apart that compromise was seen as unacceptable to both sides.[129]

But ideological polarization among followers is not the whole story either. For Bush's own rhetoric was also critically important in undermining the president's desire to deflect blame onto subordinates. When Bush promised to be the "environmental president," he invited voters to judge him on the basis of his administration's actions in this policy area. Yet the environment was, as Kraft and Vig point out, in fact "a low salience issue for the president."[130] Bush was thus asking voters to hold him personally accountable for an area of public policy in which he would play little role and in which policy direction was hotly contested within his party. Rhetoric is never mere rhetoric. Those who favored environmentalist positions used Bush's own words to hold the president's feet to the fire. A *New York Times* editorial, for instance, argued that "Mr. Bush takes pride in his innovative clean air bill and his decision to join an international agreement to abolish ozone-threatening chemicals. Those are fine achievements, but *they do not unhook him from a campaign promise* he made on Aug. 31, 1988. 'Those who think we are powerless to do anything about the 'greenhouse effect' are forgetting about the 'White House effect,' he said. 'As President, I intend to do something about it.' Do what?"[131] Such widely publicized campaign commitments may have given the president a popular issue on which to run but by lifting his profile on the issue those same promises made it more difficult for him later to deflect blame onto subordinates.

Yet why did Bush find it so difficult to slip the harness of his rhetoric? Why didn't the rhetoric serve as a signal of the president's good intentions, and why weren't the deeds understood as the work of overly zealous aides or the product of unfortunate but necessary compromises with his conservative electoral base? Why was the rhetoric instead seen as largely hollow and the deeds viewed as a sign of Bush's hypocrisy and opportunism? After all, Eisenhower made visible campaign commitments to retain price supports for farmers, and yet farmers did not accuse Eisenhower of hypocrisy so much as they charged Secretary Benson with betrayal.[132] Eisenhower's pledges were widely seen as genuine expressions of his desire to help farmers, while the administration's policies that backed away from price supports were widely interpreted in terms of Benson's zealousness or knavery.[133] Why was Bush unable to emulate Eisenhower's success?

Part of the answer is relatively straightforward. Farmers in the 1950s were overwhelmingly Republican and thus had a strong predisposition to support Eisenhower. Many environmentalists, on the other hand, were strongly predisposed to distrust Republicans, especially after eight years of the Reagan administration. As Russell E. Train, a Bush friend and ex-EPA boss and president of the World Wildlife Fund, says, "Most environmentalists are not predisposed to support a Republican president."[134]

Another part of the answer is that Eisenhower never promised to be the "agriculture president" and was thus able to keep a greater personal distance from the issue of price supports, despite the specific pledges he made during the campaign. In 1952, Eisenhower campaigned largely on the themes of "Communism, Korea, and Corruption"; agriculture was relatively peripheral. Bush's pledge to be "the environmental president," on the other hand, played a central role in defining the Bush candidacy. Only Bush's "no new taxes" pledge had greater visibility in the campaign.

Moreover, Sununu's proximity to the president made him a more risky lightning rod than Benson, who was lodged some distance away from the president in a second-tier department. People can believe that a president may not know or understand or particularly care what his secretary of agriculture is up to; it is much harder to persuade people that a president doesn't approve of, doesn't know about, or doesn't understand what his chief of staff is doing.

Sununu's extensive involvement with environmental issues, however, reflected a larger problem for Bush, namely the deep disagreements within the administration in this policy area. The Eisenhower administration included diverse views on agriculture, but most of these differences were small enough that they could be compromised and settled well below the presidential level. Reagan's initial top environmental appointments to a large degree shared a common ideological orientation, which often muted the scope of conflicts within (though not outside) the administration. Bush's strategy of including people with large philosophical differences meant, as Kraft and Vig point out, that decisions were inevitably thrust into the upper reaches of the Bush White House.[135]

Bush's experience, then, teaches us some of the difficulties of avoiding blame in a deeply polarized policy environment. Part of what made Eisen-hower's strategy of blame avoidance viable was that the differences between opposing sides were small enough that it was possible to carve out a middle ground where both sides could believe the president was still with them. Where the differences become too large, a president finds it difficult to keep his commitments ambiguous and to persuade opposing sides of his good in-tentions. The greater the ideological divisions, the greater the pressure on the president to choose sides and to become involved in the disputes. Ideological polarization thus undermines the two factors—detachment from decision making and ambiguity about intentions—that enable a president to deflect blame onto subordinates.

4
The Vice President as
Lightning Rod: Richard Nixon
and Hubert Humphrey

Long dismissed as an insignificant political office, the vice-presidency has undergone a marked rehabilitation in recent decades. As the vice president's advisory role has been upgraded, so too has the study of that institution.[1] This increase in scholarly attention to the vice-presidency is consistent with the dominant tendency within presidential studies to examine members of the executive branch in terms of their contribution to the formulation of public policy. Viewed as a policy adviser, the vice-presidency did not become important until Walter Mondale, or perhaps Nelson Rockefeller, occupied the office. Viewed as a presidential spokesman and lightning rod, however, the vice-presidency came into its own with the tenure of Richard Nixon.

Nixon was the first vice president to become a highly visible political spokesman. During Nixon's first four years in office he received as many entries in the *New York Times Index* as his four predecessors—Alben Barkley, Henry Wallace, John Nance Garner, and Charles Curtis—had received in a combined twenty years in office. Moreover, Nixon's model of a visible vice president has been emulated by most of his successors. Whereas from 1933 to 1952, the vice president received an average of 109 entries a year, in the twenty years following Nixon's tenure, the vice president averaged 482 entries a year (see Table 4.1).

The transformation in the public visibility of the vice president thus preceded the development of the vice president as policy adviser.[2] This chapter examines two vice presidents, Nixon and Hubert Humphrey, both of whom assumed highly visible roles as promoters of administration policies even though neither were important policy advisers within the administration. Both were used by their presidents as lightning rods and salesmen for policies they didn't shape. How did this vice-presidential role affect their ability to act as presidential lightning rods, and how can their success or lack

TABLE 4.1. Average annual number of entries in the *New York Times Index*.[a]

1921–1922	Calvin Coolidge	69
1925–1928	Charles Dawes	141
1929–1932	Charles Curtis	56
1933–1940	John Nance Garner	73
1941–1944	Henry Wallace	139
1949–1952	Alben Barkley	152
1953–1959	Richard Nixon	528
1961–1962	Lyndon Johnson	295
1965–1967	Hubert Humphrey	514
1969–1972	Spiro Agnew	708
1975–1976	Nelson Rockefeller	582
1977–1980	Walter Mondale	276
1981–1987	George Bush	180

[a]Excluded are those years (1960, 1968, and 1988) when the vice president was a presidential candidate, when there was no vice president (1924, 1946–1948, 1964), and when there was a presidential or vice-presidential death or resignation (1923, 1945, 1963, 1973, 1974).

thereof in deflecting blame contribute to our understanding of lightning rods generally?

JOHNSON AND HUMPHREY: COSTS OF A CREDIT-CLAIMING STRATEGY

Vice President Humphrey was a leading spokesman for the Johnson administration's war effort in Vietnam. President Johnson hoped to use Humphrey not only to persuade audiences about the rightness of the administration's course, but also to have someone other than the president carry what was a highly unpopular message in many parts of the nation. Did Humphrey's outspoken defense of the administration's handling of the Vietnam War help to deflect blame for the war away from President Lyndon Johnson? The short answer is no.

Humphrey failed to deflect blame away from Johnson in large part because Humphrey was viewed by many people as little more than an extension of Johnson, a sentiment summed up in a cover picture of *Esquire* magazine portraying a wooden Humphrey puppet being manipulated from behind by President Johnson.[3] As one scholar has put it, "For millions of Americans—protesters and non-protesters alike—Hubert Humphrey appeared to be a stand-in for Lyndon Johnson."[4] Humphrey's "basic problem," comments another scholar, "was that too many Americans regarded him as a Lyndon Johnson without the Texas accent."[5] To more caustic critics, Humphrey was "all too unhappily known as the parrot in Lyndon Johnson's blue room."[6]

Public opinion surveys show that a great majority of the mass public did not distinguish much between Humphrey and Johnson. Asked by Gallup at the end of 1966 to rate Humphrey and Johnson on a ten-point scale, 40 percent of respondents gave Humphrey and Johnson identical scores. Sixty-eight percent placed them within one point or less of each other, and 81 percent placed them within two points or less.[7] Some critics have suggested that "one cannot expect in the nature of the arrangement that the image of a vice president will be too different from that of the president."[8] But this interpretation is belied by a poll conducted at the outset of 1956 showing that only 11 percent of respondents gave Nixon and Eisenhower the same rating, only 28 percent placed them within a point of each other, and only 44 percent placed them within two points.[9]

Even after Johnson had withdrawn from the 1968 race and Humphrey had begun his own campaign for the Democratic nomination, the public perception of Humphrey and Johnson continued to remain strongly joined. In a poll conducted in May 1968, about one month after Johnson had announced his decision not to seek reelection, 30 percent placed Humphrey and Johnson at the same position on the ten-point scale, 60 percent put them within a point, and 76 percent put them within two points. Another survey taken several weeks before the 1968 election arrived at almost identical results: 31 percent gave the two men the same rating, 62 percent placed them within a point of each other, and 80 percent put them within two points.[10]

Why did so many citizens lump Johnson and Humphrey together? People thought they heard Johnson's voice when Humphrey spoke in large part because of the president's close (and well-advertised) control over his vice president's activities. "From the moment he [Humphrey] took office," reports Humphrey's biographer Carl Solberg, "the text of all his prepared speeches had to be sent to the White House in advance, and practically all suffered excisions."[11] A former Humphrey aide confirms that they "had to get every syllable cleared with the White House."[12] Johnson's close supervision of Humphrey's behavior did not go unnoticed by contemporaries. As early as February 1965, *Time* reported that "Johnson keeps him on a close leash, wants to know at all times where he is, what he is doing and, most important, what he is saying or planning to say."[13] The *Reporter* informed its readers that all of "Hubert Humphrey's public statements have to be cleared by the White House."[14]

Johnson's control over Humphrey's behavior descended to trivial, even ridiculous, depths. Johnson insisted, for instance, that Humphrey get presidential clearance before taking out a presidential yacht. The same restrictions applied to Humphrey's use of official planes. A Humphrey aide recalls: "If he had three out-of-town speaking engagements that week, three memos would go from his military aide to Johnson's military aide to Marvin

Watson to Lyndon Baines Johnson's overnight reading file, and he would mark them yes or no. That kept up for three and a half years and there were many cases where the memos came back marked 'no.' "[15]

The president made few, if any, efforts to conceal Humphrey's lack of autonomy. Indeed Johnson occasionally went out of his way publicly to put Humphrey in his place. Shortly after the election, for instance, Humphrey gave a speech in New York calling for a "massive investment" to improve American education. Such an investment, Humphrey declared, would be "the single most important step toward building the Great Society."[16] Johnson, David Halberstam recounts, "was furious; this was his terrain and Humphrey was told this in no uncertain terms. Just so there would be no mistake about it, Johnson called in the White House reporters who were with him on the Ranch and told them, 'Boys, I've just reminded Hubert that I've got his balls in my pocket.' "[17]

This incident reveals, among other things, Johnson's obsessive desire to show those in the political stratum who was in charge and his reluctance to let other members of the administration share in the credit for the Great Society. Johnson was particularly fearful that liberals, with whom he had never had particularly close relations, might credit the impetus for the administration's landmark social legislation to Humphrey, a cofounder of Americans for Democratic Action (ADA) and longtime champion of liberal causes.[18] According to Solberg, Johnson "begrudged any shaft of public light that fell on his . . . vice president. He often chided Humphrey when he felt the vice president was getting too much newspaper space. And to make sure that Humphrey did not, Johnson forbade him to take any member of the national press with him on his out-of-town trips."[19] Humphrey himself later complained that "the President not only frustrated ordinary human desire for praise or recognition, he openly clamped down."[20]

A Gallup poll conducted in November of 1965 showed that Johnson's policy of keeping Humphrey out of the limelight was having an impact. The mass public knew little about Humphrey, and what little they did know was not particularly positive. Only 23 percent said they would like to see Humphrey become president sometime in the future. Although this news alarmed Humphrey and his staff, Johnson was undisturbed. "Wrapping a big arm around Humphrey's shoulder," Johnson told Humphrey "that he had never had a press secretary as vice president and Humphrey didn't need one either." The president advised Humphrey "to concentrate on being a good, loyal vice president and not pay attention to his image." Humphrey dutifully fired his press secretary.[21]

Johnson's efforts to deny Humphrey positive publicity in the opening years of the administration retarded Humphrey's effectiveness as a lightning rod when he was later called upon to defend the war in Vietnam. Because Johnson had been unwilling to build Humphrey up and because he had taken special pains to demonstrate to others how little autonomy the vice president had, it is hardly surprising that Humphrey was unable to provide Johnson with much in the way of political cover.

After spending the opening years of his administration persuading those inside and outside of the Washington community that he was responsible for all the good things that happened, Johnson now found it difficult to duck responsibility for the increasingly negative outcomes. Johnson's credit-claiming style helped his public prestige while things were going well, but when events turned sour there was nothing to insulate him from calamity. By the time the war began to go badly, too many people had already been schooled to believe that, as one White House aide had confidently boasted in earlier, less troublesome days, "there is only one leader of this orchestra."[22]

DEFENDING VIETNAM

Although Humphrey was to become one of the administration's most vocal and enthusiastic defenders of the administration's war effort, he did not begin his tenure that way. In a meeting in early February 1965, Humphrey had argued, along with George Ball and Ambassador Llewellyn Thompson, against bombing North Vietnam. A week later, in a lengthy memorandum to the president on "the politics of Vietnam," Humphrey argued that if the war was escalated, "political opposition will mount steadily," particularly among the party's core constituency of "liberals, independents, labor." He warned Johnson that a protracted war would undermine the administration's other cherished policies. "It is always hard to cut losses," Humphrey conceded, "but the Johnson administration is in a stronger position to do so now than any Administration in this century. 1965 is the year of minimum political risk for the Johnson Administration. Indeed it is the first year when we can face the Vietnam problem without being preoccupied with the political repercussions from the Republican right."[23]

For his pains, the vice president was frozen out of foreign policy deliberations. Johnson had been upset that Humphrey had expressed his dissent in front of other members of the administration, and the president's anger was compounded when Humphrey committed his opposition to paper.[24] If the contents of the memo were leaked, Johnson had reason to fear that Humphrey would be made into an apostle of peace, leaving Johnson cast as the warmonger.[25]

Johnson's freeze-out of Humphrey had the desired effect of modifying Humphrey's behavior. Humphrey worried aloud to his aides about the need to "find a way to convince this man of my loyalty."[26] The quickest way to regain the president's confidence was to bring his public statements and private convictions about Vietnam into closer accord with the president's. Humphrey slowly climbed back into Johnson's good graces by flattering the president,[27] criticizing opponents of the war,[28] and sounding an increasingly optimistic note about the prospects for success in Vietnam.

Abandoning his previous reservations, Humphrey now became among the administration's most outspoken defenders of the war. Humphrey's change of heart about the wisdom of the war can be dated from his trip to Southeast Asia in February 1965. Upon his return, Humphrey announced to the press, "The tide of battle has turned in Vietnam in our favor."[29] From this point on, the vice president was seen (in the words of *Newsweek*) as "the scrappiest warrior in the White House phalanx."[30]

Humphrey was widely portrayed in the media as a "salesman" for Johnson's policies.[31] Those who wanted to place a more derogatory spin on Humphrey's role labeled him a "cheerleader."[32] Few people, however, are inclined to blame a salesman or cheerleader for the poor performance of a product or team. Rather, their wrath is likely to be reserved for those who are believed to be responsible for creating the product. While liberals might express disgust with Humphrey for selling and applauding a product they believed to be unwise and amoral, this in no way lessened their animosity toward the one man they held responsible for the war in Vietnam—Lyndon Johnson.

Indeed, Humphrey's "betrayal" seemed only to heighten liberal distrust and criticism of Johnson. To the president's many sins liberals now added the emasculation and intimidation of one of their staunchest allies and greatest heroes. Many of Humphrey's old liberal allies continued to believe that the vice president was suppressing his true feelings out of loyalty to the president. ADA cofounder Joseph Rauh, for instance, was convinced that "if Hubert were president, his visceral liberalism, which I believe is there, would get us out of the war."[33] In a similar vein, *The Nation* editorialized that defending the war was "a wretched assignment for any politician—even one of Hubert's gifts. If he makes one misstep Lyndon will be on his back. And Hubert is apt to step wrong in his new assignment, precisely because a residue of liberalism remains in his bosom."[34] When Humphrey came to deliver the main address at the ADA convention in April 1966, the word went out to "be kind to Hubert" because he was "locked in" by Johnson.[35] In the summer of 1967, the *Atlantic Monthly* reported that "disenchanted liberals . . . have already written him off as a prisoner of Johnson."[36]

The overriding reason why Humphrey could not serve as a presidential lightning rod was that he had no hand in making the war he was called on to defend. From the early days of the administration, he had been banished from the decision-making process. Even after he assumed a highly visible public profile on Vietnam, Humphrey was still excluded from the Tuesday luncheon sessions where Johnson, Rusk, McNamara, Bundy (and later Rostow) discussed high-level Vietnam strategy.[37] People might be persuaded or angered by Humphrey, but they were unlikely to hold him responsible for decisions over which they knew he had no influence. As long as Humphrey was seen only as a "mouthpiece" for Johnson,[38] the vice president could not deflect blame away from the president.

The Johnson/Humphrey relationship illustrates in an extreme form the importance of an adviser being at least perceived as responsible for a policy if he is to function as a lightning rod. Humphrey's limited utility as a lightning rod stemmed from both his role as vice president and Johnson's leadership style. Johnson's domineering style of leadership created a presumption among many people within the political stratum that if a member of the administration (whether staff, cabinet member, or vice president) took some action he must be carrying out the president's wishes.[39] Minimizing both the appearance and reality of subordinates' discretion makes it difficult for a leader to avoid blame when things go wrong. For if a subordinate is only following presidential orders, then it is the president and not the subordinate who deserves blame.

Humphrey's ineffectiveness as a lightning rod was also compounded by the limitations of the vice-presidential role, particularly as it existed at that time. Because the vice-presidency is often caricatured as a do-nothing role, vice presidents find it more difficult to deflect blame than do cabinet members or top presidential staff. In contrast to a chief of staff, who is placed at the vortex of the decision-making process, or to a department secretary, who is expected to have significant discretion in making public policy, vice presidents are always at risk of being presumed to be simply carrying out a president's orders, defending a policy they had no part in making.

One must be careful, however, not to overstate the inherent limitations of the vice-presidential role, even as that role existed in the 1960s. After all, the Gallup surveys cited earlier suggest that in contrast to the Humphrey/Johnson relationship, people did tend to distinguish sharply between Nixon and Eisenhower. Despite the widespread expectation that the first duty of a vice president is to be loyal to the president, Nixon was not seen as Eisenhower's tool, as simply an extension of the president. How did Eisenhower counteract the weakness of the vice-presidential role and build his vice president into a plausible lightning rod?

NIXON AS A POLITICAL LIGHTNING ROD

Presidential scholars have long recognized that all presidents must wrestle with the conflict between their roles as chief of state and chief of party. The expectation that a president assumes the leadership of his party becomes particularly problematic in a context in which the president's party is in the minority.

Eisenhower's behavior as president was constrained by the fact that he was a Republican president in a preponderantly Democratic nation. An Andrew Jackson or a Harry Truman could hope to get elected and even govern by rallying the party faithful, but Eisenhower required the support of a significant number of the opposition party in order to succeed. Eisenhower was well aware of this, acknowledging in his memoirs that "I have never enjoyed the luxury of being head of a majority party. Perhaps the leader of such a party can be uniformly partisan. But the leader of a minority party has a different set of references. To win, he . . . must merit the support of hundreds of thousands of independents and members of the opposition party. Attitudes, speeches, programs, and techniques cannot be inflexibly partisan."[40]

Avoiding the appearance of inflexible partisanship helped Eisenhower run almost six million votes (or 10 percent) ahead of his party in 1952 and again in 1956.[41] Eisenhower's success in projecting a nonpartisan image is evident from a Gallup survey conducted in July 1955 which found that 57 percent of the people felt Eisenhower was "at heart" somewhere in between the Republican and Democratic parties.[42]

In part, of course, Eisenhower's nonpartisan image was a result of his nonpartisan past.[43] Before assenting to be a candidate in 1952, he had refrained from professing an allegiance to either political party. But it is not enough to suggest, as one former administration official does, that the people thought: "Here is a man who's above partisan politics. He's the kind of man I like in the White House."[44] For this leaves unanswered the question of how Eisenhower managed to *sustain* a nonpartisan hero image throughout his eight years as president of the United States. Public images are not set in stone. They can change with incredible speed, as Nancy Reagan's turnaround from frivolous clotheshorse to respected first lady[45] or George Bush's transformation from wimp to winner during the 1988 presidential campaign attest.

Eisenhower sustained his nonpartisan public image by delegating partisan responsibilities to other administration officials, the most prominent of whom was his vice president, Richard Nixon. Since Eisenhower could not afford (nor was he particularly comfortable with) public expressions of partisanship, Nixon was assigned the task of slugging it out with the Democrats, particularly during election years. As a result, the vice president became a target for Democratic attacks.[46]

Eisenhower's intention to use Nixon as a partisan lightning rod was conveyed to Nixon immediately after he was selected as the vice-presidential nominee. After being informed of Eisenhower's choice by Brownell, Nixon was immediately rushed over to talk to the general. From this meeting,

Nixon concluded that "it was clear that he [Eisenhower] envisaged taking an above-the-battle position, and that whatever hard partisan campaigning was required would be pretty much left to me." Eisenhower instructed Nixon that he "should be able not only to flail the Democrats on the corruption issue but also to personify the remedy for it."[47] As the campaign was set to begin in earnest in mid-September, Nixon went to see Eisenhower at his Denver headquarters to review campaign strategy. The plan, Nixon recalled, was "for General Eisenhower to stress the positive aspects of his 'Crusade to Clean Up the Mess in Washington' . . . [while] I was to hammer away at our opponents on the record of the Truman administration, with particular emphasis on Communist subversion."[48]

Nixon did not disappoint. He kept up a steady barrage of hard-hitting attacks on the Democrats and their presidential nominee, Adlai Stevenson. Nixon characterized Stevenson as "a weakling, a waster, and a small-caliber Truman." "Adlai the appeaser," he told a partisan audience in southern California shortly before the election, "got a Ph.D. from Dean Acheson's College of Cowardly Communist Containment." On another occasion, Nixon accused Stevenson, Acheson, and Truman of all being "traitors to the high principles in which many of the nation's Democrats believe."[49] Meanwhile Eisenhower, who rarely met up with Nixon on the campaign trail, carefully cultivated an apolitical image.

Subsequent campaigns followed a roughly similar script. While the president would tell audiences that "no party has a monopoly on brains or idealism or statesmanship," Nixon would accuse Democrats of secretly wanting to "socialize basic American institutions" and harboring "diseased ideas . . . from the Marxist virus."[50] Nixon was assigned the role of answering Democratic criticisms of the administration, enabling Eisenhower to avoid replying to the Democrats. While the vice president repeatedly criticized Stevenson, Eisenhower rarely if ever mentioned his opponent.

While out on the campaign trail, Nixon had a large degree of discretion about what attacks to answer and how to answer them. On occasion, however, Eisenhower would give Nixon specific instructions on what needed saying. At the formal kickoff for the 1956 campaign at Eisenhower's farm in Gettysburg, for instance, the president enlisted Nixon to rebut Stevenson's charges of administration corruption and heartlessness. On the morning of the picnic, Eisenhower called Nixon with instructions:

Everybody is now noting that you are taking the new high level. However, I think today you ought to take notice of some of these attacks that have been made on the administration and on me. . . . I think that when Stevenson calls this administration racketeers and rascals, when they say we are heartless in dealing with the problems of the people and the problems of the farmers, when they say we have no peace and no prosperity, I want them to be called on it. I would like for you to do so, and if you have to praise me that will be okay. . . . I suggest something along the lines: Do you want to go back to war in order to have prosperity under the Democrats. . . . Of course, it isn't necessary to attack [Stevenson] personally but we should point out that he is wrong.[51]

Just in case Nixon had missed the message, Brownell got on the phone and advised Nixon: "I don't think we could win with a so-called high level campaign. It has to be fair but you have to take the opposition on. It has to be hard-hitting."[52]

Nixon's speech closely followed Eisenhower's outline. One by one, Nixon refuted the Democratic charges enumerated by Eisenhower. The vice president also went on the offensive, charging that for Stevenson "to suggest one day that 'we're losing the cold war' and the next day that we might get rid of the draft . . . is the height of political fakery and irresponsibility." While vowing that communism at home should not be an issue in the upcoming campaign, Nixon nevertheless called on Stevenson to repudiate Truman's comment that Alger Hiss was not a Communist. After Nixon had finished answering Democratic charges as well as making a few of his own, Eisenhower then gave a talk that completely ignored the Democratic campaign. The president gave an informal pep talk on the virtues of increasing voter registration ("If you find it necessary to vote against us, all right, we would rather have you do that than not vote at all"), the nature of leadership, and the defining principles of the Republican party.[53]

Stevenson followed a similar script when he launched the 1954 campaign by criticizing Eisenhower in a nationally televised speech for his handling of McCarthy and the "New Look" defense policy that downgraded conventional forces in favor of deterrence through the threat of massive atomic retaliation. The president immediately turned to Nixon to make the formal reply. At a strategy meeting with Republican leaders, Eisenhower suggested that "we probably ought to use Dick more than we have been. . . . He can sometimes take positions which are more political than it would be expected that I take."[54]

The day before Nixon was to deliver the televised speech, Eisenhower summoned his vice president to the White House. The president prefaced his remarks by allowing that Nixon did not need advice on "a political speech" but then went on to give him detailed advice anyway. Eisenhower laid particular stress on the need to get across to people that he had "a progressive, dynamic program which benefited all the people." Evidently worried that Nixon might come across as mean-spirited, Eisenhower suggested that he "might work [in] a smile with regard to . . . comments on Stevenson." Nixon told Eisenhower that he "planned to stick a few barbs into him [Stevenson]." The president was "perfectly content" that Nixon do so but "thought it was best to laugh at him rather than to hit him meanly." He also advised his vice president to remind the audience that he had commanded five million troops in Europe. "What qualification," the president demanded, "does Stevenson have on this subject? Who is he?"[55]

Nixon took the hint. In his speech, he built his defense of the administration's "New Look" policy upon President Eisenhower's position as "one of the greatest military leaders in the world today." In contrast, the vice president pointed out, Stevenson, like a great many of the rest of us, was no military strategist. Because Eisenhower was a military expert, Nixon believed that "we can and . . . should have confidence in his . . . policy, particularly when the nonexpert who criticizes it offers nothing but a return to a policy which failed and . . . was rejected overwhelmingly by the American people in the election of November 1952."[56] Immediately afterward, Eisenhower called to congratulate Nixon on a "magnificent" speech,[57] but many in the press were considerably less laudatory. The liberal Catholic weekly, *Commonweal,* characterized Nixon's reply to Stevenson as "low-key demagoguery." The editors were particularly critical of Nixon's "condescending" suggestion that Eisenhower's military experience was reason enough for the citizenry to place confidence in the president's policy. Were it possible to locate Eisenhower "behind the phalanx of advertising men and merchandising experts," the editors were certain that the general "would agree with us."[58] In actual fact, however, as Eisenhower's chat with Nixon the day before the speech indicates, the "condescension" (if that is what it is to suggest that the opinion of experts deserves greater weight than that of nonexperts) was Eisenhower's, not Nixon's.

That Nixon was sometimes explicitly instructed by Eisenhower to go after Stevenson and the Democrats should not obscure Nixon's relish for the role of partisan hit man. When Dulles was being criticized by congressional Democrats for his Middle East policies in 1956, for instance, the vice president called Dulles and told him to "let me know if you want anyone attacked."[59] Nixon the partisan, as he himself admitted, enjoyed "sticking a few barbs" into the likes of Stevenson, Acheson, and Truman.

Hard-hitting partisanship came naturally to Nixon, and he found these instincts difficult to repress. In his memoirs, Nixon recalls Eisenhower coming out to the Washington National Airport to see him off on the first campaign swing of 1956 and warning the vice president against indulging in "the exaggerations of partisan political talk." The president's parting admonition was "Give 'em heaven." Nixon followed Eisenhower's advice for the first few days but found it difficult to inspire his partisan audiences without exaggerated partisan rhetoric. After adding some "hard-hitting additions" to his basic speech, Nixon recounts feeling that "suddenly I felt as if a great weight had been lifted from me. I had not realized how frustrating it had been to suppress the normal partisan instincts."[60]

Nixon's attacks on the Democrats sometimes went beyond what Eisenhower regarded as proper or wise. Early in the summer of 1954, for instance, in McCarthy's home state of Wisconsin, Nixon accused "the Acheson policy" of being "directly responsible for the loss of China." Worried that such attacks would jeopardize Democratic support for administration policies, Eisenhower promptly instructed Nixon to cease such inflammatory attacks. Such accusations, Ike told Nixon, not only threatened to undermine his foreign policy but were inaccurate. "The reason we lost China," Eisenhower explained, "was because the U.S. insisted upon Chiang Kai-shek taking Communists into his government." And it was George Marshall, he pointed out, not Acheson, who had recommended this policy.[61]

Another presidential reprimand came during the 1958 campaign after Nixon attacked the Democratic party's "sorry record of retreat and appeasement," and the "defensive, defeatist fuzzy-headed thinking which contributed to the loss of China and led to the Korean war." This time Eisenhower made public his displeasure with Nixon's rhetorical excesses. At his weekly press conference, Eisenhower stated his belief that "foreign policy ought to be kept out of a partisan debate. . . . America's best interests in the world will be served if we do not indulge in this kind of thing."[62]

The occasional reprimand notwithstanding, Nixon's attacks on the Democrats largely met with Eisenhower's approval, for they satisfied the president's and the Republican party's need for effective counterpunching against the opposition. When Democratic leaders in Congress protested that Nixon's attacks during the 1954 campaign had reflected on their patriotism, Eisenhower's private response, as reported by Samuel Lubell, was that "Nixon must have done a good job if the Democrats complain so much."[63] Sherman Adams confirmed that Eisenhower did not, "as some Republicans seemed to think, . . . [want] his spokesmen to be kind to Democrats in their campaign oratory. He told Nixon and others, including myself, that he was well aware that somebody had to do the hard-hitting infighting, and he had no objections to it as long as no one expected him to do it."[64]

Nixon's hard-hitting attacks upon the opposition earned him praise from the president and Republican politicians but also secured him the undying enmity of Democrats. The Democratic party, declared one Democratic representative, has announced "open season on the Vice President." Nixon was denounced by another Democrat as an "inept, naive, Piltdown statesman, . . . a broken-down, maladjusted, purblind Throttlebottom." "So far as we're concerned," Speaker Sam Rayburn concluded, "his name is mud."[65]

According to one interpretation, Democratic attacks upon Nixon were purely strategic. Nixon himself advances this thesis in *Six Crises,* in which he argues that as vice president he had "been the whipping boy for those who chose not to direct their political attacks against Dwight D. Eisenhower, the most popular president in recent history."[66] Others concurred that "Nixon is being shot at now because he appears the obvious candidate and the attacks are directed at him instead of a popular Eisenhower. Were Nixon to step out and another appear . . . he'd get the same treatment."[67] *Time* magazine echoed this view, arguing that "Nixon was a favorite target of Democrats who felt it unprofitable to criticize Dwight Eisenhower."[68]

There is substantial truth in this view, but it underestimates the genuine antipathy that Nixon aroused among many Democrats. Truman, who never forgave Nixon for his "traitor" remark, later told Merle Miller that Nixon was "a shifty-eyed goddamn liar. . . . All the time I've been in politics, there's only two people I hate, and he's one."[69] Stevenson, too, is reported to have said that Nixon was the only man in public life he ever "really loathed."[70] Nixon was attacked not only for strategic reasons, but because his role (and the way he played that role) of answering and making partisan charges generated a deep-seated dislike for the vice president.

At the level of the mass public, Nixon-haters often liked Ike. Public opinion surveys show that citizens commonly combined an intense dislike for Nixon with great admiration for President Eisenhower. A poll conducted in February 1956, for instance, found that of those who gave Nixon the lowest possible rating of minus five (about one in seven of those who had formed an opinion of Nixon), only 7 percent gave that same low rating to Eisenhower. Better than three in ten of the people who felt most negatively toward the vice president actually gave Eisenhower the highest possible rating of plus five, and eight in ten evaluated Eisenhower positively (i.e., gave him a rating of between plus one and plus five).[71]

This divorce between the public perception of Nixon and Eisenhower is all the more remarkable when contrasted with the Johnson/Humphrey pattern. A Gallup poll conducted in December 1966 shows that extreme dislike (i.e., a minus five rating) of Humphrey was about as common as that uncovered for Nixon in the February 1956 survey. The difference is that while only 7 percent of those who gave Nixon a rating of minus five also gave President Eisenhower the lowest rating, 61 percent of those who gave Humphrey the lowest possible score also gave Johnson a minus five rating. Moreover, less than 3 percent of those who felt highly negative toward Vice President Humphrey gave Johnson the highest possible rating of plus five, and only one in ten even gave Johnson a positive rating.[72]

People had little difficulty reconciling a deep dislike for Nixon with a high regard for Eisenhower, because they did not view Eisenhower as in any way responsible for Nixon's partisanship. Most people did not see a vice president fulfilling a role assigned by the president, but simply Nixon being Nixon. Nixon, not Eisenhower, appeared to be the political mastermind behind Republican campaigns. Writing during the fall of 1954 in the *New York Times,* Cabell Phillips described Nixon as "the chief strategist" of the GOP.[73] In January 1955, *U.S. News & World Report* informed its readers that Richard Nixon is "the man at the helm of the Republican Party, busily shaping policy and strategy for the 1956 presidential contest." The vice president, the magazine concluded, "has become the President's political mentor."[74]

Eisenhower did little to discourage such notions, however inaccurate. In private, he would occasionally acknowledge that he considered himself "a better politician than most so-called professionals,"[75] but in public he took any number of occasions to build up the perception of himself as a political neophyte needing the guidance of more sophisticated professional politicians. Asked how he felt about politics in a news conference during the spring of 1955, Eisenhower confessed to "having no great liking for . . . politics . . . in the general derogatory sense."[76] And at the outset of his second year in office, he announced to the assembled press that he was "not very much of a partisan."[77] Eisenhower sensed that the perception of him as a political innocent served him well with an electorate that regarded politicians and politics as dirty words[78] and understood that his nonpartisan stance helped him to win the support of Democrats and Independents.

Part of what made Eisenhower's nonpolitical, nonpartisan image believable, however, is that it was grounded in reality. It was not all dissembling. Eisenhower did distrust party professionals, whom he viewed as too shortsighted to serve the national interest.[79] Patronage, he confided in his diary, "is almost a wicked word—by itself it could well-nigh defeat democracy."[80] In private "thinking-aloud sessions," Eisenhower occasionally discussed the possibility of forming a new party that would better reflect his views.[81]

But the nonpolitical, nonpartisan Eisenhower was only part of the story. If Ike did not share the fervent commitment to the Republican party qua party that animated Nixon, he disliked Stevenson, Truman, and Kefauver as intensely as the most partisan of Republicans.[82] If patronage-seekers were distasteful to Eisenhower, he had few qualms about throwing out New Deal and Fair Deal Democrats,[83] and he always encouraged cabinet members to cooperate with the party chair on appointments.[84] If Eisenhower showed disdain for party professionals who talked only about how an issue would play in the next election, it was he, Eisenhower, who had advised his cabinet on the need to promote the administration's accomplishments as if they were selling a product.[85]

Eisenhower's ambivalence toward politicians was mirrored in his ambivalence toward Nixon.[86] On the one hand, he recognized that Nixon played a valuable role by answering Democratic charges and rallying the party faithful. Moreover, he agreed with much of what Nixon said about Stevenson and the liberal wing of the Democratic party. On the other hand, Eisenhower's conception of a good president was one who lifts himself above the partisan fray, thereby becoming a leader of the whole people rather than of only a part. (His dislike for Truman stemmed in large part from what he saw as his predecessor's unseemly partisanship.) Eisenhower felt that Nixon was perhaps "too political" to be president.[87] In the spring of 1956, he acknowledged to Emmet Hughes that "I've watched Dick a long time, and he just hasn't grown. So I just haven't honestly been able to believe that he is presidential timber."[88] Those whom Eisenhower regarded as "presidential timber" tended to be men, like himself, who were relatively nonpartisan in orientation, such as Robert Anderson, a Democrat from Texas, or his own brother Milton Eisenhower.[89] Nixon was thus caught in a double bind, for Eisenhower (as well as local and national party officials) asked him to play a role that required behaving in ways that seemed to disqualify him, at least in Eisenhower's eyes, from the office of the presidency.

THE ART OF CASTING

Historian Stephen Ambrose, who has written definitive biographies of both Nixon and Eisenhower, has argued that President Eisenhower "used Nixon in the most cynical fashion." In this respect, Eisenhower is little different from any other president, because, as Ambrose also notes, "to be used is what a Vice-President is for."[90] But the comparison with the Johnson/Humphrey relationship suggests that it is potentially misleading to place undue stress upon Eisenhower's manipulation of his vice president. For President Eisenhower's use of Nixon pales in comparison to Johnson's ruthless manipulation of Humphrey.

The key to Eisenhower's success was not just that he used Nixon but that he cast Nixon in a role in which he needed minimal prodding or monitoring. Partisan attack and counterattack came naturally to Nixon. Indeed, so suited was Nixon to the role of partisan hit man that it was difficult even to tell that he was playing a role. In contrast, it was painfully obvious that Humphrey (who was defending a policy he had had no part in making and had initially opposed, and was criticizing longtime friends and allies) was playing a part that had been foisted upon him by the president. Not surprisingly, people who disapproved of the performance blamed the director in the case of Johnson and Humphrey and the actor in the case of Nixon and Eisenhower.

The Humphrey/Johnson relationship alerts us to a crucial point that is sometimes lost sight of in Eisenhower revisionism, at least in its popularized forms. It is true, as revisionists claim, that Eisenhower tried to conceal the strings by which he controlled his vice president while Johnson advertised his control. But it is also true (to continue the metaphor) that Eisenhower used many fewer and much thinner strings than did Johnson. Not only was Humphrey more tightly controlled than Nixon, it was much easier for outsiders to witness that control. Eisenhower's aim as a political leader was both to conceal the ways in which he controlled others *and* to select performers who could act with a minimum of presidential control.

THE CHANGING VICE-PRESIDENTIAL ROLE

Since Nixon and Humphrey's time, the vice president's advisory role has become substantially upgraded and even institutionalized. Where Nixon occupied an office on Capitol Hill and was strictly a visitor at the White House, every vice president since Walter Mondale has occupied an office in the West Wing of the White House. Where Nixon and Humphrey had only infrequent access to the president, Mondale, Bush, Quayle, and Gore have all had a regular, weekly slot in the president's schedule. Starting with Mondale, moreover, the vice president has received the president's daily briefing on foreign policy. Nixon's office budget was not to exceed that of a senator from a one-district state, and his staff numbered only a handful of people; today the vice president has a budget well over two million dollars and employs about a hundred people.[91] Indeed, as Paul Light observes, "the Vice-President's office is now a replica of the President's office, with a national security adviser, press secretary, domestic issues staff, scheduling team, advance, appointments, administration, chief of staff, and counsel's office."[92]

What does this transformation in the institutional capacity and advisory role of the vice-presidency mean for the job's availability as presidential lightning rod? With increased policy-making power one might expect that vice presidents would be better positioned to provide presidents with political cover. But Light suggests that there may actually be a trade-off for vice presidents between "external visibility" and "internal impact."[93] Mondale's influence on policy, Light suggests, rested on his "hidden-hand" approach. He "kept his advice to Carter private. He was reluctant to speak at cabinet meetings and did not want his staff taking highly visible stands."[94] Bush followed much the same low-profile strategy in gaining the trust of President Reagan and those around him.

Neither Mondale nor Bush could be described as lightning rods on any policy issue. Mondale avoided the role of policy advocate in public and did not allow himself to become identified with any one policy area, preferring instead to remain a generalist. As one Carter official remarked: "He couldn't be hit because he never made a clean target. He was moving in and out of issue areas, and didn't stay long enough to get hurt. He was a genius at staying out of the line of fire."[95] George Bush emulated the Mondale model only more so, publicly downplaying his influence in policy making, staying out of the public eye, avoiding controversial assignments, and shunning long-term duties that might make him a target for critics.[96]

Of the post-Mondale vice presidents only Dan Quayle, in his capacity as chair of the President's Council on Competitiveness, has translated the institutional changes in the vice president's policy-making role into something resembling lightning rod status. By the third year into the Bush administration, Quayle began to be portrayed by the environmentalists as an influential administration advocate of loosening environmental regulations. In the summer of 1991, for instance, *The Nation* could describe Quayle's "preemptive power [as] so considerable that he can overrule heads of agencies like E.P.A. Administrator William Reilly."[97] California Democrat Henry Waxman described Quayle's Competitiveness Council as a sinister "shadow government"[98] and said that on clean air, "Quayle seems to have made the transition from irrelevant to dangerous."[99] As head of the Competitiveness Council, Quayle has shown that by sticking to an issue a vice president can assume the role of policy lightning rod. Yet, as Waxman's comment also indicates, before this point few Washingtonians had seen Quayle as an important player in White House policy making.

Indeed, for all the changes in the office that political scientists have documented, the media and public image of the office seem to remain little changed. Recent news stories have dismissed the vice-presidency as a "high office without power," as "the least exciting job in national politics," as a job in which "traditionally, the role . . . is to do essentially nothing." "The vice president," we are told, "is in charge of very little"; the job amounts to little more than being "the president's understudy and [showing] as little independence as possible."[100] With these popular stereotypes of the office still firmly engrained, a stereotype that the "hidden-hand" vice-presidencies of Mondale and Bush have done little to dispel, it remains difficult for vice presidents to act as policy lightning rods.[101]

Moreover, the emergence of what Light calls "the policy vice presidency" in the mid-1970s may have made vice presidents more reluctant to be used as political lightning rods in quite the same way that Eisenhower used Nixon or Nixon used Agnew. When a vice president's choice was largely between the ceremonial vice-presidency (attending funerals, symbolic participation in task forces and councils, and the like) and the political vice-presidency (presidential spokesman, promoter, hit man, and campaigner), the ambitious vice president would prefer the controversial role of partisan hit man to the demeaning role of professional mourner.[102] Taking the partisan low road while the president takes the presidential high road not only gained the vice president presidential gratitude but also earned the vice president the loyalty of local party officials and fund-raisers. Now that vice presidents have access to the administration's innermost policy-making circles, however, they may be less inclined to play the divisive role of partisan hit man—a role that, as Nixon found out in 1960 and Humphrey discovered in 1968, is a reliable route to the nomination but can create a less than presidential image that may be a liability in the general election. The policy vice president will never displace the political vice president—vice presidents as well as presidents need the political/partisan function performed—but future vice presidents will be reluctant to act in ways that might jeopardize their new-found role as trusted adviser to the president. As a result, future vice presidents will most likely be reluctant to emulate the Nixonian model of vice president as slashing partisan. What future presidents would do well to emulate, though, is Eisenhower's skill at casting subordinates—vice presidents included—in roles that they can play convincingly with a minimum of presidential direction.

5

The Secretary of State as Lightning Rod: John Foster Dulles, Dean Acheson, and Henry Kissinger

Of all the members of a president's cabinet, the secretary of state is invariably the most prominent. No other member of the administration outside of the president himself so readily commands the attention of the media. During the first year of the Reagan presidency, when the administration's focus was overwhelmingly on the economy, Secretary of State Al Haig was still by far the most visible Reagan administration official. His 646 references in the *Vanderbilt Televisions News Abstract and Index* dwarf the next most prominent administration officials, who had less than half that number (Defense Secretary Caspar Weinberger, 272; OMB director David Stockman, 226; Vice President George Bush, 200). The most prominent officials in Congress, Senate Majority Leader Howard Baker and House Speaker Tip O'Neill received only about one-third of Haig's coverage (220 and 182, respectively). And Haig received roughly ten times the coverage of even reasonably prominent figures such as CIA director William Casey (66), Press Secretary Larry Speakes (77), Interior Secretary James Watt (63), Senator Bob Dole (75), and House Ways and Means chair Dan Rostenkowski (57).

Lest it be thought that this greater visibility reflects Haig's peculiarly colorful personality, one need only look at the coverage of the more understated Jim Baker in the first year of the Bush presidency. Secretary of State Baker's 322 references were still well over twice those of his nearest administration rival, Defense Secretary Dick Cheney (148), and three times those of Vice President Dan Quayle (119). Even Speaker of the House Jim Wright, despite being engulfed in a prolonged and public scandal, was only half as visible as Baker. And Baker had six times the prominence of Chief of Staff John Sununu (53) and four times that of Drug Czar William Bennett (88), neither of whom could be described as shy of the public spotlight. Baker's visibility was more than ten times as great as that of OMB director Dick Darman (32), Treasury Secretary Nicholas Brady (24), Federal Reserve chair

Alan Greenspan (23), Chief Justice William Rehnquist (29), and Senate Finance chair and 1988 Democratic vice-presidential candidate Lloyd Bentsen (30).[1]

The abundant attention the press gives to the secretary of state would seem to make this cabinet post a prime candidate for the role of presidential lightning rod. Three postwar secretaries of state stand out as particularly visible and controversial occupants of this office: John Foster Dulles, Dean Acheson, and Henry Kissinger. Surveys show that about 90 percent of the American public claimed to recognize each of these men. More significantly, close to 80 percent of the public could correctly identify Kissinger's job after four years in the Nixon administration;[2] upward of two-thirds of the public could correctly identify Dean Acheson's job as President Truman's secretary of state,[3] and close to 60 percent could "recall offhand" the name of the secretary of state by the end of Dulles's tenure in the Eisenhower administration.[4] That these individuals were well known even to the general public seems beyond question. That they were controversial and much criticized is well established. Less obvious and more interesting is the question of whether these individuals, prominent and controversial though they were, served as presidential lightning rods. In examining these three individual cases, we find a pattern that suggests some general lessons about the suitability of the secretary of state as a lightning rod.

DULLES AS LIGHTNING ROD

An oft-repeated corollary of Eisenhower revisionism is that President Eisenhower slyly used his secretary of state, John Foster Dulles, as a lightning rod. "The truth," according to one of the earliest revisionists, Peter Lyon, is not only "that Dulles did Eisenhower's bidding in matters of high policy" but that Dulles "also served as the convenient butt for any criticism of that policy so that Eisenhower's avuncular image might be preserved." Historian Robert Divine echoes this view: "Dulles could serve as the lightning rod, absorbing domestic criticism and warding off attacks from the right wing with his moralistic fervor." And Fred Greenstein writes that the secretary of state was an "object of animosity that in another presidency would have been directed toward the chief executive." Eisenhower biographer Stephen Ambrose agrees that having "Dulles available to serve as a lightning rod served Eisenhower's purposes and helped maintain Eisenhower's popularity."[5]

This view of Dulles as lightning rod is not without validity. An implicit division of labor does seem to have evolved, as Greenstein says, in which Dulles "issued the bulk of the 'get tough' foreign policy statements," while Eisenhower made the "gestures toward international humanitarianism and detente—for example, Atoms for Peace, Open Skies, goodwill trips, and summitry."[6] One can certainly point to individuals who blamed Dulles rather than Eisenhower for particular decisions or even for the overall course of the administration's foreign policy. The lightning rod hypothesis well describes the way certain liberal journalists conceived of the Dulles/Eisenhower relationship. *New Yorker* columnist Richard Rovere, to take one of the more extreme examples, believed that Eisenhower "more or less subcontracted the whole thing out [to Dulles]."[7] According to Rovere, Eisenhower was a man of peaceful, moderate instincts who was always having to resist his bellicose secretary of state. In contrast to Eisenhower's "restraint and circumspection," Dulles was a "righteous, godly man, . . . repelled by the thought of striking bargains with men as steeped in sin as the Russian leaders are." As Rovere saw it:

The periods in which our foreign policy . . . appears to reach the maximum of flexibility and sobriety are those periods when Mr. Dulles is out of the country and making the rounds of the chancelleries. Then it is the President who speaks and who gives a powerful sense of being profoundly aware not only of the danger of Communist expansion but of the danger of war. After these interludes, Mr. Dulles flies in for a few days, delivers a couple of dour Calvinist forecasts of doom and retribution, then heads back out to Bangkok or Rio or wherever. It is believed in Washington that the President . . . winces each time he is notified that Mr. Dulles is about to touch down at National Airport.

Rovere even went so far as to speculate that Eisenhower had recruited Harold Stassen for the job of the president's special adviser on disarmament in hopes that "Mr. Stassen should embarrass Mr. Dulles."[8]

For certain events, too, a good case can be made that Eisenhower consciously used Dulles to shield himself from criticism. The controversy over the Bricker amendment, which would have limited the president's power to make international agreements as well as limiting the impact of international agreements on domestic laws, provides an early instance of Eisenhower's blame-avoidance technique and Dulles's willingness, in his own words, to be the "whipping boy."[9] Asked at a press conference in March 1953 what he thought of the proposed Bricker amendment, which was heavily favored by congressional Republicans, Eisenhower at first artfully evaded the question. When asked again the following week, he spoke against the amendment but placed the responsibility for his decision on Dulles: "As analyzed for me by the Secretary of State," Eisenhower explained, the amendment "would, as I understand it, in certain ways, restrict the authority that the President must have, if he is to conduct the foreign affairs of this Nation effectively."[10] In the ensuing months, Eisenhower met with Senator John Bricker on several occasions and gave the Ohio senator what Sherman Adams described as a "warm and sympathetic" hearing.[11] Indeed, Eisenhower had seemed so sympathetic that Bricker emerged from one such conference telling reporters that he and the president had the same objectives and a few weeks later praised Eisenhower for "supporting the principle" of safeguarding constitutional rights.[12]

Eisenhower's private expressions of sympathy for Bricker's position combined with his public deflection of responsibility onto Dulles fostered the view that it was the secretary of state who was "largely responsible" for the administration's opposition to the amendment.[13] A number of supporters of the amendment doubted that the president fully understood the issue or that the president had firm views on the subject. Chief among those who held Dulles responsible for the president's opposition was Bricker himself.[14] Dulles, Bricker told an interviewer many years later, represented the New York bankers and lawyers who "wanted to run government through treaties . . . to protect themselves and the international trade." Bricker believed that Dulles "dominated the administration's position and finally converted" the president and others in the administration to oppose the amendment.[15]

The truth, as Duane Tananbaum's recent account shows, was that Eisenhower privately had little sympathy for Bricker or his amendment. Indeed "behind the scenes, Eisenhower played a much more active part in opposing the amendment than Bricker ever realized."[16] The president tried to play down his personal opposition because he wanted to avoid a public confrontation during the first months of his presidency with people whom he would need to work with on other issues; he particularly wanted to avoid picking a fight on an issue that had broad support among congressional Republicans—virtually all the Republicans in the Senate had cosponsored Bricker's resolution. Republican leaders in Congress warned Eisenhower that a firm White House stand on the issue might cause "a serious split" in the Republican party.[17] Even had Dulles not strongly opposed the measure, moreover, there were plenty of others in the administration—including Attorney General Herbert Brownell, Secretary of Defense Charles Wilson, and Mutual Security Director Harold Stassen, not to mention every high State Department official—who urged Eisenhower to oppose the amendment. In any event, Eisenhower needed little persuasion that the amendment compromised the ability of the United States to cooperate economically and militarily with its allies. On this basic question, there was no disagreement between the president and Dulles (or indeed any of the president's foreign and defense policy advisers).[18]

If conservative Republicans faulted Dulles for the administration's opposition to the Bricker amendment, liberal Democrats blamed Dulles for the administration's Middle East policies. In particular, they held Dulles responsible for the administration's abrupt decision to withdraw promised funding for the Aswan Dam, a decision that Dulles's critics believed provoked Egyptian President Nasser to nationalize the Suez Canal and thus set off the entire

Suez crisis of 1956. That the decision was made while Eisenhower was still recovering from an operation helped bolster the view that it was Dulles who was alone responsible for the decision.[19] But as Donald Neff's account of the decision-making process makes clear, Eisenhower was intimately involved in the decision-making process throughout and the final call to withdraw the American offer of financial help was the president's.[20]

In the administration's relations with foreign governments there seems a particularly compelling case for describing Dulles as a lightning rod. Foreign leaders frequently expressed admiration for Eisenhower, while simultaneously condemning the policies pursued by the secretary of state. Soviet leader Nikita Khrushchev, for instance, professed "the deepest respect" for Eisenhower but characterized Dulles as an "imperialist" and "war-like."[21] British Prime Minister Anthony Eden, upon receiving a letter from Eisenhower warning Eden that the United States would not support the use of military force against Nasser, immediately attributed the letter to Dulles. "The only thing that's true to Ike in that [letter] is his signature and that's illegible." The truth, however, was that Eisenhower himself had written the letter.[22] European powers, particularly the British, found in Dulles a convenient scapegoat for their frustrations with their postwar role as followers of the United States. Dulles was crude, undiplomatic, moralistic—indeed, from their point of view, quintessentially American.[23] Blaming Dulles allowed Europeans to avoid having to complicate their rosy view of Eisenhower as the supreme commander of the Allied forces and liberator of Europe.

What allowed Dulles to serve as a lightning rod was a widespread perception, even among some who should have known better, that the president "let Foster Dulles do about what Foster Dulles wanted to do."[24] This view was often repeated by contemporaries and even by scholars. Typical was Herman Finer's judgment that Eisenhower picked Dulles to be secretary of state "so that he could leave in [Dulles's] hands almost all of the direct and daily responsibilities for guiding this nation in her multitudinous and complex dealings with the other nations of the world. Dulles alone was in the driver's seat."[25] Revisionist research has persuasively demonstrated that this conventional view of Eisenhower is widely off the mark.[26] Dulles and Eisenhower in fact worked together extraordinarily closely,[27] and Dulles invariably consulted the president before making public statements or sending diplomatic messages of any importance.[28] Moreover, it was Eisenhower, not Dulles, who made the final decisions.[29]

DULLES AND THE MASS PUBLIC

The finding that Eisenhower controlled foreign policy is necessary but not sufficient, however, to support the claim made by Ambrose and others that having "Dulles available to serve as a lightning rod . . . helped to maintain Eisenhower's popularity."[30] To validate this hypothesis we need evidence about how the general public felt about Dulles. Was Secretary Dulles as unpopular as this thesis implies, indeed requires? A number of secondary accounts assert that Dulles was unpopular. Political scientist Stephen Hess, for instance, reports that Dulles "was as unpopular as the President was popular." Diplomatic historian Gordon Craig agrees that "it would be difficult to think of an American Secretary of State who was less beloved during his term of office than Dulles."[31] In *The Devil and John Foster Dulles,* Townsend Hoopes contrasts "the popular President" with "the unpopular Secretary of State."[32] But in none of these cases is systematic evidence marshaled to support the claim.

This oversight is surprising because, unlike with most administration officials, there is no shortage of public opinion data relating to the public's attitude toward Dulles. In Eisenhower's first term, the National Opinion Research Center (NORC) asked the public to evaluate Dulles's job performance on no less than twenty-one occasions. Contrary to conventional wisdom, these public opinion polls indicate that Secretary of State Dulles was well liked by the American public. In the first term, Dulles's popularity among those expressing an opinion averaged 87 percent, slightly *above* the 80 percent of those with an opinion who approved of Eisenhower.[33] These results suggest an alternative to the lightning rod hypothesis: the mass public viewed Dulles and Eisenhower as a package, holding them jointly responsible for foreign policy setbacks, while crediting them both with foreign policy triumphs.

Consider, for example, the 1955 Geneva Summit, which is often cited as an instance in which the likable Eisenhower played "the warm champion of peace" to Dulles's "austere cold warrior."[34] This view is offered by, among others, Herbert Parmet, who explains that "once again the impression created was of a President seeking peace with open sincerity while his Secretary of State, more consistent with the party's right wing, held out for the hard line."[35] A contemporary version of this thesis is presented in a Herblock cartoon featuring a dour Dulles, laden with "Dulles doubts," and an eager Eisenhower, bubbling with "Eisenhower optimism," reassuring the listener at the other end of the phone that "we'll be there [at the summit], rain or shine."[36]

Public opinion polls taken before and after the July summit validate part of this hypothesis: Eisenhower's popularity did increase slightly after the summit. During the months before the summit, the president's approval rating, among those expressing an opinion, hovered around 80 percent. A special Gallup survey conducted immediately after the summit showed the president's approval rating had been pushed up to 86 percent. What Parmet's thesis neglects, however, is that Dulles's popularity was also boosted by the summit. Before the summit, 84 percent of those with an opinion approved of Dulles's performance; afterward, approval of the secretary rose to 92 percent.[37] President Eisenhower's allegedly "personal triumph"[38] was thus shared, at least in the mind of the general public, by the secretary of state.

Proponents of the "Dulles as lightning rod" thesis often point to the furor over the Suez crisis as evidence of their contention. They stress that it was Dulles, on July 19, 1956, who issued the public "slap in the face" to Egyptian President Nasser by withdrawing the American offer to help finance the building of the Aswan Dam. Although the Egyptians and congressional Democrats may have blamed Dulles, there is no indication that the American public faulted the secretary. Dulles's approval rating after the incident (61 percent approval, 16 percent disapproval, and 23 percent no opinion) remained unchanged from before (63-15-22).[39] As the Suez drama unfolded—in response to Nasser's nationalization of the canal, Israel, France, and Britain invaded Egypt at the end of October—the American public, far from blaming Dulles, rallied around the foreign policy team of Dulles and Eisenhower. After Eisenhower's landslide victory in November 1956, approval of Eisenhower among those with an opinion increased to 83 percent (75-15-10), as did approval of Dulles, which rose to 84 percent (70-13-17).[40]

The public evidently did not share the bitter antipathy felt toward Dulles in foreign capitals and, to a more uneven extent, in Congress. Dulles's "frequent references to God and the flag" may have been "tiresome" for intellectuals, but the general public, if they noticed at all, seemed to be little bothered by his moralizing.[41] Perhaps, as *Newsweek* speculated at the time, "the very [moralism] that has irritated Europeans and Asians is the very thing that many Americans admire most about him."[42] For at least some in the general public, foreign antagonism toward Dulles was probably a sign that the secretary was standing up for America.[43] Whatever the reasons, the evidence cannot sustain the view that Dulles was unpopular with the American public, at least not during the first term.[44]

Data concerning public attitudes toward Dulles's performance during Eisenhower's second term, unfortunately, are much more scanty than those that exist for the first term. The few polls taken, however, do not lend much support to the lightning rod hypothesis. During 1957, only one national survey asked respondents to evaluate the secretary of state's performance. Taken in the spring, as the "get Dulles" campaign in Washington intensified,[45] the poll found that of those with an opinion (83 percent of the sample), 76 percent approved of Dulles's performance. A Gallup survey conducted at roughly the same time showed President Eisenhower with an identical approval rating of 76 percent among those with an opinion (88 percent of the sample).[46] Up to this point, at least, there is still no evidence that Dulles helped to maintain Eisenhower's popularity in the general public by serving as a lightning rod.

Anti-Dulles sentiment in Congress and the media reached its peak at the outset of 1958. Gallup conducted two surveys during January that asked the public to evaluate the performance of both Secretary Dulles and President Eisenhower. The first poll, taken at the beginning of the month, found that among those with an opinion Dulles's approval rating had fallen to 61 percent. But support for Eisenhower had also declined; only two-thirds of those with an opinion now expressed approval of Eisenhower's performance. The drop in support for Dulles, however, is sharper than these statistics indicate. Thirty-six percent—more than double the number from the previous spring—were now undecided about how to evaluate the secretary's performance. Dulles met with the approval of only 39 percent of the sample—a dramatic decline from the 63 percent who had approved of his performance the preceding spring. In contrast, only one in ten respondents reserved judgment on Eisenhower's performance, and six in ten still approved of the president's performance.[47]

This poll suggests that the pervasive criticism of Dulles in Congress and in the press did have a significant impact on public attitudes toward Dulles. The primary impact of this criticism, however, was not to increase disapproval of Dulles—only 25 percent now disapproved compared with 20 percent the previous spring—but rather to move those people who had previously approved of Dulles into the undecided column. While this might be construed as evidence of a lightning rod effect, one must keep in mind that (1) more people (30 percent) still disapproved of Eisenhower than disapproved of Dulles (25 percent), and (2) Eisenhower's popularity had been declining steadily since his reelection and continued to erode until the spring of 1958 when it reached the low point of his administration. Mounting criticism of Dulles, in other words, corresponded closely with Eisenhower's own decline in popularity.

Bivariate analysis of the January 1958 survey provides further evidence of the high degree of linkage between public attitudes toward Eisenhower and Dulles. Only 14 percent of those who expressed an opinion about both men (62 percent of the sample) combined disapproval of Dulles with approval of Eisenhower. That figure is only marginally larger than the 11 percent who disapproved of Ike but approved of his secretary of state. More than half liked both Dulles and Eisenhower, and slightly less than one-fourth disapproved of both men. In short, three-fourths of those respondents with an opinion about both men answered the same way about the president and the secretary of state. In contrast, the same survey shows that only about half of the farmers gave Secretary of Agriculture Ezra Taft Benson the same approval rating as they gave to the president.

Another Gallup poll taken in late January strengthens the linkage thesis while throwing further doubt upon the lightning rod hypothesis. Unfortunately, this survey uses an unnecessarily stringent filter question, asking whether the respondent could "recall offhand the name of the U.S. Secretary of State."[48] Among the 58 percent who passed this hurdle, Dulles had the support of 69 percent of those who expressed an opinion about Dulles's performance. This level of support was no different from the 68 percent of those with an opinion who approved of Eisenhower.[49] Again one is struck by the trend toward consistency in public attitudes toward the president and secretary of state.

Two state polls taken near the end of 1958 point to the same conclusion that there was not a great discrepancy between the public's evaluation of Eisenhower and Dulles. A Des Moines *Register* poll of 753 Iowa residents taken in September 1958 found that among those with an opinion Dulles's performance was approved by 63 percent, while Eisenhower's performance met with the approval of 67 percent. (Benson, in contrast, met with the approval of only 47 percent.) In October 1958, the Minneapolis *Herald Tribune* polled 999 Minnesotans and found that among those with an opinion, 70 percent approved of Eisenhower and 69 percent approved of Dulles (and only 47 percent approved of Benson).[50]

The dominant impression that emerges from the available survey research is of a public that has difficulty separating evaluations of the president from judgments about the secretary of state. This contrasts markedly with public attitudes in the sphere of agriculture, where many in the public, particularly among farmers, simultaneously held a positive view of the president and a negative view of Secretary Benson. Agricultural policy was deemed by the public to be largely the responsibility of Secretary Benson; foreign policy, in contrast, seems to have been judged the joint responsibility of the president and the secretary of state.

DULLES AND CONGRESS

In contrast to the mass public, which normally pays little or no attention to foreign affairs,[51] elites closely scrutinize an administration's actions. Much of what exercises elites (the battle over the Bricker amendment is a conspicuous instance)[52] leaves the great bulk of the mass public cold. While elites debate nuances in the doctrines of massive retaliation, containment, or liberation, the general public tends to evaluate an administration's performance in foreign affairs at the more "simple and global level of getting into war or staying out of it."[53] If foreign policy "has to shout loudly to be heard even a little" by the mass public, even the faintest whisper is usually detected by political elites.[54]

Because elites pay closer attention than the mass public to questions of foreign policy, they are more likely to perceive differences in the personas and positions of the president and secretary of state. We would therefore expect the lightning rod thesis to carry greater validity at the elite than at the mass level, and indeed we have already presented evidence that this is the case for Dulles. Even at the elite level, however, the evidence that Dulles was a presidential lightning rod is much less compelling than is commonly assumed. Although elites were more attentive to the differing emphases Eisenhower and Dulles assigned to policies, the dominant tendency among the political stratum no less than the mass public seems to have been to link their evaluations of the president and Secretary Dulles.

In a heroic effort, James Rosenau has coded every comment made on the Senate floor regarding Dulles between 1953 and 1956.[55] Among those senators who engaged in "recurrent behavior," ten were consistently hostile toward the secretary of state.[56] Four were extreme right-wing isolationists: William Jenner (R-Ind.), George Malone (R-Nev.), Joseph McCarthy (R-Wis.), and Patrick McCarran (D-Nev.); the other six were liberal, "peace-minded" internationalists:[57] Paul Douglas (D-Ill.), William Fulbright (D-Ark.), Hubert Humphrey (D-Minn.), Herbert Lehman (D-N.Y.), Joseph O'Mahoney (D-Wyo.), and Wayne Morse (I-Oreg.). Contrary to the lightning rod hypothesis, none of these senators were favorably disposed toward Eisenhower. Most were scornful of the president.

Like many other liberal senators, Hubert Humphrey often drew attention to apparent differences between Dulles and Eisenhower on such issues as disarmament or summit meetings with the Soviets. But this did not mean that he absolved Eisenhower from responsibility for what he regarded as the administration's incoherent and contradictory foreign policy. Far from it. Indeed the president's willingness to permit such differences was itself grounds for condemnation. Humphrey pledged that he could not "support an administration that constantly reveals such an abysmal lack of executive leadership." In another unmistakable swipe at Eisenhower he lamented that "the great tragedy of this administration is that it seeks popularity at the expense of principle and leadership."[58] President Eisenhower no less than Secretary Dulles was responsible for what he considered to be "the deterioration of American foreign policy."[59]

From 1956 on, William Fulbright was Dulles's severest congressional critic, but by 1958 the Arkansas senator had also become one of Eisenhower's most persistent and uncompromising critics. Fulbright, like many other Democrats, did single out Dulles for deciding on his own to withdraw the offer of financial assistance to Nasser.[60] And in an interview in 1970, Fulbright attributed what he regarded as the improper handling of treaties during the Eisenhower years to Dulles rather than to Eisenhower.[61] But in criticizing Dulles for seeming "at times to be exercising those 'delicate, plenary, and exclusive powers' which are supposed to be vested in the President,"[62] Fulbright also implicitly criticized Eisenhower for abdicating his constitutional responsibilities as president of the United States. Increasingly, rather than isolating Dulles as the source of the administration's missteps, Fulbright directly criticized Eisenhower. The most extreme instance was a 1958 speech on the floor of the Senate in which he ridiculed the entire Eisenhower era as one of "luxurious torpor" in which people "were at liberty to stop thinking any more . . . [when] they could bask in the artificial sunlight of a government which did not bother them with serious things." He decried the "weakness for the easy way" and, in an unmistakable jab at Eisenhower, declared that "the age of the amateur is over."[63] Fulbright was contemptuous of what he regarded as Eisenhower's "aimless and feeble" leadership that was distinguished by its "lack of taste for the hard work of the intellect that must precede meaningful action."[64]

Another of Dulles's most vocal antagonists was Oregon Senator Wayne Morse. But Morse, who had bolted the Republican party shortly after the nomination of Eisenhower to become an Independent, had been a strident critic of Eisenhower from the outset. In 1952, he had supported Stevenson, whom he considered "a brilliant statesman," over Eisenhower, who he believed wasn't "big enough . . . for the job, [and] . . . hasn't the mind for it." During the campaign, Morse accused Eisenhower of "demagoguery, double-talk and dangerous desertion . . . of his once-professed political principles" and labeled Eisenhower's "I will go to Korea" pledge "a cheap, grandstand political ploy." The trouble with Eisenhower, Morse believed, was that Eisenhower was "a man of compromise rather than a man of determined principle." Nothing Ike did during the next eight years prompted Morse to change his opinion, and their personal relations remained frosty.[65]

Neither Herbert Lehman nor Paul Douglas, both ardent liberals, had many kind words for Eisenhower. Ten days after Eisenhower had been nominated, Douglas criticized Eisenhower on the floor of the Democratic convention for his role, as army chief of staff, in recommending the withdrawal of American troops from South Korea. Eisenhower, Douglas told the Democratic delegates, must therefore carry a large part of the blame for the North Korean invasion of South Korea.[66] Like Morse, both Lehman and Douglas regarded themselves as men of principle rather than of compromise.[67] In Lyndon Johnson's view, they were "crazies . . . bomb-thrower types."[68] Both Lehman and Douglas sought leadership "which inspires and awakens . . . people to great ends and to great sacrifices" and found Eisenhower sorely lacking. Douglas condemned Eisenhower's "rush toward the middle of the road" and ridiculed a situation in which the "bland [were] leading the bland." Similarly, Lehman longed for "an administration seeking ideas instead of nostrums." Much as Ronald Reagan's detractors talked of a Teflon presidency, so Douglas referred disparagingly to "the Eisenhower spell."[69]

Among the right-wing isolationists who were critical of Dulles, none could be counted as supportive of Eisenhower. Although initially reluctant to tangle with the popular president, their private comments were suffused with disdain for the general-turned-president. In the case of McCarthy, the private contempt bubbled up to the surface at the end of 1954, when he publicly accused Eisenhower of "weakness and supineness" in ferreting out Communists and felt it necessary to "apologize to the American people" for supporting Eisenhower in 1952.[70] The attitude toward Eisenhower among this stripe of Republican was, "He's our meal ticket now. Once we're in, the hell with him. . . . I won't give a damn about Ike the day after the election."[71] From the perspective of the extreme right wing, it was not Secretary Dulles but Eisenhower, a "Fifth-Column Democrat,"[72] who was largely responsible for the administration's failure to depart from the disastrous foreign policy of his predecessors.

Early on, Eisenhower had given up trying to work with what he termed "the McCarthy-Malone axis," which "hates and despises everything for which I stand." Instead he opted for a strategy of isolating, and thereby rendering impotent, the "reactionary fringe" of the party by wooing those less rigid among the Old Guard, such as Robert Taft, Everett Dirksen, Homer Capehart, Styles Bridges, and William Knowland.[73] With the exception of the "unappeasables,"[74] the Old Guard consistently defended Dulles (as well as Eisenhower). By Rosenau's count, five such senators (Capehart, Dirksen, Homer Ferguson, Bourke Hickenlooper, and Knowland) made a total of 233 references to Dulles between 1953 and 1956, and only four of those references were coded as unfavorable toward Dulles.[75]

Suspicions the Taft wing of the party originally harbored about Dulles on account of his past associations with the Truman administration and Thomas Dewey were dispelled by Dulles's strident anti-Communist rhetoric and by the enemies he was making, particularly in Britain.[76] One notable convert was Senator William Langer (R-N.D.), a fervent isolationist who in a debate over foreign aid in 1953 had scored Dulles for having "brought over with him to the halls and meeting chambers of the State Department the entire Truman-Acheson foreign concept almost without variation."[77] Before long, however, Langer was praising Dulles as a tireless and courageous champion of American interests. "With John Foster Dulles as his Secretary of State," Langer observed, "Dwight Eisenhower and Mr. Dulles have taken charge of the foreign relations of the United States Government, and, although cooperating with other countries, have not allowed England, France, or any other country to dictate to the United States of America."[78]

If even in Congress Dulles proved to be less of a lightning rod than is often presumed, this is in part due to his assiduous efforts to gain the support and confidence of members of Congress, particularly those (like Langer) who sat on the Senate Foreign Relations Committee. "His correspondence files and telephone memoranda," according to one scholar, "tell the story of perpetual courtship."[79] He breakfasted with the Foreign Relations chair Walter

George at the influential Democrat's apartment at least every other week and frequently stopped by for conversations in the late afternoon or early evening. Dulles kept up a "continuous dialogue" with William Knowland, who was minority (and, briefly, majority) leader as well as a member of the Foreign Relations Committee.[80] Anxious to avoid the acrimonious congressional relations that had plagued the tenure of his predecessor, Dean Acheson, Dulles made extraordinary efforts to consult congressional committees. During his six-year tenure, he testified forty-eight times before the Senate Foreign Relations Committee and always consulted the committee before and after major international conferences. He established a reputation with Congress that Senator Alexander Wiley (R-Wis.) characterized as one of "complete frankness and honesty."[81] Republicans in particular regarded Dulles's attitude as a welcome departure from the "deceit and contempt" that they believed Acheson had displayed during his appearances before congressional committees.[82]

Those senators not persuaded by Dulles's appeals usually did not exempt the president from their criticisms of the administration's foreign policy. In part this was because, in contrast to a policy area like agriculture where Eisenhower had no pretense to expertise, the president knew a great deal about national security policy and foreign affairs. The former leader of the Allied armed forces could hardly claim to be following the advice of subordinates in formulating the nation's national defense posture. Indeed playing upon Eisenhower's military experience and wisdom was a common tactic used by proponents of the administration's foreign and defense policies. In defending the policy of massive retaliation, for instance, William Knowland told his fellow senators he doubted "that any member of this body has had the experience of President Eisenhower, who led our armies in World War II and won the great victory in Europe."[83] Such arguments, which were repeated again and again, meant that Eisenhower's prestige was closely tied to his foreign and defense policies in a way that was never true in domestic policy.

Criticisms of Dulles's handling of foreign and defense policies, however, spilled over into indictments of the president for reasons that go beyond the circumstances peculiar to the Eisenhower presidency. To criticize the country's "foreign policy [as] inadequate, outmoded, and misdirected"[84] necessarily implied a critique of the president, an implication that was absent or muted when critics attacked agricultural, labor, or land policies. The Acheson/Truman relationship, which exhibits an even more pronounced tendency on the part of elites and masses to merge their evaluations of the president and secretary of state, lends support to the hypothesis that this coupling phenomenon is embedded in the peculiar nature of a president's roles and responsibilities in conducting foreign policy.

ACHESON AND TRUMAN

If ever a president was in need of a lightning rod in foreign affairs it was Harry Truman during his second term. In contrast to the perceived foreign policy successes of his initial term—the Marshall Plan, Truman Doctrine, Berlin Air Lift—1949 was, as the historian Eric Goldman phrased it, "a year of shocks."[85] First came the fall of the Nationalist Chinese government, followed by the announcement that the Soviets had acquired the atomic bomb. Within another year, the United States was embroiled in a war in Korea. Public opinion surveys reflected the administration's changing fortunes. Whereas during Truman's first term more people had approved than disapproved of "the way the officials in Washington are handling our foreign affairs," during the second term a majority consistently expressed disapproval (except for a brief "rally around the flag" immediately after North Korea invaded South Korea).[86]

Dean Acheson was sworn in as secretary of state on January 21, 1949, arriving, as Acheson later noted, "just in time to have [Chiang Kai-shek] collapse on me."[87] In many ways, Acheson was an ideal foil for conservative Republicans looking for a culprit for the "loss of China." With "his smart-aleck manner and his British clothes and that New Dealism," Acheson, in the eyes of many Republicans, stood "for everything that has been wrong with the United States for years."[88] The Republican right piled abuse upon the head of "the great Red Dean."[89] By one scholar's count, isolationist Republican senators made 7 cordial and 1,268 hostile remarks regarding Acheson on the floor of the Senate.[90] It is understandable that Acheson believed he had been singled out as "chief villain by the Republican right."[91]

If there is no doubting the level of abuse directed toward Acheson by Republican congressmen, there are grounds for questioning whether these assaults upon the secretary of state diverted criticism away from President Truman. An alternative hypothesis is that criticism of Acheson went hand-in-hand with criticism of Truman. The *Congressional Record* shows the latter hypothesis to be in closer accord with the evidence. The predominant tendency among Acheson's severest congressional critics was to condemn both the secretary of state and the president.

A glimpse of the depths of Republican hostility toward Truman was revealed when Republican congressmen heckled the president during delivery of his 1950 State of the Union message.[92] The following day, California Senator William Knowland launched an extended attack upon the administration's "defeatist attitude" and "bankrupt policy" in China. Although Knowland singled out "a small group of willful men in the Far Eastern Division of the State Department" as particularly culpable for "the debacle which has taken place in China," this did not, in his view, absolve those higher up in the chain of command, for the subordinates "had the backing of their superiors." "No group," Knowland stressed, "could so operate in the Far Eastern Division without the approval of the Secretary of State and no Secretary of State could follow such a policy without the approval of the President of the United States. The ultimate responsibility is there." The Chinese, Knowland concluded, had been "sold down the river into slavery by the President of the United States and the State Department."[93]

Perhaps the most persistent critic of the secretary of state was Styles Bridges, whom Acheson later characterized as "my faithful enemy."[94] But while Bridges may have saved his most colorful barbs for Acheson and the State Department,[95] his speeches on the floor of the Senate reveal that he considered Truman and Acheson jointly responsible for the disappointing course of events in the Far East. It was "the policy of Truman and Acheson," not that of Acheson alone, that Bridges blamed for "turning over China" to the Communists.[96] In explaining why he believed no top military expert would contradict Acheson's contention that Formosa was of little strategic value to the United States, Bridges declared that under this administration "if a top-ranking policy maker is to retain his position, he must unhesitatingly follow the line *laid down by the President*."[97]

Criticism of the secretary of state intensified after Acheson responded to news of Alger Hiss's perjury conviction by announcing at a press conference that "I do not intend to turn my back on Alger Hiss." But the same Republicans who now called for the secretary's removal believed Truman too was guilty of "coddling" Communists. As they were quick to remind the opposition, it was President Truman who had dismissed charges of subversion made by congressional investigating committees as "red herrings."[98] Many Republican congressmen shared Indiana Senator Homer Capehart's belief that there would continue to be spies "as long as we have a president who refers to such matters as 'red herrings' and a secretary of state who refuses to turn his back on Alger Hisses."[99]

The outbreak of the Korean War in June 1950 only strengthened the perceived ties between Truman and Acheson. Although the immediate effect of the North Korean invasion of South Korea was to mute criticism of Truman (but not of the secretary of state) as the country "rallied around the flag," once the war began to go badly—as it did after the entry of the Chinese in the winter of 1950–1951—there was even less scope for Truman to avoid responsibility than before. President Truman could not avoid blame because, as Senate Minority Leader Robert Taft expressed it, "the Korean War is a Truman War."[100]

The dismissal of General MacArthur in the spring of 1951 provided a fresh occasion for Republicans to air their grievances with the Truman administration. As before, criticism was aimed at the team of Truman and Acheson. North Dakota Senator Milton Young, for instance, believed the firing of MacArthur to be "in line with President Truman's and Secretary

Dean Acheson's program of everlasting appeasement to Communists." Senator Richard Nixon agreed that "the policy of the State Department—and that means the policy of the administration" was one of "bare-faced appeasement." The disastrous war in Korea, Senator Capehart argued, "was due to the foreign policy team of Truman, Marshall, and Acheson." Bridges blamed the "Truman-Acheson clique."[101]

That abuse of Acheson in no way precluded blaming (or even abusing) Truman is evident from the behavior of Senator Joseph McCarthy, whose vitriolic criticisms of Acheson are well known. In his now famous Wheeling address, for instance, McCarthy had pummeled Acheson as a "pompous diplomat in striped pants, with a phony British accent."[102] Although he obviously relished attacking the vulnerable State Department, he reserved plenty of invective for the president. Truman's dismissal of MacArthur prompted McCarthy to declare that "the son of a bitch should be impeached."[103] He intimated, moreover, that Truman had been drunk when he issued the order to recall MacArthur.[104] McCarthy was unequivocal that "we should put the blame [for tying MacArthur's hands] on our Chief Executive."[105]

Another of Acheson's most abusive critics was the newly elected senator from Idaho, Herman Welker—indeed Welker attributed his election in 1950 to his denunciations of Acheson during the campaign. While MacArthur's dismissal proved to Welker that Acheson "is riding in the saddle today," he also told his Senate colleagues that on account of the "continuous blundering on the part of the President of the United States, I have lost any confidence I ever had in Harry Truman"—although he allowed that "I never had very much in the beginning." Both Truman and Acheson, Welker intimated, were in league with the Communist paper the *Daily Worker*. In addition to repeating his call for Acheson to be "fired and replaced," he also asked for Truman's resignation—90 percent of his telegrams, he reported, asked for impeachment proceedings to begin immediately.[106] Another longtime Acheson foe, Senator William Jenner, also believed that Acheson's resignation was no longer sufficient: "It is too late now for such minor remedies. We must cut this whole cancerous conspiracy out of our Government at once. Our only choice is to impeach President Truman."[107]

Public opinion polls, though scanty, strongly suggest that the general public also perceived Acheson and Truman as an inseparable package. In the public mind, Secretary Acheson was the president's accomplice, Truman's partner in crime. After the Chinese crushed the United Nations armies in late November, public support for the war shrank dramatically,[108] as did support for President Truman and Secretary Acheson. A Gallup poll conducted early in December of 1950, immediately before the Republican caucus' vote of no-confidence in Acheson, found that six in ten of those venturing an opinion held an unfavorable impression of Acheson. Roughly the same percentage believed Acheson should be replaced. A Gallup poll taken shortly thereafter showed that 58 percent of those expressing an opinion disapproved of Truman's performance as president.[109] The percentage of people who wanted Acheson replaced was thus virtually identical with the proportion who disapproved of Truman.

In May of 1951, a month after Truman's recall of MacArthur, Gallup found that slightly more than two-thirds of those with an opinion believed that Acheson should be replaced. The same poll also showed that Truman's disapproval rating among those with an opinion had reached a new high of 72 percent. Bivariate analysis confirms that those who disapproved of Truman overwhelmingly wanted to get rid of Acheson and that those who approved of Truman were content to stick with Acheson.[110]

Four months later, the storm over Acheson had subsided somewhat. Reflecting the relative absence of elite voices now calling for Acheson's dismissal, Gallup found that the percentage of those with an opinion who believed Acheson should be replaced had dropped to just under half. The same poll, however, showed that 63 percent of those expressing an opinion disapproved of President Truman's performance. One-sixth of those who wanted Acheson to stay on, moreover, did so out of a fear that Truman might appoint someone worse.[111] No matter how unpopular a secretary of state becomes, this survey suggests, he cannot protect a president from bearing the responsibility for an unpopular war. It was Truman's war, not Acheson's.

If there had been a decline in the number of people clamoring for Acheson's dismissal, it did not mean that the public now approved of his performance as secretary of state. Far from it. A NORC survey taken in October 1951 found that although 60 percent of those with an opinion now wanted Acheson to stay on, only 42 percent of those with an opinion evaluated his handling of foreign affairs positively. Another NORC poll, taken a year later, found Acheson's approval rating roughly unchanged at about 39 percent.[112] During this last year of Truman's presidency, the president's Gallup approval rating among those with an opinion hovered in the mid-30s, somewhat below Acheson's rating.

It is tempting to attribute the widespread perception of Truman and Acheson as a package to peculiar features of Truman's leadership. Because, as Robert Donovan observes, "Truman angrily regarded attacks on any of his subordinates as attacks upon himself,"[113] the president vigorously defended Acheson when he was under attack. As any number of commentators have noted, President Truman placed a high premium on loyalty. Richard Fenno, for instance, remarks that Truman "required a close loyalty, and he reciprocated in full measure when any of his subordinates (like Dean Acheson) were under fire from the outside."[114]

The most obvious example of Truman coming to Acheson's defense occurred at the close of 1950. On December 15, the Republican caucuses in both the House and Senate requested Acheson be removed on the grounds that he had "lost the confidence of the country." At a subsequent press conference, Truman promptly "blasted back" at critics of the secretary of state.[115] To dismiss Acheson, Truman responded, would be to "weaken the firm and vigorous position this country has taken against communist aggression." In addition to reiterating his great faith in the secretary of state, Truman made it clear that such attacks upon Acheson were attacks upon the president's foreign policy. As Truman later explained in his memoirs, "They wanted Acheson's scalp because he stood for *my* policy. . . . The men who struck out against Acheson were thus in reality striking out at me."[116]

Perhaps Truman's style of never shrinking from a fight, much in evidence in his sharp, unflinching defense of Acheson, encouraged opponents to criticize the president directly. Certainly Truman's insistence on reminding the public that responsibility for a decision was the president's alone ("The Buck Stops Here") made it more difficult for opponents to criticize Acheson without also criticizing Truman. But it was not only Truman who drew attention to the fact that attacks on Acheson were necessarily attacks on the president. Democrat William Fulbright, for instance, reminded his Senate colleagues that "this attack upon Mr. Acheson is, of course, not just a personal matter between him and the Republicans. It is, in fact, an attack upon the President and his foreign policy. . . . Everyone knows that Mr. Acheson is not an independent agent, but, on the contrary, that he is but the instrumentality of the President in carrying into effect the foreign policy which the President determines."[117] Republican Senator Eugene Millikin admitted as much when he explained that at issue was something much broader than the issue of Mr. Acheson himself, and that was the "whole question of this Administration's foreign policy."[118]

An examination of how President Eisenhower acted when faced with congressional criticism of Secretary Dulles's handling of the Suez affair casts doubt upon an explanation that centers exclusively on Truman's style of leadership. Rather than allow Dulles to stand alone and absorb the fire, Eisenhower went out of his way to identify himself with his secretary of state. At a January 30, 1957, news conference, Eisenhower was asked whether Dulles's actions had "contributed to our present international difficulties." Eisenhower replied that Dulles "has never taken any action which I have not in advance approved." The policies pursued by the secretary of state, the president continued, "have my approval from top to bottom."[119] Moreover, just as Truman praised Acheson as "among the greatest of our Secretaries of State,"[120] so Eisenhower credited his secretary of state with possessing "a wisdom and experience and knowledge that I think is possessed by no other man in the world."[121]

An additional difficulty with focusing on Truman's leadership style as the critical variable in explaining the intense criticism directed at Truman is that

Presidents Truman and Eisenhower both delegated extensive authority to their secretaries of state.[122] Unlike FDR, Truman had no desire to be his own secretary of state.[123] Although Truman was hardly averse to placing himself on the firing line—indeed his motto "If you can't stand the heat, stay out of the kitchen" implied that the ultimate test of presidential mettle was how well one stood up under fire—it was Acheson who, more often than not, was the administration's spokesman in foreign affairs.

In particular, Truman largely left to Acheson the role of "educating" the public about the fall of China. For instance, Acheson used a speech, delivered on January 12, 1950, before the National Press Club—with characteristic causticity, Acheson characterized the speech as "another effort to get the self-styled formulators of public opinion to think before they wrote"[124]—to explain that Chiang's government had fallen not because of American bungling but because of the Chinese government's internal weakness. Throughout the first half of 1950, Acheson continued to make numerous speeches explaining and defending administration policy. These speeches amounted to what one scholar has called an "experiment in foreign-policy education."[125]

Even with Acheson "out front," however, the president could not avoid blame. As one Republican critic of Truman reminded his fellow members of the House, "Under the Constitution, the President of the United States has full control in shaping our country's foreign policy."[126] Even decisions announced by Acheson were blamed on Truman. Although it was Acheson, for instance, in the Press Club speech of January 12, 1950, who excluded South Korea from the American "defensive perimeter" (thus allegedly inviting a North Korean invasion of South Korea), Republican Senator Bourke Hickenlooper recalled it as a presidential announcement: "A little more than a year ago . . . the State Department and the President, or the President through the State Department, made the famous announcement that Korea was not within our perimeter of defense."[127] Equally striking was Senator Knowland's reference to the much-maligned White Paper issued by the State Department—a 1,000 plus page document recounting why the administration could not have done anything to stop China from going Communist—as "the white paper statement of the President of the United States."[128] Foreign policy, these comments suggest, was viewed as primarily Truman's responsibility or at best as the joint responsibility of the president and secretary of state.

Both Truman and Eisenhower chose strong-willed secretaries of state, delegated to them substantial authority, and encouraged them to assume a prominent public profile, yet in neither case did the general public distinguish much between their evaluation of the president and their judgment of the secretary of state. In both cases the president and secretary were judged as a team, with the major difference between the two cases being that the majority approved of the results—peace—achieved by the Eisenhower/ Dulles foreign policy and disapproved of the outcomes—war—associated with the Truman/Acheson foreign policy. The story is more complex and nuanced at the elite level, particularly in the Eisenhower case, but here too the dominant tendency is to view the secretary of state as a presidential accomplice. Is there something distinctive about the domain of foreign policy that would explain why an adviser is less likely to act as a lightning rod than to be seen as an accomplice?

WHY PRESIDENTS CAN'T OR DON'T HIDE IN FOREIGN AFFAIRS

Why might presidents be less able to deflect blame in the realm of foreign policy? Part of the answer surely lies in the nature of public expectations regarding presidential control of foreign policy. The public expects the president to be responsible for, and intimately involved in, the conduct of foreign affairs, a presumption that is absent or significantly weaker in domestic affairs. A Gallup poll conducted in 1979, for instance, found that 49 percent of those surveyed thought the president "should have the major responsibility for setting foreign policy" while only 27 percent said the same about Congress. In contrast, when asked about energy policy or economic policy, 40 percent said Congress should have the major responsibility for setting policy, and only 34 percent named the president.[129]

Nor is this expectation of presidential control limited to the general public. It is shared by party activists and elected officials.[130] Hubert Humphrey, speaking while Richard Nixon was ensconced in the presidency and opposition to the Vietnam War was near its peak, admitted that "ultimately though the President must be in charge [of foreign policy]. You cannot run foreign policy by committees. . . . It is [the] President [who] has the responsibility for really defining the . . . national security [interests] of this country."[131] The same view is expressed in the findings of the 1987 Tower Commission Report: "The President is responsible for the national security policy of the United States. In the development and execution of that policy, the President is the decision-maker. He is not obliged to consult with or seek approval from anyone in the Executive Branch. . . . As Chief Executive and Commander-in-Chief, and with broad authority in the area of foreign affairs, it is the President who is empowered to act for the nation and protect its interests."[132] More systematic evidence comes from a study of 1976 national party convention delegates that found delegates from both parties showed substantially greater trust in the president's judgment in foreign than in domestic policy, while trusting Congress more than the president in domestic policy.[133]

But there is more to the puzzle than the widespread predisposition to hold the president accountable for the conduct of foreign policy.[134] The presumption that presidents are uniquely responsible for foreign policy makes it difficult for presidents to hide, but equally important is that presidents often don't even try to hide on the foreign policy stage. If secretaries of state often make poor lightning rods it is because presidents seem more inclined to thrust themselves into the public limelight in the foreign policy domain than they are in domestic policy.

In part, this is because presidents are inclined to regard foreign policy as uniquely their own responsibility. The Constitution may be, as Edward Corwin famously put it, "an invitation to struggle for the privilege of directing American foreign policy,"[135] but few presidents, especially in the twentieth century, have seen it this way. As Harry Truman bluntly informed a gathering of Jewish war veterans, "I make American foreign policy."[136] Or, as Richard Nixon expressed the point: "I've always thought this country could run itself domestically without a President; all you need is a competent Cabinet to run the country at home. You need a President for foreign policy; no Secretary of State is really important; the President makes foreign policy."[137] Presidents don't hide, in short, because they believe foreign and national security policy is their unique constitutional and statutory responsibility.

Even presidents less inclined to define the president's role in quite the way that Nixon did invariably find themselves spending large and increasing amounts of their time on foreign policy. Those presidents who come to office focused on a largely domestic agenda, as in the case of Ronald Reagan, soon find themselves "surprised at how much a part of the job, that is how much . . . percentage of your time and effort and thinking is devoted to the international situation."[138] In the most systematic study of presidential attention, John Kessel showed that not only do presidents devote more space in their State of the Union addresses to international affairs than to any other topic, but that attention to this policy area increases substantially during the course of a president's term in office.[139] Why do presidents invariably catch what a Clinton aide recently characterized as the "foreign policy bug"?[140]

A number of incentives lure the president onto the foreign policy stage. First is the prospect of being able to accomplish more. Studies have shown that presidents are more successful in getting their way with Congress in foreign policy than in domestic policy—although how much more is a matter of some dispute.[141] What is beyond dispute is that presidents are substantially less dependent on legislative enactments in foreign affairs than in the domestic area. President Carter, as Thomas Cronin notes, freely "confessed he liked foreign policy because his capacity to act unilaterally seemed much greater in the foreign than in the domestic realm."[142]

A second incentive is the promise of a more presidential image. "As foreign policy leaders," George Edwards and Stephen Wayne explain, "[presidents] can act as unifying figures, [and] overcome perceptions of partisanship."[143] To the extent that "going international" plays up the president's nonpolitical, head-of-state image, there is less need for lightning rods in the foreign policy domain.[144] For the aim of lightning rods is precisely to distance the president from the controversial political side of the presidential role.[145]

A number of studies have shown that popularity is significantly more likely to accompany presidential action in the realm of international affairs, where the president claims to speak for the entire nation, than in domestic affairs, where he appears to represent only a part.[146] Gary Smith, for instance, finds that during Kennedy's presidency, "presidential popularity jumps when foreign conflict occurs and it slumps at times of domestic conflict."[147] Examining presidential popularity from 1963 to 1980, Michael MacKuen finds that "the average net impact of all foreign actions . . . is positive (2.42 points), but . . . for domestic events (excluding Watergate) is slightly negative (− .84)."[148] And Philip Stone and Richard Brody demonstrate that even in the case of Lyndon Johnson, "approval of Johnson goes up when announcements are made regarding foreign policy other than Vietnam . . . [and] it goes down when announcements are made regarding . . . domestic issues."[149] Even foreign policy blunders, as when an American U-2 spy plane was shot down over the Soviet Union in 1960, have often resulted in increases, at least in the short term, in presidential popularity.[150]

To the extent that presidential actions in foreign affairs accent a president's unifying image as head of state and tend to be rewarded with increases in public support, presidents have an incentive to push themselves onto the foreign policy stage. This incentive structure teaches presidents to seek a lower profile on the domestic scene, where even skillful handling of a policy may cost a president political support, and to raise their profile in foreign affairs, where even mistakes may be rewarded.

If presidents are lured onto the foreign policy stage by the prospect of greater rewards, they are also pushed onto it by the fear that letting others take the blame will leave the impression of a president not in control. A president can admit ignorance or detachment in the realm of agricultural or land-use policy without drawing into question his fitness for the presidency, but a similar admission in foreign affairs is much more hazardous to a president's public prestige. In the aftermath of revelations about the Iran-contra affair, for example, Gallup found that more people thought it was worse if the National Security Council (NSC) ran the operation without President Reagan's knowledge than if President Reagan had known and approved of the Iran-contra connection.[151] The public expectation of presidential involvement in national security matters helps explain why both Truman and Eisenhower were so reluctant to let their secretaries of state take the blame for policies that were drawing criticism. And their vigorous defenses of Acheson and Dulles suggest that part of the reason the public so closely linked their assessments of the president and the secretary of state is that both presidents worked to forestall the perception that the secretary of state alone shaped the policies affecting the nation's security.

Eisenhower's willingness to accept responsibility for, and admit complete knowledge of, the U-2 flights over the Soviet Union—at the price of the collapse of the 1960 Paris Summit—reflected his recognition that a president cannot escape blame on a national security issue without seeming to abrogate his responsibility as conductor of foreign relations. Despite CIA Director Allen Dulles's offer to take full responsibility and resign, and Khrushchev's statement that he was "quite willing to grant that the President knew nothing" about the reconnaissance flights, Eisenhower evidently felt, as Stephen Hess writes, that to do so "would have been an unconscionable admission that he did not control the country's national security apparatus."[152]

The reaction in the press to the government's denials helped to persuade Eisenhower that admitting involvement would be better than feigning detachment. In the *New York Herald Tribune,* Walter Lippmann pointed out that "in denying that it authorized the flight, the Administration has entered a plea of *incompetence.*" James Reston, columnist for the *New York Times,* believed that "the heart of the problem here is that the Presidency has been parcelled out, first to Sherman Adams, then to John Foster Dulles, and in this case to somebody else—probably to Allen Dulles." Eisenhower's style had removed him from the key decisions and left "the nation, the world and sometimes even the President himself in a state of uncertainty about who is doing what." Harry Truman wrote to Dean Acheson with the opinion that "the President of the United States ought not to admit that he doesn't know what is going on." In the wake of such talk, Eisenhower convened the NSC and announced that "we're just going to have to take a lot of beating on this—and I'm the one, rightly, who's going to have to take it."[153]

In subsequent interviews a number of former officials have suggested that Eisenhower shouldered the responsibility for the fiasco because it was not in the general's nature or training to avoid blame. Douglas Dillon, for one, has suggested that "he didn't like to blame other people. . . . He felt more strongly than a civilian leader might have. He had this thing about honesty and that was the military tradition." Similarly, Andrew Goodpaster has claimed that Eisenhower wasn't "in the business of using scapegoats. . . . That's the last thing the President would want."[154]

Although there is some validity to this view,[155] the question remains as to why Eisenhower was unwilling to deflect blame in this episode but was perfectly happy to shift blame to subordinates on any number of other occasions. The answer seems to be that he recognized that an admission of detachment on such a question would do more harm than good. What

bothered Eisenhower was not only that this would be a "glaring and perma-
nent injustice" to the subordinate, but that it would have been an intolerable
admission that the president did not "control important matters in our government."[156] To mute criticism that "the country has been humiliated by ab-
sentmindedness in the highest quarters of government,"[157] Eisenhower
found it best to take the blame. The costs of being seen as a president not in
command of foreign affairs can be further illustrated by examining the public perception of the relationship between Gerald Ford and Henry Kissinger.

UPSTAGING THE PRESIDENT: KISSINGER AND FORD

From the moment Gerald Ford became president, the White House staff,
and to a lesser extent Ford himself, worried that Kissinger, who had become
a genuine celebrity in the last years of the Nixon administration, would up-
stage the new president. Believing that the public perception that Kissinger,
not Ford, directed foreign policy hurt the president,[158] some staff members
attempted to downgrade Kissinger's importance, most visibly by stripping
Kissinger of his second hat as national security assistant.[159]
    Polling data suggest that White House concerns that Kissinger was steal-
ing Ford's thunder were justified. The Harris polling organization conducted eleven surveys between September 1974 and November 1976 asking
respondents to evaluate the job performances of Kissinger and Ford. In the
initial survey, Ford and Kissinger both received high marks, with only about
20 percent of the sample disapproving of either man's performance. Ford's
pardon of Richard Nixon, however, sent the president's approval plummet-
ing below 50 percent, while having no impact on the public's evaluation of
the secretary of state. In the ten polls subsequent to the pardon, Kissinger's
approval rating ranged from a low of 55 percent to a high of 75 percent;
Ford's fluctuated from a low of 30 percent to a high of 50 percent. The president's average approval rating of 43 percent was a full 20 points below Kissinger's average approval rating of 62 percent, and at no point did Ford have
a higher approval rating than his secretary of state.
    Follow-up questions asking respondents to evaluate the performance of
the president and secretary of state in specific foreign policy areas show that
the difference between Ford and Kissinger was due to more than the fact that
Kissinger was not being evaluated on the basis of a faltering economy. They
show that the public was much more likely to approve of Kissinger's handling of foreign policy than of Ford's. More than 60 percent of those with an
opinion approved of Kissinger's performance in handling U.S.-Chinese relations, for instance, while only 45 percent of those with an opinion approved
of President Ford's performance in this area. Ford fared little better with

U.S.-Soviet relations: 62 percent of those with an opinion expressed approval of Kissinger's handling of relations with the Soviet Union, while only 46 percent approved of Ford's handling of the Soviets. While 71 percent of those expressing an opinion believed Kissinger had done a good job in "working for peace in the world," only 56 percent were willing to say the same for the president.[160]

There is some evidence that Kissinger did help President Ford by taking much of the public heat for the fall of Cambodia and the North Vietnamese takeover of Vietnam. In a May 1975 poll, taken in the aftermath of the fall of Cambodia and the North Vietnamese takeover, only 38 percent approved of Kissinger's "handling of the Vietnam and Cambodian crises." Despite Ford's significantly lower overall job rating at the time (40 percent approval compared to 56 percent for Kissinger), 46 percent expressed approval of the president's handling of the Indochina situation.[161] Given that Kissinger had been linked in the public mind with Vietnam since early 1973, before Ford had become vice president let alone president, it is not surprising that Kissinger rather than Ford was held responsible. But these are rare circumstances indeed.

On balance, these polls suggest that Kissinger's accomplishments were of little help in boosting public approval of Ford. This pattern is well illustrated by the public reaction to the preliminary agreement Kissinger helped negotiate between Egypt and Israel. Kissinger's job approval rating, which in early August had been around 56 percent, jumped to 63 percent after signing the accord in September. Sixty-one percent (in contrast to 48 percent in May, and 50 percent in August) now expressed approval of Kissinger's efforts in "working to achieve a lasting peace in the Middle East." In contrast, Ford's job rating remained mired around 40 percent, unaffected by what was perceived as Kissinger's personal accomplishment. Only 44 percent approved of Ford's efforts in handling the Mideast crisis—only slightly higher than the 40 percent who had approved in May and July. A poll conducted the following spring, which found that Kissinger's efforts in the Middle East were approved by 56 percent of the sample while approval of Ford's efforts in this area had dropped to 31 percent, showed the persistence of this pattern in which the public withheld credit to Ford for Kissinger's peacemaking efforts.

The Kissinger case highlights both the costs to a president of not being perceived as in control of foreign policy and the credit that is foregone by abdicating the public perception of being responsible for foreign policy. Kissinger's "upstaging" relationship with Ford (and Nixon in his later years) was, however, exceptional. It is unlikely that a president will long endure a situation in which his secretary is credited for favorable developments while the president is blamed for the unpopular. This upstaging type of relationship inevitably creates friction between the departmental head and the president and his aides[162] and cannot help but generate pressures for the secretary's removal.

THE TWO PRESIDENCIES

Kissinger, Acheson, and Dulles all seemed ideally suited for the role of presidential lightning rod; they were prominent, powerful, and controversial secretaries of state. Their public personas—particularly Dulles the self-righteous, Presbyterian moralist and Acheson the haughty, pompous aristocrat—made them inviting targets for opponents. That none of them were particularly effective as lightning rods, at least at the level of the mass public, suggests that foreign affairs may be in important ways a distinctive policy domain. As Wildavsky formulated the point close to thirty years ago, "The United States has one president, but it has two presidencies; one presidency is for domestic affairs, and the other is concerned with defense and foreign policy."

For Wildavsky, presidential power in foreign policy was substantially different than in domestic policy in large part because the president's potential opponents—the citizenry, special interest groups, Congress, the bureaucracy—were substantially weaker or less assertive in foreign policy than in domestic policy.[163] Whatever the reasons, presidents do in fact do better in foreign policy. They do better in terms of public approval, and they do better in terms of congressional support. In foreign policy, moreover, presidents are more able to act unilaterally and thus are better able to convey to the public an image of strength as well as a unifying image of national leadership. In foreign policy, as a result, presidents have less to gain from lightning rods than they have to lose from being upstaged, a danger that is well illustrated by Kissinger's relationship with Ford.

The two-presidencies phenomenon is also structured by public expectations about presidential roles and responsibilities. Vietnam may have modified, at least at the elite level, the willingness to defer to the president in foreign affairs, but a widespread presumption remains that foreign policy is largely a presidential responsibility or, at least, that a president's responsibilities are relatively greater in foreign than in domestic policy. The public's predisposition to hold the president responsible for the conduct of national security (in a way the public does not hold the president responsible for education policy or agricultural policy, for example) makes it difficult for a president to avoid blame in foreign policy. The president who maintains his distance from a dispute over agricultural price supports can keep himself out of trouble, but the president who seems uninvolved with a decision vital to the country's national security risks drawing into question his fitness for governing.

Certainly there is no hiding for a president when it comes to war. The Constitution's designation of the president as commander-in-chief makes it virtually impossible for a president to hide from the wrath unleashed by an unpopular war. Although Truman delegated a great deal of authority to Acheson, and although Acheson was ideally cast as a villain for conservative Republicans, it did not prevent public anger over the Korean War from being directed at the president. Neither Truman nor Acheson could have done anything short of ending the war that would have helped Truman regain public favor.

Elites, because of their greater attentiveness to foreign policy matters, are better able to discriminate between their appraisal of the president and their evaluation of the secretary of state. There are myriad foreign policy battles that never penetrate the public consciousness—the Bricker amendment controversy is a paradigmatic example—in which secretaries of state can serve as viable lightning rods at the elite level. Yet even among sophisticated political elites, the presumption that the president is responsible for the conduct of foreign relations acts as a retardant upon a president's ability to use the secretary of state as a lightning rod, particularly in major international crises such as the U-2 affair or the Bay of Pigs. Modern presidents have often found it easier, as we see in the next chapter, to deflect elite attention and blame onto the chief of staff, a post where the norm of anonymity has repeatedly clashed with the realities of the job description.

6

The Chief of Staff as Lightning Rod: From Sherman Adams to John Sununu

Presidential staff "should be possessed of high competence, great physical vigor, and *a passion for anonymity.*"[1] So concluded the famous 1937 Brownlow report in what has become its most infamous passage. When this passage was read to President Roosevelt, he is reported to have "burst out chuckling and laughing and read the phrase out loud a second time." Presenting the report at a press conference, Roosevelt forewarned the assembled press "to sharpen your pencils and take this down. This is a purple patch, one you will never forget." More than one journalist must have thought what one said, "There ain't no such animal." The bemused reporters even ran a contest among themselves to select the best poem lampooning the proposal.[2]

The cynic's view that "there ain't no such animal" has coexisted uneasily with the reformist's earnest plea for a presidency populated with more such creatures. In the half century since the Brownlow report, political observers have frequently lamented that presidential aides have forsaken Louis Brownlow's guidance. The chorus of protest became particularly vociferous in the wake of Watergate as presidential staff were roundly criticized for supplanting cabinet members as spokesmen and formulators of administration policies.

It is not only outside observers, however, who believe presidential staff should adhere to Brownlow's precept. Presidential staff, including chiefs of staff, also profess a belief in the value of staff anonymity. Nixon's controversial chief of staff, H. R. Haldeman, admits to being "very strongly . . . [in favor of] the passion for anonymity viewpoint." "I tried," Haldeman explains, "to work behind the scenes where I felt I could be most effective." "As soon as you become the issue," Haldeman continues, "you've lost an enormous amount of your value to the president . . . as a staff person."[3] Richard Cheney, chief of staff to Gerald Ford, subscribed to much the same professional code, albeit with greater success. His function as chief of staff, he says, was to explain policy but "never to be quoted, never to be out front as a public official."[4] A similar vision of the staff role is evident in Sherman Adams's comment that "I wasn't there to accomplish things, I was there to help the President. Good staff people have to be measured by their dedication, by their hard work, by their sense of proportion. But not by their accomplishments. All the accomplishments belong to the President."[5] And Donald Regan, anything but anonymous, explained his role in the Reagan White House as "a sort of producer, making certain that the star had what he needed to do his best; the staff was like the crew, invisible behind the lights, watching the performance their behind-the-scenes efforts had made possible."[6]

Why do senior staff and especially chiefs of staff so often fail to achieve the anonymity that outside observers urge upon them and that they themselves profess to prefer? Why the discrepancy between professional creed and reality?[7] Part of the answer can be found in the media's (and the attentive public's) fascination with the powers behind the throne. FDR's skepticism about Brownlow's "passion for anonymity" idea had more to do with his jaundiced view of the press than with worries about the self-aggrandizing instincts of presidential aides. As Roosevelt told Brownlow when the latter first presented the idea to the president, "Tell your British friend [who coined the phrase] that he doesn't know his American press."[8] Foremost in Roosevelt's mind was aide Tommy Corcoran, who despite (or because of) his "instinct for anonymity" had become the target of intense press scrutiny.[9] Avoiding "Meet the Press" is no guarantee of anonymity. Indeed staying out of the public eye may only fuel anxiety about unaccountable power behind the scenes.

Another answer to this puzzle lies in a conflict within the professional creed of chiefs of staff. Chiefs of staff must reconcile a passion for anonymity with their responsibilities as *gatekeeper*, determining who and what gets access to the president, *coordinator* of policy making, determining what is and is not in accord with the president's position, and *spokesman* for the president and his policies.[10] Each of these roles conflicts with the precept of anonymity. By including some people and information and excluding others, staff inevitably create ill-feeling on the part of those who feel their message has been unfairly excluded. Coordination, in the absence of consensus, is another word for coercion,[11] and coercion may induce fear but rarely loyalty or lasting support. Finally, seeing that the president and his policies are viewed in a positive light entails explaining the president's policies in private and public forums. Protecting the president, in sum, is thus likely to earn the chief of staff a notoriety and enmity that override any passion for anonymity.

"THE SMALL END OF THE FUNNEL"[12]

Presidents, like the rest of us, cannot possibly pay attention to everything at once. No president can afford to listen to, let alone grant, even a fraction of the requests made of him. Selectivity is essential. The staff's function is thus to filter out those communications that are not essential to a president's ability to make informed decisions.[13] Staff are positioned between the president and other governmental officials and given the job of screening which communications get through to the president. Such a function is indispensable. That selectivity is inevitable, however, is slight consolation to those whose messages have been excluded.

Those who have served as chief of staff are virtually unanimous in defining their role as an "honest broker" who presents all sides of an issue. At a recent conference that brought together a number of former chiefs of staff, Haldeman, Cheney, Donald Rumsfeld, and Jack Watson all eagerly endorsed the honest-broker ideal.[14] Each of Reagan's chiefs of staff have also publicly described their role in these terms, as has Bush's chief of staff John Sununu.[15] A chief of staff, explains Cheney, will not "survive very long if he, in effect, warps the flow of information to suit his own bias with respect to policy."[16] If others in the administration do not have confidence that their views are being communicated in an even-handed manner they will bypass the chief of staff and establish alternative channels to the president.[17]

No doubt it is true that a chief of staff who insisted on expressing unsolicited personal policy preferences would not last long in the job. But the notion of chiefs of staff as nothing more than "honest brokers," like the media's claim to being an "electronic mirror" of society, severely underestimates the biases that necessarily intrude in making decisions about what is more important and what is less important. Discretion is unavoidable. When Haldeman says that the chief of staff "functions as an honest broker in the sense of eliminating or bringing together repetitious material . . . and organizing the material in an orderly manner so that the president can proceed through it," he disguises the substantial power involved in deciding what is repetitious and what is not, what should be organized in and what should be organized out. Of course "the president shouldn't have ten piles of irrelevant or unrelated paper that he's got to wade through, sort out, and figure out what to do with," but the power to decide what is and is not relevant or related is critically important in framing and reaching a decision.[18] Even a chief of staff committed to ensuring that the president hears all sides of an issue has the discretion to decide which advice needs to be "counterbalanced" and by whom.[19]

If chiefs of staff see themselves as honest brokers, those who believe their message is not getting through to the president invariably portray that power in more sinister terms. As Michael Medved points out, "No one likes to believe that he has been denied an audience with the chief executive because his opinion is insignificant or irrelevant; it is much easier to blame a conspiratorial aide for cutting off advice 'the President needs.' "[20] Haldeman was "the keystone of a Berlin Wall around Mr. Nixon," the "Iron Chancellor" with "a gaze that could freeze Medusa";[21] Regan was portrayed as the "Iron Major" with "a look that would stop a locomotive in its tracks";[22] Adams was referred to as "the great stone face," the "abominable no-man" with "the disposition of a grizzly with a barked shin";[23] and Rumsfeld was dubbed the "Praetorian."[24]

The role of chief of staff may be a twentieth-century response to the tremendous growth in the size of "the presidential branch," but the belief that top aides close to the president are preventing presidents from hearing valuable advice is as old as the republic. Typical was the lament of a former congressman, who complained to Lincoln's friend and campaign manager David Davis that an opinion was "quite prevalent" that John Hay and John Nicolay deliberately prevented letters from reaching the president. A sympathetic Davis forwarded the congressman's letter to "the impassable Mr. Nicolay," prompting an unapologetic response from Nicolay: "Literally considered this is true. . . . A moment's reflection will convince you that the President has not time to read all the letters he receives, and also that [among any] hundred miscellaneous letters there will be a large proportion which are obviously of no interest or importance. These the President would not read if he could."[25] The need for aides to exclude "unimportant" or "irrelevant" communications has become increasingly critical in a political environment where more and more groups look to the president for answers to their problems.

Complaints about a chief of staff isolating the president frequently come from what political scientist Thomas Cronin calls the "outer cabinet," departments such as Health and Human Services, Housing and Urban Development (HUD), transportation, agriculture, interior, commerce, and labor.[26] In the Nixon White House, for instance, the earliest and most vocal critics of the "Berlin Wall" allegedly isolating the president were Interior Secretary Walter Hickel,[27] Transportation Secretary John Volpe,[28] HUD Secretary George Romney,[29] and top health administrators within Health, Education, and Welfare (HEW).[30] Cabinet heads from these peripheral departments want to enlist presidential support for what they deem to be a worthy cause; the president, on the other hand, often prefers to maintain his distance from the outer cabinet, thereby preserving political capital for those central issues on which he holds the most intense preferences. Chiefs of staff protect the president by guarding against a run on the bank, thereby avoiding the dissipation of precious political capital.

If such complaints more commonly arise from the periphery of the administration, they are by no means limited to the periphery. In almost every administration, officials from the "inner cabinet" (state, defense, justice, and treasury) can also be found lamenting their inability to gain adequate access to the president. During Reagan's first term, for instance, Secretary of State Alexander Haig complained bitterly about the White House staff's unwillingness to let him see the president alone, and National Security Assistant Richard Allen found that even his supposed ally, Ed Meese, was a "400-pound obstacle."[31] Eisenhower's defense secretary, Charles Wilson, felt that Adams was blocking his access to the president, although the truth was that Eisenhower found Wilson tedious.[32]

The role of gatekeeper places a chief of staff in the unenviable position of saying "no" to powerful people. Some, like Cheney or Jim Baker, have tried to deliver the negative in a relatively diplomatic manner. Others, like Adams, Haldeman, Regan, and Sununu, seem to have relished, and embellished, the image of the gruff, even autocratic no-man. Chiefs of staff have frequently blended personal characteristics with the strategic demands of the no-man role in such a way as to make it nearly impossible to tell where personality ends and role commences. Eisenhower aide William Bragg Ewald considered Sherman Adams's abrupt gruffness "artfully ingenious rudeness."[33] But Richard Strout was perhaps closer to the truth when he wrote: "Perhaps [Adams] realizes that a reputation for gruffness is a buckler against bores. But it must be said that, for Adams, the switch between make-believe and real has the gliding ease of automatic transmission."[34] More recently, John Sununu has insisted "that contrary to the legend, any strong statements on my part are . . . controlled, deliberate and designed to achieve an effect. There is no random outburst. It all is designed for a purpose."[35] But even granting Sununu his strategic outbursts, it is difficult to avoid the conclusion that Sununu's combative personality seems well suited to the gatekeeper role.

All chiefs of staff, no matter what their personalities, have been highly self-conscious of their role as presidential buffers. They have acted on the assumption that "every President needs a Darth Vader in the White House to thwart special pleaders and scrutinize even apple-pie issues."[36] Adams understood the division of labor perfectly: "Never make the mistake of giving me credit for everything. I just take the blame around here."[37] "If there's a dirty deed to be done," echoes Cheney, "it's the chief of staff who's got to do it. The president gets credit for what works, and you get the blame for what doesn't work. That's the nature of the beast."[38] Although some chiefs of staff have in fact reaped substantial credit for positive outcomes, as in the case of Jim Baker,[39] more often they have left office with sullied or at least diminished reputations; the list includes Sherman Adams, H. R. Haldeman, Hamilton Jordan, Don Regan, and John Sununu.

"A HEADKNOCKER"

The president can personally settle only a fraction of interdepartmental disputes. Thus on many issues, a senior staffer is given the responsibility for settling interagency disputes. This staff person, as Richard Rose puts it, is designated "to knock together the heads of the disputants in order to arrive at an outcome."[40] But not just any outcome will do. Senior staff are responsible not only for seeing that disputants reach an arrangement that both sides can live with but also for seeing that the negotiated outcome is consistent with presidential preferences. Coordination entails not just umpiring disputes but transmitting presidential preferences.

The headknocker function has figured prominently in the job descriptions of most chiefs of staff. Sherman Adams described his "routine" work as including "the settlement of occasional conflicts between Cabinet Secretaries and among agency heads." "I always tried," Adams explained, "to resolve specific differences on a variety of problems before the issue had to be submitted to the President. Sometimes several meetings were necessary before an agreement was reached. But with a few exceptions I was successful."[41] Cheney recalls "repeatedly" being called upon to settle "a major conflict between two willful cabinet members."[42] Jim Baker, tagged the "velvet hammer" by admiring aides, regularly called disputatious department heads into his office to "settle [disputes] on the spot."[43]

Placed in the position of determining what is and is not consistent with the basic objectives of the administration, a chief of staff is always vulnerable to criticism from others within the administration who believe the president's real preferences are (or should be) different from those laid down by staff. In the Ford White House, for instance, Rumsfeld and Cheney were frequently the target of Nelson Rockefeller's wrath because the vice president felt that senior staffers were scuttling his policy proposals. Rockefeller's proposals were invariably found to be "totally inconsistent with the basic policy of the Ford administration," and it was left to the chief of staff to confront the vice president with this awkward fact. By serving as "that cushion, that rubber . . . between the president and vice-president," Cheney points out, the staff enabled the president to continue to have an excellent working relationship with Rockefeller.[44]

Even presidents who have eschewed a chief of staff have had somebody fill the function of coordinating policy and ensuring that the outcome is consistent with presidential objectives. Joseph Califano, for instance, filled such a role under President Lyndon Johnson. Califano's office, remembers one Bureau of the Budget official, became a "command post for directing the Great Society campaigns, an operational center within the White House itself, the locus for marathon coffee-consuming sessions dedicated to knocking heads together and untangling jurisdictional and philosophical squabbles."[45] Knocking heads together antagonized many within the administration who saw Califano as an aggressive "empire builder."[46]

In the Nixon White House, John Ehrlichman performed much the same function that Califano had in the Johnson White House.[47] When Attorney General John Mitchell and HEW Secretary Robert Finch squared off over school desegregation guidelines, when Arthur Burns complained that Pat Moynihan was issuing unauthorized policy statements to the press, or when Mitchell and Treasury Secretary David Kennedy clashed over jurisdiction of foreign drug busts, it was Ehrlichman who was called in to settle the dispute and to ensure that the settlement conformed to presidential objectives.[48] Like Califano, Ehrlichman quickly made some powerful enemies within the White House. Within months of the new administration, reports surfaced in the *New York Times* that "complaints are coming in from senior officials who find themselves negotiating with Ehrlichman instead of Nixon."[49] Complaints about Ehrlichman's intrusiveness became increasingly bitter over time.

Serving as a "headknocker" makes it difficult for a top staffer to remain anonymous because the role places the staff person at the vortex of intergovernmental conflicts. Such conflict is likely to attract public attention, especially because losers in intra–White House power struggles often have an incentive, in E. E. Schattschneider's language, "to enlarge the scope of conflict," to alter the balance of political forces by introducing new actors into the equation.[50] An antagonist who chooses to go public in this manner can catapult even the most self-effacing and discreet aide into the public eye. As a consequence it is difficult for a senior staffer to follow Brownlow's twin precepts of coordinating administration policy and remaining anonymous.[51]

THE ROLE OF SPOKESMAN

Those who cannot speak to the president seek out those who can speak for the president. Absent direct access to the president, reporters or congressmen or department heads ferret out those senior aides who confer with the president throughout the day, travel with the president, and know the president's mind on a broad range of issues. Such people are few and not difficult to identify. President Eisenhower told the nation that his chief of staff "knows *exactly* what I believe, what are my convictions, my policy."[52] During the Nixon administration, attentive elites understood that Haldeman's power rested on the fact that he "knew at all times *exactly* what the President was doing, what his current priorities were, what he was expecting others to accomplish."[53] "I meet with the president dozens of times during the day," John Sununu told reporters. "[As a result] I know enough about the president to do *exactly* what he wants done."[54] Carter instructed his cabinet members to "speak with Stu [Eizenstat] if you want to know my position,"[55] and Johnson told his cabinet, "When Joe [Califano] speaks, that's my voice you hear."[56] The same intimate knowledge of the president's mind that enables a top aide faithfully to transmit presidential preferences to other actors within the political system also makes anonymity an unattainable ideal because an intimate knowledge of presidential intentions, preferences, and priorities unavoidably thrusts the aide into the role of presidential spokesman.

Some chiefs of staff have tried to preserve their anonymity by speaking to the press only on background. This was the practice followed by Cheney who, although he "talked to the press frequently," made it a rule to do so "always on background, always to explain policy, never to be out front as a public official."[57] But if a low profile was Cheney's aim,[58] he was only partially successful in achieving his objective.[59] Especially as the fight for the Republican nomination heated up, Cheney's name surfaced increasingly frequently as the spokesman for the president on the subject of the Reagan candidacy.[60] Who else could speak authoritatively for the president?

Even when a chief of staff avoids public statements, it is often difficult to avoid the limelight. In the spring of 1982, for instance, a *New York Times* reporter observed that "while Mr. Baker eschews public pronouncements, his name has replaced Mr. Stockman's in the headlines."[61] Because Baker spoke for the president in budget negotiations with Congress, Baker was news whether he spoke directly to the press or not. A picture of Baker going into the meeting made the front page as did his private, behind-closed-doors comments that were leaked by other participants to the press. Because the president is news, those vested with the authority to act for and speak for the president also become news.[62]

It is often said that the "big shift [toward a staff member serving as policy spokesman] has really been with the Reagan administration."[63] In part this is accurate. Appearances by top presidential aides on television news shows seem to have greatly and irreversibly increased during the Reagan years. But the chief of staff's role as presidential spokesman does not emerge fully formed from the Reagan administration. In fact, here as elsewhere, the Eisenhower administration established a pattern that was developed during subsequent presidencies.[64]

Sherman Adams, according to the conventional view, was the administration's "anonymous man" who "carried on his monstrous toil in a secrecy that was as zealously guarded as an atomic bomb stockpile."[65] But Adams was much less shy of the limelight than people often remember or than Adams wanted people to remember.[66] Adams was not only among the most publicly visible members of the Eisenhower administration,[67] but he is also among the most visible chiefs of staff in modern presidential history.[68] Adams may not have held press conferences, as some of his critics suggested he should, but on many occasions he spoke to groups of reporters or represented the administration point of view in public forums. A careful study of the record cannot support the claim made by Eisenhower's staff secretary Andrew Goodpaster that the Eisenhower administration "really had only two spokesmen in the White House. One was the press secretary, Jim Hagerty, and the other was none other than Dwight D. Eisenhower."[69] Besides ignoring the important role Vice President Nixon played in presenting administration views, Goodpaster overlooks Adams's substantial role in publicizing the administration's views. Adams gave a large number of public speeches,[70] most of which promoted administration policies, and some of which vigorously assailed Democratic leaders and policies.[71]

Even when Adams did not make public pronouncements, letters and telegrams that he sent to congressmen, governors, mayors, and interest-group leaders explaining the administration position were often made public and reported in the press.[72] What Adams told officials in private meetings also frequently made its way into print as, for instance, when Colorado Governor Dan Thornton publicly quoted Adams as having assured him that the president was not committed to continuation of the grant-in-aid system.[73] However much Adams might have preferred anonymity, his role as presidential surrogate thrust him unavoidably into the public eye.

"MY LORD HIGH EXECUTIONER"[74]

Few human beings enjoy having to personally fire other people. Certainly no president in recent memory has relished the task. One biographer after another tells how each president disliked such confrontations. Ronald Reagan, Lou Cannon finds, "detested confrontations, particularly over personnel."[75] For all their differences, President Carter fully shared Reagan's aversion to face-to-face confrontations. Gerald Ford, too, as Hedley Donovan reports, "simply hated to lay down the law," preferring to leave unpleasant tasks to others.[76] It is well known that President Nixon, as William Safire tells us, "never has enjoyed telling anybody bad news, firing anybody, or running down associates to their faces."[77] Likewise, President Eisenhower "always had to be the nice guy. . . . [He] always had to have someone else who could do the firing, or the reprimanding, or give any orders which he knew people would find unpleasant to carry out."[78]

Has chance ensconced in the presidency a peculiar bunch of conflict-avoiders? Perhaps. More likely, there is significantly more than personality at work here. President after president avoid such confrontations less out of psychic need than out of organizational necessity. Delegating unpopular tasks to those who are expendable helps a president maintain a positive image and thereby maintain political support. Presidents may indeed dislike personal confrontations, but so do most presidential aides. Mike Deaver, who frequently wielded the ax for President Reagan, explains, "I would find it as hard as anyone to fire somebody who worked for me. But I could do it for someone else, if doing so served Ronald Reagan."[79] Senior staff are not necessarily less sensitive people than presidents, but they are expendable in a way that presidents are not.

Deaver's case illustrates the extreme enmity that can accrue to the person assigned to be "the bearer of bad news" and explains why presidents have farmed out this job to top subordinates. In his memoirs, Deaver observes that because of "the President's distaste for an unpleasant scene" and because "both Baker and Meese were reluctant to . . . tell someone his or her services were no longer required, I was the guy who wielded the ax." As Deaver emphasizes, "That is a guaranteed way to develop a flock of ill-wishers."[80] A White House aide agreed that Deaver "was the heavy all the time. He had to dump on the old friends. He was the bearer of the bad news," and the result was that people "thought he was power-crazy" and "one royal pain in the ass."[81] The depth of resentment and bitterness against Deaver bubbled to the surface shortly after the 1984 election when a White House aide commented to a *New York Times* reporter: "Wait till he's on the outside. A lot of people he worked over will want to settle scores when he tries to call back."[82]

If the senior staffer is perceived to be doing nothing more than carrying out the president's bidding, the bearer of bad news saves the president an awkward scene but little else. Dismissal of administration officials, however, is frequently accompanied by great uncertainty about what role the president has played. Even scholars looking at the facts years later may have a difficult time reconstructing exactly what role the president played in a personnel decision. Many are the officials who have been dismissed by a senior staffer and who have left Washington thinking the president was uninformed or at least misled about the facts. And more often than not, such perceptions have a solid basis in reality. For a chief of staff is not just the "executioner," not just the one who breaks the bad news. The chief of staff can also often be the prosecutor, the principal architect of a campaign to discredit a person who is felt not to be acting in accordance with the president's best interests.

SEEING THROUGH THE RUSE

During his years as chief of staff, Haldeman is said to have boasted: "Every President needs a son of a bitch, and I'm Nixon's. I'm his buffer and I'm his bastard. I get done what he wants done and I take the heat instead of him."[83] Interviewed some years later, Haldeman gave a somewhat different, more reflective view of his role: "If I told someone to do something, he knew it wasn't me—he knew exactly what it was; it was an order from the President. They knew an appeal wouldn't get anywhere."[84] These two statements raise a puzzling question. If Haldeman's effectiveness as chief of staff rested on others believing that his wishes reflected the president's preferences then how could he serve as a lightning rod? If others clearly perceived that Haldeman was only carrying out Nixon's orders then why should they blame the chief of staff rather than the president?

One answer is supplied by Gerald Warren, former press aide under Nixon, who explains: "I hope . . . the American press understands that when Bob Hartmann leaks to Evans and Novak that Haig is keeping all those Nixon folks in the White House, he's doing that because he doesn't want to attack Jerry Ford. It's Jerry Ford who's doing it, not Al Haig."[85] Warren's answer suggests that political elites are not fooled by the lightning rod ruse. They see through it, realizing that aides are only an extension of the president himself, but fabricate feelings of hostility toward the underling in order to avoid directly criticizing the president.

The further removed one is from the inner circle the more difficult it becomes to determine whether or to what extent a directive from a top aide reflects the president's views. Even the most attentive political elites have few opportunities to directly check for themselves whether an aide is carrying out explicit presidential instructions or is creatively interpreting positions near the outer limits of the zone of presidential indifference. Even the detached scholar who has access to the voluminous records of a presidential library will often have a difficult time determining where presidential will leaves off and subordinate discretion begins.

The difficulty that others have in determining whether an aide is speaking for the president will also depend on the president's leadership style. A president who barks out directives to subordinates and keeps a close eye on the implementation of those orders will create a presumption within the administration that the aide is carrying out the president's will. A president who shuns direct instructions and detaches himself from the day-to-day operations of the White House will generate much greater uncertainty about whether and when an aide speaks for the president.

The Reagan presidency provides a vivid illustration of the latter phenomenon. Martin Anderson, who served as a senior aide in both the Nixon and Reagan White Houses, was struck by the fact that Reagan "made no demands, and gave almost no instructions."[86] Reagan's passive, detached style meant that many officials within the administration suspected (sometimes correctly) that top aides were not so much carrying out presidential directives as making presidential policy. Education Secretary Terrel Bell was convinced that Ed Meese ("the keeper of the radical right dogma") and his aides were carrying out their own agenda rather than the president's.[87] Jeanne Kirkpatrick, the U.S. representative to the United Nations, believed that Jim

Baker was doing far more than just carrying out the president's wishes in blocking her appointment to the National Security Council.[88] Secretary of State Alexander Haig professed to be at a loss to ascertain which staff directives represented presidential wishes. "Did a demand for action by a Cabinet council come from the President himself?" asks a puzzled Haig. "It was impossible to know." When Meese and Baker appeared on talk shows to speak on foreign policy questions, Haig notes that "no one knew if what they were saying was the President's policy." Indeed, Haig confesses, "I myself was never altogether certain on this point."[89]

President Nixon's directive style of leadership provides a stark contrast to Reagan's approach. Where Reagan rarely issued instructions except at the most general level, Nixon showed no hesitation in issuing detailed directives on even the most trivial of matters. Nixon would instruct Haldeman, for instance, to "tell Haig that when Henry [Kissinger] has his picture taken with Le Duc Tho, he's not to smile."[90] Those familiar with Nixon's operating style had little reason to doubt (as those in the Reagan White House certainly would) that a directive from the chief of staff originated with the president. Kissinger, who understood that Nixon systematically used Haldeman to do his dirty work, was under no illusions that Nixon was behind the messages he received from Haldeman, even petty directives advising him to "present a sterner appearance" in pictures with Le Duc Tho.[91] Haldeman seems justified in claiming that "every White House insider knew that I was [acting] at the President's direct order." He may even be correct when he adds, "so did most of the outsiders."[92]

Certainly when Haldeman appeared on national television in early 1972 and charged Nixon's critics with "consciously aiding and abetting the enemy of the United States," Washington elites had little difficulty seeing through the ruse.[93] Haldeman was too close and too loyal to Nixon, they believed, for him to have made such comments on his own initiative. Moreover, such a statement seemed perfectly consistent with what many believed to be the "real" Nixon. In reporting Haldeman's comments, the *Times* stressed that "the Administration's critics quickly assumed today that Mr. Haldeman was reflecting the President's view in saying that those who attacked the latest Nixon plan to end the Vietnam war were 'consciously aiding and abetting the enemy of the United States.' "[94] As Senator Alan Cranston (D-Calif.) put it, Haldeman's attack only showed that "the old Nixon is emerging again."[95] A *Times* editorial on "The Haldeman Smear" pointed out that "the President cannot so easily isolate himself . . . from the public comments of a man who has been a close personal associate for many years who currently serves as coordinator of White House affairs."[96] For the *Times,* both Haldeman's position and his past made it implausible to assume he did not express the president's views. Haldeman, as James Reston pointed out, "is a loyal Nixon man" who was simply "being shoved into the act."[97] Because Haldeman lacked independent stature and was positioned at the president's right hand, the White House efforts to disavow his comments as "his own personal point of view," and not necessarily those of Nixon, only fueled a "credibility gap."[98]

Even after Nixon, in a televised speech two days later, adopted a more conciliatory position than the one taken by Haldeman, most elites still seemed unwilling to let Nixon evade responsibility for Haldeman's statement. "The Nixon technique," Mayor John Lindsey said, "is all too familiar. . . . [It is] McCarthyism pure and simple."[99] "Nixon's softer tone," reported the *Times,* "had not removed McGovern's suspicion that Haldeman's comments had been programmed by the President himself."[100] And many months later, columnist William V. Shannon recounted the incident to his readers by noting that "Nixon *sent* Haldeman . . . on a television interview show to say that Muskie and others were 'consciously aiding and abetting the enemy.' "[101]

Haldeman's spectacular failure as a lightning rod was due to several factors. First, because he was a top staff person with extremely close ties to Nixon, it strained credibility that Haldeman was acting on his own. When Nixon was asked about Haldeman's statement at a press conference, the reporter prefaced his question by saying, "Do you think that Mr. Haldeman's statement, since he is so close to you, and a lot of people interpret his thinking as very close to yours."[102] Second, Haldeman's behavior seemed to conform to what many people perceived to be a Nixonian pattern. This sentiment was reflected in a letter to the editor, which pointed out that Haldeman's statement "strikingly recalls the similarly irresponsible cries of the dark days of Richard M. Nixon, who is alive and well and now living in the White House. Let's not forget Helen Gahagan Douglas and all the others."[103] Nixon's reputation for deviousness and dissembling made it difficult to sustain Haldeman as a plausible lightning rod.

Using chiefs of staff as lightning rods, as this episode illustrates, is risky business. Because chiefs of staff are so close to the president, for them to engage an issue is to bring controversy only a step away from the president's door. The advantage of using cabinet members as lightning rods is that they are further removed from the president. This is particularly true for departments in the outer cabinet. Their distance from the president, as Richard Rose explains, means they are particularly well suited to acting as "buffers that keep subgovernment problems from becoming White House problems."[104] For instance, when Carter's transportation secretary, Brock Adams, suggested to a congressional committee that some of the revenue from a proposed gas-guzzler tax be used for mass transit, Press Secretary Jody Powell could plausibly reject the idea (even though Carter had personally cleared Adams's testimony), insisting that "Secretary Adams was speaking for himself."[105] As an issue becomes engaged by those aides closest to the president, however, it becomes much more difficult for the president to disown knowledge or involvement without seeming at best disengaged and at worst disingenuous or even dishonest.

AN INTERNAL LIGHTNING ROD

A chief of staff's critics typically look significantly different from a cabinet member's critics. The bitterest critics of a cabinet member are most often partisan critics on the outside. Criticism of Secretaries Benson, Watt, Dulles, Acheson, Kissinger, and Brownell emanated largely from members of the opposition party or from groups with weak ties to the administration. The severest critics of a powerful White House aide, in contrast, are frequently found within the president's own party and especially within the president's own administration. As Cheney points out, the chief of staff's function "is to be the cushion that takes the pain and the heat, oftentimes not only externally but also internally."[106] Adams, Haldeman, Regan, and Sununu were hardly beloved by Democrats, but it was Republicans in each case who clamored the loudest for their scalps. The explanation for this pattern is not hard to find: it is members of the president's own party and especially members of the president's own administration who are most likely to feel they have a need or a right to see the president. In carrying out their gatekeeper function it is thus largely to members of their own party that chiefs of staff must say no.

This is not to say that strong chiefs of staff do not have vigorous critics on the other side of the aisle. Indeed, their role as promoter of administration policy means that they inevitably expose themselves to criticism from opponents of administration policy. Moreover, many chiefs of staff have been aggressive critics of the opposition, especially around election time. In 1954, for instance, Sherman Adams lashed out at the Democrats as "political sadists" who were trying to talk the country into a depression, substituting the "Fear Deal" for the "Fair Deal." Unless a Republican Congress were elected, Adams declared, the nation would be "turned back once more to the spending sprees and political orgies to which the American people called a halt in 1952."[107] And in 1958, Adams climbed back onto the political stump to blame the Democrats for Pearl Harbor, "the tragic loss of China," and "the scientific catastrophe of losing our atomic secrets." The "befuddled" Democratic party, he railed, was "a political monstrosity" with "two heads, two hearts, and two souls," united only by "lust for privileges of public office."[108] On national television, as we have already seen, Haldeman accused Democratic critics of the president's peace plan of "consciously aiding and abetting the enemy of the United States."[109] So, too, did Sununu plant his share of partisan barbs into the opposition's hide.

These public attacks on the opposition make it all the more remarkable that a chief of staff's bitterest enemies so often come from within the administration and from congressmen of the same party. Democratic dislike for Adams, for instance, could not compare with the hostility felt by leading Republicans. Republican National Chairman Leonard Hall told Adams, "Some of my people think you've got horns that are halfway between a Washington snowslide and a bundle of icicles. The fact is they think that in you where the milk of human kindness ought to be, there is only ice-water."[110] Republican antipathy toward Adams went beyond that felt by Old Guard Taft Republicans, who believed Adams was moving administration policy in a liberal, New Deal direction. Republicans of every ideological stripe, historian Stephen Ambrose has observed, "were furious with Sherman Adams for not handing out enough jobs fast enough for their deserving constituents."[111] Adams angered every supplicant who expected or wanted a "yes" and received a "no." The disappointed, not surprisingly, came largely from Republican ranks: from cabinet members wanting a presidential speech in support of a department initiative, from Republican congressmen seeking administration support for a pet project,[112] from local party leaders wanting the president to campaign for Republican candidates, and from various Eisenhower supporters wanting some small favor.

Hamilton Jordan would not have won any popularity contests among Republicans, but his severest critics were Democrats, not Republicans. So intense was House Speaker Tip O'Neill's hostility toward Jordan that he took to calling him "Hannibal Jerkin," thus capturing what O'Neill perceived to be both Jordan's autocratic style and political ineptitude.[113] Democratic Congressmen and members of the cabinet continually groused that Jordan "never returns a phone call."[114]

Even someone like Dick Cheney, who generally strove to be accommodating rather than confrontational in interpersonal relations,[115] was the target of a considerable amount of internal carping, especially after a string of primary losses in May 1976.[116] Many within the Ford White House, the most prominent of whom were presidential counselor Robert Hartmann and Vice President Nelson Rockefeller, complained that Rumsfeld and Cheney came between them and the president. According to John Osborne, prominent cabinet members such as Secretary of State Henry Kissinger, Treasury Secretary William Simon, and Defense Secretary James Schlesinger also thoroughly "detested the White House staff under Rumsfeld and his successor, Richard Cheney."[117] Their relationship with Rumsfeld and Cheney, Osborne wrote, was surrounded by a "welter of suspicion and hatred [and] the word hatred is justified."[118] As an aide to Cheney explained, "Cheney ran the one 'pipeline' for political communications in and out of the White House and . . . many of the President's other advisers felt shut out of the political process."[119]

Rumsfeld relates a trivial but telling example of the way in which he functioned as an internal lightning rod for Ford. A cabinet member came to Rumsfeld to complain about being left off the invitation list for a state dinner. Rumsfeld told the disgruntled cabinet member he would take the question to the president, which he did. Ford instructed Rumsfeld to leave the cabinet member off the list. Several days later the cabinet officer saw the president and mentioned that he was not on the list. Ford feigned surprise and told the cabinet officer he would see what he could do. That evening Rumsfeld received a note from the president, "Let's put that fellow back on." The result is the president gets to play the nice guy, while the chief of staff is seen as the bad guy who schemed to bump the cabinet member off the list.[120]

John Sununu delivered and took his share of partisan hits, yet the most vitriolic attacks aimed at Sununu came from inside his own party. Senate Minority Whip Alan Simpson denounced Sununu as a "beadyeyed guy out there figuring out how to use" the budget talks "for political advantage."[121] Robert Dole, the Senate minority leader, labeled Sununu "the chief of chaff."[122] After Sununu dismissed Senator Trent Lott as "insignificant" to the process, an incensed Lott told reporters that Sununu "is going to have to crawl over here and BEG for [forgiveness]. . . . He just stuck the wrong pig."[123] Newt Gingrich, meanwhile, was described as barely on speaking terms with Sununu.[124] House Minority Leader Robert Michel was more measured in his public comments, but an aide to Michel acknowledged that "our relationship with Sununu has been no bed of roses."[125] As the relationship hit bottom at the end of 1990, the *Washington Post* reported that "angry Republicans want [Sununu's] head."[126] And by early 1991, Sununu's "lagging relations" with key cabinet members close to Bush had become a prominent item in the national press.[127]

Given that hostility to chiefs of staff so often arises from within the president's own party and administration, it is little wonder that when chiefs of staff fall from grace they are often hurled into a political abyss. Fulfilling the role of internal lightning rod leaves a chief of staff with few allies and many intense enemies within his party and the administration. In contrast to cabinet secretaries, who typically spend large amounts of time and energy nurturing support from key constituencies within their party, chiefs of staff are aware that they have "a constituency of one."[128]

Sherman Adams's precipitous fall from power was typical of the experience of many powerful chiefs of staff. When Adams got in trouble for accepting gifts from industrialist Bernard Goldfine, the opposition was the first to jump on the issue, but it was pressure from Republican ranks that ultimately produced Adams's resignation.[129] As one administration member confided, "Mr. Adams is a difficult man to sympathize with."[130] Adams's dismissal, Robert Keith Gray points out, came less from the charges themselves than from "not building himself a cadre of support to lean on when trouble came."[131] What Gray does not say is that building such support is difficult for a person cast in the role of buffer between the president and those within the president's own administration and party. However much Eisenhower might feel Adams was a valuable assistant, he also knew that no important political constituencies would be offended by dumping Adams, in marked contrast to the high costs among key political constituencies that would be incurred by jettisoning a Nixon or even a Benson.[132]

Similarly, pressure for Don Regan's removal in the wake of the Iran-contra revelations came more from Republicans than from Democrats.[133] Republican Senator Larry Pressler demanded Regan's immediate resignation, saying Regan "epitomizes the arrogance of power."[134] Republicans Richard Lugar and Robert Michel echoed Pressler's call for Regan's resignation.[135] Regan had no constituency to which he could turn, having made many enemies and few friends during his two years as chief of staff. But Regan faced still another problem, one that plagues all chiefs of staff to a greater or lesser degree: an inflated reputation for power.

THE DOUBLE BIND OF EXAGGERATED POWER

In his memoirs, Don Regan complains bitterly that "somehow the press had got the idea that Poindexter, and MacFarlane before him, had reported to me and I was therefore responsible for their performance. I explained that neither man had ever worked for me, but there was no dispelling this mistaken idea." Why was there no dispelling this "mistaken idea?" Why were reporters not prepared to accept Regan's version that he had no knowledge of the Iran-contra connection? Regan's answer: "They had heard that I was an autocrat who knew . . . when every sparrow fell on the White House lawn." Although true, this begs the question of where reporters and other political elites got this mistaken impression. Regan's effort to pin the blame for his image as "an ex officio prime minister" on "a press campaign" ignores his own role in fostering this myth.[136]

No public official, of course, can be held entirely responsible for his public image. Some get tagged with an undeserved image that, try as they might, they cannot shake. One thinks, for instance, of Gerald Ford's undeserved reputation as a klutz. The mass media, no doubt, by favoring instant analysis over cautious reflection, are not always good at separating fact from fiction. But more than media malice or miscue is responsible for the inflated estimates of Don Regan's power. Regan's reputation for power was exaggerated for many of the same reasons that the reputations of Sherman Adams,[137] H. R. Haldeman, and John Sununu[138] were inflated in contemporary press accounts: many political actors, including the chief of staff and the president, have an interest in exaggerating that power.

In order to be effective, senior staffers must persuade other officials that they have the authority to speak for the president. To function successfully as a "headknocker," for instance, a staffer must have sufficient prestige within the White House that the disputants will accept the staffer's decision rather than appeal to the president.[139] Because the effectiveness of a senior staffer depends on others within the administration respecting that staffer's power, an incentive exists for staffers to exaggerate (or to permit others to exaggerate) their reputation for power. The dilemma for the senior staff person is that an inflated reputation for power also means, as Don Regan found out, being held accountable for things outside one's control.

Presidents, too, have an incentive to acquiesce in having their chiefs of staff portrayed as more powerful and autonomous than in fact they are. Not only does it mean fewer appeals to the president but, as political scientist Bruce Buchanan points out, it means that the president can "use his own power without paying the price for doing so."[140] If others believe the chief of staff exercises considerable discretion, they will be more inclined to blame the staffer and absolve the president for policies they disagree with or that have gone awry. If a congressman gets turned away at the president's door, it is in the president's interest that the congressmen "go away thinking that that S.O.B. at the door kept him out instead of that that S.O.B. on the other side of the door didn't want to see him."[141]

Other public officials within and outside the administration have a strong incentive to exaggerate a chief of staff's power because it allows them to criticize presidential policy without directly criticizing the president. Exaggerating the power of senior staff enables disgruntled elites to express displeasure with the current direction of the administration without personally affronting the president. Thus critics of administration policy, the president, and the chief of staff himself all play a role in creating the overestimation of a chief of staff's power.

Regan's claim that "because I was not in fact a prime minister, but a servant of the Presidency, I did not think it mattered what the press wrote and said about me" is not just naive but disingenuous.[142] Regan found that a reputation for near-total mastery of the White House improved his own strategic position as well as suited President Reagan's desire to remain aloof from day-to-day management squabbles and policy conflicts. Opponents undoubtedly did exaggerate Regan's power for their own purposes, but Regan made no effort to rectify the inflated estimation of his position. On the contrary, many of his actions seemed calculated to foster such an inflated reputation.

After Bitburg, Regan clearly indicated to other elites that such fiascoes would not recur because in the future he, Don Regan, would assume control over the president's schedule. Regan's aides told Bernard Weinraub of the *New*

York Times that Regan had decided "to be more careful in watching the schedule, to be in full charge." According to Weinraub, "Mr. Regan plainly seeks to send a signal across the Administration that he is in total control over Mr. Reagan's schedule."[143] When Regan found out that President Reagan and King Hussein were answering reporters' questions, Regan immediately summoned Speakes to his office and demanded to know: "Why don't I know about this? . . . Damn it, I'm in charge of scheduling around here, and anybody that's going to do anything like that has to get my approval. . . . Don't you ever let this happen again."[144] On another occasion, when Regan's driver informed him there had been a small fire at the White House, Regan exploded at one of his aides: "Dammit! I'm the chief of staff! I've got to know when these things happen! . . . You guys have got to keep me posted on these things and I don't want this ever to happen again."[145] Upon Poindexter's appointment as national security assistant, Regan was quoted as telling Poindexter "that he didn't like surprises, he wanted to be told what's going on."[146] Regan's insistence on being seen as the person who knew everything that was going on in the White House meant, as William Niskanen sagely foresaw, "there's no way for him to avoid responsibility for every mistake."[147]

Regan apparently made no effort to stop friendly White House aides from talking to the press about his control over White House operations. One Regan aide boasted, "Don has positioned himself to be an extremely powerful chief of staff who's in charge of the whole show."[148] Another aide agreed: "Don is clearly in charge. He sees the staff as his staff. He's the one the President relies on."[149] "Everyone works for Regan," agreed a third aide, who praised Regan because "he understands that all the power centers need to be subservient to him."[150] Given the image propagated by his aides, it is little wonder that, as Regan complained at one point, "if someone gets a cold in this town, I get blamed."[151] Little wonder, too, that after the Iran-contra revelations, the press insisted that Regan "cannot escape responsibility for recent developments by feigning noninvolvement."[152] Or that 65 percent of the American people believed Regan knew "that money from the Iranian arms sales was going to help the contras."[153] As a former White House aide explained, "Don Regan would never have got in this trouble if he hadn't gone around telling everyone that he ran everything and knew everything."[154] For chiefs of staff no less than for presidents, a reputation for knowing everything means being blamed even for those things one knows little or nothing about.

IS A CHIEF OF STAFF NECESSARY?

Gerald Ford entered the presidential office determined not "to have a powerful chief of staff . . . [and instead] be my own chief of staff."[155] Along with many others in Washington, Ford felt that the lesson to be learned from Watergate was that a hierarchical White House organized around a chief of staff dangerously isolates the president from diverse ideas and information. His experience as a legislator reinforced his preference for a "spokes of the wheel" system in which he would be the wheel's hub. The president would thus be assured of multiple sources of information and senior aides would be guaranteed direct access to the president.[156]

Within two months, however, the much ballyhooed "spokes of the wheel" structure was being phased out. Ford quickly recognized the validity of what his top aides had been telling him for several months: without some person acting as a funnel, the president would be overloaded with unwanted information and unwelcome visitors. "Everyone," Ford later explained, "wanted a portion of my time." Ford's answer was to bring Donald Rumsfeld into the White House to serve as staff coordinator and gatekeeper. As Ford explained to the assembled staff shortly after Rumsfeld's appointment as assistant to the president, "The responsibility is on you to work through Don . . . [and to] make sure that Don is cognizant of what is happening." By the end of 1974, Dick Cheney (then Rumsfeld's deputy) recalls, "we were really, without ever formally announcing it, back to a model that was very close to the Haldeman model." Disgruntled staff agreed that Rumsfeld was "another Bob Haldeman, only he smiles."[157]

Much the same evolution of roles occurred, albeit more slowly, in the Carter White House. Like Ford, Carter entered office committed to being his own chief of staff. Ignoring the Ford administration's unsuccessful experiment with the "spokes of the wheel" concept, the people around Carter fixated instead on the centralized structure of the Nixon White House they deemed to be partially responsible for Watergate.[158] Fearing, as Press Secretary Jody Powell explained, that "an excessively powerful White House staff in general and a chief of staff in particular, . . . would tend to choke off the flow of information to the president,"[159] Carter opted for much the same organizational structure of direct access to the president that Ford had tried and discarded. Jack Watson, who served briefly as Carter's chief of staff in 1980, explains that Carter "felt very strongly that he didn't want to set up any barriers or obstacles between the free and full expression of opinion to him directly from Stu, Jack, Hamilton, Jody, Frank. And, he didn't want it to be filtered."[160] It took Carter two years to reach essentially the same conclusion that Ford had reached in two months: filtered information might be bad but unfiltered information is worse.

Distress signals emerged among senior White House staffers almost from the outset. In the fall of 1977, Hamilton Jordan asked for a written opinion on the advisability of selecting a chief of staff. The answer he got back from A. D. Frazier, a staff person from the president's reorganization project, was that "designating someone as chief of staff or better, as staff coordinator, would be most helpful to the President." Shortly thereafter, Eizenstat wrote to the president: "I continue to believe that our most serious structural problem is the lack of internal White House coordination. . . . No one has been given the directive to sort out the various priorities of our work, to coordinate our work and make sure it is all going in the same direction, before it all pours in to you."[161] Finally in July 1979, Carter relented to his advisers' pleas and appointed Jordan as chief of staff.

Former members of the Carter administration today seem almost unanimous in concluding that not having a chief of staff was a mistake. "Without question," Eizenstat admits, "one of the most serious errors that was made, I would say near fatal error, was not having a chief of staff." The White House, Eizenstat flatly declares, "cannot function properly without a strong and effective chief of staff." Jack Watson agrees that Carter "should have designated a chief of staff almost immediately." Even Jody Powell now concedes that "we should have had . . . a chief of staff. [It] could have saved time for everybody, including the president."[162]

Natural experiments are rare in politics, and rarer still in a field like the presidency that is so open to personal idiosyncrasy and historical contingency. This makes the Carter and Ford experiences that much more noteworthy. For here are two presidents, of vastly different political backgrounds, personalities, and operating styles who both, for different reasons, came into office predisposed against the idea of a chief of staff. Ford resisted the chief of staff concept because his extensive congressional experience had taught him the value of exposing oneself to diverse sources, and Carter resisted because of his desire "to be on top of everything, to manage everything, to know everything."[163] That both men nevertheless ended up appointing a chief of staff forces one to ask whether the chief of staff is not a functional necessity in today's presidency.

A number of presidential scholars have reached precisely this conclusion. Even those like Richard Neustadt, who once vigorously opposed the idea of a chief of staff, now concede that "in administrative terms [a chief of staff], or something like it, has become a practical necessity."[164] Michael Medved concurs that "a central figure on the staff—whether he is called White House Secretary, Staff Coordinator, Assistant President, or Chief of Staff—is necessary for the efficient functioning of the White House." "Chiefs are necessary," echoes Samuel Popkin, "because a president's time must be rationed, decisions must be paced, and access by the staff and cabinet need to be refereed."[165]

The startling rapidity with which "lessons" of the presidency are learned, unlearned, and relearned leads one to regard any "iron laws" or "functional requisites" of the presidency with a healthy skepticism. Still it is striking that a position that so many people have deplored continues to persist in the modern presidency. Future presidents could with profit follow Reagan's first-term model and opt not to concentrate power in the hands of a single chief of staff,[166] but Carter and Ford's experiences teach us that it would be unwise for any future president to try, in the manner of Franklin Roosevelt or John Kennedy,[167] to be his own chief of staff.[168]

A president cannot be his own chief of staff for reasons that go beyond the crushing administrative burdens of running the modern presidency. Given the ever-increasing number of groups that look to the presidency for solutions to problems, modern presidents cannot afford to become involved in, let alone be held responsible for, all the problems that are dumped at the White House door. The president, as the Brownlow report stated, does need help. But that help cannot come only in the form of anonymous administrative aides, tirelessly toiling in the president's shadow. For in today's political environment, presidents also need top aides who can share the glare of the limelight, speak for the president, say "no" for the president, and take the blame for the president. A president who tries to do all or much of this himself will become personally embroiled in too many political disputes and will find himself increasingly unable to sustain political support inside Washington and in the country as a whole.

7

Limits of the Lightning Rod: Eisenhower, Brownell, Southern Whites, and Civil Rights

On October 23, 1957, exactly one month after President Eisenhower issued an executive order sending federal troops into Little Rock, Arkansas, to enforce the court-ordered integration of Central High School and only six weeks after the president had signed the nation's first civil rights legislation since Reconstruction, Attorney General Herbert Brownell announced his resignation. Many in the South could hardly contain their glee. "From Harper's Ferry to the Rio Grande," proclaimed the Richmond *Times-Dispatch,* "no tears are being shed for the retirement of Herbert Brownell, Jr. as Attorney General. The frightful mess the South, and the country, are in is probably as much his responsibility as that of any living man." The *Times-Dispatch* went on to chronicle Brownell's offenses:

> It was Brownell who journeyed to California in 1953 to confer with Earl Warren before that worthy was named Chief Justice of the United States. It was Brownell who pressed the government's case in the integration suits before Chief Justice Warren, and told the nine justices that it was their "duty" to rule out segregation in the public schools. It was Brownell who either drafted or sponsored the unspeakable "civil rights" bill, as originally introduced in Congress, and who convinced President Eisenhower that it was a mild and moderate piece of legislation. And finally, it was Brownell who had Eisenhower's ear throughout the Little Rock affair, and who is generally credited with persuading the President that Governor Faubus should be put in his place with bayonets.[1]

Editorial pages across the South echoed this sense of relief at Brownell's departure.[2]

Southern politicians also rejoiced at the news. Georgia's Governor Marvin

Griffin felt "encouraged and delighted that Mr. Brownell has resigned."[3] A local pol could hardly contain his enthusiasm: "That's the greatest news I've ever heard in a long time. . . . I don't care who replaces Brownell, nobody could be worse, we are bound to get an improvement. . . . I'm just delighted."[4] The chair of the Alabama Democratic Executive Committee told reporters he was "glad [Brownell's] out . . . [because] Brownell has been the moving factor in the integration movement of the present administration, as well as having advised the use of federal troops in Little Rock." With Brownell out of the way, there was now hope that "the President will look to someone else who might show a little more consideration to the South." An Alabama man who had been the Republican candidate for governor in 1954 declared that he was "delighted to hear [that Brownell] is out of government." While admitting that as "captain of the ship . . . President Eisenhower must still bear his part of the blame," he nevertheless believed that "Brownell has been the agitator, the pusher of the integration plan," and must therefore "accept the blame for the president's decision to send troops to Little Rock, the most tragic incident in American history."[5] Arkansas Governor Orval Faubus was certain that Brownell had been "fired because of the bad advice or misinformation he gave the President about Little Rock."[6]

ATTORNEY GENERAL BROWNELL AS LIGHTNING ROD

It is tempting to interpret such reactions as evidence of another triumph for Eisenhower's blame-avoidance leadership style. Certainly these reactions to Brownell's resignation suggest that many southern whites held Attorney General Brownell personally responsible for actions taken by the Eisenhower administration in the area of civil rights for blacks. Moreover, the enmity directed at Brownell was not due to Eisenhower's luck or some magical "Teflon" but rather was part of a conscious effort on Eisenhower's part to have Brownell out in front on divisive issues like civil rights.

From the outset, Eisenhower made it clear to Brownell that he expected his attorney general to exercise decision-making power and to provide the president with political cover. Among the first tasks Eisenhower delegated to Brownell was to review and make recommendations on pardon applications. Brownell diligently prepared a list of recommendations, and in one of his first official meetings with the president "started to recite the facts of each case." After about ten minutes Eisenhower cut his new attorney general off. "What are you doing reciting these details to me? Give me your recommendations and I'll approve them." A chastened Brownell turned to leave, and Eisenhower added, "But, remember, you and I initiated a policy of making these pardon actions open to the public. If anything proves to be misrepresented or incomplete about these cases, it's your responsibility."[7]

Eisenhower, according to Brownell, believed that the president "was most effective as president if he maintained his tremendous popularity and support with the public and did not get beaten down by the day-to-day political fights."[8] Eisenhower's "preferred strategy," Brownell explains, was "delegating authority to his cabinet officers—when he deemed they could be trusted with it—and having them serve as his political front men and lightning rods, and projecting an image of being above the political fray." "In my own case," Brownell continues, "it meant I was given responsibility and authority in a number of controversial areas such as civil rights, antitrust, and internal security, all of which were likely to be divisive."[9]

In private meetings and correspondence with southern leaders, Eisenhower often conveyed both his detachment from the administration's actions in the area of civil rights and his sympathy for their predicament. In July of 1953, for instance, with the White House considering how to respond to the Supreme Court's invitation to file a brief in the pending school desegregation case of *Brown v. The Board of Education,* South Carolina's Governor (and former secretary of state under Truman) James F. Byrnes met with Eisenhower in hopes of persuading the president either to decline the Supreme Court's invitation or take the southern side in submitting arguments to the Court. The president reassured his "great friend" that he felt "improvement in race relations is one of those things that will be healthy and sound only if it starts locally." Prejudice, Eisenhower agreed, would not "succumb to compulsion."[10]

Several months later, Byrnes wrote Eisenhower to lobby again for upholding the "separate but equal" doctrine; overturning *Plessy v. Ferguson,* Byrnes argued, would be inconsistent with "the position you have consistently taken, that the states should have the right to control matters that are purely local."[11] In a prompt reply, Eisenhower not only reiterated his appreciation for the South's plight, but carefully distanced himself from the legal proceedings: "In the study of the case," he explained,

> it became clear to me that the questions asked of the Attorney General by the Supreme Court demanded answers that could be determined only by lawyers and historians. Consequently, *I have been compelled to turn over to the Attorney General and his associates full responsibility in the matter. He and I agreed that his brief would reflect the conviction of the Department of Justice* as to the legal aspects of the case. . . . In rendering an opinion as to these phases of the case, it is clear that *the Attorney General had to act according to his own conviction and understanding.*[12]

"No matter what the legal conclusions might be," he assured Byrnes, "the principle of local operation and authority would be emphasized to the maximum degree consistent with [the attorney general's] legal opinions."[13]

When questioned at press conferences about the administration's position on civil rights questions, Eisenhower frequently referred the questioner to the attorney general. Questioned on March 7, 1957, as to how he felt about an amendment to the administration's civil rights bill that would provide for jury trials in cases of contempt, for example, Eisenhower refused to comment because the question "is so legal in its character that you ought to go to the Attorney General. . . . I don't know anything about . . . [these] legal quirks."[14] Asked again a few months later about southern objections to the absence of a jury-trial provision in the civil rights bill, the president responded in much the same fashion: "I am not enough of a lawyer to discuss that thing one way or the other. . . . You will have to go to the Attorney General. He knows more about it than I do."[15] By defining the jury-trial issue as a legal matter best handled by the attorney general, Eisenhower hoped to deflect the anger felt by southern whites onto Brownell.

Perhaps the most conspicuous illustration of Eisenhower's studied aloofness from the wrangling over civil rights came in a press conference during the summer of 1957, in which he was asked to comment on Senator Richard Russell's criticism that the administration's civil rights bill was "a cunning device" designed to enforce integration of public schools. Rather than repudiate Russell's charge, Eisenhower replied only that this was not *his* objective, which was only to "prevent anybody from illegally interfering with any individual's right to vote." He added, however, that "naturally, I am not a lawyer and I don't participate in drawing up the exact language of the proposals"—leaving the implication that perhaps this may have been the objective of others in his administration who drafted the bill. Expressing puzzlement that "highly respected men" could think this "a very extreme law, leading to disorder," Eisenhower allowed that he was "always ready to listen to anyone's presentation to me of his views on such a thing." Asked if that meant he would be willing to rewrite the bill so that it dealt only with the right to vote, Eisenhower declined to answer on the grounds that "I was reading part of that bill this morning, and there were certain phrases I didn't completely understand. So, before I made any more remarks on that, I would want to talk to the Attorney General and see exactly what they do mean."[16] This was a vintage Eisenhower performance, designed to distance himself from controversial aspects of the bill by deferring to the expertise of a trusted cabinet member.[17]

That Eisenhower's intent was to distance himself from the divisive issue of civil rights seems clear enough. How successful, though, was Eisenhower's strategy of having Brownell absorb the blame for unpopular or controversial policies? To answer that question requires us to ask at least three different questions. First, we need to ask whether Eisenhower actually did maintain public support in spite of controversial administration policies in the area of civil rights. Second, we need to know whether or to what extent the pursuit of presidential popularity came at the expense of achieving Eisenhower's policy objectives. Finally, we must inquire whether Brownell pursued civil rights objectives the president shared, or whether delegating to Brownell entailed sacrificing presidential control over the civil rights agenda.

DID THE SOUTH LIKE IKE?

During Eisenhower's first term, the administration was associated with a number of civil rights positions and actions that were violently opposed by many southerners. Most important among these were the Justice Department's brief arguing that "separate but equal" was unconstitutional, the appointment of Earl Warren as chief justice (both of which were critical in producing the Supreme Court's unanimous decision in *Brown v. Board of Education*), and the civil rights bill of 1956. Yet Gallup polls during Eisenhower's first term reveal consistently high public support for Eisenhower in the South and only relatively minor discrepancies between Eisenhower's approval rating in the South and in the rest of the nation.[18] These approval scores suggest that at least through his first four years Eisenhower did successfully avoid becoming personally associated with administration policies in the minds of most southerners.

Eisenhower distanced himself from *Brown* by refusing publicly to endorse the decision.[19] When, at a press conference two days after the decision was handed down, a reporter remarked that the decision had been "brought out under the Republican Administration," the president promptly, and somewhat testily, retorted that "the Supreme Court, as I understand it, is not under any administration." Asked whether he had any advice for the South about how to react to the decision, Eisenhower quickly replied, "not in the slightest" and then took the occasion to praise Governor James Byrnes: "I thought that Governor Byrnes made a very fine statement when he said, 'Let's be calm, and let's be reasonable, and let's look this thing in the face.' "[20] Eisenhower later insisted on having the words "Eisenhower administration" stricken from the section of the 1956 Republican platform endorsing the Supreme Court's desegregation decision[21] and publicly repudiated Vice President Nixon's boast, made during the 1956 campaign, that the desegregation verdict had been issued by a "Republican Chief Justice."[22]

Eisenhower remained almost equally aloof from his administration's 1956 civil rights bill, which consequently never made it out of committee. He kept the bill at arm's length by having the attorney general recommend the program to Congress rather than having it sent in a presidential message, leav-

TABLE 7.1.   Eisenhower's approval rating among southern whites and the rest of the population, April 1957–December 1958.

	Approval			Disapproval		
	South. Whites	Rest of Nation	Diff.	South. Whites	Rest of Nation	Diff.
April 25–30, 1957	63	64	−1	23	23	0
June 6–11	60	65	−5	23	22	−1
June 27–July 2	49	67	−18	27	22	−5
July 18–23	59	66	−7	21	23	+2
August 8–13	52	65	−13	29	18	−11
August 29– September 4	50	62	−12	25	22	−3
September 19–24	46	63	−17	33	25	−8
October 10–15	28	65	−37	53	21	−32
November 7–12	41	62	−21	41	24	−17
January 2–7, 1958	48	64	−16	42	27	−15
January 24–29	42	62	−20	39	24	−15
April 16–21	40	59	−19	41	28	−13
December 3–8	43	61	−18	44	29	−15

Sources: Gallup polls; data provided by Roper Center. The "rest of the nation" category includes nonwhite southerners.

ing the two most controversial of the bill's recommendations (those parts calling for protection of voting rights and protection of civil rights more generally) off his legislative "must" list and refusing to endorse these provisions until late in his reelection effort.

The president's landslide reelection over Adlai Stevenson in 1956 confirmed what the polls had been saying. In 1956, Eisenhower held every southern state he had carried in 1952 (Florida, Oklahoma, Tennessee, Texas, and Virginia), while adding victories in Kentucky, Louisiana, and West Virginia. Moreover, he increased his share of the vote in virtually every southern state. In Virginia, for example, where he had received 56 percent of the vote in 1952 (becoming the first Republican since Herbert Hoover to carry the state), he increased his share of the vote to 59 percent. In Alabama, to take another instance, he improved from 35 percent in 1952 to 41 percent in 1956.

Not until the summer of 1957, as the administration's civil rights bill made its way through Congress, was there a drop-off in southern support for Eisenhower (see Table 7.1). A Gallup survey conducted in late April showed no difference in support for Eisenhower among southern whites and citizens in the rest of the nation, and even as late as the first weeks of June, the difference between the president's popularity among southern whites and his support in the rest of the country was still only marginal. But by the end of June, southern support for Eisenhower had declined significantly, a decline that would appear to be directly attributable to the House of Representatives having passed the administration's civil rights bill on June 18. This gap between support for Eisenhower among southern whites and the rest of the population persisted throughout the summer as the Senate debated and then passed its own, significantly weaker version of the bill on August 7 and then approved the reconciled version of the bill on August 29. Three surveys conducted in the two-month span between the House passage of the bill on June 18 and final Senate approval of the Civil Rights Act on August 29 show an average gap of almost 13 percent between approval of Eisenhower among southern whites and the rest of the nation.[23] Another poll taken immediately after final passage of the 1957 Civil Rights Act showed the persistence of the same 12–13 point gap between southern whites and the rest of the nation.

The shift in southern attitudes toward Eisenhower during the summer of 1957 is evident, too, in the editorial pages of leading southern newspapers. Previously inclined to blame Brownell for the administration's course on civil rights, editors increasingly began to pin responsibility on the president. The Richmond *Times-Dispatch,* for instance, ran an editorial on May 19, 1957, laying the blame on Attorney General Brownell for misleading a well-meaning and honorable president. The commentary began by citing Eisenhower's remarks at a May 15 press conference that the proposed "civil rights bill is a very moderate thing done in all decency" and that those with questions about the bill's denial of jury trials should ask the attorney general who "knows more about it than I do." "Herein," the editors informed their readers,

> lies the tragedy of this whole presidential effort to ram the "civil rights" bill through Congress. Mr. Eisenhower is no lawyer and he has been told by Mr. Brownell that the civil rights bill is a mild piece of legislation. . . . If anybody could get Mr. Eisenhower to read the minority report of the Senate Subcommittee on Civil Rights . . . he might see what vast and far-reaching evil lies in this legislation.

A month later, the editors were still hopeful that "in time, Mr. Eisenhower can be brought to see how utterly nonsensical it is for him to describe this bill as 'moderate.' "[24]

By mid-summer, however, the paper's tone had shifted dramatically. The editors ceased to hold out hope that Eisenhower would recognize that he had been deceived and repudiate the bill and his attorney general. While still complaining of a "Warren-Brownell coup," they no longer spared Eisenhower, whom they now accused of "surrender to the left." After the president issued a statement on August 2 declaring that the Senate's passage of a jury-trial amendment had weakened "our whole judicial system," the *Times-Dispatch* directly attacked the president for presenting an "absurd" opinion that "only adherents to the Warren school of thought could hold." The editors also criticized Eisenhower for "guilelessly" relying on the legal advice of "that astute politician with both ears to the ground, Attorney General Brownell." A few days later the editors continued the trend of placing responsibility on the president for following the advice rather than on the advisers for giving it. As if it only had just dawned on them, they wrote, "Not only has the President endorsed federal civil rights legislation of the most extreme character, but he must have approved the action of Attorney General Brownell in telling the Supreme Court prior to its anti-segregation decision of 1954 that the court was in duty bound to render the decision, annihilating the rights of the states to operate their own public schools."[25]

A similar pattern of change is evident in the editorial pages of the *Mobile Register.* Alienated by the Democratic party of Truman, Harriman, and Stevenson, the *Register,* like the *Times-Dispatch,* had been a consistent supporter of Eisenhower and had endorsed his candidacy in 1952 and 1956. An April 10 editorial provided the first indication of uneasiness with the discrepancy between Eisenhower's professions of support for states' rights and the civil rights course being pursued by his administration. A week later, the editors suggested that the reason for this inconsistency was that the president had been getting bad advice: he had been "sold a bad bill of goods" by "the loud-mouthed anti-South busy beavers" and "political radicals." If Eisenhower had "more advisers with a political philosophy that makes horse sense," he would quickly "recognize the need for correcting the errors of his administration's ways."[26]

The first hint of personal criticism of Eisenhower for his handling of the civil rights issue came on June 8. Bemoaning the administration's sponsorship of the civil rights bill, the *Register* concluded that "the South . . . has deserved better from Mr. Eisenhower than he has given it." The following day, the editors called attention to the contradiction between the president's performance and his promises. Eisenhower's address to the annual conference of state governors at Williamsburg, Virginia, (delivered on June 26) advocating a return of power to the states was met with deep suspicion: "It does not make sense to us for Mr. Eisenhower to talk up states' rights while his administration batters down states' rights."[27]

Throughout July and August, as the bill made its way through Congress, the *Register* continued to criticize in the severest terms the "wretched" civil rights bill but largely refrained from criticizing Eisenhower directly.[28] Instead the editors preferred to blast "anti-Southern radicals" in Congress, such as Paul Douglas and Hubert Humphrey. But after the bill had passed both houses of Congress, and with Eisenhower set to sign the bill into law, the editors publicly expressed, for the first time, the extent of their disillusionment with Eisenhower's leadership. In a September 6 editorial, they admitted that the *Register* "once had great hope that Mr. Eisenhower could . . . lead America away from . . . federal intermeddling and racial anxiety" but now conceded that they had been mistaken. Instead the Eisenhower administration had "carried the country deeper into the night of racial misfortune than the Roosevelt and Truman administrations left it." "The disillusionment of the people with the Republican administration of Mr. Eisenhower," they concluded, "must be close to complete."[29]

Despite Eisenhower's efforts to have the Justice Department take the lead on the civil rights bill, he ultimately was unable to avoid political fallout from this controversial measure. In large part, this was because Eisenhower had been faced with a choice of placing his prestige behind the civil rights bill or watching the bill fail. He had largely avoided identifying himself with the 1956 civil rights bill, and as a result the bill died in committee. In July of 1957, faced with the strong possibility that the Senate would attach a jury-trial amendment to the bill—which he believed would "nullify the purpose of the legislation"[30]—Eisenhower felt compelled to take an unequivocal public stand against the amendment. In a press conference at the end of July, he emphatically stated his opposition to a trial-by-jury amendment and urged the Senate to pass the bill "as it now stands."[31] Eisenhower's more visible public profile became necessary because the lightning rod strategy that he had hitherto pursued was now playing into the hands of the bill's opponents.

Although southern support for Eisenhower slipped markedly during this period, one must be careful not to overstate the extent of the decline. If, as the Richmond *Times-Dispatch* reported on August 17, "the bloom was off the I-like-Ike boom,"[32] it was also true that a Gallup poll conducted at the end of August showed that twice as many southern whites approved of the president's performance as disapproved. Gallup polls showed that although there had been a large decrease in the number of southern whites who approved of the president, there was not a comparably large increase among those expressing disapproval. By far the greatest increase was in the number of southerners who were uncertain about how to evaluate Eisenhower's performance.[33] This public indecision changed rapidly, however, with the dramatic events in Little Rock that followed closely on the heels of the president's signing of the 1957 Civil Rights Act.

"BY GOD I HATE HIS GUTS NOW"

Whatever distance Eisenhower had been able to maintain from civil rights issues ended overnight with his decision to send federal troops into Little Rock to uphold a federal court order to integrate Central High School.

Eisenhower's confrontation with Arkansas Governor Orval Faubus, who had called out the Arkansas National Guard and ordered the troops to prevent black students from entering Central High, proved so costly in terms of political support because it was no longer possible for Eisenhower to remain in the background and allow others to take the heat. The press portrayed events in Little Rock as a personal clash between President Eisenhower and Governor Faubus. Typical was the front page of the Richmond *Times-Dispatch* the day after troops had been ordered into Little Rock, which placed Faubus's picture in the upper left-hand corner and Eisenhower's in the upper right.[34]

After having made the decision to send troops in, Eisenhower made no effort to distance himself from the controversy. In the president's radio and television address to the nation on September 24, explaining why he had sent in troops, he left no doubt that it was his decision. No mention was made of advice received from those within his administration or requests from local officers in Arkansas. Similarly, at his first press conference after sending troops into Little Rock, Eisenhower did not refer questioners to the attorney general, nor did he redefine questions as purely legal ones that he was not competent to answer. Press Secretary James Hagerty reiterated that "the action taken in Little Rock was the President's responsibility and his alone."[35]

This pose was necessary in part because for the president to seem disengaged from such a momentous decision would call into question his competence. It was also required because Governor Faubus was attempting to discredit the administration by portraying Brownell and the "palace guard" as the cause of the problem.[36] By not criticizing the president directly, Faubus tried to avoid the impression that he was challenging presidential authority. Faubus argued, in effect, that Brownell rather than he was the usurper. It thus became essential for Eisenhower to make it clear to others that the conflict was between the president of the United States and a governor.

Thrust unprotected onto center stage, criticism rained down upon Eisenhower (Table 7.1). A Gallup poll conducted between September 19 and September 24, at the height of the showdown but before the decision to send in troops, shows further deterioration in support for Eisenhower among southern whites. But it was the sending in of troops that caused Eisenhower's popularity among southerners to sink to unprecedented lows. A survey taken between October 10 and October 15, while federal troops were still in Little Rock, found that almost twice as many southern whites disapproved (53 percent) of Eisenhower's performance in office as approved (28 percent)! The president's approval rating among southern whites was close to forty points below that which he received from the rest of the nation. Even after the last of the federal troops had been withdrawn in November, Eisenhower's approval rating among southern whites still lagged about twenty points behind the support he received from the rest of the nation, a pattern that endured for well over a year. An Arkansas woman summed up the feelings of a great number of southerners: "I voted for Ike twice, but by God I hate his guts now. He's wrong, wrong, wrong."[37]

A flood of hostile letters to the editor revealed the depth of southern animosity toward the president. One letter expressed "shame" at having a president "so callous, so lacking in patriotism, and so lacking in judgment." Another believed Eisenhower had "shown himself to be incapable and unworthy of public office," and another condemned him for his "super arrogance." Eisenhower was reviled for having shown "the spirit of a dictator." One reader suggested the formation of an "I don't like Ike club."[38] Believing Eisenhower had "broken faith" with the South, many letters demanded that we "get a new President."

The *Mobile Register,* which had expressed guarded disillusionment with Eisenhower over his handling of the civil rights bill, now vilified Eisenhower for his "horrifying" decision to send troops into Little Rock. The editors lamented: "Something has happened to the Eisenhower who was first elected President in 1952. The old Eisenhower is gone from the White House. A different Eisenhower, an unfamiliar Eisenhower and a contradictory Eisenhower is there now." The Eisenhower of today was "unrecognizable as the man who only last year pleaded earnestly for patience and understanding." The Eisenhower of today, the editors complained, had joined with Brownell to usher in dictatorship and drive out freedom.[39]

The *Register*'s assault on the president only intensified the following day. It announced that "Dwight Eisenhower should be the last sample of career military brass who will be seen in the White House as an elected President of the United States." Eisenhower had proven that a military man could not be trusted as president. "Behind the facade of Eisenhower's ingratiating manner stood a personality long accustomed to snapping military commands that none dared disobey or ignore." Mindless of the inconsistency, the editors also maintained that Eisenhower's "military mind" had become "political putty recklessly influenced by men like the incompetent attorney general Brownell."[40]

Previous criticisms of Brownell had accentuated the differences between the opinions of the president and those of his attorney general, but the *Register* now referred to "the team of Eisenhower and Brownell." Before, the nonpolitical Eisenhower had been contrasted to "the politicians" like Brownell and Nixon, who were allegedly pandering to the black vote, but the *Register* now spoke of the "high Republican politicians from Eisenhower down."[41] Little Rock had sullied Eisenhower's carefully cultivated image of being above the political fray.

The confrontation in Little Rock over integration vividly reveals the limitations on a president's ability to use advisers to deflect criticism, a fact one might miss if one looked only at Eisenhower's overall national approval ratings, which throughout this period show little change (August 29–September 4: 59 percent; September 19–24: 59 percent; October 10–15: 57 percent; November 7–12: 58 percent; and January 2–7, 1958: 60 percent). It would be easy but badly mistaken to interpret these national approval numbers as remarkable evidence of Eisenhower's invincible Teflon coating. Probing beneath the misleading national approval average shows that Eisenhower was anything but Teflon coated in the case of Little Rock. Southern support for Eisenhower dropped precipitously after the president sent federal troops into Little Rock, and even after Brownell's resignation at the end of October, southern support for Eisenhower remained substantially below pre–Little Rock levels for well over a year.

POPULARITY AT WHAT PRICE?

Assessing presidential success or failure is, of course, far more complex than determining whether a president's popularity rose or fell. Achievement of policy objectives matters too. One can make a reasonable case that before Little Rock, Eisenhower had significant success in deflecting responsibility for the administration's civil rights agenda onto Attorney General Brownell. After all, even after the Civil Rights Act had passed both houses of Congress at the end of August 1957, twice as many southern whites approved of Eisenhower's performance as disapproved. To what extent, though, did Eisenhower's distancing of himself from crucial provisions of the 1957 civil rights bill get in the way of achieving his administration's policy objectives?

The civil rights bill President Eisenhower signed into law on September 9, 1957, differed significantly from the original administration proposal. Gone was section three, which would have empowered the attorney general to seek injunctions against anyone interfering with civil rights broadly defined. Amended to the bill was a jury-trial provision, which required that anyone cited for contempt be given a jury trial if the sentence exceeded forty-five days in jail or a $300 fine. Believing that no white jury would convict another white person for preventing a black person from voting, many black leaders felt the bill had been so emasculated that they urged the president not to sign it.[42] Indeed the president himself, after the Senate had passed an earlier version of the jury-trial amendment that called for juries in all contempt cases, had blasted the amendment for making "largely ineffective the basic purpose of the bill—that of protecting promptly and effectively every American in his right to vote."[43]

The president's anger at the Senate for tacking on a jury-trial amendment was genuine—he told the cabinet the next morning that the vote was "one of the most serious political defeats of the past four years"[44]—but the president himself was at least partly to blame for that serious defeat. On three separate occasions during the spring of 1957, he had asserted at news conferences that he didn't know enough to say whether a jury-trial amendment "would be a crippling or disabling amendment"[45] and had referred questions about the subject to the attorney general. The president did not publicly take a stand in opposition to the jury-trial amendment until July 31, just two days before the Senate passed its amendment. Those opposed to the administration's civil rights policies were able to make Eisenhower's strategy of distancing himself from controversial provisions of the civil rights bill serve their own ends. By ceding Eisenhower his popularity, opponents of civil rights legislation could achieve their own political ends.

Eisenhower's statement in his July 3 press conference that there were "certain phrases" in the civil rights bill he didn't "completely understand" was particularly critical in giving southerners a means to attack the bill without attacking Eisenhower. Senator Sam Ervin of North Carolina, who called the bill the "most drastic and indefensible" legislation ever submitted to Congress, assured his Senate colleagues that President Eisenhower would not favor the civil rights bill in its present form "if he understood its provisions and implications."[46] Virginia Senator Harry Byrd used the same opening gambit to launch his attack upon the bill:

> If there is any doubt about this being a bad bill, we can start with the President of the United States as the first authority on the deception which has been perpetrated on him, on the Congress, and on the public. He has repeatedly said he looks on the bill primarily as covering only so-called voting rights. But at a news conference several weeks ago, he appeared to be getting a glimmer of the injustice to which he was being made a party. He said he did not understand what he called the "legal quirks" in the bill. Then at a later conference, he went further, and said he had been reading the bill and did not understand all of its language.

Byrd then went on to analyze for his Senate colleagues twenty "quirks" that he found in the bill.[47] Eisenhower's press conference remarks were successful in deflecting criticism away from the president in large part because they enabled opponents of the civil rights bill to attack the administration's bill as being inconsistent with the president's stated intentions.

Eisenhower's refusal to refute directly Senator Richard Russell's charge that the bill was cunningly designed to hasten integration of southern schools—Ike would say only that was not *his* intention—allowed the bill's opponents to hammer away at those in the Justice Department for perverting the president's honorable intentions. Mississippi Senator John Stennis, for instance, called the bill an evil concoction of some "crafty and designing lawyers," a sentiment echoed by the other senator from Mississippi, James Eastland, who described the measure as "a slick, devious scheme."[48]

Section three of the civil rights bill was attacked not for the power it would give to Eisenhower but for the power it would grant to Attorney General Brownell. Senator Ervin asserted that the bill would make the attorney general "dictator of all the Southern states." It would "create a little Hitler out of the Attorney General," declared South Carolina Senator Olin Johnston. Georgia Democrat Herman Talmadge told his Senate colleagues that the provision would turn the attorney general into a "civil rights czar" superior to the Constitution. Echoing these statements, Harry Byrd warned that the bill would make Brownell "a 20th century American Caesar."[49]

That Brownell rather than Eisenhower was attacked as an aspiring tyrant may have helped Eisenhower maintain his personal popularity but it also helped weaken the administration's civil rights bill. It is difficult, of course, to determine whether these southern senators really believed Brownell was the culprit or whether their motivation was purely tactical. For our purposes, however, it is sufficient to observe that acquiescing in Eisenhower's lightning rod strategy—by accentuating the divergence between the president and the attorney general—helped further their aim of stripping the administration's civil rights bill of its most stringent provisions.[50]

The charge that Eisenhower's performance, particularly at the July 3 news conference, hurt the civil rights bill is not new. It was made by many contemporaries and has been repeated subsequently by several scholars.[51] What is different is that rather than viewing this episode as an instance of Eisenhower's political ineptitude—the usual explanation—it can now be understood as the unintended result of an overall presidential strategy designed to avoid blame and maintain political support. A lightning rod strategy is not a presidential panacea, for considerable costs accompany its benefits.[52] Not the least of these costs is that to the extent that presidential support is critical to realizing policy objectives, presidential distancing may come at the expense of achieving those objectives.

WHOSE VOICE?

The Little Rock episode reveals a further cost of using advisers as lightning rods: it generates uncertainty as to whether one is hearing the president's voice or the voice of the adviser. If, as Richard Neustadt argues, "the first factor favoring compliance with a presidential order is assurance that the President has spoken,"[53] then a lightning rod strategy makes compliance with a presidential directive less likely. It seems possible that Eisenhower's reliance on Brownell as a lightning rod, by creating ambiguity in Governor

Faubus's mind about Eisenhower's position, played a significant role in forcing the president to send federal troops into Little Rock.

Faubus and Eisenhower met on September 14 in Newport, Rhode Island, to discuss the tense situation in Little Rock. After this meeting, Neustadt asserts, "there is no doubt that Faubus knew it was the President who wanted something done."[54] If Faubus's own testimony is to be given credence, however, Neustadt's claim must be called into question. For, according to Faubus, it was on precisely this point that the governor harbored doubts.

Faubus explained that he "felt that the only possibility of ironing it out was through the innate good will and good nature of the President who, I always felt, was a good-intentioned man, who wanted to do the right thing." From the moment the interview began, Faubus recalls, it was evident that the president's advisers "simply hadn't informed him on anything."[55] Faubus proceeded to tell Eisenhower how far Arkansas had progressed in desegregating public schools, universities, and even some private institutions. The president, Faubus recalled, was "impressed" by his presentation. The governor then told Eisenhower that "the only hope of solving it right now without the use of force is a delay, to give the tempers a chance to cool off, to give emotions a chance to subside." Eisenhower seemed in agreement with the governor on this. At this point, Faubus reports, the president called in Brownell and asked him, "Can't you go down there and ask the court to postpone the implementation of this order for a few days, ten days or three weeks?" The attorney general, according to Faubus, responded, "No, that's impossible. It isn't legally possible."[56]

The effect of this interview was to leave Faubus with the impression that it was Brownell, and not the president, who wanted the court order enforced. By having the attorney general play the "no-man," Eisenhower conveyed an impression of sympathy for the governor's plight, consistent with the impression the president had communicated in conversation and correspondence with various other southern elites.[57] While effective as a means of maintaining the support of southern whites, it was ill suited to getting Governor Faubus to comply with the president's wishes. By allowing Faubus to believe that "the attitude of the federal government" did not express the president's views but instead "was principally due to Brownell,"[58] Eisenhower had inadvertently given Faubus reason to hope that he could defy the court order.

The Little Rock episode is thus best seen neither as an illustration of the inherent limitations on presidential power nor as an example of the political ineptitude of President Eisenhower. Rather, it reveals the weakness of a particular blame-avoidance style of presidential leadership. It was both the strength and shortcoming of Eisenhower's style that it created ambiguity about whether it was the president or the adviser speaking. In the case of Little Rock, unfortunately, ambiguity over whose voice was being heard undermined Eisenhower's immediate objective, which was to prevent a public showdown over integration between the president of the United States and a governor of a southern state.

WHOSE POLICY?

Eisenhower's objectives in the case of Little Rock are clear enough. The president wanted to uphold the federal law while at the same time avoid a public showdown with Faubus that he felt would inflame race relations and place the president in a politically vulnerable position. Faubus's refusal to cooperate made it impossible for Eisenhower to avoid a public showdown if he was also to uphold federal law, not to mention presidential power. Unlike the case of Joseph McCarthy, whom Eisenhower helped to undercut without ever having to go public,[59] Eisenhower was forced to meet Governor Faubus's challenge by abandoning his low-profile, blame-avoidance posture in favor of a highly visible, buck-stops-here mode of presidential leadership complete with prime-time television announcements, presidential proclamations, and unambiguous statements of presidential responsibility.

Determining President Eisenhower's objectives in the area of the civil rights bill, on the other hand, is more difficult.[60] To what extent did the civil rights bill reflect the goals of the president, and to what extent did delegating responsibility to the attorney general result in a bill that departed substantially from the president's own preferences? Put another way, was Eisenhower's public standoffishness toward certain elements in the civil rights bill merely a strategic ploy disguising his private commitment to Brownell's public positions, or did his public behavior accurately reflect his ambiguous and even confused private feelings? This question goes to the heart of the revisionist claim that there was a fundamental division between what Eisenhower said (and did) in public and what he said (and did) in private.

Was the president being disingenuous or was he genuinely confused about the objectives of the civil rights bill when he informed reporters at his July 3 press conference that he didn't fully understand "certain phrases" of the bill? A telephone conversation Eisenhower had with Brownell immediately after the press conference indicates that the latter may be closer to the truth. Eisenhower told Brownell (as reported by the president's personal secretary, Ann Whitman) "that some two years ago when they had discussed civil rights legislation, he had understood verbally from the Attorney General that the right of the Attorney General to go into the South was to be concerned with interference of the right to vote." He wondered "whether this bill was not somewhat more inclusive in that particular factor than had been intended." Eisenhower added that he did not understand what "any civil right" meant since "it varied from state to state and city to city."[61] While reaffirming his commitment to ensuring the right to vote, the president insisted (just as he had in the press conference) that it was not his intention to go beyond the protection of voting rights.

The 1957 civil rights bill had its origins in a draft statement Brownell presented to the full cabinet on March 9, 1956, thus fulfilling a pledge in the president's State of the Union Address that "there will soon be recommended to the Congress a program further to advance the efforts of the Government, within the area of Federal responsibility" to ensure that "every person [is] judged and measured by what he is, rather than by his color, race or religion." The attorney general made four proposals: (1) creation of a bipartisan commission mentioned in the State of the Union message; (2) amendment of existing statutes to further protect the right to vote; (3) amendment of existing statutes to further protect other rights; and (4) creation of an assistant attorney general to head a new civil rights division.

In the subsequent discussion, Ezra Taft Benson, HEW Secretary Marion Folsom, Treasury Secretary George Humphrey, and Harold Stassen all questioned the wisdom of going beyond the establishment of a bipartisan commission. Progress, argued Humphrey, "must be evolutionary . . . [and] must accent *moderation.*" Benson echoed that we must "be on the side of patience," and Folsom hoped the president would "find occasion to speak clearly on [the] need for calmness and *moderation.*" The "great danger," Stassen agreed, was in "moving too fast." Brownell's counterargument was that these proposals—by allowing the Department of Justice to employ civil rather than criminal remedies—would give the department more flexibility and enable them to avoid having to resort to more drastic measures such as sending in troops. Without them, he maintained, "we have no basis for acting in these incidents except to throw people in jail. These would allow us to take moderate action." This debate shows that both Brownell and his opponents on this issue were keenly attuned to the fact that to sway the president it was necessary to show how one's suggestions served the cause of moderation.[62]

The March 9 meeting shows Eisenhower in essential agreement with Brownell's objectives. The president thought the four-point program was "O.K." as long as the attorney general included in the presentation a statement "that what is needed is calmness and sanity." Eisenhower believed the proposals—especially the emphasis on civil rather than criminal recourse—were, as Brownell claimed, "ameliorative," "moderate," and "mild" and dissented from the critics' view that they were "moving too rapidly." The attorney general, Eisenhower concluded, "should put forward what he has got here, but with a statement that many Americans understandably are separated by deep emotions on this subject," a message that Eisenhower tirelessly preached in all of his public statements on the subject.[63] Although Ike closed by instructing Brownell to bring the revised statement back for a final review before submitting it to Congress, he gave no indication that he would balk at any of these proposals.[64]

A revised message, presented to the cabinet on March 23, began, as Eisenhower had requested, by recognizing the "deep emotions" that divided the country on this issue and called for "restraint, calm judgment and understanding." This time, however, Brownell's proposal met with a decidedly more chilly reception from the president. The session opened with Eisenhower telling Brownell that he was having a "terrible time getting through your brief." As in the previous meeting, Brownell insisted that "going under civil law rather than criminal would have a calming effect." But Eisenhower now expressed doubts that section three would have the ameliorative effect predicted by Brownell. The attorney general tried to reassure the president that the Justice Department "wouldn't use the power to the extreme" and argued that it would have "good preventive effect." Perhaps sensing the president's concern, Brownell said he was "willing and eager to accept lay judgement on this," admitting that "as lawyers we may take too technical a view." What was needed, Eisenhower reminded Brownell, was "good sense and moderation—rather than get[ting] more laws on [the] books only to have them defied."[65]

The danger of legislating social mores, and the consequent need for a more gradual approach, was echoed by Dulles, Benson, Folsom, and Wilson. Folsom argued that the controversial sections should be left to the bipartisan commission, a proposal that appealed to Eisenhower's instinct for remaining aloof from controversy.[66] Realizing that he was losing the battle over the definition of what constituted a moderate program, Brownell now retreated from his earlier tack and instead insisted that leaving the voting rights and wider civil rights provisions for a commission to study "would be moderation but no progress."

Throughout the cabinet discussion, Eisenhower exhibited a bewildering mix of conflicting sentiments. He wanted "to put something that [we] can show as an advance" but also wanted "to make sure that we don't go further than moderate intelligent people." Although the president still believed that the voting rights section was "moderate," he could not deny Folsom's point that the South "won't see it that way" and acknowledged that "any broadening of authority is going to be resented." While complaining that "Southern Democrats have gone so far that anything ameliorating we propose and regard as an advance gets attacked," Eisenhower simultaneously criticized civil rights advocates who didn't understand "how deep this emotion is in the South" and would, by pressing too hard for advances, provoke a backlash that would set back race relations. The president finally confessed that he was "at sea on this." With the cabinet at an impasse, the president asked Brownell to come and see him later.[67]

That afternoon Brownell met with the president and gave him a revised statement of the civil rights program. Although Eisenhower repeated his concern that "the program would be regarded in the southern states as an extension of Federal power," he agreed to let Brownell "go ahead with it if he wished." Eisenhower thus disregarded the advice of Sherman Adams and Gerald Morgan that "the statement should not go up unless and until the President was more convinced in his own mind that it was the right thing to do."[68] Brownell has explained that Eisenhower allowed him to send up the controversial parts of the program (as departmental rather than administration proposals) because he "knew how deeply I felt about the importance of them."[69] The president's decision to defer to Brownell, despite not being fully persuaded that the program was "the right thing to do," is testimony to the president's strong predisposition to allow (in the absence of strong, contrary presidential preferences) a trusted cabinet member like Brownell to pursue what that cabinet member believed to be good public policy.[70]

In view of Eisenhower's grave reservations about the wisdom of the Justice Department plan—particularly section three, which dealt with federal protection of undefined "civil rights"—one should be wary of glib talk of lightning rods. Brownell was not a passive agent announcing and administering Eisenhower's policy, as the lightning rod metaphor might suggest, but instead was himself actively involved in the formulation of that policy. If Brownell took most of the heat for section three it was only proper because it was he, and not the president, who pressed for it. Delegation was thus not without its hazards for Eisenhower, because it pulled him into controversies that he might otherwise have avoided.

One must be careful, however, not to exaggerate the differences between Eisenhower and his attorney general. The evidence does not support the claim made by J. W. Anderson, in *Eisenhower, Brownell, and the Congress* (1963), that there was a "profound difference [on the civil rights bill] . . . between the President and his Justice Department," nor that Brownell had "overstepped the line that divided initiative from insubordination" by sending up the voting rights provision and section three over White House objections.[71] Some White House staff members might grumble about the "Department of Just Us," but Eisenhower himself did not.[72] Brownell did not, as Anderson argues, slyly defy Eisenhower's wishes; rather, in the case of section three Eisenhower deferred to the judgment of a cabinet member he admired and trusted immensely, and in the case of the voting rights provision Eisenhower and Brownell were in close accord.[73]

Although Eisenhower was at first reluctant to have himself publicly identified with the voting rights provision (and hence unwilling to put it on his legislative "must" list in 1956), Eisenhower's private comments reveal that he fully supported this provision—in contrast not only to section three but also to the *Brown* decision about which he harbored severe misgivings.[74] As he explained in a press conference the following year, "If in every locality every person . . . is permitted to vote he has got a means of . . . getting what he wants in democratic government."[75] He echoed these sentiments to Republican legislative leaders, telling them that section three had only "beclouded the issue," for if blacks can get the right to vote they can protect themselves, and "the Republican party can stand on that."[76]

The president's strong commitment to the voting rights provision and his uncertainty over section three can be seen from his sharply contrasting reactions to setbacks to the respective provisions. When Congress eliminated section three from the bill, Eisenhower expressed no regret, publicly or privately.[77] Passage of the jury-trial amendment to the voting rights section, however, put the president in a foul mood. He opened the cabinet meeting the day after the Senate action by telling the assembled members that there was "not much forgiveness in my soul. We've taken political defeats in the past four years, but this one is the worst" because it affected "a basic principle of the United States."[78] This private expression of disgust was followed by a public statement excoriating the jury-trial amendment for tending to "weaken our whole Judicial system" and making "largely ineffective the basic purpose of the bill—that of protecting promptly and effectively every American in his right to vote."[79]

Until late July, Eisenhower had carefully maintained his distance from the heated controversy over the jury-trial amendment. In public he repeatedly said that such a question was too complicated and legalistic for a nonlawyer like him. Go ask Brownell instead, he would say. In private, however, he expressed unqualified support for Brownell's position. It was "wrong," Eisenhower told Press Secretary James Hagerty in a prepress conference briefing in mid-April, "to put [voting rights violations] in the hands of a jury."[80] Eisenhower's handling of the jury-trial amendment thus reveals, as Greenstein's "hidden-hand" thesis predicts, a substantial discrepancy between the public and private Eisenhower. Here Eisenhower's ambiguous public stance does seem to have been part of a conscious (albeit, as we have seen above, flawed) strategy to deflect responsibility for a controversial position that he fully endorsed onto his attorney general.

But to see Eisenhower's behavior on the civil rights bill as fully vindicating Greenstein's hidden-hand thesis would be inaccurate. Although the hidden-hand thesis makes sense of Eisenhower's actions in the case of the jury-trial amendment, the concept does not do justice to Eisenhower's involvement with section three of the bill. Here Eisenhower's public uncertainty mirrored his own private doubts and even confusion. Although his own political instincts and his other political advisers clearly warned the president of the political dangers of Brownell's more controversial proposals, Eisenhower reluctantly decided to defer to Brownell's judgment and preferences. In part, this decision must be seen as evidence of Eisenhower's own conflicting emotions on the subject of race, torn as he was between feeling that lasting progress on race relations required gradual measures that moderate southern whites could accept and his equally strong feeling of the injustice of denying blacks basic civil rights. But in part, too, the decision reveals Eisenhower's preference for deferring to trusted cabinet members whenever possible. The evidence, in this case at least, points not to Machiavellian guile but to an administrator who genuinely believed in giving subordinates the authority to make their own judgments and mistakes.

Both the "hidden hand" Ike of the jury-trial amendment and the deferential Ike of section three are an integral part of the Eisenhower blame-avoidance leadership style. Indeed it was Eisenhower's delegation and deference to trusted aides that made the periodic dissembling of his hidden hand possible. Because in so many cases he genuinely did defer to his aides' judgment it then became possible in other cases for the president to avoid responsibility for views or policies he fully endorsed. To try the hidden hand without the deference would soon expose any president to deafening, even disabling, cries of deception, distortion, even lying.

LIMITS OF THE LIGHTNING ROD

Presidents who pursue a lightning rod strategy must be prepared for the strategy's limits. Those limits are probably most evident in the Little Rock confrontation. Eisenhower's decision to send federal troops into Little Rock necessitated putting the president onto the front lines unflanked and unprotected. Such a decision had to be announced and defended publicly by the president, and the president had to take full responsibility for it privately as well.[81] Neither Brownell nor anyone else could protect Eisenhower at this point from bearing the brunt of the wrath of southern whites. Moreover, and more interesting, Eisenhower's reliance on Brownell as a lightning rod before the showdown may have contributed to the need for a public confrontation by giving Faubus the mistaken impression that it was Brownell rather than Eisenhower who wanted Faubus to comply with the federal court order.

In the struggle over civil rights legislation, Eisenhower was faced with a trade-off between deflecting blame onto Brownell and getting civil rights legislation through Congress.[82] To defeat the administration's civil rights bill, congressional opponents of the bill were more than willing to vilify the attorney general and grant that the president did not know what was in the bill. In the case of the proposed jury-trial amendment, Eisenhower was confronted with the choice of publicly identifying himself with a controversial provision of the bill or seeing the bill compromised by an amendment that he privately opposed. Only in late July, far too late to affect congressional deliberations, did the president publicly and unambiguously oppose the jury-trial provision. To the extent that Eisenhower regarded such a compromise as making (in his words) "largely ineffective the basic purpose of the bill," his strategy of distancing himself from this provision seems to have poorly served his policy objectives.

Finally, the civil rights case study reveals limitations to the lightning rod metaphor as such. More specifically, the metaphor can be misleading if one assumes that a cabinet member who absorbs criticism is only announcing and executing policy set by the president. In order to make Brownell a plausible lightning rod, Eisenhower delegated not only responsibility but authority. Brownell was not simply taking the heat for the president's policy; he was instrumental in making that policy.

As Brownell's recently published memoirs make clear, it was the attorney general and not the president who took the initiative in pressing for civil rights legislation. "The initiatives," Brownell freely concedes, "rested on my shoulders." Brownell admits that he "could have responded to the political pressures on the administration to propose new civil rights legislation with a weak bill that offered a lot of pious words about racial equality and simply brought forward again the orthodox solutions previously proposed."[83] Implicit here is the admission that Eisenhower would have had no difficulty supporting Brownell if the attorney general had proposed a watered down civil rights bill.

While Brownell received the greatest burden of public criticism for section three, the attorney general was also the person responsible for the provision.[84] Left to his own instincts for shunning controversy in this contentious area, Eisenhower would certainly have preferred to avoid such a contentious proposal, instead limiting the legislation to voting rights and proceeding in the area of more broadly defined civil rights only where the federal government had clear authority to act unilaterally—as Eisenhower did in desegregating the armed forces—or where he could effect change indirectly and gradually—as he did in appointing moderate federal judges.[85] Delegating decision-making power to Brownell, although intended to deflect criticism away from the president, thus helped contribute to the very political firestorm that Eisenhower had hoped to avoid.

Having accented the limits of Eisenhower's lightning rod strategy, it is also worth remembering what Eisenhower did achieve. After all, Eisenhower did pass the first civil rights bill since Reconstruction, something that Franklin Roosevelt and Harry Truman had failed to do. Though Eisenhower was genuinely upset about the inclusion of the jury-trial amendment, the Civil Rights Act of 1957 did take a credible first step in the direction of protecting voting rights for blacks. The opposition to the final bill among both black civil rights leaders and southern segregationists, moreover, suggests that the law struck the sort of balance between progress and moderation that Eisenhower originally sought. At the same time, before Little Rock Eisenhower had been able to contain much of the political fallout in the South. Though hardly Teflon coated, Eisenhower did manage to deflect a substantial amount of blame for the administration's civil rights positions onto Brownell.

If Eisenhower would have done better, in view of his own misgivings, to instruct Brownell unequivocally in the spring of 1956 to omit section three from the bill, it is the type of mistake that inevitably accompanies an administrative style that gives cabinet members genuine autonomy and discretion. Richard Neustadt might with reason chide Eisenhower for forgetting that "no on else sits where he sits, or sees quite as he sees,"[86] yet it is equally true that the president cannot afford to sit where everybody else sits. A president who consistently tries to substitute his own judgment for the judgment of even his most trusted aides is a president who will be continually overextended and overexposed. The president who is serious about blame avoidance must be prepared to cede not only responsibility but power. If that is a limit of the lightning rod strategy, it is also its strength.

8

Blame Avoidance and
Political Accountability:
What Have We Learned?

The reader searching for the Rosetta stone that will turn presidential lore into presidential laws will be sorely disappointed. We have unearthed no precise formulas for identifying let alone predicting the existence of lightning rods. Nor have we discovered invariable laws that specify how presidents can deflect blame onto subordinates. Politics, unfortunately, is not like physics. The cases are too few, the variables too numerous, and our ability to hold variables constant too limited.[1]

Generalizations about lightning rods must be constructed upon an inhospitable terrain in which exceptions leap readily to mind and contingency and idiosyncrasy abound. For some people this will suggest that time spent on such ground is wasted. Let us rather devote our limited time and resources, some will suggest, to fields of inquiry better able to support cumulative bodies of theory. But this allows methodological techniques to dictate the questions we allow ourselves to ask. That we cannot bring a mathematical or statistical precision to the lightning rod relationship does not make the relationship any less important. If a unified theory of lightning rods is too much to expect, political scientists can still hope to contribute to our understanding of lightning rods by questioning the premises that political actors take for granted.[2] Political science's contribution comes in showing how proverbial wisdom ("look before you leap") is contradictory ("he who hesitates is lost") and thus empty or misleading. By identifying conditions under which such claims are valid, political science can help reconcile the contradictory certainties so characteristic of conventional wisdom. If this is a relatively unheroic conception of political science, it is also a more relevant conception for the enduring questions relating to political leadership in general and blame avoidance in particular.

THE LIGHTNING ROD CONCEPT REEXAMINED

What then have we learned about lightning rods and blame avoidance in the modern presidency? The patient reader, having made her way through the cases examined in this book, may have learned, at a minimum, to approach the lightning rod concept with caution. Such caution is mandatory, first, because it is difficult empirically to distinguish presidential lightning rods from liabilities and, second, because the metaphor often obscures critical aspects of the relationship between president, adviser, and audience. Such caution, unfortunately, is all too often missing in journalistic accounts, which use the term casually and on the basis of scant evidence.

More reason still to be skeptical of lightning rod claims is that they are more often than not political claims. Lightning rod status is often ascribed to justify or advance personal and policy agendas rather than to describe accurately an empirical relationship.[3] When James Watt and his allies, for instance, described Watt as a lightning rod, they were not trying to describe reality so much as to shape it. In claiming the mantle of lightning rod, Watt could justify his actions (to himself and to others) as being in the best interests of the president and thus neutralize those critics calling for his resignation.

Watt is not alone in using the lightning rod designation to justify his actions. In 1986, for instance, Reagan's communications director, Pat Buchanan, countered Democratic charges that his inflammatory rhetoric[4] had been largely responsible for the defeat of a bill to aid the Nicaraguan contras by insisting: "Pat Buchanan is a lightning rod. . . . The Democrats attacked Pat Buchanan because they are not comfortable attacking the President."[5] Obscured by Buchanan's lightning rod self-designation is the question of whether his rhetoric made it easier for Democrats to oppose the president's policy. In the wake of the 1988 presidential campaign, to take another example, those around Dan Quayle peddled a version of the campaign that had Quayle serving a valuable function as a lightning rod for President George Bush.[6] A number of Democrats, too, bought into this version of events because it allowed them to attribute Michael Dukakis's defeat to strategic failures rather than to failures of party policy or ideology. That the evidence for such claims was weak did not matter to the principals involved for whom this was a political rather than a scientific question.

Talk of "lightning rods" is often little more than administration officials attempting to put the best gloss on a bad situation. This is arguably the case, for instance, with the previously mentioned comment (see Chapter 3) by an unnamed presidential aide who told reporter Steve Weisman that President Reagan "feels that he ought not to be answering questions about the B-1 bomber or anything else that specific. . . . His job is to announce broad policy. Let Cap Weinberger take the heat on the B-1."[7] Weisman does not point out that the unnamed aide's comment came only a few days after Reagan announced to reporters a plan to modernize U.S. forces by building one hundred B-1 bombers. After reading a prepared statement, Reagan announced he would answer a few questions and then turn the podium over to Weinberger "for all the technical matters." But Reagan, as Lou Cannon observes, "couldn't deal with even the nontechnical matters." After stumbling through three or four questions, in what Cannon characterized as a "sorry performance," Reagan turned the questions over to Weinberger.[8]

As these examples suggest, the rhetoric of lightning rods is often little more than a way of covering up failure, from oneself as well as from others. Rather than opening up inquiry, the lightning rod label can become a way of closing it off, of wrapping oneself or others in a righteous mantle of self-justification while ignoring the damaging consequences of provocative or inept behavior. That political actors try to portray themselves in the most positive light is hardly remarkable. More surprising is that journalists so frequently and uncritically repeat these claims. Conventional wisdom is made, unmade, and remade with such startling rapidity because its empirical underpinnings are so slight and its conceptual foundations so sloppy.

The lightning rod concept can be particularly unhelpful or misleading because of what it allows us to overlook or assume. By wrapping himself in the lightning rod mantle, Pat Buchanan obscures the question of whether in the absence of his charged rhetoric congressional Democrats might have supported the president's policy. One needs to ask not just Buchanan's question—are the Democrats attacking Buchanan because they don't want to attack the president directly—but also the question of effectiveness. Would the Reagan administration have been more successful in achieving its ends in this domain by taking a less confrontational approach? It would be dangerous indeed if presidents were to assume that a subordinate serving as a lightning rod was sufficient to justify the adviser's behavior, for it avoids the tough counterfactual question of whether the president's policy objectives would be better served by public confrontation or behind-the-scenes conciliation.

In the case of Watt, Reagan failed to ask himself this question early enough. Even if Reagan had concluded that Watt's behavior was not damaging to him personally (a conclusion, I believe, that was mistaken, at least by 1982), he still needed to ask whether Watt's confrontational style was getting in the way of achieving his objectives in environmental and land-use policy. The evidence strongly suggests that Watt undermined these objectives by discrediting Republican positions and bolstering the cohesiveness of the opposition. Moreover, the subsequent tenure of Donald Hodell suggests that the Reagan administration was able to get much more of what it wanted at less cost through Hodell's low-key approach than through Watt's high-voltage politics.[9]

To say that presidents need to think seriously about staying out of trouble and avoiding blame is not, therefore, to recommend that a president rush out to fill his ranks with confrontational cranks and vocal extremists. A concern for blame avoidance means, if anything, more rather than less compromise. Nor is it to suggest that high-visibility advisers are necessarily preferable to low-profile advisers. Quietly working behind the scenes to bring the rival sides together may defuse conflict and keep the president out of trouble. To say that a president should think about blame avoidance *is* to say that presidents need always to think about what will happen when (not if) things go badly. Among the things that will help when things go wrong is having subordinates of sufficient stature and independent authority that they can plausibly serve as targets of criticism.

To think about lightning rods is inevitably to think counterfactually. Because we can never rerun the reel of history to definitively determine what would have happened if a particular actor had behaved in one way rather than another, lightning rod claims will always be politically contested. That the lightning rod concept may be used for political purposes, however, does not mean that the concept is empty or that we should abandon it. It is possible to marshal empirical evidence to falsify such claims through systematic data collection and carefully chosen comparisons. Moreover, under whatever label the concept goes, the lightning rod idea raises questions that are central to any political science worthy of that name: How is blame deflected and attributed? How does presidential leadership style affect popular support? And how does what elites say affect what the wider public thinks?

THE BLAME GAME: IS IT DIFFERENT FOR ELITES AND THE MASSES?

What is the relationship between a president's support among elites and a president's approval among the mass public? How do elite criticisms of a president or his advisers influence public opinion? Are the dynamics of the lightning rod different for elites and for the mass public? We do not know, as Bert Rockman points out with understatement, "all that we need to about the causal dynamics between presidential esteem in various elite sectors and that in the general public."[10] Presidential scholars do have a fairly good sense of the ways in which public prestige affects presidential influence at the elite level,[11] but they understand much less well how presidential effectiveness and elite judgments about that effectiveness affect a president's popularity.

One school of thought suggests that a president's standing in the Washington political community bears at best only a tenuous relationship with his popularity in the country as a whole. Because politics for most people is "a sideshow in the great circus of life,"[12] the determinant of presidential approval at the mass level is not what elites say or how they say it, most of which the public doesn't follow, so much as the outcomes, particularly economic ones, that directly affect the day-to-day life of citizens. "Behind [the public's] judgments of [presidential] performance," Richard Neustadt argues, "lie the consequences in their lives . . . paychecks, grocery bills, children's schooling, sons at war."[13] "Inside the beltway" stories about a president's administration, in this view, are too distant from people's lives to shape their evaluation of a president.

Support for this theory comes from the striking success some economic models have had in predicting the presidential vote. Using only a few basic economic variables, Yale economist Roy Fair predicted Bush's 1988 victory over Dukakis within three-tenths of a percent, without taking into account any information about Boston Harbor, Willie Horton, or even Michael Dukakis. In 1992, however, Fair's model (indeed all economic models) fared poorly: Fair predicted that Bush would receive 55.7 percent of the two-party popular vote when in fact he got less than 47 percent.[14] In the 1992 election there was clearly significant slippage between objective economic reality and the perception of that reality. Enter elite evaluations.

A second hypothesis is that the mass public's judgments about presidential performance are significantly cued by elite judgments. David Gergen articulates this view: "Once the Washington crowd takes your measure and finds you wanting, that has a ripple effect. It's like throwing a stone into a pond. It ripples out across the country and eventually does hurt a president."[15] This view of the relationship between elite judgments and public approval was frequently invoked to explain President Carter's difficulties. Haynes Johnson, for example, argued that "private judgments [of Carter] quickly became public ones—and were transmitted to the country at large."[16]

Empirical support for this version of the elite-mass linkage can be found, among other places, in Richard Brody's study of the determinants of presidential popularity. Brody demonstrates the crucial role played by politicians' responses and media coverage in shaping public perceptions of a president's performance.[17] Citizens rally around the flag in the face of an international crisis not out of an instinctive patriotism, Brody shows, but because elite assessments of presidential performance become more positive during such events. Even economic figures, Brody shows and Bush's experience confirms, do not directly impress themselves on citizens. Rather, these events are mediated by elite evaluations.

Samuel Kernell reconciles these two rival hypotheses by suggesting that during the time of Truman and Eisenhower it may have been true that a president's standing among elites bore little relation to his approval in the country but that this no longer holds for today's presidents. "Washington has changed," argues Kernell. This transformation came about not because citizens have gotten more attentive to or more sophisticated about politics but simply because "citizens are exposed to more—and more critical—information about the president than ever before." This transformation in the extent to which "the American public has become privy to political relations in Washington" means that today, unlike in Eisenhower's time, "what others in Washington have to say about the president may shape what the rest of the country thinks of him."[18]

If Kernell is correct, his thesis has important implications for our understanding of blame avoidance. To begin with, it suggests that Eisenhower's popularity (though not his support at the elite level) was largely unrelated to his use of subordinates as lightning rods and to his hidden-hand strategy more generally. It also means that contemporary presidents may become increasingly reliant on lightning rods to maintain public support. An additional implication of Kernell's argument is that conclusions drawn from Eisenhower's time may be inapplicable to today's presidents.

Kernell's synthesis is intuitively plausible, but ultimately, I think, it fails.[19] To sustain his thesis, Kernell needs to show that citizens have become more aware over time of "political relations in Washington." Because comparisons over time are fraught with difficulties, it is not easy to prove or disprove such an assertion. In the early years of survey research, pollsters asked all sorts of questions that probed what the public knew about politics. But the results were so overwhelming—most of the public didn't know much—that scholars soon lost interest in the subject and pollsters stopped asking such questions.[20]

One question that researchers have consistently asked over a long period of time probes voters' ability to recall the name of congressional incumbents and challengers. These questions indicate no change in public knowledge over a thirty-year time span. Neither is there any evidence of an increase in the public's political knowledge about which political party controls the House of Representatives, a question that researchers have asked since 1960. Questions that ask people what they like or dislike about a presidential candidate or political party show no appreciable increase in the number of responses offered. Nor has there been an increase over time in the electorate's ability to perceive differences between the parties.[21] In short, those few questions that address change over time in the electorate's political knowledge undercut Kernell's claim that there has been a change, let alone transformation, in public awareness of political relations in Washington since Eisenhower's time.[22]

If we are to reconcile the two rival hypotheses about the elite-mass relationship, we must do it some other way than fitting the two into distinct, chronological stages. Moreover, such a formulation must account both for the continuing low levels of political awareness or knowledge and for the continuing discrepancies between objective, especially economic, indicators and presidential support. Such a formulation must begin by recognizing the tremendous variation in political awareness within the mass public and the consequent variation in the levels of exposure to elite discourse.

Within the general public there is an extraordinary range of attentiveness to and knowledge about politics. Many people are almost totally inattentive to elite discourse. A 1986 National Election Study (NES), for instance, found that close to 20 percent of the American public could not identify any of the government jobs held by George Bush, Caspar Weinberger, William Rehnquist, Paul Volcker, Robert Dole, or Tip O'Neill.[23] For this segment of the electorate, attention to political relations in Washington is far too sporadic for elite discourse to have much, if any, impact upon how these voters view a president. Presidential lightning rods can play no significant role here.

At the other end of the spectrum is a highly informed segment of the population who, as Neustadt says, "make an avocation of the watchfulness vocationally imposed on Washingtonians."[24] This part of the population would certainly include the 4 percent of the general public who were able to identify each one of the jobs held by Bush, Weinberger, Rehnquist, Volcker, Dole, and O'Neill. It might also reasonably be extended to include the additional 13 percent who were able to identify four or five of these individuals. This segment of the general public often pays sufficient attention to differentiate between the positions and personas of presidents and certain prominent subordinates. Moreover, though these people are attentive enough to be influenced by elite discourse, they are probably not close enough to the drama to be able to see through the lightning rod ruse. Among this highly informed part of the population, then, we might expect lightning rods to play an important role.

In between these extremes, of course, lies a range of attentiveness and knowledge. It would be a mistake to write off more than four-fifths of the population as totally immune to elite discourse about the presidency. Halfway through Eisenhower's second term, close to 60 percent of the general public could "recall offhand" the name of the secretary of agriculture and the secretary of state.[25] Indeed more people could recall the names of Ezra Taft Benson and John Foster Dulles than could recall the name of their own congressman.[26] Benson and Dulles were, to be sure, unusually visible cabinet officials, but it is not uncommon for a third or more of the population to be able to identify correctly the jobs of prominent cabinet officials. In the above-mentioned 1986 NES survey, for instance, one-third of respondents were able to identify Caspar Weinberger's job as secretary of defense.[27] Even George Humphrey, Eisenhower's relatively low-profile treasury secretary, was correctly identified by 28 percent of respondents.[28]

Attentiveness to politics, moreover, varies not just among individuals but within individuals. For farmers, for instance, the Department of Agriculture is more salient than are the Departments of Labor or Education. Individuals who are inattentive to most issues may be highly attentive to a narrow band of issues that directly affect them or people like them. The concrete, personal consequences of policies that Neustadt highlights thus may generate closer attentiveness to the flow of elite messages on the part of particular segments of the public in particular policy areas. This may, in turn, open up an avenue for elite messages to shape public opinion and thus create the conditions necessary for the construction of presidential lightning rods.

Such a dynamic appears to have operated in the case of Benson. Farmers were more likely to know who Benson was and to have an opinion about Benson than was the general population. A survey conducted by Gallup at the outset of 1958, for instance, found that the general population (44 percent) was almost twice as likely as farmers (23 percent) to have no opinion about Benson's performance.[29] Because price-support policies affected farmers directly, farmers paid significantly closer attention than the general public to elite discourse in this area.[30] Contra Neustadt, the existence of a direct personal or group interest in a policy thus can generate the attentiveness to elite messages necessary for a lightning rod strategy to affect public perceptions of a president.

Attentiveness and information are, of course, no obstacle to the effective use of lightning rods at the elite level. Those within the Washington community pay close enough attention to national politics that they can readily differentiate between even the most subtle differences in administration personas and positions. One might thus expect lightning rods to be most viable at the elite level. However, elites are also much more likely to be able to see through the ruse. As participants rather than just spectators in the political drama they are often in a position to know or at least strongly suspect that an administration official is doing something at the direct request of a president.

Elites who see through the ruse, however, may still criticize a presidential subordinate and spare the president direct attack for strategic reasons of their own. After being selected Senate majority leader, Lyndon Johnson explicitly instructed his fellow Democrats to "lay off of Eisenhower. If you want to attack somebody, attack one of his Cabinet members or something of that sort, but just don't get yourself out on a limb harping at the President and get the party identified with too much opposition to Eisenhower."[31] Many of the elite criticisms of Brownell, as we saw in Chapter 7, are best viewed as a product of the strategic calculations of civil rights opponents not to criticize directly a popular president. Similar strategic calculations by elites can be found throughout presidential history, particularly when an incumbent president is popular.[32]

The strategic calculations made by elites in attributing blame make the blame-attribution process a significantly different phenomenon at the elite than at the mass level. Because elites are players in the political game they have interpersonal relations to preserve and objectives to gain. Who to blame is thus in large part a strategic question. Political strategy, in contrast, almost by definition plays no role in the public's decision about who to blame. An explanation for the public's decision about where to place blame can be framed almost exclusively in terms of the flow of information and the social psychological ways that information is processed.[33]

This is not to imply that all lightning rods at the elite level reflect elite strategy. Indeed the need to preserve access can make the psychological pressures on political elites to believe in a leader's good intentions even greater. Elites are no different from other people in wanting to believe that the president is sympathetic to their views. Strategy matters in understanding blame avoidance at the elite level, not because elites are more clear headed or rational than the mass public, but rather because, unlike the mass public, political elites have strategic interests that can be rationally advanced by placing blame upon presidential subordinates.

Even at close proximity to a president, however, it is often extremely difficult for political elites to tell when a subordinate is speaking for a president or for herself. Even Secretary of State Al Haig, as we saw in Chapter 6, professed to be uncertain whether what Ed Meese or Jim Baker said in public reflected the president's or their own views on foreign policy. Because there is an inevitable ambiguity about who is talking when a subordinate speaks in the name of a president, skillful presidents have plenty of room, even at the elite level, to create effective lightning rods.

That elites see through a lightning rod may, in any event, not matter much, so long as elites carry on as if they believe it. For the attentive public, it is not the motives of the critics but the critics' message that matters most in their appraisal of presidential performance. Popularity thereby becomes its own shield. Reluctant to criticize a popular president, elites aim their criticism at other targets, thus helping to sustain a president's popularity. But the moment a president's popularity drops, the distinction introduced in Chapter 1 between the "strong" lightning rod hypothesis—that critics attack a subordinate because they believe that person is corrupting a president's good intentions—and a "weak" lightning rod hypothesis—that opponents, for tactical reasons, choose to criticize the subordinate rather than the president—becomes enormously consequential.

In Chapter 3, for instance, we saw that environmental elites were suspicious of Reagan from the start but initially held back from criticizing him directly for tactical reasons. As Reagan's popularity began to tumble and without any evidence that the president was or would become sympathetic to their cause, environmental groups abandoned their initial strategy of targeting Watt alone in favor of direct attacks on President Reagan as well. The steady flow of negative elite evaluations badly tarnished Reagan's environmental image with the wider public until, by the beginning of 1983, he was widely seen as a co-conspirator in the effort to despoil America's land, water, and air.

The general public, then, is far from immune to elite discourse. What elites say does seem to matter to how the public evaluates a president. President Bush fell so far and so fast in public estimation in 1992 not just because the economy was weak but also because when he appeared vulnerable, disaffected elites buried him with a volley of direct, personal criticism. This is not to disregard the well-established maxim of survey research that the issues and controversies that animate those inside the beltway often leave the larger public untouched. It is well to remember that at the height of Watergate, more than 30 percent of the American public admitted having never heard the name of H. R. (Bob) Haldeman.[34] And as David Stockman was supposedly becoming a "household name" as the point man for the Reagan administration's budget initiatives in the early 1980s, more than 40 percent of the American public conceded that they hadn't heard enough about Stockman to form an impression of him.[35] After Jim Baker had served four years as Reagan's chief of staff, 50 percent of the American public confessed to being "not familiar with that person at all."[36] Nothing new here.

But public opinion data also suggest that it would be a mistake to regard the lightning rod phenomenon purely as an elite phenomenon. Significant segments of the general public can identify prominent administration officials. Moreover, important segments of the public do make distinctions between their evaluation of a president and their evaluation of a subordinate. In the case of Benson, for instance, close to 40 percent of the general public (and 50 percent of farmers) with an opinion about both Eisenhower and Benson evaluated the secretary differently than they did the president. Even in the case of Dulles, where attitudes toward the president and secretary of state were much more closely coupled, almost one quarter of the public evaluated Dulles and Eisenhower differently.[37] Although the mass public cannot be written out of the lightning rod equation, it must be conceded that as we move the lightning rod concept into the area of elite-mass linkages we move onto much more uncertain and uncharted ground. We know very little about how criticism or praise at the elite level is processed at the mass public level. We do not know, for instance, the extent to which elite criticisms of a presidential subordinate are processed by the mass public as negative evaluations of the president himself. To answer this sort of question requires further research of a different, more experimental kind that goes beyond the scope of this book.[38] It is research that needs to be done, however, if we are to get beyond the contradictory certainties that characterize conventional wisdom on this topic.

If this book cannot speak as directly to this particular issue as one would

like, the evidence compiled here does provide compelling reasons for rejecting Neustadt's view that elite discourse and public evaluations are largely independent realms and for rejecting Kernell's argument that the elite-mass
linkage has been transformed over the last several decades. The data from
the Eisenhower administration strongly suggest that any transformation in
public awareness of political relations in Washington had already taken
place by Eisenhower's time. What I want to highlight is neither the low levels
of public awareness of elite discourse, as Neustadt's model would, nor the
transformation in levels of public awareness of elite discourse over time, as
Kernell's model does, but rather the great variations in public awareness of
administration officials that occur within and across presidencies. Why in
some cases is the difference between how a president is perceived and how a
subordinate is perceived rather large and in other cases quite small? What, if
anything, is it possible to say about the conditions under which presidents
will be able to deflect blame and to distance themselves from controversial
policies or subordinates? These are the questions I want to take up in the
subsequent sections.

THE EISENHOWER MODEL: MAKING LIGHTNING
RODS WORK

What was it that enabled President Eisenhower to deflect blame onto key subordinates? Eisenhower certainly was not unique in wanting to deflect responsibility for negative outcomes or controversial policies onto subordinates. Any
number of accounts testify to the ubiquity of this impulse among modern presidents. Even Lyndon Johnson, despite his hunger for occupying the center of
the political stage, often expressed concern with keeping bad or controversial
news away from the president. On one occasion, for instance, when White
House aide Harry McPherson informed the president that House Ways and
Means chair Wilbur Mills and majority floor leader Carl Albert were contest-
ing an anticipated Department of Agriculture decision on milk price supports,
the president responded, "Get Mills and Albert with [Secretary of Agriculture
Orville] Freeman and get [the] president out of this."[39] Not long after the Kennedy assassination, Johnson told Secretary of the Interior Stewart Udall: "I'm
from an oil state; oil's a very controversial subject. I want to have a relationship
that Roosevelt and Ickes had. I want you to make all the oil decisions, you to
run the oil program; I want oil out of the White House." Johnson instructed
Udall to go out and "tell the reporters this," which Udall promptly did, informing the press that the president "expects the major and final responsibility [on
oil prices] to rest with me and my department."[40]

   Such anecdotes suggest that President Johnson did try to use cabinet members as lightning rods. This should come as no surprise. He was a highly skilled

politician and understood the risks of being drawn into politically controversial or unpopular ventures. And if he forgot, members of his staff kept up a steady stream of advice extolling the virtues of lowering the president's public profile and building up cabinet members as lightning rods. White House special assistant Tom Johnson, for example, informed the president:

> It is my view that you have become so closely associated with all the major issues which face this country that you are suffering from it. . . . I believe a better course would be to have your decisions and feeling on a particular matter voiced through the Cabinet and through the agency heads who are most directly concerned with the issue. Let them shoulder more of the burden for the faults of their programs. Rather than the President losing popularity for weaknesses, it seems more appropriate for the department head to receive the criticism.[41]

The puzzle is explaining why such efforts failed.

The first impediment was Johnson's desire to get credit for all the good things that happened on his watch. "Whenever an agency of the government had good news," political scientist Nelson Polsby reports, "there was a standing order to send it to the White House for announcement."[42] This practice of taking credit for the positive might seem, at first glance, to be perfectly consistent with a lightning rod strategy of deflecting responsibility for negative outcomes. But taking credit for all that is good makes it difficult to avoid being blamed for the bad. A credit-claiming strategy is incompatible with a blame-avoidance strategy.[43] For starters, good news can quickly sour. A leader cannot credibly take credit for a positive turn of events on one day, and the next day expect the blame to fall on others when conditions suddenly deteriorate. The secret to President Eisenhower's success was that he allowed subordinates to take credit as well as blame. By building subordinates up, they were also there to be torn down.

Johnson's difficulty, as Rowland Evans and Robert Novak put it, was that he "did not care for limelight-sharing."[44] Perhaps more than any other president in American history, Johnson worried about being upstaged by subordinates getting positive press.[45] We have already shown the lengths Johnson went to deny positive press to his vice president. Humphrey, however, was by no means unique in this regard. National Security Assistant McGeorge Bundy too found that "Johnson became annoyed when he felt that Bundy was getting too much personal publicity."[46] Perhaps one of the reasons that Dean Rusk and Johnson got along so well was that, according to Rusk's biographer, "it was part of his [Rusk's] personality to be reserved, to stay out of the spotlight."[47] President Johnson's distrust of administration officials engaging in self-aggrandizement manifested itself in a directive forbidding any staff member to talk to the press without getting clearance from the press secretary. Violations of this order brought strict reprimand. For instance, when Joseph Califano wrote to President Johnson informing him that he had met with journalist Joseph Kraft to discuss a number of issues before Congress, including Medicare-Medicaid and tax credits for social programs, a furious Johnson scrawled at the bottom of the memorandum: "Joe—may I again—again ask you and all your associates to please meet with press members during your association with my administration upon request of Press Secretary [George] Christian only. This request has been made before and will not be made again."[48]

In contrast, Eisenhower never expressed concern about subordinates receiving positive publicity. On the contrary, reports Milton Eisenhower, "during his presidency, as he had done as Supreme Commander in war, [Eisenhower] almost instinctively wished to 'build up' those who worked with him."[49] "If there was something favorable to be announced from one of his Departments," recalls former White House aide Don Paarlberg, "the Secretary would do that."[50] "You'd be amazed how much you can accomplish," Eisenhower told his associates, "if you're willing to see the credit go to someone else."[51] Moreover, Eisenhower understood, as Reagan did also, that a president rarely has to worry about being upstaged by subordinates. When things go right, the president gets the credit.[52]

The image that Johnson propagated of a president in control of all facets of government—a master of Congress as well as his own administration—undermined his halting efforts to get others to absorb blame. Fostering the impression that Johnson was attentive to every policy arena had the benefit for Johnson of instilling respect and fear in the political stratum. The disadvantage was that cabinet members, staff, and vice president, even when prominently displayed, were widely perceived as little more than deputies executing a presidential directive. Generating the perception that government was a one-man show could not be reconciled with a lightning rod strategy.

Attempts to deflect blame, moreover, only increased the perception of Johnson as a dissembling politician, thus feeding the so-called credibility gap. Those advisers who urged Johnson to set up lightning rods did not sufficiently appreciate the underlying conditions that made such a strategy unviable. It was not just a matter of giving cabinet members and staff a higher public profile nor, as many within the administration argued, of the president being "overexposed."[53] The root cause of Johnson's "flypaper presidency" was his reluctance to relinquish control over decision making.

Johnson wanted to fashion cabinet members into an extension of himself. "When I looked out at the heads of my departments," Johnson explained to Doris Kearns, "I realized that while all of them had been appointed by me, *not a single one was really mine.* I could never fully depend on them to put my priorities first. . . . I was determined to turn those lordly men into good soldiers."[54] To ensure that cabinet members followed presidential preferences, Johnson instituted what one student has described as a "systematic and extensive monitoring of departments and agencies" aimed at keeping the president abreast of department activities and reminding the cabinet member that the president was watching.[55]

Eisenhower was able to deflect responsibility in large part because he was willing to cede a significant degree of control over policy making to department heads.[56] The wide band of discretion that Eisenhower granted his cabinet members is evident in the relatively free hand they had in staffing their departments,[57] as well as their license to make public statements without prior White House approval.[58] The cost of granting cabinet members autonomy, as with Brownell on civil rights, is that public policy may not always develop in precisely the direction the president prefers.[59] The benefit is to generate a climate in which it is plausible (rather than seeming disingenuous) to blame a cabinet member for a policy gone amok.

The difference between Presidents Johnson and Eisenhower, then, was not only that Eisenhower's hand was hidden while Johnson's was visible, but that Eisenhower's hand was far less intrusive. Against the backdrop of the "traditional" view of the Eisenhower presidency, one may be impressed by Ike's behind-the-scenes activism, but, set against the standard of presidents who came after, what stands out about Eisenhower is his genuine deference toward and tolerance of cabinet members.

Eisenhower's political sagacity, to repeat, did not lie solely, or even mainly, in his recognition that advisers could serve as lightning rods. Few are the presidents who have been unaware of the utility of deflecting blame onto subordinates.[60] Rather, what distinguishes Eisenhower from other presidents is that his behavior—such as tolerating discrepancies between his preferences and departmental actions and not begrudging subordinates positive publicity—contributed to a public perception that Eisenhower's subordinates operated with a significant degree of discretion. It was this perception (a perception strongly rooted in reality) of subordinate discretion that enabled Eisenhower to build up a network of effective, because plausible, lightning rods.

Detachment (or at least the appearance of detachment) from decision making is a necessary but perhaps not sufficient condition for the creation of effective lightning rods. To keep hostility targeted at the subordinate rather than the president, relevant groups must believe that were the president better informed he would be more sympathetic to their policy position than the adviser. My argument is that this belief is easier to sustain for those leaders who cloak their stance in ambiguity (or who have a genuinely ambiguous position) because it allows them to be different things to different people.

No modern president has been more successful in being different things to different people than Dwight Eisenhower.[61] A Gallup survey conducted in

May 1955 illustrates this phenomenon at the mass level. Asked whether they considered President Eisenhower "to be liberal or conservative in his political views," 49 percent believed Eisenhower to be a conservative and 42 percent pronounced him a liberal. Moreover, of those respondents who thought of themselves as liberals, 65 percent believed Eisenhower was, like them, a liberal, and only 28 percent identified him as a conservative. Of those who considered themselves conservatives, 61 percent thought the president was also a conservative, while only 32 percent felt he was a liberal.[62]

This proclivity to read into Eisenhower's political views one's own political preferences was not limited to the mass public. Highly sophisticated political elites exhibited the same tendency to see Eisenhower's underlying political predilections as being in sympathy with their own. To read memoirs or oral histories of the period is to encounter the same tale over and over again: the "real" Eisenhower was the one who agreed with the person relating the story.

One example of this is Emmet Hughes's well-known memoir, *The Ordeal of Power*. A liberal Republican and foreign-policy speech writer for Eisenhower, Hughes's account is suffused with the sense that Dulles's cold war bellicosity was perverting the underlying pacific instincts of Eisenhower. From Hughes's vantage point, there appeared to be a "chasm" between the president and his secretary. To talk of a "Dulles-Eisenhower" foreign policy, Hughes argued, was "no more sensibly descriptive than some fantastic diplomacy proclaiming itself 'radical-reactionary' or 'bellicose-pacific.' "[63] Eisenhower apparently did little to discourage Hughes's perception. In a wide-ranging discussion of foreign and domestic policy lasting an hour and a half, Hughes recalls, "We struck . . . not one troubling note of dissent between us."[64]

The only black man on the White House staff, E. Frederic Morrow, believed that Eisenhower "instinctively said and did the right thing" on civil rights issues. Morrow attributed the president's hesitance about proceeding in this area to his reliance on an old network of southern friends for advice.[65] Meanwhile southern Democrats blasted the liberal coterie of Sherman Adams, James Hagerty, and Herbert Brownell for leading astray a well-meaning, prosouthern president.

Chapter 2 documents this phenomenon with respect to agricultural policy. Secretary Benson, as well as his defenders like Barry Goldwater, were convinced that Eisenhower was a fervent believer in applying free-market principles to agriculture. At the same time, a number of supporters of continued high price supports, such as Senators Edward Thye and Milton Young, continued to believe that Eisenhower was sympathetic to their viewpoint.

In this respect, Eisenhower resembles Abraham Lincoln, who also had a remarkable capacity to be different things to different people.[66] Lincoln stated his war aims ambiguously enough that those in favor of eradicating slavery came away persuaded that the president intended to eliminate slavery, while those in favor of limiting the war effort to preserving the Union were convinced that this was Lincoln's real aim. So profound was his ambiguity that historians today still argue about what it was that Lincoln really intended.

President Reagan, particularly in the first term, differed from both Eisenhower and Lincoln in that his objectives tended to be unequivocal. Reagan's conservative credentials were impeccable and his ideological agenda was, to an extent unusual in American politics, explicitly laid out before and during the 1980 campaign. Because conservatives believed, with good reason, that his instincts were fundamentally conservative, he was usually able to deflect right-wing criticism. The rallying cry, "Let Reagan be Reagan,"[67] reflected conservatives' confidence that a Reagan free of the influence of "pragmatists" such as James Baker would pursue their policy agenda.

But Reagan's unmistakable ideological commitments left him exposed on the left flank. As the case study of Watt showed, there was little, if any, sense among critics of the administration's environmental policies that the president's preferences diverged from Watt's. Thus, although Reagan's ideological character insulated him from right-wing critics when he failed to push conservative causes, it left him vulnerable to attack from liberals when pursuing the conservative agenda. As a result, Reagan often found it safer to abandon the right-wing agenda. Witness his two major second-term initiatives—arms control and tax reform—both of which moved in directions more likely to be criticized by conservatives than liberals.

Eisenhower's equivocal stance on most issues of the day, in contrast, often protected him from both liberal and conservative critics. Many liberals felt that, at heart, Eisenhower was really more liberal than his administration's policies indicated and were consequently quick to blame conservative advisers (whether Benson, Dulles, or George Humphrey) for stunting his natural liberalism. Many conservatives, on the other hand, felt that the president's natural instincts were conservative and so faulted liberal advisers (whether Herbert Brownell, Sherman Adams, or James Hagerty) for perverting the president's good intentions.

IT WORKED FOR IKE, BUT WILL IT WORK TODAY?

Are Eisenhower's strategies and experiences relevant to today's presidents? Have we entered a new era of the "postmodern" presidency in which old axioms and assumptions no longer hold?[68] Much is certainly different for contemporary presidents. The office is bigger, the responsibilities are greater, and the citizenry is more suspicious of political leadership. Increasing demands coupled with decreasing support is not good news for presidents.

Add to this an increasing ideological polarization among elites, and one has plenty of reason to wonder whether lessons drawn from Eisenhower's tenure are relevant today.

These objections force us to look beyond presidential style and strategy and toward the environmental conditions that are largely beyond a president's control. This section focuses on two of these environmental conditions: (1) ideological polarization among political elites, and (2) expectations of presidential involvement among the general public.[69] In both of these areas, there is reason to think that the political environment may have been radically transformed since Eisenhower's time.

In the concluding chapter of *The Hidden-Hand Presidency,* Fred Greenstein explicitly confronts the question of the relevance of the Eisenhower model for today's presidents. To those who dismiss the 1950s as "static and politically uneventful," Greenstein points out that if the 1950s seemed uneventful it was in part a product of Eisenhower's leadership. Eisenhower, Greenstein reminds us, "took office in the midst of a stalemated, unpopular war" but achieved a truce within six months and refused to become entangled in further military conflicts in Vietnam. Moreover, Greenstein cautions that "it is largely in retrospect that his presidency is remembered as conflict-free in the realm of foreign policy. There were sharp disagreements within and between the parties over whether the nation's foreign policy should be basically internationalist and over how aggressively the cold war should be prosecuted." Add to this not only McCarthyism but "major domestic political conflicts over such issues as civil rights, education, welfare, and regulatory policy" and one has a decade that was both eventful and full of conflict.[70]

Valuable as it is in dispelling popular myths about the allegedly serene 1950s, Greenstein's answer still leaves open a number of important questions about change over time in political climate and context. Most political scientists will have little trouble accepting Greenstein's refutation of the popular stereotype of the 1950s as a decade in which nothing happened and nobody argued. Yet those same political scientists may still point to specific institutional and cultural changes—the rise of an adversarial media and a distrustful public; rising public expectations of presidential control combined with diminished institutional capacity; increasingly polarized political parties—that have arguably transformed the political landscape within which presidents act.

What is the evidence for these hypothesized changes, and what is the effect of those changes that can be reliably documented on the applicability of Eisenhower's blame-avoidance model of leadership? Let us begin with the issue of party polarization. Greenstein is right that there were sharp differences over American foreign policy throughout the 1950s. But the evidence shows, too, that there was significantly less conflict, at least between parties,

TABLE 8.1. Differences in support for the president between congressional Republicans and Democrats.

	House Domestic	House Foreign	Senate Domestic	Senate Foreign	Summed Domestic	Summed Foreign
Eisenhower					34	8
Key votes	22	6	47	12		
Nonunanimous	27	1	38	14		
LBJ/JFK					36	25
Key votes	48	36	25	11		
Nonunanimous	48	39	24	12		
Nixon/Ford					30	24
Key votes	30	25	32	25		
Nonunanimous	27	17	30	28		
Carter					32	26
Key votes	35	20	34	27		
Nonunanimous	34	29	23	29		
Reagan, 1981–1986					40	48
Key votes	34	50	44	52		
Nonunanimous	36	44	41	44		
Totals					34	26
Key votes	34	27	36	25		
Nonunanimous	34	26	31	25		

Source: Calculated from congressional support scores reported in George Edwards, At the Margins (New Haven, Conn.: Yale University Press, 1989), 59–63. The numbers are arrived at by subtracting support among the opposition party from support among the president's own party. The "summed" statistics on the right represent the average of the sum of key votes and nonunanimous votes in both the House and Senate.

on foreign policy questions in Eisenhower's time than in subsequent administrations.

Data compiled by George Edwards, for instance, show that on "key" foreign policy votes there was only a 6 percentage point difference between the support Eisenhower received from House Republicans and the support he received from House Democrats (see Table 8.1).[71] In contrast, Kennedy/ Johnson averaged a 36 percentage point difference, Nixon/Ford a 25 percentage point difference, Carter a 20 percentage point difference, and Reagan (through his first six years) a 50 percentage point difference. The data on key votes from the Senate differ in important ways but still show a similar gap between the relatively bipartisan Eisenhower pattern (a 12 percentage point gap between Republican and Democratic support) and the highly polarized pattern of the Reagan years (a 52 percentage point gap between Republican and Democratic support). Using a summary statistic that combines key votes and nonunanimous votes in the Senate and House, two things stand out: the extraordinarily low degree of partisan polarization during Eisenhower's term and the extraordinarily high degree of partisan polarization during the Reagan period.[72]

If the data presented in Table 8.1 confirm a pattern of dramatic increases in levels of party polarization in the foreign policy arena, the domestic policy arena tells a far different story that is much more supportive of Greenstein's argument. Comparing "key" votes again we find in Eisenhower's term relatively low levels of polarization in the House (a 22 percentage point difference between Republican and Democratic support) but relatively high levels of polarization in the Senate (a 47 percentage point difference). Indeed, no subsequent president has had more polarized support in the Senate. Averaging the sum of key votes and nonunanimous votes in both the Senate and House, we find that Eisenhower's 34 percentage point gap between Republican and Democratic support is virtually identical to the average differential among all subsequent presidents. The evidence suggests a somewhat increased polarization during the Reagan presidency in domestic policy, but the overall picture in domestic policy is one of roughly comparable and quite high levels of party polarization throughout the last forty years.

Further evidence that the 1950s were not nearly as consensual as conventional wisdom would have it comes from Herbert McClosky's seminal study of 1956 national convention delegates. McClosky stressed that "despite the brokerage tendency of American parties, their active members are obviously separated by large and important differences."[73] Consistent with the data presented in Table 8.1, McClosky found that partisan differences on foreign policy issues were significantly less pronounced than partisan differences in domestic policy. Especially on issues involving the government's role in the economy, the differences between Republican and Democratic delegates were consistently large (see Table 8.2).[74]

Subsequent studies of convention delegates have all reaffirmed this basic pattern of large absolute differences between the parties on the issues of the day.[75] But have these partisan differences become larger since the 1950s?[76] This question is difficult to answer because issues and their importance inevitably change over time. Yet some preliminary answers can be had by comparing questions McClosky asked of the 1956 delegates with questions about preferred budgetary allocations asked of the 1984 convention delegates.[77] To facilitate comparisons across issue areas, McClosky constructed a "ratio of support" index by "assigning a weight of 1.0 to each 'increase' response in the sample, of 0 to each 'decrease' response, and of .50 to each 'remain as is' (or 'same') response."[78] Using this "support ratio" index McClosky found that the average difference on domestic issues between Democratic and Republican convention delegates was .22, and on foreign policy issues, the average difference was .12 (see Table 8.2). If we construct similar "ratio of support" scores for the budgetary allocation questions

TABLE 8.2. Issue positions among 1956 convention delegates.

	Increase	Same	Decrease	Ratio of Support	Diff. in Ratios
Public ownership of natural resources					.39
Republicans	12.9	35.2	51.9	.30	
Democrats	57.5	23.8	18.6	.69	
Level of farm price supports					.38
Republicans	6.7	25.8	67.4	.20	
Democrats	43.4	28.5	28.1	.58	
Federal aid to education					.36
Republicans	22.3	34.5	43.2	.40	
Democrats	66.2	20.4	13.4	.76	
Corporate income tax					.33
Republicans	4.0	34.5	61.5	.21	
Democrats	32.3	44.4	23.3	.54	
Government regulation of business					.33
Republicans	0.6	15.3	84.1	.08	
Democrats	20.2	41.3	38.5	.41	
Tax on large incomes					.28
Republicans	5.4	37.7	56.9	.24	
Democrats	27.0	49.9	23.1	.52	
Slum clearing and public housing					.27
Republicans	40.1	38.3	21.6	.59	
Democrats	78.4	16.0	5.6	.86	
Regulation of public utilities					.26
Republicans	17.9	64.5	17.6	.50	
Democrats	59.0	34.6	6.4	.76	
Social Security benefits					.22
Republicans	22.5	64.4	13.1	.55	
Democrats	60.0	36.1	3.9	.78	
Tax on business					.22
Republicans	1.0	27.8	71.1	.15	
Democrats	12.6	49.1	38.3	.37	
Minimum wage					.21
Republicans	15.5	72.0	12.5	.52	
Democrats	50.0	45.2	4.7	.73	
Enforcement of antimonopoly laws					.20
Republicans	44.9	46.1	9.0	.68	
Democrats	78.0	19.1	2.9	.88	
Regulation of trade unions					.18
Republicans	86.4	9.2	4.5	.91	
Democrats	59.3	28.3	12.4	.73	

(Continued)

TABLE 8.2. (continued)

Public control of atomic energy					.18
Republicans	45.0	39.7	15.3	.65	
Democrats	73.2	19.6	7.2	.83	
Enforcement of integration					.12
Republicans	25.5	42.8	31.7	.47	
Democrats	43.8	29.5	26.6	.59	
Tax on middle incomes					.12
Republicans	0.8	35.3	63.9	.18	
Democrats	2.7	47.1	50.2	.26	
Level of tariffs					.11
Republicans	19.2	54.5	26.3	.46	
Democrats	13.0	43.9	43.0	.35	
Immigration					.10
Republicans	18.4	51.7	29.9	.44	
Democrats	36.1	36.9	27.0	.54	
Tax on small incomes					.08
Republicans	2.9	32.1	65.0	.19	
Democrats	1.4	19.4	79.2	.11	
Restrictions on credit					.07
Republicans	20.6	58.8	20.6	.50	
Democrats	24.8	35.9	39.3	.43	
Reliance on United Nations					.21
Republicans	24.4	40.7	34.8	.45	
Democrats	48.9	33.5	17.6	.66	
American partici- pation in military alliances					.14
Republicans	22.7	51.6	25.7	.48	
Democrats	41.5	40.9	17.6	.62	
Foreign aid					.10
Republicans	7.6	30.7	61.7	.23	
Democrats	17.8	31.1	51.0	.33	
Defense spending					.03
Republicans	13.6	52.8	33.6	.40	
Democrats	20.7	44.8	34.4	.43	
Domestic policy average					.22
Foreign policy average					.12
Domestic and foreign policy combined					.20

Source: Adapted from Herbert McClosky et al., "Issue Conflict and Consensus among Party Leaders and Followers," *American Political Science Review* 54 (June 1960): 410–15.

TABLE 8.3.   Preferred budgetary allocations among 1984 national convention delegates.

	Increase	Same	Decrease	Ratio of Support	Diff. in Ratios
Education					.55
Republicans	14	36	50	.32	
Democrats	77	19	4	.87	
Minorities					.38
Republicans	3	43	64	.25	
Democrats	40	46	14	.63	
Medicare					.35
Republicans	6	56	38	.34	
Democrats	44	50	6	.69	
Social Security					.26
Republicans	6	65	29	.39	
Democrats	37	56	6	.65	
Science					.10
Republicans	40	45	15	.63	
Democrats	52	41	8	.73	
Crime					.01
Republicans	52	40	8	.72	
Democrats	46	49	5	.71	
Star Wars					.62
Republicans	57	29	14	.72	
Democrats	4	11	84	.10	
MX missile					.47
Republicans	32	45	23	.55	
Democrats	2	11	88	.08	
Foreign aid					.15
Republicans	2	25	73	.15	
Democrats	9	41	50	.30	
Domestic policy average					.28
Foreign policy average					.41
Domestic and foreign policy combined					.32

Source: Calculated from Nelson W. Polsby and Aaron Wildavsky, *Presidential Elections: Contemporary Strategies of American Electoral Politics,* 8th ed. (New York: Free Press, 1991), 149.

asked of the 1984 delegates, we get an average difference on domestic issues of .28 and an average difference on foreign policy issues of .41 (Table 8.3).[79]

The relatively small number of questions reported in the 1984 survey counsel caution in interpreting these results,[80] yet it does seem possible to draw a few conclusions from Tables 8.2 and 8.3. First, one finds further confirmation of the finding in Table 8.1 that foreign policy has become much more polarized since Eisenhower's time. Contemporary presidents do seem to face a degree of partisan polarization in foreign and defense policy that is unlike anything faced by Eisenhower. Second, three of the nine issues probed in 1984—federal spending on education, Star Wars, and the MX missile—were much more polarized than the most polarized issue in 1956! Two others—aid to minorities and federal spending on Medicare—would have ranked among the top four polarized issues in 1956. In sum, then, these data seem to lend strong support to the increasing polarization thesis, especially in the foreign-policy domain.[81]

If politics has become more polarized at the elite level, what difference does this make for presidents who want to deflect blame? Quite I bit, I think. Partisan polarization presents a serious obstacle to a president trying to deflect blame because to use lightning rods effectively requires that those doing the blaming have a sense that a president is really on their side (but is being thwarted or misinformed by advisers) or at least that the president can be persuaded to take their side (and so better to blame the adviser and not burn their bridges with the only president they have). The more polarized the political climate the more difficult it is for a president to sustain either of these beliefs. The tighter the constraint across issue positions (i.e., knowing a person's position on global warming, for instance, allows one to predict that person's position on military intervention in Latin America, government spending on defense, and aid for the homeless), the more likely an opponent on one issue will be an opponent on the next issue. Polarization thus weakens the force of what social scientists refer to as "crosscutting cleavages." Crosscutting cleavages moderate conflict by making opponents on one issue into allies on the next.[82] But crosscutting cleavages also create incentives for political elites to avoid criticizing the president directly on issues about which they may disagree in order to maintain the president's ear on subsequent issues on which they may hope to find common ground. Increasing partisan polarization therefore makes it more difficult for presidents to create effective lightning rods and to avoid blame.

It would be wrong, however, to assume that presidents are prevented from deflecting blame simply because an issue is polarized. In view of our findings in Chapter 2 about Eisenhower's success in deflecting blame onto Secretary Benson, it is worth a second look at McClosky's data about elite attitudes regarding farm price support policies. Table 8.2 shows that Democratic and Republican elites in 1956 were more divided on agricultural price-support policies than on any other issue except public ownership of natural resources. Among Republican elites only 7 percent favored increasing price supports, while 67 percent of Republican elites favored decreasing them. In contrast, 43 percent of Democratic elites favored increasing price supports and only 28 percent favored decreasing them. Even more striking, farm price supports was the only issue on which McClosky detected anything approaching significant evidence of polarization at the mass public level.[83] Our case study of Eisenhower and Benson, then, strongly suggests that lightning rods are not precluded by polarization.

What threatens the effective use of lightning rods may be less the extent of polarization on any given issue than the extent of polarization across issue domains. Lyndon Johnson, for example, instructed his fellow Democrats not to attack Eisenhower personally not just because Eisenhower was popular but also because the Democrats needed and counted on Eisenhower's support on other issues, especially on foreign-policy questions. George Bush, though he self-consciously set out to emulate Eisenhower's inclusive, consensual approach to governing,[84] faced a radically different situation than did Eisenhower when he entered office. Democratic lawmakers who disagreed with Bush on the environment, for example, were highly likely to disagree with him on a whole range of other issues, including foreign policy. With the battle lines in foreign policy drawn in much the same configuration as the battle lines in domestic policy,[85] Bush could not count on Democratic opponents drawing the same sort of fire line they created for Eisenhower.

Is Eisenhower's "low profile, anti-conflictual approach to politicking"[86] a poor guide for presidents in an era of more polarized politics? Perhaps Reagan's more confrontational, more ideological approach is better suited to these more polarized times. This is the argument made by Thomas Edsall, who argues that "Reagan's strength lay in his willingness to deal with a polarized electorate. Rather than seeking broad consensus—a goal that may be currently impossible, given the conflicts within American society as a whole—Reagan accepted a divided electorate."[87] Edsall errs in positing increased polarization at the level of the mass public—study after study documents the lack of change among ordinary citizens[88]—but Edsall's challenge still remains: Is Reagan's model a better guide for contemporary presidents than Eisenhower's model?

A stark dichotomy between the Eisenhower and Reagan presidential models may be misleading, however, because in some crucial respects the two presidencies are quite similar. Both Reagan and Eisenhower delegated extensively and neither seemed concerned about being upstaged by subordinates. Both presidents focused their personal attention on a few issues and kept themselves off the front lines as much as possible on most other issues. Both presidents, in short, pursued a blame-avoidance rather than a credit-claiming strategy. Is it just a coincidence that the only two presidents to serve two full terms in the last half century are also the only two presidents who have consciously propagated public images emphasizing their detachment from White House decision making?

No doubt, growing elite polarization makes it more difficult to emulate Eisenhower's success in being different things to different people. Bush's difficulties in straddling rival positions would seem to confirm this. Yet one should be careful about inferring too much from Bush's experience. Both Eisenhower and Bush lacked the clear ideological agenda and convictions of a Reagan or a Robert Taft, but Eisenhower, unlike Bush, did have a clear sense of the direction he wanted to take the Republican party—from isolationism to internationalism in foreign policy and reconciling the party to the New Deal in domestic policy.[89] Strategic ambiguity is one thing, an absence of objectives quite another.[90] Moreover, it is well to remember that Bush's average public approval score (61 percent) was actually substantially higher than Reagan's (52 percent)—indeed of the postwar presidents Bush's average public support ranks behind only Eisenhower (65 percent) and Kennedy (71 percent).[91] To remember Bush as a public opinion failure and Reagan as a public relations success is thus to distort history.[92] Finally, as Chapter 3 documents, Reagan's firm ideological commitments impeded his ability to deflect blame and maintain support. Whatever success Reagan had at deflecting blame was in spite of rather than because of his clear ideological agenda. Those pundits and politicians who have been confidently touting the "lesson" of the Reagan and Bush presidencies as something like, "nothing succeeds like high-definition presidents with a clear, unambiguous ideological vision," will find that such an understanding of our recent past provides an impoverished guide to success in the White House.

A more polarized politics makes blame avoidance more difficult, but it does not fundamentally alter the basic requirements for success nor does it diminish the desirability of a blame-avoidance posture. If anything, a more contentious politics means presidents need to place an even greater premium on a leadership style that keeps presidents out of the direct fire of competing interests and views. Now as before, the key to keeping out of trouble is to create ambiguity about where one stands, to let subordinates stand in the limelight whenever possible, and to limit severely the number of issues on which one becomes directly and extensively engaged. Presidents who do not keep themselves off the front lines and out of harm's way are likely to find their presidencies untenable.

Have there been changes at the mass public level that might affect a president's ability to deflect blame? One of the recurrent themes in the presidency literature over the past two decades has been the theme of rising and increasingly unrealistic public expectations about presidential roles and responsibilities.[93] If such a change in public expectations has occurred it has important implications for contemporary presidents' ability to deflect blame. For the success of a lightning rod strategy is contingent on the degree to which people expect a president to be in command of a policy area. The greater the expectation of presidential involvement and control, the less likely a president will be able to deflect blame for administration actions onto subordinates. We need to ask therefore whether changes over the last forty years in what the public expects from a president have so radically altered the political environment as to narrow greatly or even foreclose the effective use of lightning rods. Are public expectations today such that it is impossible for contemporary presidents to distance themselves from particular policy areas in the same manner that Eisenhower did?

The rising expectations position is compelling. Rising, unrealizable expectations are said to account for the string of troubled presidencies that the United States has experienced since the late 1960s.[94] Others have suggested that rising expectations account for presidents' increasing tendency to centralize operations in the White House and to politicize the bureaucracy.[95] Moreover, the thesis comports with the public's own feeling that the public's expectations of the president are higher than in the past.[96] The rising expectations thesis has almost become enshrined as the common-sense understanding of presidential development. But, as Jagdish Bhagwati usefully reminds us, "common sense is precisely the quality that makes people assert that the earth is flat, since that is how it appears to the naked eye."[97]

What evidence is there of a rising tide of public expectations? The answer, somewhat surprisingly in view of the widespread acceptance that this proposition engenders, is very little.[98] One of the only studies that marshals empirical evidence in support of the claim that public "expectations about [presidential] roles and responsibilities have grown substantially in recent years" is Stephen Wayne's essay on "Expectations of the President."[99] Wayne arrives at this conclusion by comparing the results of surveys conducted in 1968 and 1979. The 1968 survey asked, "In making the nation's foreign policy (policy in economic or welfare laws)(policy dealing with racial problems) who do you think should have the major responsibility—the president, Congress, or both about equal," and found that on average 62 percent said "about equal," 11 percent chose the president, and 27 percent chose Congress. The 1979 survey posed the question, "Some people think that the president ought to have the major responsibility for making policy, while other people think that Congress ought to have the major responsibility. In general, which do you think should have the major responsibility for setting policy?" and found that 22 percent said both, 37 percent said the president, and 36 percent said Congress.[100]

Although these differences may capture change over time in the public's view of presidential roles and responsibilities, at least several other more or at least equally plausible interpretations are possible. As Wayne himself concedes, the observed differences may reflect little more than the particular historical circumstances. In 1968 the country was in the midst of an unpopular "presidential" war, while in 1979 the country was perceived as suffering from weak executive leadership.[101] More troubling still is the significantly different wording employed in the two questions. In view of what we know about the power of question wording to affect responses (especially where respondents do not have firmly held attitudes), it is a strong possibility that the different results are simply an artifact of different questions.[102] Other survey results that predate the 1968 study provide further grounds for treating the rising expectation thesis with skepticism—at least in so far as the thesis is intended to distinguish the 1950s from the contemporary period. In a 1966 article, Roberta Sigel reported the results of a survey conducted in Detroit, Michigan, in the early 1960s, which showed that more people preferred presidential leadership than preferred congressional leadership.[103] Indeed it was against the backdrop of such evidence that Glenn Parker had originally presented the 1968 survey results as a *"challenge* [to] the premise held by some that the populace prefers presidential, in contrast to congressional, leadership in public policy."[104]

More damaging still to the thesis of rising public expectations is evidence from *New York Times*/CBS News surveys conducted during the 1980s that showed the public placed the locus of responsibility for governing squarely on the shoulders of Congress. In November 1985, at the peak of President Reagan's popularity, respondents were asked, "Who should have the most say about what cuts should be made to balance the budget—the president or Congress?" Seventy-one percent answered Congress, and only 20 percent answered the president. At the outset of Reagan's second year in office, the same polling organization asked a roughly similar question—"In your opinion, whose responsibility for balancing the budget is greater, the president's or that of Congress"—and got roughly similar results. Sixty-three percent placed the responsibility with Congress, and only 23 percent said the president's responsibility was greater.[105] Most striking of all, Gallup asked exactly the same question in 1936, and there was actually a slightly higher percentage back then saying that balancing the budget was a presidential responsibility (31 percent) and somewhat lower percentage saying balancing the budget was a congressional responsibility (50 percent)![106]

The available survey evidence, in sum, offers scant support for the thesis that today's presidents are afflicted with a rising tide of public expectations about their roles and responsibilities. At best, we could render the Scotch verdict of "not proven." Moreover, it would be unwise to ignore or even downplay the tremendous public expectations that faced President Eisenhower. Eisenhower was still president when Richard Neustadt wrote that "everybody now expects the man inside the White House to do something about everything."[107] We can agree with contemporary scholars that today's presidents are hampered by a gap between public expectations and institutional capacity, but we must remind ourselves that this was the starting point for Louis Brownlow's analysis fifty years ago. "The nation," Brownlow reported, "expects more of the President than he can possibly do."[108] It was true then, and it is true today.

My purpose is not to deny that public expectations of the presidency have seen a massive transformation during the past century or even that public expectations of the president are often unrealistically high. What I do want to suggest is that the undeniable transformation in public expectations about the role of the president had largely taken place by Eisenhower's time. Eisenhower, in this respect at least, inhabits much the same modern universe that today's presidents inhabit—a universe in which presidents are at the center of public attention and are expected to maintain peace, prosperity, and national security.

Institutions, attitudes, and expectations, of course, do change. Elite partisan polarization in foreign policy seems to be one such area where substantial change does appear to have occurred. The decline in public trust in political leaders in Washington appears to be another,[109] as does the rise of a more adversarial media.[110] We need to take note of these changes and their consequences for governing. But we should be wary of too readily writing off the hard-earned experiences of past presidents as irrelevant to our contemporary problems. Presidential leadership, then and now, is a hazardous proposition—doubters need only remember that Eisenhower's predecessor in office, Harry Truman, has the *lowest* average approval scores of any president for which Gallup has polling data.[111] We would do well to heed the warning of Arthur Schlesinger, Jr., that it is necessary to "avoid the fallacy of self-pity that leads every generation to suppose that it is peculiarly persecuted by history."[112] Among journalists especially there is too often a born-yesterday quality to analysis and a too ready willingness to accept that things are totally different today than yesterday.[113]

Whatever the changes that have occurred during the last forty years—and they are often greatly exaggerated—they have not altered the basic choice in leadership style that presents itself to every modern president. That is a choice between a leadership style premised on blame avoidance and one based on credit claiming.[114] In this sense, Eisenhower's blame-avoidance model (with all of its limitations[115]) is just as relevant today as it was in the 1950s.

WHERE ARE PRESIDENTS LIKELY TO FIND THE MOST EFFECTIVE LIGHTNING RODS?

What can this study tell us about the positions within an administration that are most likely to be able to sustain effective lightning rods? Is it better to set up lightning rods in what Thomas Cronin styles the "inner cabinet" or the "outer cabinet?"[116] Should presidents try to build their cabinet members into lightning rods, or will those within the White House work just as well? What about president's wives? Have changes in the importance of some offices, like the vice-presidency, meant changes in the office's utility as a source of lightning rods? The deflection of blame onto subordinates is easiest in those policy areas where public expectations of presidential involvement and control are least pronounced. Thus we might expect the most successful lightning rods are likely to emerge from the ranks of the outer cabinet—Agriculture, Commerce, Education, Energy, Health and Human Services, Housing and Urban Development, Interior, Labor, and Transportation. It is in these more peripheral domestic-policy areas, where the president is not necessarily expected to be engaged or knowledgeable, that lightning rods are most likely to flourish.

What made Benson a successful lightning rod was not only Eisenhower's blame-avoidance leadership style but also the widespread expectation that a president had other duties that took precedence over agricultural policy making. In the context of the outer cabinet, presidential claims of ignorance or lack of involvement are both more plausible and less damaging. Presidents, of course, may act in ways that connect them more closely with the actions of these departments. Reagan's well-publicized antienvironmental views helped link him in the public mind with the actions of the Interior Department and the Environmental Protection Agency. In a different way, Bush tied himself to the fate of these departments by promising to be the environmental president. And Clinton has done much the same by personally attending, indeed presiding over, a Northwest forest summit in the opening months of his presidency.

If the outer cabinet's distance from the president can make these department heads effective lightning rods, that same distance from the president can also make it more difficult to get the sort of media coverage that is necessary to become an effective lightning rod. The departments of the outer cabinet tend to get much less media coverage than the big four—Defense, State, Treasury, and Justice (Cronin's inner cabinet). In his study *Washington Reporters,* Stephen Hess found a large discrepancy between press coverage of the inner and outer cabinets, especially in television network news. Stories about the inner cabinet made up 19 percent of Washington stories, while the outer cabinet constituted only 4 percent of the total. The discrepancy was smaller among newspaper stories, but even here 12 percent of coverage of Washington stories involved the inner cabinet compared with 9 percent involving the outer cabinet.[117] My own research has shown a similar imbalance between news coverage of the outer and inner cabinets and also replicates Hess's findings that the imbalance is significantly greater in television news, although this overall imbalance is significantly skewed by the tremendous amount of coverage the secretary of state typically receives (see Table 8.4). In the years I examined, 1981 and 1989, the secretary of state made

TABLE 8.4.   Media coverage of department secretaries.

	1981		1989	
	Television	Times	Television	Times
State	646	745	322	225
Defense	272	356	148	94
Treasury	156	239	24	64
Attorney General	121	153	100	98
Inner cabinet	1,195	1,493	594	481
Interior	63	184	18	30
HHS	73	64	32	58
Agriculture	38	52	3	6
HUD	10	19	42	60
Labor	72	100	12	12
Energy	24	54	14	29
Education	20	60	6	15
Transportation	90	73	45	32
Commerce	31	64	12	30
Outer cabinet	421	670	184	272
Percent of stories on inner cabinet	74	69	76	64
Percent of stories on inner cabinet minus State	55	53	60	48

Sources: Computed from entries in the New York Times Index and Vanderbilt Television News Index and Abstracts.

up 54 percent of the television coverage and slightly under one-half of the newspaper coverage received by the inner cabinet.

As Table 8.4 indicates, as does evidence previously presented in Chapter 5, the secretary of state is by far the most visible member of the president's cabinet. With such visibility, the secretary of state would seem to be an ideal candidate for lightning rod status. However, we saw in Chapter 5 that even in the cases of the three most influential and prominent postwar secretaries of state, little evidence showed that they served as public lightning rods. Kissinger, whose stature (80 percent of the public could identify him before he'd even been appointed secretary of state) and circumstances (President Ford had never been elected) were highly exceptional, probably did serve as a lightning rod for the fall of Cambodia and the North Vietnamese takeover of Vietnam, but for the most part Kissinger seems to have upstaged Ford rather than to have deflected blame. For John Foster Dulles and Dean Acheson, there was little evidence of a lightning rod role, at least at the level of the mass public. The ups and downs in the popularity of both were closely tied to the fortunes of their president.

The widely shared expectation that a president is uniquely responsible for the conduct of foreign relations makes it difficult for a president to avoid blame in the area of foreign policy. This is particularly true concerning war or major international crises such as the U-2 affair or the Bay of Pigs. Although Truman delegated a great deal of authority to Acheson, it did not prevent public anger over the Korean War from being directed at the president. Similarly, although Johnson sent out a number of prominent spokesmen (Dean Rusk, Hubert Humphrey, Walt Rostow, among others) to defend the war effort, this did not prevent him from being blamed for setbacks in Vietnam. Just as the Korean War was Truman's war (and the War of 1812 had been Madison's war), so Vietnam became Johnson's war. The costs of seeming not to be in control during a major international crisis, moreover, are such that no president can afford to let subordinates take the heat. More likely, presidents will have to bear the blame for events that they tried to prevent or decisions that were not of their making.

Similarly, the public's well-documented tendency to hold the president responsible for the general state of the economy limits the extent to which a president can distance himself from economic performance. Presidents are less likely to create lightning rods out of their secretary of treasury than they are to take the blame (or credit) for economic conditions not of their making. Although this book has not examined the treasury secretary specifically, one cannot but be struck by how infrequently modern presidents have made any concerted effort to fashion a lightning rod out of the head of the Treasury Department.[118] Eisenhower's treasury secretaries, George Humphrey and Robert Anderson, for instance, were both highly influential players within the administration, yet neither ever served any sort of lightning rod function. Not long after Bill Clinton selected Senate finance chair and former Democratic vice-presidential nominee Lloyd Bentsen to be his treasury secretary, the president immediately felt it necessary to tell reporters that he, Bill Clinton, would "be the chief economic adviser in my Administration" and that he personally "would take responsibility for addressing both the short and long-term economic challenges facing us."[119] Even discounting Clinton's proclivity to immerse himself in the details of policy making, it is hard to imagine him needing or wanting to make such statements in the areas of transportation, education, labor, or even the environment.

One of the defining changes in the presidency over the last half century has been the tremendous growth in the White House staff and the increasing involvement of White House staff in departmental operations.[120] What are the implications of this increased centralization for a president's ability to deflect blame? Can staffers make effective lightning rods, or are they likely to be limited by their proximity to the president? By bringing problems and policies into the White House, the president may indeed find it harder to distance himself from problems when they go unsolved or policies when they go awry. By virtue of the problem being brought into the White House it has become a presidential problem. Moreover, staffers are largely creatures of the president who lack the independent standing of cabinet members. If this makes cabinet members less controllable that is also part of their value. To presidents already overburdened with decisions and demands, delegating real decision-making authority to those outside the White House helps presidents focus on the decisions about which they and their followers care most.[121]

Yet it must also be noted that Reagan's experience in the Iran-contra affair suggests that sometimes the key may be less the degree of White House involvement in decisions than the degree (perceived at least) of presidential involvement in White House decisions. That Admiral John Poindexter and Lieutenant Colonel Oliver North were within the White House certainly meant that the Iran-contra scandal damaged Reagan much more directly and personally than it would have had some comparable scheme been uncovered in the State Department. Yet at the same time, Reagan was able to secure deniability and was able to recover in part because his claims of noninvolvement fit with a widespread understanding of his decision-making style. That Reagan was "out of the loop" did not seem implausible to many in the Washington community who had been saying much the same thing for several years before the scandal.

Senior staffers' proximity to the president is a double-edged sword. Their positions of power, particularly in the case of the chief of staff, make them natural targets for critics who dislike the direction an administration is going. Disgruntled elites blaming the leader's errors on the influence of evil advisers are a perennial feature of human history. But the internal power of a chief of staff also stems from his ability to faithfully reflect the president's preferences, and the willingness of others to listen to and follow the chief of staff's directives depends on their believing that he speaks for the president. Thus a chief of staff serving as a lightning rod may simultaneously be undermining his ability to act as an effective staff person. The lightning rod role is thus an especially unstable and precarious role for chiefs of staff.

Moreover, as a controversy becomes something more than inside-the-administration griping and blossoms into a full-blown public debate, chiefs of staff are particularly unlikely to make effective lightning rods. As we saw in Chapter 3, sustained scrutiny of the Bush administration's environmental policy record ultimately led critics to conclude that someone as close to the president as John Sununu must be expressing the president's own policy preferences. When the chief of staff publicly speaks out on an issue, it is difficult for a president to disown knowledge or involvement without seeming at best dangerously disengaged and at worst disingenuous or even dishonest. We saw in Chapter 6 how difficult it was for Nixon to distance himself from Haldeman's public statement charging critics of the Vietnam War with "consciously aiding and abetting the enemy of the United States." Most elites interpreted Nixon's distancing as further evidence of the president's duplicity.

If proximity militates against distancing where does that leave the president's spouse? For most of American history this point has been moot because presidents' wives have largely taken on nonpolitical tasks, have usually been relatively noncontroversial, and are thus often more popular than their husbands.[122] Barbara Bush fit this pattern particularly well, as did Rosalynn Carter and Betty Ford.[123] All this has changed with the presidency of Bill Clinton. Of particular importance is President Clinton's decision to appoint Hillary Rodham Clinton as head of the task force on health reform, but also of note is her extensive role in the appointments process, particularly in the areas of domestic policy.

At the time of her appointment to head the task force on health reform, a number of voices were raised expressing misgivings about the decision on the grounds that it would become difficult for Bill Clinton to deflect blame if things went badly. Sheila Tate, Nancy Reagan's former press secretary, explained that "the problem is that if her task force is a stink bomb, Bill Clinton can't distance himself. It lays the responsibility right at his feet."[124] Moreover, if Hillary Clinton becomes a liability (and any lightning rod can rapidly become a liability), Clinton can not jettison his wife in the same way that Eisenhower dumped Adams, Reagan dismissed Regan and Watt, or Bush got rid of Sununu.

On the other hand, the peculiar dynamics of a husband-wife relationship could make Hillary Rodham Clinton an effective lightning rod, at least at the elite level. Among conservative and moderate Democrats as well as among once-hopeful Republicans, Hillary Clinton is bearing much of the blame for diverting the Clinton administration away from the president's Democratic Leadership Council instincts and in the direction of a more liberal, activist agenda.[125] A few like Mickey Kaus of the *New Republic* have suggested that her influence may be rooted in the leverage she has over the president as a result of her knowledge of the president's "wrongdoing."[126] Others have implied that romantic attachment may obscure policy judgment or that the president's understandable desire to "do what Hillary wants" may come at the expense of Clinton's own more conservative policy preferences. Such explanations allow critics to absolve Bill Clinton of the responsibility for the perceived leftward tilt of the Clinton administration.

Yet it is not clear how much good this really does Bill Clinton. Because

Clinton can't dismiss his wife there is no incentive for political elites to single out Hillary Clinton instead of directly attacking the president. Criticism might as well be aimed directly at the president. Elite critics of Sununu or Watt or Benson or Brownell hoped to indicate displeasure with a particular policy direction without permanently alienating the president. Who will feel that the way to keeping the president's ear is to criticize his wife? Combine this with Clinton's well-publicized penchant for showing how much he knows about every conceivable policy area (and he does know a lot), not the least of which is health policy, and the prospects for an effective Hillary lightning rod seem dim indeed. But then Bill Clinton is anything but a blame-avoidance president.

What, finally, about the vice-presidential role? Humphrey's status as lightning rod, as suggested in Chapter 4, may have been undermined not only by Johnson's leadership style but also by the vice-presidential role itself, which allowed Humphrey little or nothing in the way of a policy-making role. Humphrey was essentially little more than a cheerleader on the sidelines, and while cheerleaders may distract or irritate they cannot be blamed for what is happening on the playing field. Since Humphrey's tenure, however, the vice presidents' policy-making role has become substantially more important. Indeed, political scientist Paul Light suggests that "as Vice-Presidents have moved beyond ceremonial duties into the political and policy arenas, they have come to resemble senior members of the White House staff."[127] And indeed they have. But, as Light also recognizes, a number of things still distinguish the vice-presidential role. Intense presidential ambition for one.

In marked contrast to the largely dead-end job of chief of staff,[128] the vice president, at least since Nixon's time, always has one eye on the presidency and one eye on the president. Vice presidents must loyally serve the needs of their presidents (both to be renominated and to gain the president's blessing when the baton is passed), but they must also carefully mind their own needs if their presidential ambitions are to be fulfilled. They cannot afford to go down in flames, in the manner of Adams, Haldeman, Regan, or Sununu. Nor can they afford too much of the sort of negative press doled out to Benson or Watt. The political ambitions of vice presidents thus tend to place limits on how they will allow themselves to be used by the president.

Vice presidents differ from senior staff, too, in that the former's loyalty to the president must always, to a lesser or greater degree, be in question. Senior staffers are picked for their loyalty to the president;[129] vice presidents are selected for their political appeal to key constituencies. They may even, as in the case of Reagan and Bush, have been rivals for the nomination. Because of their independent political base and because a vice president's interests cannot always be the same as the president's interests, presidents and their staffs may view with suspicion vice presidents' assuming a prominent public profile in a policy area. "Credit claiming and posturing [by a vice president or his staff]," Light writes, "are highly threatening to the White House."[130] Vice presidents may react to this anxiety on the part of presidents and their staff, as Bush did, by exercising their influence quietly. Fear of stealing the show and thereby incurring presidential disapproval encourages contemporary vice presidents to keep a low profile on public policy issues, and thus undermines their availability as lightning rods.

An individual's availability and effectiveness as a lightning rod, in sum, depends not only on the president's leadership style or the subordinate's actions but also on the particular pattern of expectations and incentives that accompany a given institutional role. Although one would be hard-pressed to predict in advance which individuals would serve as lightning rods simply by virtue of the role they occupy, the preceding discussion suggests it is possible to anticipate the types of problems and dilemmas that each role poses for a president who wants to think seriously about staying out of trouble.

LIGHTNING RODS AND POLITICAL ACCOUNTABILITY

Lightning rods may be good for presidents, but how should we as citizens look on the phenomenon of presidential lightning rods? As a lie by which presidents avoid accountability, or as a justifiable means for beleaguered presidents to maintain their authority and effectiveness? One's answer to this question depends on one's view of the nature of the American political system and of the president's place within that system.

American political science has a long and honored tradition which maintains that the fundamental weakness of the American political system is its "division of authority and concealment of responsibility." Among the earliest advocates of this view was Woodrow Wilson who, in his classic treatise *Congressional Government,* argued that it is "manifestly a radical defect of our federal system that it parcels out power and confuses responsibility." The American political system, Wilson lamented, allows "every suspected culprit . . . [to] shift the responsibility upon his fellows." With power divided, Wilson asked rhetorically, "how is the schoolmaster, the nation, to know which boy needs the whipping?"[131]

Modern-day advocates of "responsible parties" have shared Wilson's concern with making it easier for the public to assign blame when things go awry. The division of power between the legislative and executive branches, party government advocates contend, not only makes for a less effective government, but hopelessly confuses the poor voter. In "Toward a More Responsible Two-Party System," the American Political Science Association's Committee on Political Parties advanced its members' vision of a political system in which the governing party (with the president at its head) would have the power to carry out a clearly articulated program, on which the electorate could then pass judgment.[132] Only by concentrating authority, in this view, can the electorate hold elected officials responsible for their behavior.

Wilson's concern with making government more "responsible" is also echoed in modern writings on public administration. The report issued by the first Hoover Commission, for instance, began from the premise that "the President . . . must be held responsible and accountable to the people . . . for the conduct of the executive branch." This goal was being thwarted, the commission reported, because power within the executive branch was diffused and lines of authority were confused. Without "a clear line of command from top to the bottom" it was impossible to have "a return line of responsibility and accountability from bottom to the top." The executive branch (which the commission described as "a chaos of bureaus and subdivisions") was consequently both weak and unaccountable.[133]

If one sides with the Wilsonian tradition that the flaw in the American political system is that fragmented authority (both within the executive branch and between the executive and legislative branches) produces "irresponsible" government, then the use of advisers as lightning rods, by providing yet another skirt for presidents to hide behind, must be condemned as only exacerbating the political system's existing deficiencies. Presidential lightning rods make an already irresponsible system even more irresponsible. From this point of view, lightning rods are symptomatic of the inadequacies of American politics.

Echoes of this scholarly tradition can be heard all around us. Presidents, we are told, should articulate their program (in the singular, as if it were all of a piece) clearly and unambiguously.[134] They should tell us where they stand on everything from gun control to abortion to offshore oil drilling. Presidents should, moreover, be publicly visible. Attempts to retreat from public (particularly press) scrutiny are regarded as cowardly or manipulative or both.

A very different way of viewing presidential lightning rods is suggested by an alternative tradition in American political science, perhaps best exemplified by the writings of Pendleton Herring,[135] which stresses the need to minimize conflict within society and maintain public support for authority. Rather than concentrating government power to make it more effective, Herring was concerned with facilitating the adjustment of conflicting interests. Making presidents more responsible for government actions, Herring believed, would only result in discrediting the president and incapacitating the political system.

Unlike a British prime minister, who can be removed by a parliamentary vote of no-confidence if people lose faith in him or her, an American president serves a fixed term. Because of this, Herring argued, it is important for

presidents to insulate themselves from the daily policy battles to avoid becoming discredited before their term expires. "In halcyon days," Herring
warns, "a discredited occupant of the White House is an inconvenience; in
times of emergency such institutionalized futility may become tragic."[136]

Herring's political theory begins from the premise that the United States
executive branch more closely resembles a "feudal pattern of fiefs, baronies,
and dukedoms than . . . an orderly and symmetrical pyramid of authority."[137] Given that a president's power over his subordinates is severely limited, Herring suggests that a president is well advised to redefine his job in
such a way that expectations of what the president is responsible for more
closely coincide with the president's limited ability to control the decisions
of subordinates.[138] In contrast to the Wilsonian tradition, which advocates
systemic change to increase both presidential power and responsibility, Herring's tack is to assume that presidential power is relatively fixed and to
avoid overload by decreasing presidential responsibility.

Herring's sensitivity to the dangers of overloading a president with responsibilities that will outstrip his resources is evident in his concern for insulating presidents from the work of independent commissions. In marked
contrast to the Brownlow Committee, which recommended that independent
commissions be brought under the control of the president (so as "to restore
our constitutional ideal of a fully coordinated Executive Branch responsible
to the President"[139]), Herring suggested that "independent commissions,
while sometimes inconvenient to presidential policy, may yet relieve the chief
executive of a greater burden of political responsibility than any one man
can effectively carry."[140] Those who advocate having all roads of responsibility lead to the White House door, Herring intimates, are, contrary to their
intentions, weakening rather than strengthening the presidency.

Pervading Herring's political theory is a feeling for the frailty of the
American political system.[141] Herring acknowledges that the American political system's dispersal of authority and responsibility "does not appeal to
men of strictly logical mind" but defends the institutional arrangement on
the grounds that "it at least tempers the intensities of feeling that arise when
the onus of decision making is centered upon one governing agency or even
one individual."[142] Diffusion of responsibility, in this view, helps to diffuse
conflict and thus sustain societal consensus.

Herring applauds evasion and ambiguity for their role in muting conflict.
In contrast to Wilson, who urged "an open war of principle against principle," Herring counseled "caution, and even reticence, . . . when disagreements arise."[143] Just as a rigid adherence to truth-telling in one's personal life
would soon result in the deterioration of personal relations, Herring argued,
so in the political realm harmonious relations depend to some extent on
equivocation, hedging, and even deception.[144] Indeed if the president is to be
a "president of all the people" (given that "the people" are rarely if ever

agreed on a course of action), he *must* cloak his intentions in ambiguity. Lightning rods thus enable a president to govern while still fulfilling his function as chief of state.

From the perspective of proponents of consensus government, advocates of responsible party government who recommend the president assume command of "his" party are flirting with a dangerously divisive mode of politics. Herring's emphasis on consent leads to a preference not only for a less visible president but for a president who emphasizes the more detached role as chief of state over that of party head.[145] While fears of system breakdown may be exaggerated (though not unfounded as the South's secession in response to Lincoln's election in 1860 demonstrates), polarization, at least among the political stratum, must be expected if a president is to follow the script of party responsibility.[146]

"The politics of combat," to be sure, is not without its virtues.[147] Vigorous, open debate about pressing issues of the day may help to clarify those issues and to expose the weaknesses of proposed policies.[148] A president who avoids the controversial issues or puts off the "tough choices" may be keeping out of trouble at the expense of allowing the country to travel down the road to ruin. Indeed, some would maintain that the *definition* of leadership is taking unpopular stands and letting the chips fall where they may. A blame-avoidance strategy, in this view, is thus akin to abdicating leadership.

Certainly, as we saw in the case study of Eisenhower and the civil rights issue, it is difficult for a president simultaneously to pursue a blame-avoidance strategy and to mobilize support for his objectives. Without the public backing of the president, a cabinet member will find it difficult if not impossible to enlist the necessary public or congressional support for a controversial initiative. The Reagan White House's decision to package social security reform as Dick Schweiker's plan rather than Ronald Reagan's ensured, as Schweiker recognized, that it would be "dead on arrival" when it got to Capitol Hill.[149] When a president doesn't care intensely about an outcome, blame avoidance may be a fitting strategy, but when a president feels strongly about achieving something he will probably have little choice but to put his prestige on the line.

Eisenhower's conduct as president was largely consistent with the political theory of consensus government.[150] His leadership was aimed more at minimizing conflict and obtaining consent than enacting programs. It was a leadership strategy that stemmed from a belief that the president not only should not, but could not afford to dominate the political system. Contrary to received wisdom about his presidency,[151] Eisenhower well understood the non-hierarchical character of presidential authority in the United States and consequently directed his efforts as much or more toward sustaining political support as toward exercising presidential power.

One may concede that Eisenhower pursued a leadership strategy designed to avoid rancorous divisions within society, maintain personal popularity, and build up presidential authority, and yet still question the wisdom of such a strategy. The McCarthy episode, the halting efforts toward civil rights legislation, and the dragging out of the controversy over the Bricker amendment could all be cited as illustrating the limitations of Eisenhower's blame-avoidance leadership style.

The question of whether a president should put a premium on keeping out of trouble (as Eisenhower did) or doing good (as Johnson and Carter did) is thus intimately tied up with evaluations about the nature and purpose of the American political system. Although the debate about what a president is responsible for is inextricably tied up with these larger philosophical debates about accountability and the scope of the federal government, these traditionally opposed conceptions of presidential responsibility may still find common ground.

Champions of a strong programmatic presidency have traditionally urged a more active and visible president, in whom power and responsibility are concentrated, but today's supporters of presidential effectiveness might do well to look for scaled-back presidential power.[152] Given the president's position as the "most important continuing story that the media deal with,"[153] maintaining presidential authority and effectiveness may entail ceding power and dispersing responsibility for particular policies. Presidents may have to be more selective about the areas in which they want to have an impact.[154] Placing a premium on keeping out of trouble, far from conflicting with effective presidential leadership, may turn out to be a prerequisite for doing good.

Appendix

Many of those who argue that public expectations of presidential leadership have risen during the last three or four decades cite indirect evidence drawn from analyses of changes in media coverage of the presidency. Following the cue of Elmer Cornwell's seminal work on "the expansion of the Presidential image," they proceed "on the assumption that a measure of Presidential news content in a representative sample of the media can be taken as a rough measure of the relative public preoccupation with the Presidential office."[1] Cornwell examined front-page headlines in the *New York Times* and *Providence Journal* in selected years from 1885 to 1957 and documented what he argued was "a long-term upward trend in overall Presidential news, both in absolute terms and relative to news about Congress."[2] Cornwell is correct that his data provide incontrovertible evidence of an increase in the absolute number of presidential stories but is wrong that his data support the proposition that presidential news increased relative to congressional news. Although the ratio of presidential to congressional news shows short-term fluctuations there is no evidence of a long-term change over time (see Table A.1). Still, one can accept Cornwell's basic conclusion of an expanding presidential image without it touching our immediate concern, which is whether that image has expanded so much since the 1950s as to make lessons drawn from one era potentially misleading in another era.

More directly relevant for us is a study by Alan Balutis, which updated Cornwell's study through 1974. Balutis found what he claimed was a continuation of the trends identified by Cornwell. In fact, however, his data suggested important differences between the period examined by Cornwell and the period studied by Balutis. Cornwell's data identified a clear break between the period before World War I, which averaged 226 column inches of presidential news in the *New York Times,* and the period after the war, which averaged 809 column inches in the *Times.* But Balutis's research

185

TABLE A.1. Ratio of presidential to congressional news.

New York Times		Providence Journal	
1885	1.3	1894	1.7
1893	2.5	1899	3.1
1901	10.5	1906	2.3
1909	2.4	1910	2.5
1917	1.9	1914	2.6
1925	2.0	1922	2.2
1933	6.4	1926	1.1
1941	1.7	1930	0.8
1949	0.8	1934	2.8
1957	2.8	1949	1.0
		1954	1.0

Source: Calculated from Table 1 in Elmer E. Cornwell, Jr., "Presidential News: The Expanding Public Image," in Aaron Wildavsky, ed., The Presidency (Boston: Little, Brown, 1969), 314.

showed that for the entire period between 1958 and 1974, presidential news coverage in the Times averaged 707 column inches, actually somewhat below the average obtained in Cornwell's survey. Moreover, within the period surveyed by Balutis there was no evidence of any progressive increase over time in the front-page space that the Times allotted to presidential stories (Table A.2).[3]

Interestingly, though, if one looks at the ratio of presidential to congressional news reported by Balutis, one finds an unmistakably strong pattern of increasing coverage of the presidency relative to Congress (Table A.2). In this respect, too, Balutis's data are quite different from Cornwell's, which provide no evidence of change over time in the ratio of presidential to congressional news. What Balutis's data suggest is less an expanding presidential image than a declining congressional image. Caution is needed, however, in interpreting the data in Table A.2 because of the distorting effect of extraordinary years. For example, omitting 1972 and 1973 would lower the ra-

TABLE A.2. Front-page coverage of the presidency in the New York Times.

	Column Inches	President/Congress News Ratio
1957–1960	779	1.8
1961–1968	642	2.6
1969–1974	776	3.5

Sources: Calculated from Table 1 in Alan P. Balutis, "Congress, the President and the Press," Journalism Quarterly 53 (Autumn 1976), 511; 1957 data calculated from Elmer E. Cornwell, Jr., "Presidential News: The Expanding Public Image," in Aaron Wildavsky, ed., The Presidency (Boston: Little, Brown, 1969), 314.

tio of presidential to congressional news for the Nixon years from 3.5 to 2.2, a figure that is only slightly higher than the average ratio for Eisenhower's years. Even if one accepts that Balutis's data indicate an increasing relative prominence for the president, one could hardly conclude that they support the view that Eisenhower inhabited a qualitatively different universe than his successors.

A final word of caution is necessary in interpreting the Cornwell-Balutis data. Coding decisions made by Cornwell and subsequently by Balutis mean that the numbers showing the presidency predominating in the contemporary media may be highly misleading. Cornwell opted to count as congressional stories only those that included the terms "Congress," "Senate," "House," or the name of a specific congressional committee in the headline. Excluded altogether were headlines that named individual legislators, even though Cornwell chose to count as presidential stories those that included not only the words "president," "presidency," and "White House," but the name of the incumbent president. Thus headlines such as "Majority Leader Mitchell Responds to Bush's Speech" or "Republican Senators Successfully Filibuster Clinton's Plan" would be coded as presidential stories! Also pictures of presidents (even pictures of a president meeting with congressional leaders) were counted as presidential news, while pictures of congressmen were not counted as congressional news.[4]

Subsequent research by Stephen Hess confirms that the Cornwell-Balutis data probably greatly exaggerate presidential dominance of print journalism. For one week in April 1978, Hess analyzed the coverage of 22 newspapers and found that of the 921 stories about the president and the Congress, 54 percent of the time the subject of the story was the Congress, and 46 percent of the time the subject was the president. "Newspaper stories," Hess concluded emphatically, "do not pay more attention to the president [than to Congress]."[5]

Perhaps the most reliable evidence of the print media's increasing attention to the president comes from Michael Baruch Grossman and Martha Joynt Kumar's study of the *New York Times* and *Time* magazine from 1953 through 1978.[6] Grossman and Kumar show that for *Time* magazine there is a clear increase in the amount of coverage devoted to the White House beginning with the presidency of Richard Nixon (Table A.3). The *New York Times,* however, tells a somewhat different story, with the significant increase in coverage occurring with the Kennedy presidency. From Kennedy through Carter, however, Grossman and Kumar's evidence suggests no appreciable change in attention given to White House stories—a finding that is largely consistent with a careful reading of Balutis's data gathered from the *Times.*[7]

On balance, then, the evidence from newspapers (especially from the *New York Times*) tends not to support the thesis that the last thirty to forty years

TABLE A.3.   White House stories in each issue or broadcast, by administration.

	Time	New York Times	CBS News
Eisenhower	3.2	6.6	
Kennedy	3.8	9.1	
Johnson	2.8	8.3	
Nixon	5.1	11.1	4.2
Ford	4.5	8.8	3.8
Carter[a]	5.9	9.3	3.7

Source: Michael Baruch Grossman and Martha Joynt Kumar, Portraying the President: The White House and the Media (Baltimore: Johns Hopkins University Press, 1981), 259. Reprinted with permission of Johns Hopkins University Press.
[a]Data for Carter through 1978 only.

have seen the sort of massive increase in media attention to the presidency that would make Eisenhower's experience irrelevant.[8] It does suggest that the pattern of coverage in the latter half of the twentieth century is radically different from the nineteenth- or early twentieth-century pattern,[9] but that is not the relevant issue here. The evidence from news magazines like Time and Newsweek, on the other hand, does suggest an impressive increase in attention to presidents in recent decades.[10] Without better data about how the increase in coverage of presidential news compares with changes in congressional news, however, it is often difficult to interpret the significance of the increase in presidential news in news magazines.[11]

Unmistakable evidence of presidential dominance comes from studies of national television network news. Particularly striking is a study by Robert Gilbert, who examined lead stories on all three major networks for 1975, 1979, 1981, and 1985 and found that presidential stories dwarfed congressional news: the president garnered 934 lead stories and 235,640 seconds, while Congress had only 76 lead stories and 14,550 seconds.[12] Hess, too, found that television network stories paid more attention to the president, though his numbers (59 percent to 41 percent) are much less overwhelming, probably because he analyzed the entire news segment rather than just lead stories.[13] Michael J. Robinson, who examined television network news in 1969 and 1977, confirms Hess's findings that the presidency has about a sixty percent to forty percent edge on Congress.[14]

Each of the above studies confirms that television news today pays significantly greater attention to the presidency than to Congress. The evidence is more mixed, however, on the question of change over time. Gilbert does find that the presidential advantage in news coverage was significantly less in 1975 than in subsequent years, but it is difficult to know whether 1975 was an atypical year. Grossman and Kumar, who surveyed coverage on CBS in every year from 1968 to 1978, found high levels of attention to the White House but detected no evidence of any increase over time (Table A.3). Similarly, Robinson's comparison of 1969 and 1977 uncovers no evidence of increased network attention to the presidency, although some evidence suggests a slight decline in stories focusing on the legislative branch.[15] None of these studies, moreover, goes back to the Eisenhower era, so it is difficult to say precisely how or whether television coverage of the presidency has changed since then.[16] Even if it were true that newspaper and television coverage of presidents had changed only modestly, the public's increasing reliance on television news relative to newspapers might still lead one to expect that the presidency would assume greater salience in people's minds.

This conclusion may err, however, in two respects. First, though the data do indicate important and unquestionable change toward greater reliance on television, one should not exaggerate the changes of the last forty years.[17] Television was an important source of information during the Eisenhower period, and newspapers remain an important source of information for people today. Indeed by some measures, W. Russell Neuman finds that newspapers "have remained dominant in terms of the primary flow of political communications." Studies have found, for instance, that "in a single day only 23 percent of the adult population see a network newscast, while 69 percent see a newspaper."[18] Second, many people who indicate to pollsters that they rely on television for their news rely primarily or even exclusively on local news rather than national network news. And local television news, it appears from a 1987–1988 study by Steven Hess, is markedly different in its coverage of the president than network news. Hess found that "local broadcasts covered executive and legislative branches of the national government in about equal proportions" and that if one leaves out appearances by executive officials other than the president, Congress has about a two to one edge on the president. Moreover, "the 'quality of the legislators' appearances on local news is better . . . in that they are more often seen and heard, while the president is more often merely mentioned."[19]

Whatever the patterns of media coverage, it is well to return to more direct measures of how people think about the president's role in the political system. As early as 1968, a poll showed that close to 70 percent of the public reported that of the three branches of the national government, they followed the presidency most closely. Only 23 percent named the Congress. Yet in spite of this, the same poll showed that more people believed the Congress affected their day-to-day life than thought the president did. And more people believed Congress should have the greater say in decision making than believed the president should. Even in 1978, at a time when studies have shown presidential news swamping congressional news on television, the public was evenly divided about whether Congress or the president should have a greater role in decision making. Moreover, in the 1980s, as the Reagan presidency was dwarfing Congress in national network coverage, far more people felt that balancing the budget was Congress's responsibility than felt it was the president's. Such findings suggest that one needs to be extremely cautious about inferring too much about popular expectations of presidential roles from media coverage.

Notes

CHAPTER 1. THE LORE OF LIGHTNING RODS

1. John Hersey, *Aspects of the Presidency* (New Haven, Conn.: Ticknor and Fields, 1980), 83.

2. See, e.g., Aaron Wildavsky, "The Past and Future Presidency," in Nathan Glazer and Irving Kristol, eds., *The American Commonwealth* (New York: Basic Books, 1976), 56–76, esp. 73, and Fred I. Greenstein, *The Hidden-Hand Presidency: Eisenhower as Leader* (New York: Basic Books, 1982), 238.

3. *The Portable Machiavelli,* ed. and trans. Peter Bondanella and Mark Musa (New York: Penguin, 1979), 139.

4. "Advice to Sir George Villiers, afterwards Duke of Buckingham, when he became favourite to King James," in *The Works of Francis Bacon,* 3 vols. (Philadelphia: A. Hart, 1853), 2:375–88, quotation at 375. Barry Goldwater reports that among the Hopi Indians it was "custom that the chief rarely if ever spoke publicly on important matters. A promising young brave always did so. If anything went wrong, it was the brave's fault. If things went right, the chief was praised" (Barry M. Goldwater with Jack Casserly, *Goldwater* [New York: Doubleday, 1988], 270).

5. Pendleton Herring, *Presidential Leadership* (New York: Farrar and Rinehart, 1940), 111–15.

6. Harold J. Laski, *The American Presidency: An Interpretation* (New York: Harper and Brothers, 1940), 90–91, 93–94; emphasis in quotation is in original.

7. Patrick Anderson, *The President's Men* (Garden City, N.Y.: Doubleday, 1968), 6.

8. James Bryce, *The American Commonwealth,* 2 vols. (1893; reprint, New York: Macmillan, 1924), 1:93.

9. Arthur Krock, *Memoirs: Sixty Years on the Firing Line* (New York: Funk and Wagnalls, 1968), 384.

10. John Ehrlichman, *Witness to Power: The Nixon Years* (New York: Simon and Schuster, 1982), 111. In a similar vein, James Hagerty confided in his diary, "A Cabinet member, even though he is expressing his own opinion, is looked upon as talking for the administration" (Robert H. Ferrell, ed., *The Diary of James C. Hagerty: Eisenhower in Mid-Course, 1954–1955* [Bloomington: Indiana University Press, 1983], 193).

11. Fred I. Greenstein, "Reagan and the Lore of the Modern Presidency: What Have We Learned?" in Fred I. Greenstein, ed., *The Reagan Presidency* (Baltimore: Johns Hopkins University Press, 1983), 159–87, quotation at 159.

12. Compare, for instance, Patrick Anderson's judgment that Harry Hopkins had been "used as a political lightning rod to draw criticism away from the President" (*President's Men,* 4) with Robert Sherwood's claim that Hopkins "was unquestionably a political liability to Roosevelt, a convenient target for all manner of attacks directed at the President himself" (*Roosevelt and Hopkins: An Intimate History* [New York: Harper and Brothers, 1948], 1). Or contrast Rosalynn Carter's judgment that Carter needed to fire Joseph Califano because, "Joe was hurting him [Carter] politically" (*First Lady from Plains* [Boston: Houghton Mifflin, 1984], 155) with Fred Greenstein's judgment that the firing of Califano was a mistake because Califano was "a public figure with a sufficiently independent reputation and personal disposition to be effective as a deflector" (*Hidden-Hand Presidency,* 238).

13. The most sustained treatment of the subject that I am aware of is Fred Greenstein's *Hidden-Hand Presidency,* esp. 90–92, 147, 179, 238–40. Two other books that are well attuned to the adviser's role in deflecting blame are Patrick Anderson, *President's Men,* and Joseph G. Bock, *The White House Staff and the National Security Assistant: Friendship and Friction at the Water's Edge* (Westport, Conn.: Greenwood Press, 1987).

14. See, for example, Henry C. Kenski, "The Impact of Economic Conditions on Presidential Popularity," *Journal of Politics* 39 (August 1977): 764–73; Kristen Renwick Monroe, *Presidential Popularity and the Economy* (New York: Praeger, 1984); and David J. Lanoue, "Economic Prosperity and Presidential Popularity: Sorting Out the Effects," *Western Political Quarterly* 40 (June 1987): 237–45.

15. John E. Mueller, "Presidential Popularity from Truman to Johnson," *American Political Science Review* 64 (March 1970): 27, 34.

16. The most important work in this vein is Samuel Kernell, "Explaining Presidential Popularity," *American Political Science Review* 72 (June 1978): 506–22.

17. Richard A. Brody, "Daily News and the Dynamics of Public Support for the President" (Paper presented at the 1986 Annual Meeting of the Western Political Science Association, Eugene, Oreg., March 20–22, 1986), 1.

18. Kernell, "Explaining Presidential Popularity," 518.

19. Charles W. Ostrom, Jr., and Dennis M. Simon, "Promise and Performance: A Dynamic Model of Presidential Popularity," *American Political Science Review* 79 (June 1985): 334–58, quotation at 351.

20. Time-series analysis, Lee Sigelman has warned, is "a statistical minefield, where a single misstep can cause the entire analysis to blow up in the face of the unwary researcher" ("Presidential Popularity: Some Unresolved Issues," Presidency Research Group *Newsletter* [April 1981], 9). A fine discussion of some of the limits of time-series analysis can be found in George C. Edwards III, *The Public Presidency: The Pursuit of Popular Support* (New York: St. Martin's, 1983), 257–60.

21. See, for example, Robert Y. Shapiro and Bruce M. Conforto, "Presidential Performance, the Economy, and the Public's Evaluation of Economic Conditions," *Journal of Politics* 42 (February 1980): 49–67; Helmut Norpoth and Thom Yantek, "Macroeconomic Conditions and Fluctuations of Presidential Popularity: The Question of Lagged Effects," *American Journal of Political Science* 27 (November 1983): 785–807, esp. 802–3; and Edwards, *Public Presidency,* 211–67.

22. The phrase is used in Mark Peffley and John T. Williams, "Attributing Presidential Responsibility for National Economic Problems," *American Politics Quarterly* 13 (October 1985): 395.

23. James Reston, "The Blame Game," *New York Times,* October 17, 1982, E15.

Hedrick Smith, *The Power Game: How Washington Works* (New York: Random House, 1988), 656–60.

24. A wide-ranging discussion of possible blame-avoidance strategies can be found in R. Kent Weaver's important essay, "The Politics of Blame Avoidance," *Journal of Public Policy* (October–December 1986): 371–98.

25. *The Hoover Commission Report* (New York: McGraw-Hill, 1949), 25; also see 21.

26. Leonard D. White, *The Jacksonians: A Study in Administrative History, 1829–1861* (New York: Free Press, 1954), 87.

27. See, e.g., Richard Tanner Johnson, *Managing the White House* (New York: Harper and Row, 1974); Alexander L. George, *Presidential Decisionmaking in Foreign Policy: The Effective Use of Information and Advice* (Boulder, Colo.: Westview Press, 1980), chap. 8; and Richard E. Neustadt, *Presidential Power* (New York: John Wiley, 1980), chap. 7.

28. Neustadt, *Presidential Power,* 31; Graham Wilson, "Are Department Secretaries Really a President's Natural Enemies?" *British Journal of Political Science* 7 (July 1977): 273–99.

29. See, e.g., Richard P. Nathan, *The Administrative Presidency* (New York: John Wiley, 1983).

30. Richard F. Fenno, Jr., *The President's Cabinet* (Cambridge, Mass.: Harvard University Press, 1959), 171.

31. Anderson, *President's Men,* 348. Of Bill Moyers, George Reedy said: "What Bill did was pin responsibility upon the President in private conversations with the press. . . . It was no accident that the President's popularity started to fall abruptly as soon as Bill took over" (Larry Berman, "Johnson and the White House Staff," in Robert A. Divine, *Exploring the Johnson Years* [Austin: University of Texas Press, 1981], 193).

32. Maureen Dowd and Thomas L. Friedman, "Baker Rides to the Rescue and Straight into Trouble," *New York Times,* September 6, 1992, A10. Some people on Vice President Quayle's staff fretted that Quayle's chief of staff, William Kristol, got too much credit for Quayle's successes, particularly after the surfacing of news reports characterizing Kristol as "Dan Quayle's brain" (Kevin Sack, "Quayle's Right Hand: A Contrarian Tries to Turn Boss's Image Inside Out," *New York Times,* September 9, 1992, A11).

33. Dick Kirchsten, "Keeping the Image Clean," *National Journal,* August 22, 1981, 1515.

34. George Sergiovanni, "The 'Van Buren Jinx': Vice Presidents Need Not Beware," *Presidential Studies Quarterly* 18 (Winter 1988): 67.

35. Larry Speakes, *Speaking Out: The Reagan Presidency from inside the White House* (New York: Scribners, 1988), 85. Also confusing is Hedrick Smith's suggestion that Don Regan had to quit because he "was becoming too much of a lightning rod" (address to the Commonwealth Club of San Francisco, July 8, 1988). If the term lightning rod denotes deflection of criticism (and this definition is consistent with Smith's usage of the term in his splendid book, *The Power Game* [New York: Random House, 1988]), then it is difficult to see how, at least from the president's point of view, an adviser can become "too much" of a lightning rod. An adviser may, of course, become so controversial that rather than deflect criticism (i.e., act as a lightning rod) he draws criticism to the president (i.e., becomes a liability).

36. Juan Williams, "John Sununu, the White House Chief of Gaffe," *Washington Post National Weekly Edition,* December 2–8, 1991, 22.

37. See Martin Landau, "On the Use of Metaphor in Political Analysis," in *Political Theory and Political Science* (New York: Macmillan, 1972), 78–102, and Robert

A. Nisbet, *Social Change and History* (New York: Oxford University Press, 1969), esp. 4-7.

38. "Peck" Russell of the *New York Times,* quoted in James Reston, "Not a Political Movement but a Love Affair," September 11, 1955, reprinted in *Sketches in the Sand* (New York: Alfred A. Knopf, 1967), 422.

39. *Newsweek,* September 4, 1967, 19.

40. Earl L. Butz, Oral History-95, January 15, 1968, Columbia Oral History Project, Eisenhower Library, 49, 51 (hereafter cited as COHP, EL). Butz was assistant secretary of agriculture from 1954 to 1957 and served as secretary of agriculture under Presidents Nixon and Ford.

41. Fred Steeper, quoted in *Wall Street Journal,* June 23, 1988, 58; Robert J. Donovan, *Eisenhower: The Inside Story* (New York: Harper and Row, 1956), 71.

42. Fenno, *President's Cabinet,* 165.

43. Ibid., 165-67.

44. The distinction between the "inner cabinet" (State, Defense, Treasury, and Justice) and the "outer cabinet" is from Thomas E. Cronin, *The State of the Presidency,* 2d ed. (Boston: Little, Brown, 1980), 282 ff.

45. More precisely, the postmaster general averaged 260 mentions a year, the secretary of interior 137, the secretary of labor 104, the secretary of agriculture 95, and the commerce secretary 93.

46. Averaging Benson's numbers over the duration of Eisenhower's presidency would not affect the results much. I have not calculated such an average, however, because after 1950, the *Times* changed the way it indexed names, making it necessary to cross-reference in order to obtain data about front-page references or even to obtain total mentions that are comparable with the earlier data.

47. I have excluded defense secretary designate John Tower from the list of administration officials. Tower had 143 mentions in 1989, almost all the result of his contentious confirmation hearing. Coverage of Sam Nunn, who was chair of the Armed Services Committee, was substantially increased by the Tower confirmation. The coverage of Jim Wright and John Glenn was greatly inflated as a result of ethics investigations directed at them.

48. For vivid illustrations of this truth see Michael Jay Robinson and Maura Clancey, "Teflon Politics," *Public Opinion* 7 (April/May 1984): 14-18.

49. Neustadt, *Presidential Power,* 72.

50. Ibid., 64.

CHAPTER 2. IKE'S LIGHTNING ROD

1. During his eight years in office, Eisenhower averaged a 65 percent approval rating. In contrast, Ronald Reagan averaged 52 percent, Jimmy Carter and Gerald Ford each 47 percent, Richard Nixon 48 percent, and Lyndon Johnson 56 percent (see George C. Edwards III with Alec Gallup, *Presidential Approval: A Sourcebook* [Baltimore: Johns Hopkins University Press, 1990], 156).

2. Fred I. Greenstein, *The Hidden-Hand Presidency: Eisenhower as Leader* (New York: Basic Books, 1982), 92.

3. Ibid., esp. 90-92, 147, 238-39.

4. Ibid., 91-92.

5. Herbert Brownell, "From Campaigning to Governance," in Kenneth W. Thompson, ed., *The Eisenhower Presidency* (Lanham, Md.: University Press of America, 1984), 168.

6. Emmet John Hughes, *The Ordeal of Power: A Political Memoir of the Eisenhower Years* (New York: Atheneum, 1963), 251.

7. Greenstein, *Hidden-Hand Presidency,* 91. Krock's memoirs, it needs to be mentioned, were not published until eight years after Eisenhower left the presidency, but there are plenty of reasons to think that this was not something that occurred to Eisenhower only after watching Johnson's failure.

8. No evidence exists that Eisenhower selected his secretary of agriculture (or any other controversial cabinet member) for the purpose of being a lightning rod (Greenstein comes to the same conclusion in *Hidden-Hand Presidency,* 91). Rather, Benson seems to have been chosen in large part because he had widespread support within the farming community, particularly from the powerful Farm Bureau (see, e.g., Richard F. Fenno, Jr., *The President's Cabinet* [Cambridge, Mass.: Harvard University Press, 1959], 51-87; Jeffrey E. Cohen, *The Politics of the U.S. Cabinet: Representation in the Executive Branch, 1789-1984* [Pittsburgh: University of Pittsburgh Press, 1988]; Edward L. Schapsmeier and Frederick H. Schapsmeier, *Ezra Taft Benson and the Politics of Agriculture* [Danville, Ill.: Interstate, 1975], 13-14, 35-36; and George Aiken, Oral History-28, April 27, 1967, COHP, EL, 12. In addition, the administration saw the appointment of Benson, who had backed Taft in 1952, as an opportunity to unite the Republican party (Herbert Brownell, Oral History-282, April 7, 1971, COHP, EL, 14). Eisenhower also definitely wanted someone who shared his view that government control over agriculture needed to be reduced (see Herbert Brownell, Oral History-157, January 31, 1968, COHP, EL, 108; Ezra Taft Benson, *Cross Fire: The Eight Years with Eisenhower* [Garden City, N.Y.: Doubleday, 1962], 11; and Dwight D. Eisenhower, *Mandate for Change* [Garden City, N.Y.: Doubleday, 1963], 90.

9. Greenstein, *Hidden-Hand Presidency,* 91. The Benson-as-lightning-rod hypothesis is also suggested by David Miller Tiffany, "Agricultural Policy-Making in the Eisenhower Administration" (Ph.D. dissertation, State University of New York at Binghamton, 1973), 207, 382; and Charles C. Alexander, *Holding the Line: The Eisenhower Era, 1952-1961* (Bloomington: Indiana University Press, 1975), 164. Neither Tiffany nor Alexander, however, provide evidence to support the hypothesis.

10. Rep. Frank Chelf of Kentucky, for instance, warned Eisenhower that if Benson remained in the cabinet, "he will do more to undermine the confidence of the farmers in your administration than anything that could happen" (Sherman Adams, *Firsthand Report* [New York: Harper and Brothers, 1961], 202; also see Edward L. Schapsmeier and Frederick H. Schapsmeier, "Eisenhower and Ezra Taft Benson: Farm Policy in the 1950s," *Agricultural History* 44 [October 1970]: 377; Milton R. Young, Oral History-248, April 28, 1967, COHP, EL, 8-9; and Edward J. Thye, Oral History-22, July 17, 1967, COHP, EL, 19.

11. See Schapsmeier and Schapsmeier, *Benson and the Politics of Agriculture,* 150-55; Tiffany, "Agricultural Policy-Making," 160-65, 172-74; and Benson, *Cross Fire,* 218.

12. Fenno, *President's Cabinet,* 183.

13. Stephen E. Ambrose, *Eisenhower: The President* (New York: Simon and Schuster, 1984), 159.

14. Adams, *Firsthand Report,* 202. Eisenhower was certainly well aware that in a context of declining farm prices, policies aimed at reducing price supports were bound to draw fire from aggrieved interests. In a meeting with legislative leaders held at the outset of his second term, for instance, Eisenhower acknowledged that in the agricultural area "any change will be criticized" (Legislative Leadership Meeting, April 16, 1957, Legislative Meeting Series (Official File, Eisenhower Library, hereafter cited as OF, EL). "None of us was blind to the fact," Eisenhower later wrote,

"that in attempting to liberate agriculture from the artificial system of marketing in vogue since World War II, we were undertaking an effort that would call forth angry protests from vote-seeking politicians and from certain sectors of the agricultural community" (*Mandate for Change,* 290). A number of prominent Republicans shared the view that criticism of the secretary of agriculture was inevitable given the farm situation and the administration's policies. See, for example, Adams, *Firsthand Report,* 203; Meade Alcorn, Oral History-163, February 8, 1967, COHP, EL, 128, 130; Edward Thye, *Congressional Record,* August 4, 1954, 13247.

15. American Institute of Public Opinion-593, January 3-7, 1958. The questions asked by Gallup were, Do you approve or disapprove of the way Secretary of Agriculture Ezra Taft Benson is handling his job? and Do you approve or disapprove of the way Eisenhower is handling his job as President? Essentially the same results showed up in an earlier Gallup poll, taken in March 1956. The March poll found that 60 percent of farmers approved of Eisenhower's job performance while only 25 percent approved of Benson's; 36 percent of farmers combined disapproval of Benson with approval of Eisenhower (AIPO-561, March 8-13, 1956).

16. The exact wording of the questions were, On the whole, do you think President Eisenhower is doing a good, fair, or poor job for the nation at Washington? and On the whole, do you think that Ezra Taft Benson is doing a good, fair, or poor job as secretary of agriculture?

17. Herbert S. Parmet, *Eisenhower and the American Crusades* (New York: Macmillan, 1972), 320.

18. Survey of Iowa farmers conducted by *Wallace's Farmer,* January 24-29, 1955.

19. Survey of Iowa farmers by *Wallace's Farmer,* June 22-July 1, 1957; also see July 7-14, 1958.

20. Survey of Iowa farmers by *Wallace's Farmer,* October 8-15, 1958.

21. Benson, *Cross Fire,* 399.

22. *The Gallup Poll: Public Opinion, 1935-1971,* 3 vols. (New York: Random House, 1972), 2:1421. This poll, the data for which have evidently been lost, was conducted at some point between April 16 (the day of the president's veto) and May 13 (the date of the press release).

23. Parmet, *Eisenhower and the American Crusades,* 322.

24. All of the data in this section were kindly provided to me by the Miller Publishing Center in Minneapolis.

25. In July 1981, 15 percent disapproved of Block, and 12 percent disapproved of Reagan. In July 1982, 38 percent disapproved of Block and 35 percent disapproved of Reagan. In January 1984, 25 percent disapproved of Block and 27 percent disapproved of Reagan. In July 1984, 32 percent disapproved of Block and 35 percent disapproved of Reagan.

26. A July 1985 poll showed a slightly larger discrepancy, with 65 percent disapproving of Block and 54 percent disapproving of Reagan. This is still a tightly coupled set of attitudes, however, when compared with the Eisenhower-Benson pattern.

27. In March 1981, 2 percent disapproved of Block and 6 percent disapproved of Reagan. In September 1981, 9 percent disapproved of Block and 11 percent disapproved of Reagan. In January 1982, 14 percent disapproved of Block and 18 percent disapproved of Reagan. In September 1982, 22 percent disapproved of Block and 27 percent disapproved of Reagan. In February 1983, 16 percent disapproved of Block and 29 percent disapproved of Reagan. In September 1983, 15 percent disapproved of Block and 22 percent disapproved of Reagan. In March 1984, 14 percent disapproved of Block and 19 percent disapproved of Reagan.

28. This average is computed from six polls conducted twice a year (January and July) between 1978 and 1980.

29. In both the Illinois and Indiana samples, the questions were asked twice a year, once in the early spring and once in early fall. I have omitted the polls conducted in March 1977, because of its proximity to the beginning of the term.

30. More specifically, in May 1975, 26 percent disapproved of Butz and 24 percent disapproved of Ford. In December 1975, 25 percent disapproved of Butz and 28 percent disapproved of Ford. In June 1976, 26 percent expressed disapproval of Butz, while 30 percent expressed disapproval of Ford, and in September of that year, 32 percent disapproved of Butz and 32 percent disapproved of Ford.

31. There were, of course, exceptions. North Carolina Democrat Kerr Scott, for instance, professed to being "one member of this body who from the beginning of this administration has placed the responsibility for its sorry record on one man, and that one man is Dwight Eisenhower" (*Congressional Record,* April 24, 1956, 6848). In general, it was the most liberal senators, such as Wayne Morse (January 26, 1954, 806–9; March 12, 1954, 3201–2), Paul Douglas (January 27, 1956, 1453), and beginning in 1956 Hubert Humphrey (March 1, 1956, 3687), who attacked Eisenhower directly. By the same token, there were conservative Republicans who forthrightly defended Benson, such as Arthur Watkins of Utah (January 30, 1956, 1527–28) and Everett Dirksen of Illinois (January 30, 1956, 1527; February 1, 1956, 1779; February 21, 1957, 2383).

32. Ibid., April 16, 1958, 6483.

33. Rep. Cannon (D-Mo.), in ibid., July 22, 1958, 1646.

34. Ibid., February 19, 1954, 2041.

35. Ibid., January 29, 1957, 1060.

36. Ibid., January 27, 1956, 1460.

37. Ibid., April 4, 1957, 5151.

38. Rep. Reuss (D-Wis.), in ibid., March 25, 1958, 5317.

39. Senator Kerr (D-Okla.), in ibid., February 16, 1954, 1768.

40. Ibid., January 30, 1956, 1539.

41. Ibid., March 31, 1958, 5761. Also see August 7, 1958, 16512.

42. Ibid., March 31, 1958, 5762.

43. Beginning early in the election year of 1956, Humphrey changed his tune, attacking both Benson and Eisenhower. He took special pains, for the first time, to identify the administration's program as "the Eisenhower-Benson farm program" (see, for example, ibid., March 6, 1956, 4025–52; also see March 1, 1956, 3696 and April 18, 1956, 6489). To press the point home, he told his Senate colleagues: "I have stated on the floor at times that I thought the Secretary of Agriculture ought to be dismissed, but I think that was an unkind remark. I do not believe it would make a bit of difference if he were dismissed. He is carrying out the policy of the administration from right up at the top" (March 1, 1956, 3687).

44. Ibid., March 22, 1954, 3654; March 4, 1954, 2642. Commenting on a *Wall Street Journal* report that Eisenhower had decided to veto any extension of present levels of farm price supports, Humphrey believed that if the president "will consult his own conscience" rather than following Benson's advice, there would almost certainly be no veto (June 16, 1954, 8355).

45. Farmers Union's *Washington Newsletter,* September 20, 1957.

46. Telegram, William Proxmire to DDE, September 12, 1957, cited in Adams, *Firsthand Report,* 203; and Schapsmeier and Schapsmeier, *Benson and the Politics of Agriculture,* 193, emphasis added.

47. Annual Message to Congress on the State of the Union, February 2, 1953, *Public Papers of the Presidents: Dwight D. Eisenhower, 1954–1961,* 8 vols. (Washington, D.C.: U.S. Government Printing Office, 1960–1961), 27.

48. "General Statement on Agricultural Policy," February 5, 1953, reprinted as Appendix D in Benson, *Cross Fire,* 602-5.

49. Address at the Annual Convention of the Future Farmers of America, Kansas City, Mo., October 15, 1953, *Public Papers,* 667-76.

50. Adams, *Firsthand Report,* 82.

51. Eisenhower, *Mandate for Change,* 290; also see 562-63. Sherman Adams observed that "the so-called Benson farm policies that everybody indignantly called to Eisenhower's attention were actually Eisenhower's own farm policies" (*Firsthand Report,* 203). Also see Ambrose, *Eisenhower,* 159-60; William E. Leuchtenburg, *In the Shadow of FDR: From Harry Truman to Ronald Reagan* (Ithaca, N.Y.: Cornell University Press, 1983), 53-56; Schapsmeier and Schapsmeier, "Eisenhower and Ezra Taft Benson," 369, 378; and Parmet, *Eisenhower and the Crusades,* 321.

52. Notes of meeting with secretary of agriculture, October 29, 1955, Box 6, Administration Series, Ann Whitman File (hereafter cited as AWF), EL. Also present at the meeting were Milton Eisenhower, Sherman Adams, and Jim Hagerty.

53. The Soil Bank included a temporary "Acreage Reserve" program, through which farmers were paid to take soil out of production, and a more long-term "Conservation Reserve" program, through which farmers would receive federal money for shifting their land into forage, trees, or even reservoirs.

54. Thye, Oral History-22, 24, 40.

55. Herschel D. Newsom, Oral History-306, March 21, 1968, COHP, EL, 5-7, 13, 22, 26, and passim. Also see Don Paarlberg, Oral History-52, January 17, 1968, COHP, EL, 97.

56. Young, Oral History-248, 8, 9, 18, 19.

57. Benson, *Cross Fire,* 394.

58. News Conference, February 26, 1958, *Public Papers,* 187.

59. Dwight D. Eisenhower to Edward J. Thye, March 13, 1958, OF, EL; cited in Schapsmeier and Schapsmeier, *Benson and the Politics of Agriculture,* 200-201, emphasis added.

60. Thye, Oral History-22, 38-39.

61. Young, Oral History-248, 18.

62. Herbert Brownell with John P. Burke, *Advising Ike: The Memoirs of Attorney General Herbert Brownell* (Lawrence: University Press of Kansas, 1993), 297. Brownell here is talking about Eisenhower's style generally not about Benson in particular.

63. Ibid., 72-73, 189. Stewart L. Udall, interior secretary under John Kennedy and Lyndon Johnson, points out that "visible, or apparent, Presidential support is vital to [a cabinet member's] authority and credibility; without it he cannot be a successful administrator or a national leader of power and prestige" ("Lame-Duck Cabinet," *New York Times,* December 28, 1972, A31).

64. Similarly, during the Reagan presidency, White House staffers constantly worried about distancing Watt from the president. See, for example, "Keeping the Image Clean," *National Journal,* August 22, 1981, 1515; and *New York Times,* March 7, 1983, II:6.

65. Benson, *Cross Fire,* 164. Benson to Eisenhower, January 5, 1954, Administration Series, AWF, EL.

66. *New York Times,* January 12, 1954, 8. Following the press conference, Benson participated in a half-hour television interview in which he discussed the message, as well as making a radio broadcast later that evening. Benson later described the day the president's message was delivered to Congress as "one of the busiest times in my eight years" (Benson, *Cross Fire,* 170).

67. Benson, *Cross Fire,* 174.

68. *U.S. News and World Report,* March 5, 1954, cited in Benson, *Cross Fire,* 184.

69. Early in his administration, Eisenhower signaled his reluctance to be drawn into the farm-policy debate. At a press conference in early April 1953, he was asked what he would do to deal with the problem of butter being stockpiled and spoiling and replied, "Well, of course, you are talking about something where you could far better go to the Secretary of Agriculture and get a really definitive answer to such a question" (News Conference, April 2, 1953, *Public Papers,* 155).

70. Benson, *Cross Fire,* 195. Also see 191.

71. See Robert J. Spitzer, *The Presidential Veto: Touchstone of the American Presidency* (Albany: State University of New York Press, 1988), 72 ff.

72. As George Bush found out. One of the fundamental contradictions of the Bush presidency was that the frequent recourse to the veto undermined his efforts at blame avoidance.

73. Ambrose, *Eisenhower,* 300.

74. Eisenhower, *Mandate for Change,* 560.

75. *Congressional Record,* April 16, 1956, 6322.

76. Ibid., April 16, 1956, 1638.

77. Ibid., April 18, 1956, 6489. In truth, Humphrey had publicly come to this conclusion a month earlier: "For a time I thought it was all Mr. Benson's idea, but I do not think it is. I think we have been unfair to the Secretary. He is carrying out orders from some place in the White House. I am not sure where they originate. I would assume he is carrying out President Eisenhower's orders. Possibly they are orders from Sherman Adams. But someone is giving orders" (ibid., March 1, 1956, 3687).

78. Ibid., April 18, 1956, 6511-13.

79. Eisenhower, *Mandate for Change,* 560. Tiffany, "Agricultural Policy-Making," 200-201.

80. *The Gallup Poll,* 1421. Also see "14 Farm States: Checking Ike's Strength," *Newsweek,* April 30, 1956, 28-29.

81. Eisenhower had anticipated that a veto would leave him vulnerable to criticism. A month before the legislation passed, Eisenhower told aides that "the Democrats are going to . . . write a bill that has something for everybody and if I then veto it, a lot of people will be mad" (Ambrose, *Eisenhower,* 300).

82. Ambrose, *Eisenhower,* 461. Jack Z. Anderson, a White House staff member and former aide to Benson, recalls the president calling Benson into his office to express his extreme displeasure at having to veto this bill. Eisenhower lectured Benson: "You've backed me into a corner. As a military man, I don't like this. Sometimes you have to lose a battle to win a war. . . . I guess I'm going to veto the bill as you've indicated you want done, but I'm in a horrible predicament" (Oral History-321, February 2, 1971, COHP, EL, 57).

83. Ezra Taft Benson to Eisenhower, March 18, 1958, Administration Series, AWF, EL.

84. Eisenhower to Benson, March 20, 1958, Administration Series, AWF, EL. Further instances of Eisenhower instructing Benson in the art of politics are recounted in Benson, *Cross Fire,* 70, 203, 321; and Paarlberg, Oral History-52, 12-13.

85. Meade Alcorn, then Republican party chair, recalls a meeting in which the president "cut Ezra Benson . . . cold out of the discussion. . . . He said, 'Now, look, Ezra this man over here is the National Chairman, and the reason he is National Chairman is because he's supposed to know something about politics. You're supposed to know something about agriculture. Now, you stick with the agriculture but you leave the politics to him' " (Alcorn, Oral History-163, 35).

86. President Eisenhower to Benson, November 15, 1958, Administration Series, AWF, EL.

87. Parmet, *Eisenhower and the Crusades,* 324. Adams, *Firsthand Report,* 204-5, 211-12.

88. Minnich minutes of meeting with legislative leaders, June 21, 1954, DDE Diary Series, AWF, EL.

89. Eisenhower to Hazlett, March 18, 1954, in Robert Griffith, ed., *Ike's Letters to a Friend, 1941-1958* (Lawrence: University Press of Kansas, 1984), 121. Typically, he added that "I want to stress, too, that there is no man in government more dedicated and devoted, and more selfless and sincere, than is Ezra Benson."

90. August Andresen to Eisenhower, February 27, 1954, Administration Series, AWF, EL.

91. Newsom to Karl D. Butler, February 23, 1954, cited in Schapsmeier and Schapsmeier, *Benson and the Politics of Agriculture,* 81.

92. Paarlberg, Oral History-52, esp. 15.

93. Adams, *Firsthand Report,* 206.

94. A "knowledgeable White House staffer," cited in William Bragg Ewald, Jr., *Eisenhower the President: Crucial Days, 1951-1960* (Englewood Cliffs, N.J.: Prentice-Hall, 1981), 163.

95. Chapter 7, a case study focusing on Eisenhower's relations with Attorney General Herbert Brownell, explores in greater depth the control over the direction of policy that a president forfeits in delegating to a subordinate.

96. Barry Goldwater, for instance, recalled that Eisenhower "was violently opposed to federal regulation of farming, prices, acreage and so forth" (Oral History-21, June 15, 1967, COHP, EL, 62).

CHAPTER 3. REAGAN'S LIABILITY

1. Mark Hertsgaard, *On Bended Knee: The Press and the Reagan Presidency* (New York: Farrar, 1988), 32. This view of the Carter presidency as oblivious to the problems of overexposure is exaggerated. After the Three Mile Island nuclear accident, for instance, Carter carefully avoided associating himself with events. As Jack Watson explained: "We didn't want to get the president out front and involved because we thought that the president's speaking about that and being personally involved in it would escalate the matter beyond where our knowledge would permit us to go. . . . So while we were keeping him informed internally at every turn of the day, he was not, either through a spokesman or otherwise, actively takng much of a role or saying much about it" (Samuel Kernell and Samuel L. Popkin, eds., *Chief of Staff: Twenty-Five Years of Managing the Presidency* [Berkeley: University of California Press, 1986], 36).

2. Steven R. Weisman, "Reagan Dissipates Heat by Delegating Authority," *New York Times,* October 11, 1981, V:4.

3. Hertsgaard, *On Bended Knee,* 32-33. Also see Hedrick Smith, "Reagan's Men: The Exercise of Power in the White House," *New York Times,* April 19, 1981, VI:64. Reagan's strategy of "presidential distancing" is analyzed in Bruce Buchanan, *The Citizen's Presidency* (Washington, D.C.: Congressional Quarterly, 1987), 125-29.

4. Larry Speakes, *Speaking Out: The Reagan Presidency from inside the White House* (New York: Scribners, 1988), 85.

5. David Stockman, *The Triumph of Politics: Why the Reagan Revolution Failed* (New York: Harper and Row, 1986), 189-91. The effort to distance Reagan from the

Social Security controversy was not particularly successful. A CBS/*New York Times* poll, conducted in September 1981, found that only 44 percent of the respondents said they could "trust the President to make the right decisions on social security" (press release, October 4, 1981). In contrast, six in ten trusted Reagan on military and budget issues.

6. Donald T. Regan, *For the Record: From Wall Street to Washington* (New York: Harcourt, 1998), 240.

7. Hertsgaard, *On Bended Knee,* 33.

8. See, e.g., *New York Times,* January 17, 1982, 20; James Reston, "Who Advises Reagan," *New York Times,* April 27, 1983, 27.

9. Lou Cannon, *President Reagan: The Role of a Lifetime* (New York: Simon and Schuster, 1991), 191-92; also see 145, 160. Similarly, in the wake of charges that the White House was being run by a "palace guard" and that President Eisenhower was uninformed about important matters of state, Sherman Adams felt the need to defend Eisenhower publicly as the "best informed man in the country today" and "the policy maker" (*New York Times,* November 19, 1957, 26), a comment that produced such unflattering headlines as "Adams Insists Ike Is Really President" (*New York Times,* January 22, 1958, 16).

10. Lou Cannon writes, the "low opinion of Reagan [among those in Washington] deprived him of credit for some of his accomplishments but also spared him the blame for his shortcomings" (*Role of a Lifetime,* 13; also see 87).

11. *New York Times,* January 10, 1982, 24. Also see Dick Kirschten, "White House Strategy," *National Journal,* February 21, 1981, 300-303.

12. Ann Reilly Dowd, "What Managers Can Learn from Manager Reagan," *Fortune,* September 15, 1986, 32-41.

13. In "Ronald Reagan—Another Hidden-Hand Ike?" Fred I. Greenstein points to the similarities in public image as well as probable differences in the behind-the-scenes reality. If Ike was really a hidden hand president, Greenstein concludes, Reagan was likely a "no-hands president" (*P.S.: Political Science & Politics* 23 [March 1990]: 12). The same apellation is used in Jane Mayer and Doyle McManus, *Landslide: The Unmaking of the President, 1984-1988* (Boston: Houghton Mifflin, 1988), chap. 2.

14. Political scientists seem to agree that Reagan was the most ideological president in recent history. Fred I. Greenstein writes that Reagan "is unique among the modern presidents in his depth—and one might add, duration—of ideological commitment" ("Reagan and the Lore of the Modern Presidency: What Have We Learned?" in Fred I. Greenstein, ed., *The Reagan Presidency* [Baltimore: Johns Hopkins University Press, 1983], 171). Richard E. Neustadt echoes this view, suggesting that Reagan "seems to be, ideologically, the most committed President since Herbert Hoover (is this fair to Hoover?)" ("Does the White House Need a Strong Chief of Staff?" in James Pfiffner, ed., *The Managerial Presidency* [Pacific Grove, Calif.: Brooks/Cole Publishing, 1991], 32). Bert Rockman agrees that a distinguishing feature of President Ronald Reagan is that he "believes in a few things with great passion and holds to them uncompromisingly" ("The Style and Organization of the Reagan Presidency," in Charles O. Jones, ed., *The Reagan Legacy: Promise and Performance* [Chatham, N.J.: Chatham House, 1988], 7).

15. Lou Cannon cautions that "while Reagan tried to stuff everything he heard or read into the view of the world he had brought with him to Washington, he appreciated the value of compromise and negotiation. . . . Reagan did not fit the neat ideological stereotype that was presented in alternative forms by movement conservatives and liberal activists. . . . On nearly all issues, Reagan was simultaneously an ideologue and a pragmatist. He complained to aides that true believers on the Republican

right such as Senator Jesse Helms preferred to 'go off the cliff with all flags flying' rather than take half a loaf and come back for more." Cannon speculates that Reagan's intense desire to win tended to "prevail even at the expense of his program [and] served as a check on ideology" (Cannon, *Role of a Lifetime,* 185–86).

Fred Greenstein reaches a similar conclusion, though by a somewhat different route: "Reagan is less than the compleat ideologue in two senses. In an Eric Hoffer world of 'true believers'—individuals who rely on detailed elaborations of doctrine to guide their day-to-day actions and even to lend meaning to their lives—Reagan is a tame specimen. His beliefs are important to him, but so are his wife, his family, his friends, his avocations, and much else that keeps him from being a Savonarola descended upon Washington to purge it of evil" (Greenstein, "Reagan and the Lore," 171). Also see James David Barber, *Presidential Character,* 4th ed. (Englewood Cliffs, N.J.: Prentice-Hall, 1992), 236–38.

16. Rockman, "Style and Organization," 9.

17. Martin Anderson was struck by the fact that as an executive, Reagan "made no demands, and gave almost no instructions" (*Revolution* [New York: Harcourt, 1988], 289). Also see Don Regan, *For the Record,* 142–43.

18. Mayer and McManus, *Landslide,* chap. 1.

19. In foreign policy, writes Lou Cannon, Reagan "had impulses . . . rather than policies" (*Role of a Lifetime,* 182). According to Cannon, Don Regan believed Reagan "was fundamentally a centrist and therefore gave a different meaning to 'let Reagan be Reagan' " (ibid., 565).

20. Mayer and McManus, *Landslide,* 53.

21. See Everett Carl Ladd, "The Brittle Mandate," *Political Science Quarterly* 96 (Spring 1981): 1–25; William Schneider, "The November 4 Vote for President: What Did It Mean?" in Austin Ranney, ed., *The American Elections of 1980* (Washington, D.C.: American Enterprise Institute, 1981); and Warren E. Miller and J. Merrill Shanks, "Policy Directions and Presidential Leadership: Alternative Interpretations of the 1980 Presidential Election," *British Journal of Political Science* 12 (July 1982): 299–356. Also see George C. Edwards III, *At the Margins* (New Haven, Conn.: Yale University Press, 1989), chap. 8; Robert Dahl, "Myth of the Presidential Mandate," *Political Science Quarterly* 105 (Fall 1990): 355–66; and Raymond Wolfinger, "Dealignment, Realignment and Presidential Mandates," in Austin Ranney, ed., *The American Elections of 1984* (Washington, D.C.: American Enterprise Institute, 1985).

22. Thomas E. Mann, "Thinking about the Reagan Years," in Larry Berman, ed., *Looking Back on the Reagan Presidency* (Baltimore: Johns Hopkins University Press, 1990), 27.

23. The argument I am making in this chapter runs up against one of the most persistent myths about Reagan, namely that his popular appeal was exceptional in the way that it transcended party lines. According to David Gergen, for instance, Reagan had become "a father figure . . . [who] transcends the party" (Mayer and McManus, *Landslide,* 13). But this view of Reagan cannot bear careful scrutiny. Reagan's average approval rating among Democrats was 30 percent, which is the *lowest* Democratic support score among all Republican presidents for whom Gallup has kept records. Reagan's average Democratic support score was marginally below that registered by Nixon (34 percent) and Ford (36 percent) and well shy of Bush's 46 percent and Eisenhower's 49 percent approval ratings among Democrats. In fact, Reagan did no better with Democrats than Carter (31 percent) had done with Republicans, and much worse than Johnson (39 percent) and Kennedy (49 percent). And in 1982 and the first ten months of 1983, while Watt was in office, Reagan's support among Democrats averaged about 23 percent. Only Nixon in his final year, mired in

Watergate, received less support from the opposite party (see George C. Edwards with Alec Gallup, *Presidential Approval* [Baltimore: Johns Hopkins University Press, 1990], 119). Moreover, the gap between the support given the president by adherents of the two parties was *higher* during the Reagan presidency than at any other time during the last forty years. From Eisenhower to Carter the average difference in approval between Democrats and Republicans was roughly 35 percentage points, ranging from Carter's 26 percent to Nixon's 40 percent. For Bush the gap between Democratic and Republican approval was 37 percent. During Reagan's tenure, however, that gap ballooned to 53 percentage points. This and other evidence debunking the myth of Reagan as a "Teflon-coated" president can be found in Edwards, *Presidential Approval*, esp. 156, 179. The data for Bush were generously provided to me by George Edwards. The precise numbers for Bush may be off a percentage point or two due to a few missing polls, but this is inconsequential for the point being made here.

Edwards's findings are supported by recent work by Martin P. Wattenberg. Wattenberg counted the responses to open-ended questions (1952–1984) asking what voters liked and disliked about the presidential candidates and found that in 1984 Reagan was "the most unpopular among nonsupporters of *any* major candidate in the time series, winning or losing!" "Reagan's net unpopularity largely stems from the unprecedented, intense dislike with which he was perceived by voters who opposed him." Of those who voted for Mondale in 1984, 54 percent had more than two reasons for voting against Reagan while only 27 percent expressed any reason at all for voting for Reagan. In contrast, among those who voted for Adlai Stevenson in 1956, only 21 percent gave more than two reasons for voting against Eisenhower and 60 percent gave some reason to vote for Ike ("The Reagan Polarization Phenomenon and the Continuing Downward Slide in Presidential Candidate Popularity," *American Politics Quarterly* 14 [July 1986]: 226–27, 229–30). Other important antidotes to the facile characterization of Reagan as a Teflon president are D. Roderic Kiewiet and Douglas Rivers, "The Economic Basis of Reagan's Appeal," in John E. Chubb and Paul E. Peterson, eds., *The New Direction in American Politics* (Washington, D.C.: Brookings, 1985), 69–90; and James W. Ceaser, "The Reagan Presidency and American Public Opinion," in Jones, ed., *Reagan Legacy,* 172–210.

24. *New York Times,* April 15, 1982, 15. *Wall Street Journal,* June 2, 1982, 1. Lou Cannon, *Reagan* (New York: G. P. Putnam's Sons, 1982), 366.

25. Laurence I. Barrett, *Gambling with History: Reagan in the White House* (Garden City, N.Y.: Doubleday, 1983), 40–41. Hedrick Smith, *The Power Game: How Washington Works* (New York: Random House, 1988), 55, 658.

26. See, for example, Peter M. Benda and Charles H. Levine, "Reagan and the Bureaucracy: The Bequest, the Promise, and the Legacy," in Jones, ed., *Reagan Legacy,* 109; and Frank J. Fahrenkopf, Jr., quoted in *New York Times,* March 29, 1983, 1.

27. Kenneth T. Walsh, "James Watt, Reagan's Lightning Rod, Won't Leave Soon," *Denver Post,* August 23, 1981, 27. Also see Dick Kirchsten, "Inferior Departments?" *National Journal,* June 27, 1981, 1170.

28. Quoted in Larry Liebert, "Watt Wows Some," *San Francisco Chronicle,* August 13, 1981, 45.

29. There were, of course, exceptions. From the outset, John B. Oakes, former senior editor of the *New York Times,* aimed his criticism directly at Reagan. By nominating "the anti-environmental extremist James G. Watt," Oakes complained, "Ronald Reagan has demonstrated his contempt for the office itself, for the needs of the country, and for the advice of the most respected environmentalists of his own

party" (quoted in *Not Man Apart,* February 1981, 11). Also see Oakes, "Reagan-vironmentalism," *New York Times,* May 1, 1981, 31.

30. Excerpts from the address were reprinted in *Sierra,* July/August, 1981, 6+; and *Not Man Apart,* July 1981, 11.

31. *San Francisco Chronicle,* July 25, 1981, 9.

32. T. H. Watkins, "James Gaius Watt: An Idea Whose Time Has Gone," *Living Wilderness* (Winter 1981): 34.

33. *New York Times,* April 18, 1981, 39.

34. Ibid., March 29, 1981, 32.

35. CBS News Poll press release, September 1981.

36. Gallup-1176, June 26–29, 1981. Gallup-1183, October 2–5, 1981.

37. *San Francisco Chronicle,* August 19, 1981, 9.

38. Sierra Club President Phillip Berry suggests, I think accurately, that environmental groups' initial hesitancy to directly attack Reagan was due primarily to the president's popularity and not to a sense that Reagan was an environmentalist at heart. Also at work, Berry explains, was a "desire to give the administration a way 'out' if they chose to take it" as well as the knowledge that "you cannot easily change presidents" but "it is relatively easy to change [an] interior secretary" (Personal correspondence with author, August 2, 1991). As these comments make clear, the lightning rod phenomenon is as much if not more a product of the strategic calculations of critics as of presidents.

39. *Not Man Apart,* October 1981, 25. The same sentiments were expressed in a letter to the *Los Angeles Times,* August 29, 1981, II:2. Expressing amazement "that President Reagan has so successfully been able to escape criticism for what is in reality Reagan's own ridiculous environmental policy," the letter pointed out that Watt was appointed by Reagan "because he shares Reagan's pro-exploitation view of the environment and because Reagan was convinced he could forcefully advocate and enforce these views." "We in California," he reminded his audience, "should remember, Reagan has always been an anti-environmentalist." The letter concluded that "it is time for people who are disappointed or outraged at James Watt to pin the blame on the boss, Ronald Reagan." Also see John B. Oakes, "The Reagan Hoax," *New York Times,* November 1, 1981, IV:21.

40. *Not Man Apart,* December 1981, 26.

41. *New York Times,* February 2, 1982, 13.

42. *Not Man Apart,* June 1982, 2.

43. Joe Fontaine, Sierra Club president, quoted in Doug Scott, "Reagan's First Year: 'We Know Watt's Wrong,'" *Sierra,* January/February, 1982, 30.

44. The other groups were the Natural Resources Defense Council, the Environmental Defense Fund, the Environmental Policy Center, Environmental Action, Defenders of Wildlife, and the Solar Lobby.

45. *Ronald Reagan and the American Environment* (Andover, Mass.: Brick House, 1982), 6–7. In October 1982 the same ten groups came out with another report, entitled "Hitting Home," which kept the blame focused on Reagan ("10 Environment Groups See Reagan Marring Health and Landscape," *New York Times,* October 13, 1982, 22).

46. *Not Man Apart,* May 1982, 1, 22; *San Francisco Chronicle,* April 1, 1982, 13; *New York Times,* April 1, 1982, 23.

47. Russell W. Peterson, "Laissez-Faire Landscape," *New York Times Magazine,* October 31, 1982, 27+.

48. See, for example, the editorial in the *Los Angeles Times,* which not only blasted "the Reagan Administration . . . [for] sacrificing economics to ideology . . . [in] a fire sale . . . that will burn Americans for generations to come," but stressed

that Watt was "operating with the explicit sanction of the White House" ("A Sellout of Our Heritage," *Los Angeles Times*, August 10, 1982, II:4). Also see John Hooper, "Privatization: The Reagan Administration's Master Plan for Government Giveaways," *Sierra*, November/December 1982, 32-37.

49. *Sierra*, September/October 1983, 20-24.

50. *Not Man Apart*, May 1983, 14-15.

51. *Los Angeles Times*, February 10, 1983, II:10.

52. *New York Times*, July 9, 1981, 1; June 3, 1983, 18.

53. *Los Angeles Times*, October 3, 1983, II:4; October 11, 1983, II:6; October 16, 1983, V:4.

54. *Sierra*, November/December 1983, 10; *Los Angeles Times*, October 11, 1983, 7; *Not Man Apart*, November 1983, 1 (emphasis added).

55. Gallup-1176, June 26-29, 1981; Gallup-1196, June 11-14, 1982; Gallup-1212, April 15-18, 1983. Also see Gallup-1183, October 2-5, 1981; Gallup-203-6, July 3-August 2, 1982; and Gallup-1222, August 19-22, 1983.

56. See Gallup/Newsweek no. 20684, January 8-15, 1984. Harris surveys also indicated that jettisoning Watt helped Reagan's public image. See "Watt's Departure is Helping Reagan," *Business Week*, December 19, 1983, 14.

57. William Schneider, "The Environment: The Public Wants More Protection, Not Less," *National Journal*, March 26, 1983, 677. Barry Sussman, "Poll Says Most Think Reagan Prefers to Protect Polluters," *Washington Post*, March 5, 1993, A6.

58. The shift among environmentalists from attacking Watt to attacking Reagan must be understood, in part, as a strategic reaction to Reagan's declining popularity caused by the economic downturn. During the spring of 1981, in the aftermath of the assassination attempt, Reagan had approval ratings that were better than three to one, making it costly to directly criticize Reagan. By the following spring, however, with as many people disapproving as approving of Reagan, it had become far less risky for environmental groups to directly attack Reagan. As his job rating continued to slide over the next year, criticism of the president became increasingly painless. But this is only a partial explanation, for it neglects the role that Reagan's behavior played in making it untenable for opponents to believe that Watt was diverging from Reagan's preferred policies.

59. Anne Burford with John Greenya, *Are You Tough Enough?* (New York: McGraw-Hill, 1986), 281-82. Contrast this with Burford's insistence, while still in office, that "the President has a strong commitment to the environment" (*New York Times*, March 11, 1983, A18).

60. On the importance of ideological criteria for appointments in the Reagan presidency, see Benda and Levine, "Reagan and the Bureaucracy," 108-9; Richard Nathan, *The Administrative Presidency* (New York: Wiley, 1983); Joel D. Aberbach, "The President and the Executive Branch," in Colin Campbell and Bert A. Rockman, eds., *The Bush Presidency: First Appraisals* (Chatham, N.J.: Chatham House, 1991), esp. 227-28; and Terry M. Moe, "Interests, Institutions, and Positive Theory: The Politics of the NLRB," *Studies in American Political Development* 2 (1987): 236-99, esp. 266-70. Also see Education Secretary Terrel H. Bell's revealing account in *The Thirteenth Man: A Reagan Cabinet Memoir* (New York: Free Press, 1988), 38-51.

61. Ward Sinclair, "The Rhinestone Cowboys," *Living Wilderness* (Fall 1981): 11-13. Audubon president Russell Peterson, in a meeting with Meese in February 1982, complained that the president "has appointed to agencies involved with environmental matters almost across the board people who had been working against the very laws and regulations they were now assigned to administer" (Philip Shabecoff, "Memo: Meese and Environmentalists, *New York Times*, February 5, 1982, A14).

Sierra Club official Doug Scott commented that the administration's antienvironmental image was "reinforced by the words and actions of virtually every . . . prominent environmental appointee of the Reagan administration so far" ("Reagan's First Year," *Sierra,* January/February, 1982, 128).

62. The lack of access environmental groups had to the Reagan White House is documented in a recent study of interest-group access during the Carter and Reagan presidencies. See John Orman, "The President and Interest Group Access," *Presidential Studies Quarterly* 18 (Fall 1988): 787–92.

63. *New York Times,* February 5, 1982, 14; March 17, 1982, 20.

64. Robert Cameron, "Public Opinion and Environmental Politics in the 1970s and 1980s," in Norman J. Vig and Michael Kraft, eds., *Environmental Policy in the 1980s: Reagan's New Agenda* (Washington, D.C.: Congressional Quarterly, 1984), 71. Dale Russakoff, "The Critique: Ansel Adams Takes Environmental Challenge to Reagan," *Washington Post,* July 3, 1983. In an interview with Lou Cannon in 1990, Reagan again insisted that he had always considered himself an environmentalist (Cannon, *Role of a Lifetime,* 526).

65. Frank J. Popper, "The Timely End of the Sagebrush Rebellion," *Public Interest,* no. 76 (Summer 1984): 61.

66. Michael E. Kraft, "A New Environmental Policy Agenda: The 1980 Presidential Campaign and its Aftermath," in Vig and Kraft, eds., *Environmental Policy in the 1980s,* 35, 42. Lou Cannon comments that "Reagan compiled an environmental record as governor of California that was better than his comments during the campaign would have led anyone to believe" (*Role of a Lifetime,* 530).

67. Ron Arnold, *At the Eye of the Storm: James Watt and the Environmentalists* (Chicago: Regnery Gateway, 1982) 190. Also see *New York Times,* August 14, 1981, 10.

68. *New York Times,* March 22, 1983, 22.

69. Ibid., March 12, 1983, 8. At this press conference, Reagan also expressed the view that "environmental extremists" wouldn't "be happy until the White House looks like a bird's nest." Also see ibid., March 7, 1983, II:6.

70. Ibid., March 30, 1983, 14.

71. See Fred I. Greenstein, *The Hidden-Hand Presidency: Eisenhower as Leader* (New York: Basic Books, 1982), 73. Also see Eisenhower to John Foster Dulles, April 2, 1956, DDE Diary Series, AWF, EL; and Don Paarlberg, Oral History-52, January 17, 1968, COHP, EL, 23–24.

72. Ron Wolf, "God, James Watt, and the Public's Land," *Audubon,* May 1981, 64.

73. *Los Angeles Times,* March 30, 1983, II:4.

74. Elizabeth Drew, "A Reporter at Large," *New Yorker,* May 4, 1981, 112.

75. See sources cited in note 24.

76. Greenstein, *Hidden-Hand Presidency,* 239. Russell Peterson, for instance, observed: "By his own admission a 'lightning rod' for the President's least popular environmental policies, the Interior Secretary was doing exactly what he had been hired to do" ("Laissez-Faire Landscape," *New York Times Magazine,* October 31, 1982, 27+).

77. "If there hadn't been a James Watt," confided Doug Scott, director of federal affairs for the Sierra Club, "we would have had to invent one" (Cannon, *Reagan,* 363).

78. Cannon, *Role of a Lifetime,* 532.

79. Paul R. Portney, "Natural Resources and the Environment: More Controversy than Change," in John L. Palmer and Isabell V. Sawhill, eds., *The Reagan Rec-*

ord: *An Assessment of America's Changing Domestic Priorities* (Cambridge, Mass: Ballinger Publishing, 1984), 161.

80. Ibid., 158, 161. Similarly, Philip B. Heymann has noted that Anne Gorsuch Burford's "forced departure was as attributable to the *way* she handled her unpopular assignment as it was to *what* she did" (*The Politics of Public Management* [New Haven, Conn.: Yale University Press, 1987], 43). Much of what Heymann writes about Burford applies with equal or greater force to Watt. Reagan asked for Watt's resignation for the same reason he asked for Burford's resignation: "Not because she was ignoring his policies but because she failed to consider the policies and powers of others as well" (ibid., 7).

81. Aaron Wildavsky, "Foreward: The Human Side of Government," in *Steering the Elephant: How Washington Works* (New York: Universe Books, 1987), xiv. Also see Heymann, *Politics of Public Management.*

82. Portney, "Natural Resources and the Environment," 153–54. Also see Michael E. Kraft and Norman J. Vig, "Environmental Policy in the Reagan Presidency," *Political Science Quarterly* 99 (Fall 1984): 425.

83. See Heymann, *Politics of Public Management,* 19.

84. Cannon, *Role of a Lifetime,* 532. William A. Niskannen, *Reaganomics* (New York: Oxford University Press, 1988), 125–29. David Boaz, ed., *Assessing the Reagan Years* (Washington, D.C.: Cato Institute, 1988). Also see John D. Leshy, "Natural Resource Policy," in Paul R. Portney, *Natural Resources and the Environment: The Reagan Approach* (Washington, D.C.: Urban Institute Press, 1984), 13–46.

85. Portney, "Natural Resources and the Environment," 141, 173.

86. Riley E. Dunlap, "Polls, Pollution, and Politics Revisited: Public Opinion on the Environment in the Reagan Era," *Environment* 29 (July/August 1987): 32, 34–35. Also see Cannon, *Role of a Lifetime,* 526.

87. Dunlap, "Public Opinion on the Environment in the Reagan Era," 36.

88. In the summer of 1982, George Will correctly foresaw the danger "that Watt will discredit economic analysis by seeming sympathetic only to economic considerations" ("A Word for the Wilderness," *Newsweek,* August 16, 1982, 68).

89. See Philip Shabecoff, "Watt's Goals at Interior, But in a Different Style," *New York Times,* March 3, 1986.

90. Portney, "Natural Resources and the Environment," 162.

91. Robert Cameron Mitchell, "Public Opinion and the Green Lobby: Poised for the 1990s?" in Norman J. Vig and Michael E. Kraft, eds., *Environmental Policy in the 1990s: Toward a New Agenda* (Washington, D.C.: Congressional Quarterly Press, 1990), 91–92; Michael E. Kraft and Norman J. Vig, "Environmental Policy from the Seventies to the Nineties: Continuity and Change," ibid., 16; Dunlap, "Public Opinion on the Environment in the Reagan Era."

92. Michael E. Kraft and Norman J. Vig, "Presidential Styles and Substance: Environmental Policy from Reagan to Bush" (Paper presented at the 1990 Annual Meeting of the American Political Science Association, San Francisco, Calif., August 30–September 2, 1990), 45.

93. Kraft and Vig point to the "greater emphasis [in the EPA] to pollution prevention, source reduction, and recycling efforts," to the greater attention within the Department of Energy toward "environmental and public health issues in its management of nuclear facilities," as well as to "substantial new funds for EPA and Justice Department enforcement actions; cleanup activity at federal facilities (especially DOE weapons plants); acceleration of Superfund cleanup actions; research, protection, and enhancement of wetlands; demonstration projects to terminate 'below cost' timber sales in national forests; research on global climate change; and the

'America the Beautiful' initiative, which includes new funds for expanded land acquisition for national parks, wildlife refuges, forests and other public lands." In addition, "Bush backed an EPA-ordered phase out of asbestos use by 1997, and supported an EPA ruling that blocked issuance of a permit to construct the Two Forks Dam in Colorado" ("Presidential Styles and Substance," 25-26).

94. Kraft and Vig, "Presidential Styles and Substance," 45, 25. This perhaps explains why, when the president eventually signed the clean air bill into law on November 15, 1990, he largely left congressmen on the sidelines and tried to have his administration take all of the credit for the outcome (Richard E. Cohen, *Washington at Work: Back Rooms and Clean Air* [New York: Macmillan, 1992], 169).

95. Cathleen Fogel, quoted in *Statesman Journal,* Salem, Oregon, July 15, 1990, 10.

96. John B. Oakes, "An Environmentalist? Bush? Forget It," *New York Times,* May 8, 1992, A31.

97. Gallup asked the question, "Do you approve or disapprove of the way George Bush is handling the issue of the environment?" on six occasions during Bush's presidency. In November 1989, 46 percent approved and 40 percent disapproved; in July 1990, 42 percent approved, 46 percent disapproved; in October 1990, shortly before Bush signed the Clean Air Act, 45 percent approved, 45 percent disapproved; in March 1991, 53 percent approved, 38 percent disapproved; in January 1992, 49 percent approved, 41 percent disapproved; and in June 1992, 29 percent approved, 58 percent disapproved. See Lydia Saad, "Bush Stance on Environment Unpopular," *Gallup Poll Monthly,* June 1992, 25.

98. Kraft and Vig, "Presidential Styles and Substance," 46-47. Even the way in which these questions were asked reflects the elites' framing of the Bush record as a disconnect between what Bush said and what Bush did. Interestingly, Kraft and Vig, though critical of many parts of the Bush environmental record, found that "Bush's budgets indicate a continuing effort to live up to his campaign promises on the environment" (Kraft and Vig, "Presidential Styles and Substance," 25).

99. *New York Times,* June 11, 1992, A7.

100. Kraft and Vig, "Presidential Styles and Substance," 46.

101. Bush, for instance, reached out to the black community in a way that Reagan never did. He began his first weeks in office by giving a well-received speech honoring Martin Luther King. He met with Coretta King, who later described the session as "very warm and cordial." "We don't disagree on goals," King's widow said. "The goals that he seems to want for his administration are very similar to the goals that I would like to see" (*San Francisco Chronicle,* December 14, 1988, 20). Bush met also with Desmond Tutu, who afterward praised Bush's "warm openness" to the antiapartheid cause, comments that differed strikingly from those Tutu made after meeting in 1984 with President Reagan. Tutu called Reagan a "racist pure and simple" after he vetoed a sanctions bill (*San Francisco Chronicle,* May 19, 1989, 30). Bush invited every member of the Congressional Black Caucus to the White House in March 1989, and the dozen who came got a complete White House tour. In April 1990, Bush's approval rating among blacks reached 56 percent, the highest for a Republican since Dwight Eisenhower. A headline in a May 1990 issue of the *New Republic* blared "Why Blacks Love Bush."

102. See Bert A. Rockman, "The Leadership Style of George Bush," in Campbell and Rockman, eds., *Bush Presidency,* 1-35; and Kerry Mullins and Aaron Wildavsky, "The Procedural Presidency of George Bush," *Political Science Quarterly* 107 (Spring 1992): 31-62.

103. Philip Shabecoff, "Bush Tells Environmentalists He'll Listen to Them," *New York Times,* December 1, 1988, B15.

104. McLaughlin Group, April 21, 1989.

105. Kraft and Vig, "Presidential Styles and Substance," 19. "Most of Bush's natural resources appointments, on the other hand, were much like Reagan's: sympathetic to development interests and possessing few environmental credentials" (ibid., 19-20).

106. Maureen Dowd, "Who's Environmental Czar, E.P.A.'s Chief or Sununu?" *New York Times,* February 15, 1990, B16. Not everyone within the Bush administration viewed Reilly's efforts in the same positive light. The conservative view, expressed through Fred Barnes's column, was that Reilly "gets too much credit, Bush too little. Bush really wants to be known as the 'environmental President.' Instead he's known as the President with an ardent environmentalist at the EPA. That's not the same" ("Green Thumb," *New Republic,* January 1, 1990, 11).

107. *New York Times,* February 8, 1990, B8. Also see February 9, 1990, 16; *Washington Post National Weekly Edition,* November 26–December 2, 1990, 31; and Kraft and Vig, "Presidential Styles and Substance," 23.

108. Others who occasionally served as environmental lightning rods were OMB director Richard Darman, who publicly denounced the "radical, anti-growth green perspective" (Kraft and Vig, "Presidential Styles and Substance," 21), and Dan Quayle who, as head of the Competitiveness Council, called for relaxing many environmental regulations.

109. Philip Shabecoff, "Bush Gets Pleas over Environment: President's Policies Undercut by Sununu, 8 Groups Say," *New York Times,* February 22, 1990, A20. So intense was the criticism of Sununu that the administration felt it necessary to send out presidential spokesman Marlin Fitzwater to play down Sununu's role. Fitzwater insisted that Bush's decisions "represent his point of view and priorities." Sununu simply prepares options and "insures that all points of view are heard."

110. *Washington Times,* February 21, 1990, 4; *New York Times,* February 15, 1990, B16.

111. Patrick Jackson, quoted in Fox Butterfield, "Sununu's Role in Debates on Environmental Issues Reflects Old Patterns," *New York Times,* May 14, 1990, A14; Jay Hair, quoted in *Statesman Journal,* Salem, Oregon, July 15, 1990, 10; *New York Times,* July 11, 1990, A18.

112. Tom Wicker, "Going Easy on Energy," *New York Times,* January 5, 1991, A21; also see Tom Wicker, "Who Elected Sununu?" *New York Times,* May 14, 1990, A7. Leslie Gelb, "Sununu vs. Scientists," *New York Times,* February 10, 1991, V:17.

113. A Gallup poll of four hundred climate, atmospheric, and oceanographic scientists found that only one in five attributes increasing global temperatures to human activities rather than natural fluctuations. Ninety percent of the experts described the study of global change as an "emerging science" rather than a "mature science," and only 6 percent said the scientific community understands global climate change "very well." Forty-five percent said "fairly well," 41 percent said "not too well," and 6 percent said "not well at all." The Center for Media and Public Affairs, in a study of media coverage of the scientific and political debate over global warming from January 1985 through January 1992, found that the scientific experts quoted in the media were significantly less skeptical of the greenhouse effect than were the scientific experts polled by Gallup (*Media Monitor,* December 1992).

114. These ideas are developed in Michael Thompson, Richard Ellis, and Aaron Wildavsky, *Cultural Theory* (Boulder, Colo.: Westview Press, 1990), esp. chap. 1.

115. Kraft and Vig, "Presidential Styles and Substance," 17.

116. Ibid., 44.

117. For instance, George Frampton, president of the Wilderness Society, told re-

porters that he "remain[ed] convinced that . . . when [Bush is] educated about environmental issues, and he gets into it personally, he will tend to make good [environmental] choices" (David Hoffman, "George Bush Has His Own Environmental Problems," *Washington Post National Weekly Edition,* April 30–May 6, 1990, 12).

118. Kraft and Vig, "Presidential Styles and Substance," 21.

119. *Statesman Journal,* Salem, Oregon, July 15, 1990, 10.

120. Hoffman, "George Bush Has His Own Environmental Problems," 12.

121. *Statesman Journal,* Salem, Oregon, July 15, 1990, 10.

122. Kraft and Vig, "Presidential Styles and Substance," 47–48.

123. Ibid., 49. Grady, it should be pointed out, was no Darman-like foe of environmentalism. Indeed Grady served as Bush's environmental speech writer during the 1988 campaign, and his appointment as associate director of OMB for natural resources, energy, and science was well received by the environmental community (ibid., 19).

124. See Aaron Wildavsky, *The Rise of Radical Egalitarianism* (Washington, D.C.: American University Press, 1991), 74–81. Also see Mary Douglas and Aaron Wildavsky, *Risk and Culture* (Berkeley: University of California Press, 1982).

125. Bush and his administration were far from the only targets of environmental ire. During the debate over the Clean Air Act of 1990, a frustrated George Mitchell, the Democratic Senate majority leader, complained to reporters that the environmentalists "were not helpful in this process. . . . They spent most of their time attacking their friends" (Cohen, *Washington at Work,* 101).

126. See the profile of National Wildlife Federation president Jay Hair, by John Lancaster, "Jay Hair's Environmental Impact," *Washington Post National Weekly Edition,* September 9–15, 1991, 12–14. It is a sign of how widespread apocalyptic environmentalism has become when someone like Hair can insist that "the Bush administration's approach to compromise and consensus is killing the planet" (ibid., 12).

127. The extent of this polarization is suggested by a study of 1984 national convention delegates, which found that 73 percent of Democrats favored tightening environmental regulations and only 14 percent favored relaxing those regulations, while among Republican elites, in contrast, 65 percent favored relaxing environmental regulations and 16 percent favored tightening environmental regulations (Nelson W. Polsby and Aaron Wildavsky, *Presidential Elections: Contemporary Strategies of American Electoral Politics,* 8th ed. [New York: Free Press, 1991], 148).

128. Ann Devroy, "Environmental Presidential Politics: Bush is in the Middle of the Clean Air Fight," *Washington Post National Weekly Edition,* May 4–10, 1992, 14. The earlier debate within the administration over offshore oil drilling presented a similar problem for Bush. As one Bush adviser explained, "This has been a split-the-difference presidency, and on some issues you can't split the difference" (Hoffman, "George Bush Has His Own Environmental Problems," 12). Also see Philip Shabecoff, "In Thicket of Environmental Policy, Bush Uses Balance as His Compass," *New York Times,* July 1, 1990, I20.

129. Hoffman, "George Bush Has His Own Environmental Problems," 12; Kraft and Vig, "Presidential Styles and Substance," 10.

130. Kraft and Vig, "Presidential Styles and Substance," 17.

131. *New York Times,* July 11, 1990, A18, emphasis added. As Bert Rockman points out, "If the kinder, gentler line gave Bush partisans some pause, it also gave Democrats a hook to criticize Bush for not supporting their preferred programs" ("The Leadership Style of George Bush," 7).

132. In Kasson, Minnesota, on September 6, 1952, Eisenhower promised "here, and now, without any ifs or buts, I say to you that I stand behind . . . the price sup-

port laws now on the books. This includes the amendment to the Basic Farm Act . . . to continue through 1954 the price supports on basic commodities at 90 percent of parity. . . . I firmly believe that agriculture is entitled to a fair, full share of the national income and it must be a policy of Government to help agriculture achieve this goal in ways that minimize Government control and protect the farmers' independence; and a fair share is not merely 90 percent of parity—it is full parity."

133. Minnesota Senator Hubert Humphrey, for instance, accused Benson of "betraying both his constituency and his boss." (*Congressional Record,* June 16, 1954, 8353). Also see the comments by Senators Eastland (February 13, 1953, 1047), Fulbright (February 18, 1953, 1175–79), Kefauver (March 25, 1954, 3829, 3831), and Humphrey (March 4, 1954, 2642; June 16, 1954, 8353–55). Also see Milton Young, Oral History-248, April 28, 1967, COHP, EL, 8–9.

134. Cohen, *Washington at Work,* 105.

135. Kraft and Vig, "Presidential Styles and Substance," 21.

CHAPTER 4. THE VICE PRESIDENT AS LIGHTNING ROD

1. Most notably, the fine study by Paul C. Light, *Vice-Presidential Power: Advice and Influence in the White House* (Baltimore: Johns Hopkins University Press, 1984). Also see Michael Turner, *The Vice President as Policy Maker: Rockefeller in the Ford White House* (Westport, Conn.: Greenwood Press, 1982); Joel K. Goldstein, *The Modern American Vice Presidency: The Transformation of a Political Institution* (Princeton, N.J.: Princeton University Press, 1982); and Marie D. Natoli, *American Prince, American Pauper: The Contemporary Vice Presidency in Perspective* (Westport, Conn.: Greenwood Press, 1985).

2. Light, *Vice-Presidential Power,* 60. Light usefully distinguishes between the political vice-presidency and the policy vice-presidency.

3. *Esquire,* November 1966.

4. Marie D. Natoli, "The Humphrey Vice Presidency in Retrospect," *Presidential Studies Quarterly* 12 (Fall 1982): 606.

5. Albert Eisele, *Almost to the Presidency: A Biography of Two American Politicians* (Blue Earth, Minn.: Piper, 1972), 335.

6. Robert Sherrill, *The Accidental President* (New York: Grossman, 1967), 266.

7. AIPO-738, December 8–13, 1966.

8. Norma Krause Herzfield, "H.H.H.: Vote-getter or Scapegoat?" *Commonweal,* August 11, 1967, 492.

9. AIPO-560, February 16–21, 1956. In both the February 1956 and December 1966 survey, respondents were asked to rate the vice president immediately after having evaluated the president. Subsequent surveys conducted during the 1956 campaign, one shortly before the Republican convention and the other immediately preceding the general election, indicate that evaluations of Nixon and Eisenhower became more closely joined as the election drew closer. Those who felt favorably toward Eisenhower appeared to resolve the discrepancy in their attitude toward the Republican ticket by upgrading their evaluation of Vice President Nixon. Still, even these surveys demonstrate considerably less linkage than existed in the Johnson/Humphrey relationship. The July survey, taken about the time Harold Stassen was vainly floating the idea of dumping Nixon in favor of Massachusetts Governor Christian Herter, showed that 24 percent gave Eisenhower and Nixon the same rating, 39 percent placed them within a point of each other, and 54 percent put them

within two points (AIPO-567, July 12–17, 1956). The pre-election survey found only 23 percent gave the two men the same rating, 40 percent placed them within a point, and 57 percent placed them within two points (AIPO-573, October 18–23, 1956).

10. AIPO-761, May 2, 1968; AIPO-770, October 17–22, 1968. In both of these surveys, after rating Johnson the respondent was asked to evaluate two other public figures before being asked about Humphrey. The Eisenhower/Nixon questions, in contrast, were asked consecutively in the February and July surveys and were separated by only a single question in the October poll. Because the closer together the questions are asked the greater the likelihood that a respondent's answer will be similar, the question order may actually be attenuating some of the underlying differences between the Humphrey and Nixon cases. On the effects of question order, see Howard Schuman and Stanley Presser, *Questions and Answers in Attitude Surveys: Experimentation on Question Form, Wording, and Context* (New York: Academic Press, 1981), chap. 2.

11. Carl Solberg, *Hubert Humphrey: A Biography* (New York: Norton, 1984), 279.

12. Light, *Vice-Presidential Power,* 28. Humphrey's personal physician, Edgar Berman, reported that "it had always bothered Humphrey that he had to have all speeches cleared line by line" (*Hubert: The Triumph and Tragedy of the Humphrey I Knew* [New York: G. P. Putnam's Sons, 1979], 93).

13. "A Gruntled Man," *Time,* February 12, 1965, 15. Also see " 'I Enjoy It,' " *Newsweek,* March 15, 1965, 29.

14. Andrew J. Glass, "Hubert Humphrey's One-Man Constituency," *Reporter,* November 18, 1965, 27.

15. Eisele, *Almost to the Presidency,* 237. Also see David Halberstam, *The Best and the Brightest* (New York: Random House, 1972), 535; Solberg, *Humphrey,* 279; and Joesph A. Califano, Jr., *The Triumph and Tragedy of Lyndon Johnson: The White House Years* (New York: Simon and Schuster, 1991), 64.

16. Arnold Lubasch, "Humphrey Urges Education Drive," *New York Times,* November 25, 1964, 26.

17. Halberstam, *Best and the Brightest,* 533. Humphrey received a similar, if less public, chewing out from Johnson for his call for a "Marshall Plan for the impoverished areas of America" (Solberg, *Humphrey,* 309–10; Hubert H. Humphrey, *The Education of a Public Man* [Garden City, N.Y.: Doubleday, 1976], 428).

18. On Johnson's anxiety about being accepted by liberals, particularly liberal intellectuals, see Paul K. Conkin, *Big Daddy from the Pedernales: Lyndon Baines Johnson* (Boston: Twayne, 1986), 182; and Merle Miller, *Lyndon: An Oral Biography* (New York: Ballantine, 1980), 512 ff.

19. Solberg, *Humphrey,* 278. Also see Natoli, "Humphrey Vice Presidency," 605; and Humphrey, *Education,* 428. This aspect of the Humphrey/Johnson relationship was also widely reported in the contemporary press. For instance, the *Atlantic Monthly* reported that Johnson "was annoyed whenever Humphrey's name appeared in the newspapers" (June 1967, 8), and *Time* observed that "Johnson was nettled by the newspaper space that Humphrey garnered" (April 1, 1966, 23).

20. Humphrey, *Education,* 427; also see 367.

21. Solberg, *Humphrey,* 284; George Gallup, "Pallid View Taken of Humphrey," *Washington Post,* December 12, 1965, L4; Survey 720, November 18–23, 1965, *The Gallup Poll, 1935–1971,* 3 vols. (New York: Random House, 1972), 3:1975–76. Also see *Newsweek,* January 3, 1966, 15.

22. *New York Times,* January 1, 1966, 3.

23. Humphrey, *Education,* 318–24. Solberg, *Humphrey,* 271–75. Larry Berman,

Planning a Tragedy: The Americanization of the War in Vietnam (New York: Norton, 1982), 45.

24. Solberg, *Humphrey,* 271–74. Eisele, *Almost to the Presidency,* 232–33.

25. About the same time, Humphrey was scheduled to address a United Nations conference on Pope John's *Pacem in Terris* encyclical. The speech was submitted to the White House, and, as Humphrey later lamented, all "the innovative, peace-seeking material" was cut out (Humphrey, *Education,* 324).

26. *Atlantic Monthly,* June 1967, 8. Humphrey aide John Reilly described Humphrey as "desperate to get back into Johnson's good graces" (Eisele, *Almost to the Presidency,* 246).

27. In July 1965, for instance, Humphrey wrote to Johnson telling him that "I have a roomful of senators over here at the Capitol, and we thought that the [announcement] was tremendous. I was personally inspired, moved, and I just couldn't be happier if they had Christmas every day and every dream I ever wanted came true" (Humphrey to Johnson, July 28, 1965, quoted in Solberg, *Humphrey,* 282; also see 303).

28. See, e.g., Humphrey to Johnson, August 13, 1965, in ibid., 282.

29. Ibid., 290. Even when Humphrey was staunchly defending the war effort, Johnson often found it difficult to allow Humphrey to occupy center stage. Upon Humphrey's return from his February trip every member of Congress was invited to the White House, and although the purpose was "nominally to hear Vice-President Humphrey report on his trip to the Far East, . . . it was the President who popped up to field the questions in his old-time bantering form" (Rowland Evans and Robert Novak, *Lyndon B. Johnson: The Exercise of Power* [New York: Signet, 1966], 596).

30. "Dissenting from the Dissenters," *Newsweek,* November 6, 1967, 25.

31. See, e.g., "Life of a Salesman," *Newsweek,* March 7, 1966, 25–26; and "Humphrey's Role: Selling a Consensus," *U.S. News & World Report,* March 7, 1966, 20.

32. "Not So Ancient History," *The Nation,* May 9, 1966, 538–39, quotation at 538. "The Nervous Cheerleader," *The Nation,* December 25, 1967, 674–75. Washington columnist Mary McGrory termed Humphrey the "cheerful cheerleader."

33. Quoted in Robert Sherrill and Harry W. Ernst, *The Drugstore Liberal* (New York: Grossman, 1968), 191. Also see Lewis Chester et al., *An American Melodrama: The Presidential Campaign of 1968* (New York: Viking, 1969), 148.

34. "The Nervous Cheerleader," 774. See also William V. Shannon, "Humphrey and 1972," *Commonweal,* March 1966, 630; and Eisele, *Almost to the Presidency,* 252–55.

35. Andrew Kopkind, "Humphrey's Old Pals: An Account of the ADA Convention," *New Republic,* May 7, 1966, 19, 21.

36. *Atlantic Monthly,* June 1967, 10.

37. George Christian, *The President Steps Down* (New York: Macmillan, 1970), 148–49. Eisele, *Almost to the Presidency,* 234. Also see Henry F. Graff, *The Tuesday Cabinet: Deliberation and Decision on Peace and War under Lyndon B. Johnson* (Englewood Cliffs, N.J.: Prentice-Hall, 1970).

38. *The Nation,* December 25, 1967, 674.

39. So, for instance, Robert Sherrill could write that Attorney General Nicholas Katzenbach has "refused (on the President's orders, surely) to send more than a skeleton crew of registrars into the South" ("Cold Eye on Johnson," *The Nation,* January 3, 1966, 6).

40. Dwight D. Eisenhower, *Mandate for Change* (Garden City, N.Y.: Doubleday, 1963), 431.

41. Steven E. Ambrose, *Nixon: The Education of a Politician 1913–1962* (New York: Simon and Schuster, 1987), 299.

42. Survey 550, July 14–19, 1955, *Gallup Poll,* 1355. The question read, "In your opinion, is Eisenhower, at heart, more of a Republican, more of a Democrat, or do you think he is somewhere in between the two?" Also see Samuel Lubell, *Revolt of the Moderates* (New York: Harper and Brothers, 1956), 24–25.

43. See Herbert H. Hyman and Paul B. Sheatsley, "The Political Appeal of President Eisenhower," *Public Opinion Quarterly* 17 (Winter 1953/54): 443–60.

44. Earl Butz, Oral History-95, January 15, 1968, COHP, EL, 51.

45. Hedrick Smith, *The Power Game: How Washington Works* (New York: Random House, 1988), 393–97.

46. This division of labor created a dilemma for Nixon, whose own presidential ambitions also depended on attracting a significant block of Democrats. Consequently, Nixon's lightning rod role became less pronounced during the second term. Eisenhower's lightning rod strategy worked best when it coincided with Nixon's own political interests of solidifying his leadership role within the Republican party and less well as Nixon's attention turned toward winning a national election. For evidence that Nixon well understood this tension between his role as Eisenhower's "political point-man" and his own presidential ambitions, see Richard M. Nixon, *The Memoirs of Richard Nixon* (New York: Grosset and Dunlap, 1978), 199.

47. Nixon, *Memoirs,* 87–88.

48. Richard Nixon, *Six Crises* (New York: Pocket Books, 1962), 82. Also see Earl Mazo, *Richard Nixon: A Political and Personal Portrait* (New York: Harper and Brothers, 1960), 98.

49. William Costello, *The Facts about Nixon: An Unauthorized Biography* (New York: Viking Press, 1960), 117–18. Fawn M. Brodie, *Richard Nixon: The Shaping of His Character* (New York: Norton, 1981), 310. Ambrose, *Nixon,* 297.

50. *Newsweek,* April 30, 1956, 30. Richard H. Rovere, *Affairs of State: The Eisenhower Years* (New York: Farrar, 1956), 302. Ambrose, *Nixon,* 357.

51. Nixon, *Memoirs,* 176–77. Nixon relates this conversation as an example of the "way he [Eisenhower] worked when he wanted something political done." Emmet Hughes, who was with Eisenhower at the time, recalled the conversation similarly. According to Hughes, Eisenhower told Nixon: "Look, Dick, we've agreed that your speeches generally in this campaign ought to be on a higher level than in the past. Still I think it's perfectly all right for you to pick up some of these wild charges and throw them back at the other fellow" (Emmet John Hughes, *The Ordeal of Power* [New York: Dell, 1964], 161).

52. Nixon, *Memoirs,* 177.

53. *New York Times,* September 13, 1956, 22.

54. Nixon, *Memoirs,* 144. Also see Fred I. Greenstein, *The Hidden-Hand Presidency: Eisenhower as Leader* (New York: Basic Books, 1982), 194; and Mazo, *Nixon,* 149.

55. Nixon, *Memoirs,* 145–46.

56. *New York Times,* March 14, 1954, 44.

57. Ambrose, *Nixon,* 337–38.

58. "Mr. Nixon and the 'New Look,' " *Commonweal,* March 26, 1954, 617.

59. Telephone conversation, April 17, 1956, cited in Donald Neff, *Warriors at Suez: Eisenhower Takes America into the Middle East* (New York: Linden, 1981), 226.

60. Nixon, *Memoirs,* 177–78.

61. Ambrose, *Nixon,* 349. Eisenhower originally drafted a letter to Nixon, in which he wrote: "I quite understand the impulse—particularly before a partisan au-

dience—to lash out at political opponents. . . . But I am constantly working to produce a truly bipartisan approach, and I rather think that keeping up attacks against Acheson will, at this late date, hamper our efforts." Eisenhower then decided not to send the letter.

62. Costello, *Facts about Nixon,* 169–70.

63. Lubell, *Revolt of the Moderates,* 27.

64. Sherman Adams, *Firsthand Report* (New York: Harper and Row, 1961), 167.

65. Ralph de Toledano, *Nixon* (New York: Henry Holt, 1956), 180. Ezra Taft Benson, *Cross Fire: The Eight Years with Eisenhower* (Garden City, N.Y.: Doubleday, 1962), 206.

66. Nixon, *Six Crises,* 143.

67. John O. Hjelle, editor of the *Bismark Tribune,* quoted in *Newsweek,* April 23, 1956, 28.

68. *Time,* January 23, 1956, 14. The same view was put forth a few months later when *Time* reported that "Nixon was . . . an attractive target for Democrats who did not want to waste their ammunition on Eisenhower" (March 26, 1956, 21).

69. Merle Miller, *Plain Speaking: An Oral Biography of Harry S. Truman* (New York: Putnam, 1974), 135, 178.

70. John Bartlow Martin, *Adlai Stevenson of Illinois* (Garden City, N.Y.: Doubleday, 1976), 693.

71. Sixty-three percent gave Eisenhower a rating of between plus 3 and plus 5. AIPO-560, February 16–21, 1956.

72. AIPO-738, December 8–13, 1966.

73. Costello, *Facts about Nixon,* 129; de Toledano, *Nixon,* 178.

74. "Democrats' No. 1 Target is Ike's No. 1 Politician," *U.S. News & World Report,* January 28, 1955, 75.

75. This frank admission came in an informal talk with the journalist Merriman Smith in late 1957. Smith asked Eisenhower how he felt about the term "politician," adding that he had got the impression that Eisenhower "didn't like it and that he had never liked the role of politician." Eisenhower retorted, "What the hell are you talking about? How do you get to be Army Chief of Staff? . . . I've been in politics, the most active sort of politics, in the military most of my adult life. . . . There's no more active political organization in the country or in the world than the armed services of the United States. As a matter of fact, I think I am a better politician than most so-called professionals" (Merriman Smith, Oral History-160, January 3, 1968, COHP, EL, 4).

76. Quoted in Richard E. Neustadt, *Presidential Power* (New York: Wiley, 1980), 122.

77. News Conference, February 10, 1954, *Public Papers of the Presidents: Dwight D. Eisenhower, 1953-1961,* 8 vols. (Washington, D.C.: U.S. Government Printing Office, 1960-1961), 246. Also see Henry Cabot Lodge, *As It Was* (New York: Norton, 1976), 144–45. Even when speaking before partisan audiences such as the Republican National Finance Committee, Eisenhower would sometimes use the occasion to warn against excessive partisanship. "Our greatest enemy," the president lectured, "is not the Democrats. We certainly can't have better allies when we are fighting anybody from abroad. So let's remember that, and as I talk, let's not build up a picture that the worst enemy anyone can have is a Democrat. Far from it. We just don't think they can do as good a job as we do" (Remarks at Luncheon Meeting of the Republican National Committee and the Republican National Finance Committee, February 17, 1955, *Public Papers,* 267).

78. See the public opinion polls reported in William C. Mitchell, "The Ambivalent Social Status of the American Politician," *Western Political Quarterly* 12 (Sep-

tember 1959): esp. 689-91. Also see Maurice Klain, " 'Politics'—Still a Dirty Word," *Antioch Review* 15 (December 1955-1956): 457-66.
79. Adams, *Firsthand Report,* 20. Greenstein, *Hidden-Hand Presidency,* 54.
80. Robert H. Ferrell, ed., *The Eisenhower Diaries* (New York: Norton, 1981), 218 (entry for January 5, 1953).
81. Adams, *Firsthand Report,* 28.
82. Although initially favorably disposed toward Stevenson, Eisenhower soon came to regard Stevenson as indecisive, flippant, and naive. Indeed, so great was Eisenhower's disdain for Stevenson that, according to Nixon, "after Eisenhower's stroke the doctors ordered us to steer clear of discussion of Stevenson because it always caused the President's blood pressure to rise alarmingly" (Nixon, *Memoirs,* 111; also see Hughes, *Ordeal of Power,* 171-72).
83. In a confidential memo to Secretary of Commerce Sinclair Weeks, for instance, the president worried that a revised Civil Service procedure would protect individuals who had reached their positions "through a process of selection based upon their devotion to the socialistic doctrine and bureaucratic controls practiced over the past two decades" (Eisenhower to Weeks, March 8, 1953, cited in Herbert S. Parmet, *Eisenhower and the American Crusades* [New York: Macmillan, 1972], 209-10).
84. See Cornelius P. Cotter, "Eisenhower as Party Leader," *Political Science Quarterly* 98 (Summer 1983): 255-83, esp. 279-81.
85. Parmet, *American Crusades,* 332.
86. Eisenhower's ambivalence toward Nixon is captured in Ambrose, *Nixon,* esp. 300, 394, 620; and Ambrose, *Eisenhower,* 319-20. Also see William Bragg Ewald, Jr., *Eisenhower the President: Crucial Days, 1951-1960* (Englewood Cliffs, N.J.: Prentice-Hall, 1981), 179.
87. Arthur R. Larson, *Eisenhower: The President Nobody Knew* (New York: Scribners, 1968), 10. Later (in 1958, 1964, and again in 1967), he told Larson that he thought Nixon had "matured."
88. Hughes, *Ordeal of Power,* 152. He confided to Hughes that his decision to run for reelection stemmed in part from an absence of "fresh, young, new leadership." Eisenhower sounded a similar note in a letter to Swede Hazlett explaining his decision to run again. The first reason he offered was his feeling that he had "failed to bring forward and establish a logical successor for myself. This failure was of course not intentional. To the contrary, I struggled hard to acquaint the public with the qualities of a very able group of young men. . . . The evidence becomes clear that I had not been able to get any individual to be recognized as a natural or logical candidate for the Presidency" (Robert Griffith, ed., *Ike's Letters to a Friend, 1941-1958* [Lawrence: University Press of Kansas, 1984], 160 [March 2, 1956]).
89. President Eisenhower, observed William Ewald, "never wrote a list of possible running mates or successors without including Nixon's name . . . but Nixon was never at the top" (Ewald, *Eisenhower the President,* 177). In discussions with James Hagerty at the end of 1955 concerning possible successors, Eisenhower identified four people who he thought were "mentally qualified for the presidency": George Humphrey, Herbert Brownell, Sherman Adams, and Robert Anderson (Robert H. Ferrell, ed., *The Diary of James Hagerty: Eisenhower in Mid-Course, 1954-1955* [Bloomington: Indiana University Press, 1983], 245 [December 14, 1955]). Eisenhower's preference for Robert Anderson is noted in, among other places, Ewald, *Eisenhower the President,* 186; Hughes, *Ordeal of Power,* 217-18; and Ambrose, *Eisenhower,* 320. In his diary, Eisenhower confided his belief that his brother, Milton Eisenhower, "is at this moment the most highly qualified man in the United States to

be president" (May 14, 1953, *Eisenhower Diaries,* 238). Also see Ewald, *Eisenhower the President,* 189-90.

90. Ambrose, *Nixon,* 619.

91. Bradley H. Patterson, Jr., *The Ring of Power: The White House Staff and Its Expanding Role in Government* (New York: Basic Books, 1988), 286-89. Joseph A. Pika, "Bush, Quayle, and the New Vice Presidency," in Michael Nelson, ed., *The Presidency and the Political System* (Washington, D.C.: Congressional Quarterly, 1990), 504.

92. Light, *Vice-Presidential Power,* 63.

93. Ibid., 255. Table 4.1 offers some support for Light's proposition in so far as Mondale and Bush, both of whom gained unprecedented access to the administration's inner councils, were markedly less newsworthy than their immediate predecessors.

94. Ibid., 255; also see 50.

95. Ibid., 256. "Of all the programs that the Carter administration produced," Light observes, "only the Vietnamese boat people rescue can be identified as a pure Mondale idea" (ibid., 50).

96. On Bush's role as vice president, see ibid., 260-68; and Pika, "Bush, Quayle, and the New Vice Presidency," 511-16.

97. *The Nation,* July 29/August 5, 1991, 160.

98. *Time,* November 4, 1991, 25.

99. *U.S. News & World Report,* May 20, 1991, 23.

100. Lance Morrow, "The Strange Destiny of a Vice President," *Time,* May 20, 1991, 23; *Time,* October 19, 1992, 34; *Newsweek,* May 20, 1991, 22; *U.S. News & World Report,* May 20, 1991, 22; Kermit Lansner, "Dan Quayle and the President's Flu," *FW,* February 4, 1992, 88.

101. Shortly after Bush's election, conservative activist and fund-raiser Richard Viguerie was asked whether he took any comfort in the fact that Quayle, a conservative, was vice president. Viguerie responded, "No one that I'm aware of believes that Dan Quayle is making policy" (*New York Times,* January 31, 1989, A16).

102. Light, *Vice-Presidential Power,* 28-34. The phrase "professional mourner" is used by a Mondale aide, quoted in ibid., 29.

CHAPTER 5. THE SECRETARY OF STATE AS LIGHTNING ROD

1. During each of the twelve years of the Reagan and Bush presidencies, the secretary of state was the most visible official within the administration with only one exception. That exception came in 1988, when Vice President George Bush was a presidential candidate. The *New York Times Index* tells exactly the same story, as anyone who has ever tried to count references to a secretary of state can testify. Also see Herbert J. Gans, *Deciding What's News: A Study of CBS Evening News, NBC Nightly News, Newsweek, and Time* (New York: Pantheon, 1979), 10.

2. Gallup-864, February 16-19, 1973. Kissinger was appointed national security adviser in 1969 and was given a second "hat" as secretary of state in July 1973.

3. Between December 1950 and September 1951, Gallup asked respondents on four separate occasions to tell them "who Mr. Dean Acheson is." In each of the four surveys about two-thirds of the general public was able to correctly identify Dean Acheson as head of the State Department and usually about another 5 percent was partly correct, identifying him as a cabinet member or as a secretary of some depart-

ment. AIPO-468, December 3-8, 1950. AIPO-471, February 4-9, 1951. AIPO-475, May 19-24, 1951. AIPO-480, September 21-26, 1951. Acheson became secretary of state in January 1949 and served until the end of Truman's term.

4. AIPO-594, January 24-29, 1958. Two years into President Eisenhower's first term, the National Opinion Research Corporation asked whether the respondent had "ever heard of John Foster Dulles" (85 percent said they had) and then asked the respondent to identify Dulles's job. Close to 62 percent (52 percent of the whole sample) of those who claimed to have heard of Dulles correctly identified his job. Roughly another 10 percent had some knowledge that Dulles was a diplomat or cabinet member (NORC-54, November 29-December 8, 1954). Dulles served as secretary of state from January 1953 until resigning in April 1959, one month before dying of cancer.

5. Peter Lyon, *Eisenhower: Portrait of the Hero* (Boston: Little, Brown, 1974), 543. Robert A. Divine, *Eisenhower and the Cold War* (New York: Oxford University Press, 1981), 21. Fred I. Greenstein, *The Hidden-Hand Presidency: Eisenhower as Leader* (New York: Basic Books, 1982), 91. Stephen E. Ambrose, *Eisenhower: The President* (New York: Simon and Schuster, 1984), 442. See also Herbert S. Parmet, *Eisenhower and the American Crusades* (New York: Macmillan, 1972), 574. Also see Wm. Roger Louis, "Dulles, Suez, and the British," in Richard H. Immerman, ed., *John Foster Dulles and the Diplomacy of the Cold War* (Princeton, N.J.: Princeton University Press, 1990), 135; H. W. Brands, Jr., *Cold Warriors: Eisenhower's Generation and American Foreign Policy* (New York: Columbia University Press, 1988), 125; and Jeff Broadwater, *Eisenhower and the Anti-Communist Crusade* (Chapel Hill: University of North Carolina Press, 1992).

6. Greenstein, *Hidden-Hand Presidency,* 90. Also see Brands, *Cold Warriors,* 125. In a conversation in December 1956, Dulles told Harold Macmillan that "it was an error to believe that he and the President could be separated. He wrote most of the Presidential statements himself. When they had to be tough, they were made by the Secretary of State. . . . When they were idealistic, they were made by the President but written by the Secretary of State" (Townsend Hoopes, *The Devil and John Foster Dulles* [Boston: Little, Brown, 1973], 389).

7. Richard Rovere, Oral History-65, 1968, COHP, EL, 34.

8. Richard H. Rovere, *Affairs of State: The Eisenhower Years* (New York: Farrar, Strauss, and Cudahay, 1956), 267, 270, 266. Also see Emmet Hughes, *The Ordeal of Power: A Political Memoir of the Eisenhower Years* (New York: Atheneum, 1963); and Marquis Childs, *Eisenhower: Captive Hero* (New York: Harcourt, Brace, 1958).

9. Duane Tananbaum, *The Bricker Amendment Controversy: A Test of Eisenhower's Political Leadership* (Ithaca, N.Y.: Cornell University Press, 1987), 78. The Bricker amendment carried enormous emotional freight for conservative "Old Guard" Republicans because it tapped into their intense dislike for the agreements reached by Presidents Roosevelt and Truman at Teheran, Yalta, and Potsdam, as well as their fear that international charters like the proposed United Nations Covenant on Human Rights would override American laws and liberties.

10. Tananbaum, *Bricker Amendment Controversy,* 77-78. Parmet, *Eisenhower and the American Crusades,* 312.

11. Sherman Adams, *Firsthand Report* (New York: Harper and Brothers, 1961), 106.

12. Parmet, *Eisenhower and the American Crusades,* 311. Tananbaum, *Bricker Amendment Controversy,* 98-99.

13. Arthur Krock, columnist for the *New York Times,* quoted in Tananbaum, *Bricker Amendment Controversy,* 78.

14. Ibid., esp. 78-79, 96, 111. Also see Parmet, *Eisenhower and the American*

Crusades, 310; and Louis Gerson, *John Foster Dulles* (New York: Cooper Square Publishers, 1967), 120.

15. Tananbaum, *Bricker Amendment Controversy,* 111. The interview with Bricker was conducted by Tananbaum in 1975.

16. Ibid., 111. Tananbaum's fine case study, while supporting Greenstein's hidden-hand thesis, also provides compelling evidence of the costs of that leadership style—costs that are quite similar to those that I identify in Chapter 7.

17. Adams, *Firsthand Report,* 106. Tananbaum, *Bricker Amendment Controversy,* 79.

18. Tananbaum, *Bricker Amendment Controversy,* 111.

19. This version of events was presented in Herman Finer's influential book, *Dulles over Suez: The Theory and Practice of His Diplomacy* (Chicago: Quadrangle, 1964). Townsend Hoopes concluded that "in perhaps no other decision during his tenure at the State Dept. did [Dulles] play so lone a hand" (*Devil and John Foster Dulles,* 340).

20. Donald Neff, *Warriors at Suez: Eisenhower Takes America into the Middle East* (New York: Linden Press, 1981), esp. 258-60. Also see Robert R. Bowie, "Eisenhower, Dulles, and the Suez Crisis," in Wm. Roger Louis and Roger Owen, eds., *Suez 1956: The Crisis and Its Consequences* (Oxford: Clarendon Press, 1989), esp. 189-96; Louis, "Dulles, Suez, and the British," esp. 135, 145-46; Ambrose, *Eisenhower,* 329-30; and Parmet, *Eisenhower and the American Crusades,* esp. 475-76, 481, 485.

21. Hubert H. Humphrey, *The Education of a Public Man* (Garden City, N.Y.: Doubleday, 1976), 199-200. In his memoirs, Khrushchev characterizes Dulles as a "vicious cur" but also makes less than flattering remarks about Eisenhower. "Our people whose job it was to study Eisenhower closely," Khrushchev explained, "have told me that they considered him a mediocre military leader and a weak President. He was a good man, but he wasn't very tough. There was something soft about his character. As I discovered in Geneva, he was much too dependent on his advisors" (Nikita S. Khrushchev, *Khrushchev Remembers* [New York: Little, Brown, 1970], 398). Also see Fawn M. Brodie, *Richard Nixon: The Shaping of His Character* (New York: Norton, 1981), 379.

22. Neff, *Warriors at Suez,* 302. Also see *The Memoirs of Anthony Eden: Full Circle* (Boston: Houghton Mifflin, 1960). In his retirement, Eden described Dulles as being "as tortuous as a wounded snake, with much less excuse" (Louis, "Dulles, Suez, and the British," 158; also see 133-34, 151).

23. See *Newsweek,* January 27, 1958, 28-29; and Neff, *Warriors at Suez,* esp. 19, 143, 205, 208-9, 214-15, 302, 330. Dulles became even more unpopular in British and French circles after his widely quoted comment in January 1957 to the effect that "if I were an American soldier who had to fight in the Middle East, I would rather not have a British and a French soldier, one on my right and one on my left." A Canadian newspaper, the *Calgary Herald,* reacted by calling Dulles "an international catastrophe." "Mr. Dulles must hold the record for losing more international good will than any other United States Secretary of State in history. His stupidity is scarcely credible. Eisenhower ought to fire him forthwith" (*Congressional Record,* February 19, 1957, 2222).

24. Lewis Douglas, quoted in Robert Paul Browder and Thomas G. Smith, *Independent: A Biography of Lewis W. Douglas* (New York: Alfred A. Knopf, 1986), 385. Douglas was an ambassador to Great Britain under President Truman before backing Eisenhower in 1952 and 1956. During the first term he was one of Eisenhower's informal advisers, and he was among the names rumored to be under consideration for the treasury post after George Humphrey's resignation. Douglas became

disenchanted with Eisenhower in his second term because he felt the president had "abdicated to a pretty second-rate group of people" (390). After Eisenhower's death, Douglas rendered a less than flattering (and grossly inaccurate) verdict of his friend's presidency: "He had a very poor understanding of the structure of [the] American federal government. I think he looked upon the Presidency as though perhaps it was somewhat analogous to a crown" (391).

25. Finer, *Dulles over Suez*, 11. Similarly, Hans Morgenthau wrote that Eisenhower "trusted Dulles so completely and admired his ability as Secretary of State so unreservedly that he gave him, for all practical purposes, a free hand to conduct the foreign policy of the United States as he saw fit" ("John Foster Dulles," in Norman Graebner, ed., *An Uncertain Tradition: American Secretaries of State in the Twentieth Century* [New York: McGraw Hill, 1961], 302).

26. See Richard H. Immerman, "Eisenhower and Dulles: Who Made the Decisions," *Political Psychology* 1 (Autumn 1979): 21–38; Bennett C. Rushkoff, "Eisenhower, Dulles and the Quemoy-Matsu Crisis, 1954–1955," *Political Science Quarterly* 96 (Fall 1981): esp. 466; Divine, *Eisenhower and the Cold War;* Greenstein, *Hidden-Hand Presidency;* Ambrose, *Eisenhower;* Cecil V. Crabb, Jr., and Kevin V. Mulcahy, *Presidents and Foreign Policy Making: From FDR to Reagan* (Baton Rouge: Louisiana State University Press, 1986), 156–97; Richard A. Melanson and David Mayers, eds., *Reevaluating Eisenhower: American Foreign Policy in the Fifties* (Urbana: University of Illinois Press, 1987); and Brands, *Cold Warriors*.

27. Greenstein writes that "with Dulles, unlike any other cabinet member, [Eisenhower] entered into a collegial working relationship" (*Hidden-Hand Presidency*, 87).

28. According to Andrew Berding, assistant secretary of state for public affairs under Dulles: "The Secretary never took an action of any importance whatsoever without first consulting with the President and getting his OK. . . . Dulles never made a speech of any importance . . . that he did not send . . . to the President, and he would not make the speech until the President had sent the text back. . . . If Dulles were going to have a press conference, and he knew certain important things were going to come up at that press conference, he would check first with the President and tell the President what he himself, Dulles, expected to say" (Oral History-16, June 13, 1967, COHP, EL, 27–29).

Eisenhower said much the same thing in his memoirs: "[Dulles] would not deliver an important speech or statement until I had read, edited, and approved it." Eisenhower went on to explain that Dulles "guarded constantly against the possibility that any misunderstanding could arise between us. It was the mutual trust and understanding, thus engendered, that enabled me, with complete confidence, to delegate to him an unusual degree of flexibility as my representative in international conferences, well knowing that he would not in the slightest degree operate outside the limits previously agreed between us" (*Waging Peace, 1956–1961* [Garden City, N.Y.: Doubleday, 1965], 365).

29. The revisionist scholarship on the Eisenhower/Dulles relationship has been enormously salutary, but as Richard Immerman points out, some of these studies have left the mistaken impression that Dulles "did little more than carry out Eisenhower's directives and take the heat that they generated." The president did retain control over the making of foreign policy but, as Immerman stresses, "Dulles was an integral actor in the sphere of formulation as well as implementation. Eisenhower did not dominate Dulles any more than we once thought the reverse true. Moreover, because their levels of interest and expertise differed, their contributions to different policy issues and areas varied. On some occasions Dulles took the lead; on others it was Eisenhower. They were in a real sense a team" (Immerman, "Introduction," in *Dulles and the Diplomacy of the Cold War*, 9). To the extent that Dulles's input was

critical in shaping and not just executing foreign policy, the lightning rod idea can be a misleading metaphor that obscures more than it reveals. This is a point I pursue in greater depth in Chapter 7, which analyzes Brownell's role in shaping civil rights policy.

30. Ambrose, *Eisenhower,* 442.

31. Gordon A. Craig, "John Foster Dulles and American Statecraft," in *War, Politics, and Diplomacy: Selected Essays* (New York: Praeger, 1966), 262.

32. Stephen Hess, *Organizing the Presidency* (Washington, D.C.: Brookings, 1976), 65-66. Townsend Hoopes, *The Devil and John Foster Dulles* (Boston: Little, Brown, 1973), 489. Also see Alexander DeConde, *The American Secretary of State: An Interpretation* (New York: Praeger, 1962), 144.

33. For Eisenhower this four-year-average approval rating is based on fifty-one Gallup polls reported in "Presidential Popularity: A 43 Year Review," *The Gallup Opinion Index* (October-November 1980). For Dulles the average is based on twenty-one surveys conducted by the NORC, all of which asked: "In general, do you approve or disapprove of the way John Foster Dulles is handling his job as Secretary of State in Washington?" Those with no opinion for Dulles ranged from a low of 17 percent to a high of 40 percent; those with no opinion for Eisenhower ranged from a low of 9 percent to a high of 25 percent.

34. Greenstein, *Hidden-Hand Presidency,* 90.

35. Parmet, *Eisenhower and the American Crusades,* 402.

36. The cartoon is reproduced in both Ambrose, *Eisenhower,* and Hoopes, *Devil and John Foster Dulles,* 292.

37. NORC-372, June 1955. NORC-374, August 1955. Special Survey, *Gallup Poll,* 2:1351.

38. Parmet, *Eisenhower and the American Crusades,* 411.

39. NORC-390, June 27-July 5, 1956. NORC-393, September 1956.

40. NORC-401, December 1956. AIPO-575, November 22-27, 1956.

41. Immerman, "Introduction," 11. Relevant here is Herbert Parmet's observation that "every public address made by the Secretary was delivered with concern for its popular response. One of the frequent criticisms of such statements cited their obvious and pious moralizing, but Dulles was more conscious of his audience than were his critics. He carefully avoided complex language and rejected Latin words, which were always removed from the final drafts of his speeches. . . . While intellectuals sneered, Dulles's mail usually brought fabulous responses to his speeches from the Midwest" (Parmet, *American Crusades,* 187).

42. *Newsweek,* January 27, 1958, 29.

43. As one letter to the editor expressed it: "For the first time in many years, we have a Secretary of State who puts his country above Western Europe. His predecessor, pro-British Dean Acheson, was often called 'the best Secretary of State England ever had.' But Dulles has usually stood for our interests" (*Newsweek,* February 24, 1958, 6).

44. Nor was Dulles inattentive to or unconcerned with public opinion. Dulles was well aware of how the public regarded his performance, as a memo he sent to Eisenhower at the outset of 1957 demonstrates. Attached to the memo were two fold-out charts graphing public support for Dulles and for the administration's handling of foreign affairs (Dulles to Eisenhower, January 30, 1957, Dulles-Herter Series, AWF, EL). Dulles's attention to public opinion is also accented in Neff, *Warriors at Suez.* Howard Cook, a State Department official, agrees that Dulles was "very conscious of public relations" and even suggests that Dulles "enjoyed this sort of thing" (Oral History-175, December 31, 1970, COHP, EL, 7, also see 5-6).

45. See "The 'Get Dulles' Campaign," *Newsweek,* February 4, 1957, 21.

46. NORC-404, April 27–May 6, 1957. AIPO-582, April 25–30, 1957.

47. AIPO-593, January 3–7, 1958.

48. Research on public awareness of congressional candidates has shown that a large portion of the electorate cannot recall a name but can recognize it when they see it. See Thomas E. Mann, *Unsafe at Any Margin: Interpreting Congressional Elections* (Washington, D.C.: American Enterprise Institute, 1978), 30–34; and Thomas E. Mann and Raymond E. Wolfinger, "Candidates and Parties in Congressional Elections," *American Political Science Review* 74 (1980): 617–32.

49. AIPO-594, January 24–29, 1958.

50. Des Moines *Register,* Iowa Poll no. 150, September 1958. Minneapolis *Herald Tribune,* Survey no. 175, October 1958.

51. See Gabriel A. Almond, *The American People and Foreign Policy* (New York: Harcourt, 1950), esp. 53, 69 ff; James N. Rosenau, *Public Opinion and Foreign Policy* (New York: Random House, 1961), chap. 4; Michael Jay Robinson and Maura Clancey, "Teflon Politics," *Public Opinion* 7 (April/May 1984): 14–18; and Richard Sobel, "Public Opinion about United States Intervention in El Salvador and Nicaragua," *Public Opinion Quarterly* 53 (Spring 1989): 114–15. Eugene R. Wittkopf has recently argued that the mass public's beliefs about foreign policy are significantly more constrained and coherent than the received wisdom suggests, but Wittkopf also concedes that he does not challenge "the well-documented finding that the mass of the American people are, relatively speaking, uninterested in and ill informed about foreign policy issues" (*Faces of Interventionism: Public Opinion and American Foreign Policy* [Durham, N.C.: Duke University Press, 1990], 15).

52. A Gallup poll released in October 1953 found that 81 percent of the respondents had not "heard or read anything about Senator Bricker's proposal of an amendment to the Constitution to limit the President's treaty-making power" (Tananbaum, *Bricker Amendment Controversy,* 128).

53. See Angus Campbell et al., *The American Voter* (New York: Wiley, 1960), 199.

54. Almond, *American People and Foreign Policy,* 71. Rosenau uses the analogy of a "gigantic theatre" in which "the mass public, occupying the main seats in the balcony, is so far removed from the scene of action that its members can hardly grasp the plot, much less hear all the lines or distinguish between the actors. . . . The attentive public, on the other hand, is located in the few choice orchestra seats. Its members can not only hear every spoken line clearly, but can also see the facial expressions of the actors" (*Public Opinion and Foreign Policy,* 34).

55. James N. Rosenau, "Private Preferences and Political Responsibilities: The Relative Potency of Individual and Role Variables in the Behavior of U.S. Senators," in J. David Singer, ed., *Quantitative International Politics* (New York: Free Press, 1968), 17–50.

56. This is operationalized by Rosenau as those senators who served more than ten legislative months between 1953 and 1956 and who averaged more than 0.7 references to Dulles a month. By "consistently hostile" I mean that more than half of their references to Dulles were recorded by Rosenau as unfavorable.

57. The appellation "peace-minded" Democrats is applied to this group of senators in Gary W. Reichard, "Divisions and Dissent: Democrats and Foreign Policy, 1952–1956," *Political Science Quarterly* 93 (Spring 1978): 65; and Norman Graebner, "Eisenhower, Congress, and the Cold War Consensus," in Richard Melanson and Kenneth W. Thompson, eds., *Foreign Policy and Domestic Consensus* (Lanham, Md.: University Press of America, 1985), 81.

58. *Congressional Record,* 84th Cong., 2d sess., July 13, 1956, 12654.

59. Ibid., February 23, 1956, 3145–46.

60. Kenneth W. Grundy, "The Apprenticeship of J. William Fulbright," *Virginia Quarterly Review* 43 (Summer 1967): 393.

61. Naomi B. Lynn and Arthur F. McClure, *The Fulbright Premise: Senator J. William Fulbright's Views on Presidential Power* (Lewisburg, Pa.: Bucknell University Press, 1973), 113 n50. In that same interview, Lynn and McClure report that Fulbright "still adheres to the concept of the dichotomy between the passive President Eisenhower and the overactive Secretary of State Dulles" (117 n61).

62. This was from a 1961 article written by Fulbright for the *Cornell Law Quarterly.* Quoted in Eleanor Lansing Dulles, *John Foster Dulles: The Last Year* (New York: Harcourt, Brace and World, 1963), 31. Fulbright is quoting from *U.S. v. Curtiss-Wright* (1936), which spoke of "the very delicate, plenary and exclusive power of the President as the sole organ of the federal government in the field of international relations."

63. *Congressional Record,* 85th Cong., 2d sess., August 21, 1958, 18903.

64. Ibid., June 20, 1958, 11844. In a 1961 law review article, Fulbright wrote that Eisenhower was "an exemplary head of state" but his "failure to exercise the *full* measure of his powers and duties as 'Prime Minister' was the cause of basic failures and omissions in our foreign policy" (Lynn and McClure, *Fulbright Premise,* 114).

65. A. Robert Smith, *The Tiger in the Senate: The Biography of Wayne Morse* (Garden City, N.Y.: Doubleday, 1962), 140, 142, 146, 150, 153.

66. Parmet, *Eisenhower and the American Crusades,* 108.

67. Lehman insisted that "the first duty of liberals is not to exercise power, but to uphold principle" (*Congressional Record,* 85th Cong., 1st sess., March 2, 1957, 2950).

68. Quoted in Carl Solberg, *Hubert Humphrey* (New York: Norton, 1984), 163. In 1952 Truman told aide Eban Ayers that he considered Douglas "something of a crackpot" (Donald R. McCoy, *The Presidency of Harry S. Truman* [Lawrence: University Press of Kansas, 1984], 308).

69. *Congressional Record,* 85th Cong., 1st sess., March 2, 1957, 2950. Ibid., 2d sess., July 3, 1958, A6052. Paul H. Douglas, *In the Fullness of Time: The Memoirs of Paul H. Douglas* (New York: Harcourt Brace Jovanovich, 1971), 570.

70. Ambrose, *Eisenhower,* 220.

71. David W. Reinhard, *The Republican Right since 1945* (Lexington: University Press of Kentucky, 1983), 138.

72. Ibid., 121.

73. Robert H. Ferrell, ed., *The Eisenhower Diaries* (New York: Norton, 1981), 234 (April 1, 1953). Eisenhower to Bill Robinson, March 12, 1954, cited in Ambrose, *Eisenhower,* 164. In early March 1954, Eisenhower commented that "we just can't work with fellows like McCarthy, Bricker, Jenner, and that bunch" (Robert H. Ferrell, ed., *The Diary of James C. Hagerty: Eisenhower in Mid-Course, 1954-1955* [Bloomington: Indiana University Press, 1983], 24 [March 2, 1954]).

74. So-called by Eisenhower's friend and adviser Paul G. Hoffman in "How Eisenhower Saved the Republican Party," *Collier's,* October 26, 1956, 45.

75. Rosenau, "Private Preferences and Political Responsibilities," 41.

76. British opposition to Dulles's appointment was enough to persuade Walter Judd (R-Minn.) that Dulles would be a welcome departure from Acheson. "For too long," Judd told Eisenhower, "our State Department has been a kind of outpost of the British foreign office" (Walter Judd, Oral History-196, December 18, 1970, COHP, EL, 109).

77. *Congressional Record,* 83d Cong., 1st sess., June 30, 1953, 7647. The fear that Dulles was "a part of the old regime" was common among right-wing isolationists. See, e.g., George Malone, ibid., April 14, 1953, 3067-68; and Frank Holman to

John Bricker, November 6, 1952, and December 17, 1952, cited in Gary W. Reichard, "Eisenhower and the Bricker Amendment," *Prologue* (Summer 1974): 91; and Tananbaum, *Bricker Amendment Controversy,* 65-66.

78. *Congressional Record,* 84th Cong., 2d sess., January 19, 1956, 919-20.

79. Anna Kasten Nelson, "John Foster Dulles and the Bipartisan Congress," *Political Science Quarterly* 102 (Spring 1987): 43-64, at 47. Also see Michael A. Guhin, *John Foster Dulles: A Statesman and His Times* (New York: Columbia University Press, 1972), 184.

80. Nelson, "Dulles and the Bipartisan Congress," 46-47.

81. Alexander Wiley, Dulles Oral History, Princeton, cited in Parmet, *American Crusades,* 186-87. Also see the testimony of Alexander Smith, Dulles Oral History, Princeton, cited in Brands, *Cold Warriors,* 24; Carl McCardle, Oral History-116, August 29, 1967, COHP, EL, 43; Francis O. Wilcox, Oral History-246, April 3, 1976, COHP, EL, 15-16; and Prescott Bush, Oral History-31, August 1, 1966, COHP, EL, 317.

82. Ralph Flanders to Clark Eichelberger, January 19, 1954, cited in Tananbaum, *Bricker Amendment Controversy,* 70.

83. *Congressional Record,* 83d Cong., 2d sess., January 22, 1954, 651.

84. Fulbright, *Congressional Record,* 85th Cong., 2d sess., August 6, 1958, 16317.

85. Eric F. Goldman, *The Crucial Decade—And After* (New York: Vintage, 1960), 112.

86. See the enclosed chart in Dulles to Eisenhower, January 30, 1957, Dulles-Herter Series, AWF, EL.

87. Dean Acheson, *Present at the Creation: My Years in the State Department* (New York: Norton, 1969), 257.

88. Senator Hugh Butler of Nebraska, quoted in Goldman, *Crucial Decade,* 125.

89. *Congressional Record,* 81st Cong., 2d sess., December 6, 1950, 16178.

90. Glen H. Stassen, "Individual Preferences versus Role-Constraint in Policy-Making: Senatorial Responses to Secretaries Acheson and Dulles," *World Politics* 25 (October 1972): 96-119, at 107. Also see James N. Rosenau, "Senate Attitudes toward a Secretary of State," in John C. Wahlke and Heinz Eulau, *Legislative Behavior: A Reader in Theory and Research* (Glencoe, Ill.: Free Press, 1959), 332-47; and Rosenau, "Private Preferences and Political Responsibilities."

91. Acheson, *Present at the Creation,* 370.

92. Robert J. Donovan, *Tumultuous Years: The Presidency of Harry S Truman, 1949-1953* (New York: Norton, 1982), 131-32.

93. *Congressional Record,* 81st Cong., 2d sess., January 5, 1950, 79, 81, 96.

94. Foster Rhea Dulles, *American Policy toward Communist China, 1949-1969* (New York: Thomas Y. Crowell, 1972), 68.

95. See, for example, *Congressional Record,* 81st Cong., 2d sess., January 13, 1950, 389-90.

96. Ibid., 82d Cong., 1st sess., April 12, 1951, 3720. Also see September 27, 1950, 13283-84.

97. Ibid., 81st Cong., 2d sess., January 24, 1950, 815, emphasis added.

98. See, for example, ibid., January 23, 1950, 756; January 25, 1950, 893; January 26, 1950, 1006, 1008.

99. Donovan, *Tumultuous Years,* 163.

100. James T. Patterson, *Mr. Republican: A Biography of Robert A. Taft* (Boston: Houghton Mifflin, 1972), 489.

101. *Congressional Record,* 82d Cong., 1st sess., April 11, 1951, 3633, 3654, 3657, and April 12, 1951, 3719.

102. Goldman, *Crucial Decade,* 142.

103. David M. Oshinsky, *A Conspiracy so Immense: The World of Joe McCarthy* (New York: Free Press, 1983), 194.

104. *Congressional Record,* 82d Cong., 1st sess., April 11, 1951, 3640.

105. Ibid., April 13, 1951, 3863.

106. Ibid., April 12, 1951, 3724-25.

107. Ibid., April 11, 1951, 3619.

108. John E. Mueller, "Trends in Popular Support for the Wars in Korea and Vietnam," *American Political Science Review* 65 (June 1971): 358-75, at 361.

109. AIPO-468, December 3-8, 1950. AIPO-469, January 1-5, 1951.

110. Of those who disapproved of Truman, 81 percent believed Acheson should be replaced. Of those who approved of Truman, 70 percent thought Acheson should stay on. About two-thirds of those with an opinion about both men disapproved of Truman and believed Acheson should be replaced (AIPO-475, May 19-24, 1951).

111. AIPO-480, September 21-26, 1951.

112. NORC-313, October 3-11, 1951. NORC-329, September 2-10, 1952.

113. Donovan, *Tumultuous Years,* 114.

114. Richard F. Fenno, Jr., *The President's Cabinet* (Cambridge, Mass.: Harvard University Press, 1959), 49. Similarly, Cabell Phillips writes that "to Harry Truman a sense of loyalty was as natural as breathing, and he used every opportunity to reiterate his faith in Dean Acheson" (*The Truman Presidency: The History of a Triumphant Succession* [New York: Macmillan, 1966], 288). Also see Acheson, *Present at the Creation,* 730.

115. Margaret Truman, *Harry S. Truman* (New York: Quill 1972), 505. According to Acheson, Truman "blew up in typical fashion" (*Present at the Creation,* 366).

116. Harry S. Truman, *Years of Trial and Hope* (Garden City, N.Y.: Doubleday, 1956), 430; emphasis in original.

117. *Congressional Record,* 81st Cong., 2d sess., December 18, 1950, 16691.

118. *New York Times,* December 15, 1950, 27.

119. News Conference, January 30, 1957, *Public Papers of the Presidents: Dwight D. Eisenhower,* 8 vols. (Washington, D.C.: U.S. Government Printing Office, 1960-1961), 100.

120. Truman quoted by Senator Kem, in *Congressional Record,* 81st Cong., 2d sess., December 4, 1950, 16058.

121. News Conference, January 30, 1957, *Public Papers,* 100. Also see Eisenhower to Walter Judd, January 4, 1958, Dulles-Herter Series, AWF, EL.

122. On Truman's leadership style generally and relationship with Acheson specifically, see Crabb and Mulcahy, *Presidents and Foreign Policy Making,* 122-55; Alonzo L. Hamby, "Harry S. Truman: Insecurity and Responsibility," in Fred I. Greenstein, ed., *Leadership in the Modern Presidency* (Cambridge, Mass.: Harvard University Press, 1988), 65-67; Acheson, *Present at the Creation,* esp. 733-37; Donovan, *Tumultuous Years,* 35-36; and Alexander L. George, *Presidential Decisionmaking in Foreign Policy: The Effective Use of Information and Advice* (Boulder, Colo.: Westview Press, 1980), 151-52.

123. Harry S. Truman, *Year of Decisions* (Garden City, N.J.: Doubleday, 1955), 328-29. Also see Crabb and Mulcahy, "The President as His Own Secretary of State: FDR and Hull," chap. 3, *Presidents and Foreign Policy Making.*

124. Acheson, *Present at the Creation,* 355.

125. David S. McLellan, *Dean Acheson: The State Department Years* (New York: Dodd, Mead, 1976), 229; also see 218-19.

126. August A. Andersen, *Congressional Record,* 81st Cong., 2d sess., September 23, 1950, A6993.

127. Ibid., 82d Cong., 1st sess., April 11, 1951, 3652-53.

128. Ibid., January 13, 1951, 391.

129. The question was worded, "Some people think that president ought to have the major responsibility for making policy, while other people think that Congress ought to have the major responsibility. In general, which do you think should have the major responsibility for setting (foreign/economic/energy) policy?" Poll results are reported in Stephen J. Wayne, "Expectations of the President," in Doris A. Graber, ed., *The President and the Public* (Philadelphia: Institute for the Study of Human Issues, 1982), 19. Also see the data presented in Robert S. Sigel, "Image of the American Presidency: Part II of An Exploration into Popular Views of Presidential Power," in Aaron Wildavsky, ed., *The Presidency* (Boston: Little, Brown, 1969), esp. 299-300. Also relevant is Michael B. MacKuen, "Political Drama, Economic Conditions, and the Dynamics of Presidential Popularity," *American Journal of Political Science* 27 (May 1983): 165-92.

130. In their recent text, George C. Edwards III and Stephen J. Wayne write, "The general public, party leaders, and elected officials continue to look to the president for guidance [in foreign affairs] . . . the president is expected to take the policy-making initiative in [foreign and military affairs]. He is expected to oversee the conduct of war and diplomacy" (*Presidential Leadership: Politics and Policy Making,* 2d ed. [New York: St. Martin's, 1990], 416, 425).

131. Naomi B. Lynn and Arthur F. McClure, *The Fulbright Premise*, 110-11.

132. Tower Commission Report, reprinted in Harry A. Bailey, Jr., and Jay M. Shafritz, eds., *The American Presidency: Historical and Contemporary Perspectives* (Pacific Grove, Calif.: Brooks/Cole, 1988), 261, 262.

133. Frederick P. Lee, "The Two Presidencies Revisited," *Presidential Studies Quarterly* 19 (Fall 1980): 620-28.

134. Most presidential scholars share this view. Thomas E. Cronin, for instance, writes that "foreign policy responsibilities cannot be delegated; they are executive in character and presidential by constitutional tradition or interpretation" (*The State of the Presidency,* 2d ed. [Boston: Little, Brown, 1980], 146). Clinton Rossiter explains that "the President . . . is or ought to be in command of every procedure through which our foreign relations are carried on from one day to the next" (*The American Presidency* [New York: Harcourt, Brace and World, 1960], 27). The president, according to Richard Rose, "rightly sees national security, the object of diplomacy and military policy, as a unique concern for the White House" (*The Postmodern President: George Bush Meets the World,* 2d ed. [Chatham, N.J.: Chatham House, 1991], 215). Even those scholars critical of this tendency to view foreign relations as primarily a presidential responsibility concede that "the realm of foreign policy has come to be accepted, with important exceptions, as being primarily the domain of the President" (Robert J. Spitzer, *President and Congress: Executive Hegemony at the Crossroads of American Government* [New York: McGraw-Hill, 1993], 233).

135. Edward S. Corwin, *The President: Office and Powers, 1787-1957,* 4th ed. (New York: New York University Press, 1957), 171.

136. Rossiter, *American Presidency,* 27.

137. Theodore H. White, *The Making of the President, 1968* (New York: Atheneum, 1969), 171. In his memoirs, Nixon recounts being told by John Kennedy that "foreign affairs is the only important issue for a President to handle. . . . I mean, who gives a shit if the minimum wage is $1.15 or $1.25 in comparison to something like [the Bay of Pigs]" (Richard Nixon: *RN: Memoirs of Richard Nixon* [New York: Grosset and Dunlap, 1978], 235).

138. Harlan Cleveland, "Coherence and Consultation: The President as Manager of American Foreign Policy," in Bailey and Shafritz, eds., *The American Presidency,*

259. Thomas Cronin suggests that "White House advisers from all the recent administrations agree that a president spends a half to two-thirds of his time on foreign-policy or national-security deliberations" (*State of the Presidency*, 146).

139. John H. Kessel, "The Parameters of Presidential Politics," *Social Science Quarterly* 55 (June 1974): 10. Kessel found that attention to international affairs grew over time, "not evenly, but in a pattern that can be related to the election cycle. It mounts during the first, second and third years, then drops as a president faces reelection in his fourth year. During a president's second term, concern with international involvement grows again. During the sixth, seventh and eighth years, the loadings on this factor become substantially higher than they were during the first term." This pattern, Kessel concluded, "implies that institutional responsibilities call a president's attention to international problems whether he brings an interest in foreign affairs to the White House or not."

140. *New York Times*, June 29, 1993, A5.

141. The seminal study here is Aaron Wildavsky, "The Two Presidencies," reprinted in Aaron Wildavsky, ed., *The Presidency* (Boston: Little, Brown, 1969), 230–43. Several studies have shown that the gap in congressional support between foreign and domestic policy has declined since the period that Wildavsky examined (1948 to 1964), but even these studies reaffirm that presidents generally do get somewhat greater congressional support in foreign than in domestic policy (see Lance T. LeLoup and Steven Shull, "Congress versus the Executive: The 'Two Presidencies' Reconsidered," *Social Science Quarterly* 59 [March 1979]: 704–19; and George C. Edwards III, "The Two Presidencies: A Reevaluation," *American Politics Quarterly* 14 [July 1986]: 247–63).

More recent studies have strongly reaffirmed the two presidencies phenomenon. Richard Fleisher and Jon R. Bond found that between 1953 to 1984 every president but Johnson did better in foreign policy than in domestic policy ("Are There Two Presidencies? Yes, But Only for Republicans," *Journal of Politics* 50 (August 1988): 747–67). Examining the period from Eisenhower to Ford, Terry Sullivan finds a strong "two presidencies effect" for every president except for Johnson in the House ("A Matter of Fact: The 'Two Presidencies' Thesis Revitalized," in Steven A. Shull, ed., *The Two Presidencies: A Quarter Century Assessment* [Chicago: Nelson-Hall, 1991], 143–57), and Russell D. Renka and Bradford S. Jones find unmistakable evidence of the two presidencies during the 1980s ("The 'Two Presidencies' in the Reagan and Bush Administrations," in Shull, *The Two Presidencies*). A fascinating study by Jeffrey E. Cohen found that even in the first half of the twentieth century presidents did substantially better in foreign than in domestic policy ("A Historical Reassessment of Wildavsky's 'Two Presidencies' Thesis," *Social Science Quarterly* 63 (September 1982): 549–55). All of the above articles as well as a number of others are conveniently gathered together in Shull's useful collection, *The Two Presidencies*.

142. Cronin, *State of the Presidency*, 146. Bryce Harlow comments that "Presidents like Eisenhower and Nixon have been more immersed in foreign than domestic affairs" because "they have felt they could *do* more" (Emmet John Hughes, *The Living Presidency* [New York: Penguin, 1974], 345).

143. Edwards and Wayne, *Presidential Leadership*, 426. Also see Cronin, *State of the Presidency*, 147–48.

144. The phrase "going international" is taken from Rose, *Postmodern President*, 37–40.

145. Greenstein, *Hidden-Hand Presidency*, 92.

146. Ezra Suleiman observes much the same pattern among modern French presidents. French presidents gravitate toward foreign affairs, Suleiman suggests, because

"it creates a more prestigious presidential image than do other roles that he assumes. Here the President represents France, and not merely a political party" (Ezra N. Suleiman, "Presidential Government in France," in Richard Rose and Ezra Suleiman, eds., *Presidents and Prime Ministers* [Washington, D.C.: American Enterprise Institute, 1981], 38).

147. Gary D. Smith, "The Pulse of Presidential Popularity: Kennedy in Crisis" (Ph.D. dissertation, University of California at Los Angeles, 1978), 322 and passim.

148. MacKuen, "Political Drama, Economic Conditions, and the Dynamics of Presidential Popularity," 188.

149. Philip Stone and Richard A. Brody, "Modeling Opinion Responsiveness to Daily News: The Public and Lyndon Johnson, 1965-1968," *Social Science Information* 9 (February 1970): 117.

150. Nelson W. Polsby, *Congress and the Presidency,* 4th ed. (Englewood Cliffs, N.J.: Prentice-Hall, 1986), 73, 75.

151. Survey no. 272, January 16-19, 1987, *The Gallup Poll: Public Opinion 1987,* 15-17. The survey found that 49 percent felt it was worse if the NSC ran it without the president's knowledge, and 36 percent felt it was worse if the president knew and approved.

152. Hess, *Organizing the Presidency,* 66.

153. Michael B. Beschloss, *Mayday: The U-2 Affair* (New York: Harper and Row, 1986), 249, 251, 255, emphasis added.

154. Beschloss, *Mayday,* 243, 252.

155. According to John Eisenhower, when he told his father that Allen Dulles had let him down and should therefore be fired, the president exploded, "I am not going to shift the blame to my underlings" (Beschloss, *Mayday,* 271).

156. Eisenhower, *Waging Peace,* 553.

157. Walter Lippmann, quoted in Beschloss, *Mayday,* 251.

158. A CBS/*New York Times* poll taken in March 1975 found that only 49 percent of the public felt Ford was playing a "very important" role in foreign-policy decision making, while 73 percent felt Kissinger played such a role. Close to half (44 percent) of those polled thought Ford should play a more important role in foreign policy.

159. Joseph G. Bock, *The White House Staff and the National Security Assistant* (Westport, Conn.: Greenwood Press, 1987), 117-22. John Osborne, *White House Watch: The Ford Years* (Washington, D.C.: New Republic Books, 1977), 144. Philip Shabecoff, "Ford Foreign Policy Dims Kissinger Role: A New Imprint," *New York Times,* May 28, 1975, A1. Samuel Kernell and Samuel L. Popkin, *Chief of Staff* (Berkeley: University of California Press, 1986), 147-48.

160. These numbers are averages based on the three Harris surveys (March 1975, May 1975, and August 1975) for which these follow-up questions were asked about both Kissinger and Ford. Adding results from separate polls conducted in early 1976 reduces Ford's support scores by a point or two and has no effect on Kissinger's.

161. Harris Survey, Press Release, June 12, 1975.

162. For instances of such friction during Nixon's presidency, see Henry Kissinger, *The White House Years* (Boston: Little, Brown, 1979), especially 25, 918, 1408-10, 1424, 1455, 1468. John Ehrlichman complained that Kissinger's "press conferences were full of the President when there was bad news, but Nixon was seldom mentioned when the news was good" (*Witness to Power: The Nixon Years* [New York: Simon and Schuster, 1982], 315). Also see Barry M. Goldwater with Jack Casserly, *Goldwater* (New York: Doubleday, 1988), 270. The opening years of the Reagan presidency, to take another example, were dotted with stories like the one in which Hedrick Smith reported, "Once again, White House officials are mumbling

privately about Mr. Haig's 'grandstanding.' Some say he has not only taken center stage but even 'stolen the limelight' from President Reagan by making an extended public statement this afternoon on the Falklands crisis." (*New York Times,* April 15, 1982, quoted in Alexander M. Haig, Jr., *Caveat: Realism, Reagan, and Foreign Policy* [New York: Macmillan, 1984], 302).

163. Wildavsky, "The Two Presidencies." Also see Duane Oldfield and Wildavsky, "Reconsidering the Two Presidencies," in Shull, *The Two Presidencies,* 182. Oldfield and Wildavsky retreat significantly from the original Wildavsky thesis, going so far as to suggest that "the two presidencies" is "time and culture bound" (183). In my view, they retreat further from the original thesis than is warranted by the evidence (see Fleisher and Bond, "Are There Two Presidencies?"; Renka and Jones, "The 'Two Presidencies' in the Reagan and Bush Administrations"; and especially Sullivan, "A Matter of Fact"). Part of the problem seems to be that Oldfield and Wildavsky tend to conflate the question of partisan divisions, which have indeed increased in foreign policy (see Chapter 8), with the different (though importantly related) question of differences between congressional support in foreign and domestic policy, where differences persist. It is possible to have two presidencies and simultaneously to have strong partisan divisions in foreign policy.

CHAPTER 6. THE CHIEF OF STAFF AS LIGHTNING ROD

1. Report of the President's Committee on Administrative Management (1937), reprinted in Frederick C. Mosher, ed., *Basic Documents of American Public Administration, 1776–1950* (New York: Holmes and Meier, 1976), 117, emphasis added.

2. Louis Brownlow, *A Passion for Anonymity* (Chicago: University of Chicago Press, 1958), 381, 397. Also see Richard Polenberg, *Reorganizing Roosevelt's Government, 1936–1939* (Cambridge, Mass.: Harvard University Press, 1966), 222; and John Hart, *The Presidential Branch* (New York: Pergamon, 1987), 28.

3. Samuel Kernell and Samuel L. Popkin, eds., *Chief of Staff: Twenty-Five Years of Managing the Presidency* (Berkeley: University of California Press, 1986), 153–54, 90. H. R. Haldeman with Joseph DiMona, *The Ends of Power* (New York: New York Times Books, 1978), xx. Also see Kernell and Popkin, *Chief of Staff,* 88–89, 110, 195; and Rowland Evans, Jr., and Robert D. Novak, *Nixon in the White House: The Frustration of Power* (New York: Vintage, 1972), 47.

4. Kernell and Popkin, *Chief of Staff,* 89. President Ford concurs that "the Chiefs of Staff we had . . . weren't worried about getting their face in a picture with the President; they weren't worrying about getting recognition themselves; they ran the shop" (quoted in Bradley H. Patterson, Jr., *The Ring of Power: The White House Staff and Its Expanding Role in Government* [New York: Basic Books, 1988], 306).

5. Michael Medved, *The Shadow Presidents: The Secret History of the Chief Executives and Their Top Aides* (New York: Times Books, 1979), 259. Speaking to the Paper and Pulp Association early in 1954, Adams explained that upon being asked to address the association he decided to make an exception to a rule that he thought members of the president's staff should observe: "Keep your name out of the newspapers." "Perhaps I should do a better job of that," he added, "or, as my boss said, 'Never miss an opportunity to keep your mouth closed' " (*New York Times,* February 19, 1954, 1). Also see "The President's Buffer: Sherman Adams," *New York*

Times, June 11, 1956, 18; and W. H. Lawrence, "Presidency at Work in Time of Illness," *New York Times,* December 1, 1957, IV:5.

6. Donald T. Regan, *For the Record: From Wall Street to Washington* (New York: Harcourt Brace Jovanovich, 1988), 226. Regan further reveals that "as an antidote to the leaks to the media that had plagued the White House in the first term, I asked [the assistants to the president] all to cultivate a passion for anonymity" (237).

7. Samuel Kernell, "The Creed and Reality of Modern White House Management," in Kernell and Popkin, *Chief of Staff,* esp. 195-98.

8. Brownlow, *Passion for Anonymity,* 381.

9. "You can't just have one Executive Secretary," Roosevelt explained to Brownlow. "The damn columnists would never let him alone. They are always looking for the 'white haired boy.' Just now they are writing up Corcoran. Way back, it was Raymond Moley" (Brownlow, *Passion for Anonymity,* 381). A good example of the media's fascination with Corcoran is Alva Johnston, "White House Tommy," *Saturday Evening Post,* July 31, 1937. Also see Patrick Anderson, *The President's Men* (Garden City, N.Y.: Doubleday, 1968), esp. 41-42; and Joseph P. Lash, *Dealers and Dreamers: A New Look at the New Deal* (New York: Doubleday, 1988), esp. 307-8.

10. These three functions are identified and described in Hart, *Presidential Branch,* 127-28.

11. Jeffrey L. Pressman and Aaron Wildavsky, *Implementation,* 2d ed. (Berkeley: University of California Press, 1979), 133.

12. Don Regan, quoted in Michael K. Deaver, *Behind the Scenes* (New York: Morrow, 1987), 130. Donald Rumsfeld uses an even more telling metaphor: "[The chief of staff is] the person who sets up the staff system so that there is an orderly flow of work, meetings, paper, appointments, thought, and action, and that it satisfies the president, and serves the president. You bring those disparate threads up through a needle eye" (Patterson, *Ring of Power,* 303).

13. See Lewis A. Dexter, "Court Politics: Presidential Staff Relations as a Special Case of General Phenomenon," *Administration & Society* 9 (November 1977): 276-77.

14. See Kernell and Popkin, *Chief of Staff,* 128-29, 164, 170-71.

15. On Jim Baker, see *New York Times,* January 25, 1984, 25, and *New York Times Magazine,* May 20, 1984, esp. VI:56; on Ed Meese, see *New York Times Magazine,* April 19, 1981, VI:68; on Don Regan, see *New York Times,* January 21, 1985, IV:6, and *New York Times Magazine,* January 5, 1986, 14, 27; on Howard Baker, see *New York Times,* June 20, 1988, II:7. On Sununu, see *New York Times,* September 13, 1989, 18, and *New York Times,* February 22, 1990, 20.

16. Kernell and Popkin, *Chief of Staff,* 128. A similar line was taken by members of Cheney's staff, "almost all of [whom] concede that they are in a position of exercising enormous power, but add that it is delegated power that can be used only in a way that *exactly* matches the president's desires" (*New York Times,* May 24, 1976, 18, emphasis added). Similarly, Donald Rumsfeld insists that "the answer to the question about what influence any of the various chiefs of staff have had on their presidents is: *exactly* what the president wanted" (Kernell and Popkin, *Chief of Staff,* 129, emphasis added).

17. Kernell and Popkin, *Chief of Staff,* 164-65; James Pfiffner, "White House Staff versus the Cabinet: Centripetal and Centrifugal Roles," *Presidential Studies Quarterly* 16 (Fall 1986): 671.

18. Haldeman, quoted in Kernell and Popkin, *Chief of Staff,* 129.

19. Samuel Popkin, "The Art of Managing the White House," in Kernell and Popkin, *Chief of Staff,* 6. Also see Samuel Kernell, "Creed and Reality," in ibid.,

218-19; and Robert Hartmann's comments quoted in Patricia Dennis Witherspoon, *Within These Walls: A Study of Communication between Presidents and Their Senior Staffs* (New York: Praeger, 1991), 159.

20. Medved, *Shadow Presidents,* 318.

21. Haldeman, *Ends of Power,* 54-55. Patterson, *Ring of Power,* 306.

22. Regan, *For the Record,* 334-35. Bernard Weinraub, "How Donald Regan Runs the White House," *New York Times Magazine,* January 5, 1986, 36.

23. *New York Times,* June 3, 1956, 13; *Time,* January 9, 1956, 18.

24. Patterson, *Ring of Power,* 306.

25. Helen Nicolay, *Lincoln's Secretary: A Biography of John G. Nicolay* (New York: Longmans, 1949), 86. After showing the letter to Lincoln, Nicolay received permission to send it and then marked it "not sent" and laid it away. In his book of reminiscences, Stoddard characterized Nicolay as "the impassable Mr. Nicolay" who "has a fine faculty of explaining to some men the view he takes of any untimely persistency. . . . People who do not like him—because they cannot use him, perhaps—say he is sour and crusty. Good thing that he is. The President showed his good judgment when he put Mr. Nicolay just where he is" (ibid., 86-88).

26. Thomas E. Cronin, *The State of the Presidency,* 2d ed. (Boston: Little, Brown, 1980), 276-86.

27. See *New York Times,* November 26, 1970, A23. Also see Walter J. Hickel, *Who Owns America?* (Englewood Cliffs, N.J.: Prentice-Hall, 1971).

28. Kernell and Popkin, *Chief of Staff,* 191.

29. Richard P. Nathan, *The Administrative Presidency* (New York: Macmillan, 1983), 38.

30. Ousted administrator Joseph English was one of a number of HEW officials who charged the Nixon staff with "not placing the issue of health before the President of the United States" (*New York Times,* October 12, 1969, 28).

31. Lou Cannon, *President Reagan: The Role of a Lifetime* (New York: Simon and Schuster, 1991), 189, 197.

32. Herbert S. Parmet, *Eisenhower and the American Crusades* (New York: Macmillan, 1972), 179. Sherman Adams, *Firsthand Report* (New York: Harper and Brothers, 1961), 402-3.

33. William Bragg Ewald, Jr., *Eisenhower the President: Crucial Days, 1951-1960* (Englewood Cliffs, N.J.: Prentice-Hall, 1981), 161.

34. Richard Strout, "The Administration's Abominable Noman," *New York Times Magazine,* June 3, 1956, 13.

35. Ann Devoy, "Citing Year of Triumph, Sununu Defends Actions," *Washington Post,* December 12, 1990, cited in Colin Campbell, "The White House and Cabinet under the 'Let's Deal' Presidency," in Colin Campbell and Bert A. Rockman, eds., *The Bush Presidency: First Appraisals* (Chatham, N.J.: Chatham House, 1991), 213. Also see *New York Times,* September 13, 1989, 18.

36. *New York Times,* May 11, 1990, 34.

37. Robert Keith Gray, *Eighteen Acres under Glass* (Garden City, N.Y.: Doubleday, 1962), 51.

38. Kernell and Popkin, *Chief of Staff,* 61-62.

39. "Much of the great deal of success in Reagan's first term," Stuart Eizenstat told a *New York Times* reporter, "was due to Jim Baker, who really has been the glue that has held the Administration together. . . . Without Baker, he would not have gotten out of the starting blocks as quickly and would have had a very different image than what the President has right now" (January 22, 1985, 16). In the fall of 1981, the *Times* reported that "Jim Baker . . . has emerged on Capitol Hill as the key figure who engineered President Reagan's triumph in the Saudi arms sale. 'It was

Jim Baker and no other,' said one Senate aide. 'Baker just took over, handled the phones, got people in to see Reagan, got Reagan to make the calls, and knew who to call and who was wavering' " (November 3, 1981, II:10).

40. Richard Rose, *The Postmodern President: George Bush Meets the World,* 2d ed. (Chatham, N.J.: Chatham House, 1991), 182.

41. Adams, *Firsthand Report,* 51. Also see Andrew Goodpaster's testimony in Kernell and Popkin, *Chief of Staff,* 176-77.

42. Kernell and Popkin, *Chief of Staff,* 149.

43. *New York Times,* February 13, 1981, 4; February 8, 1982, 16.

44. Kernell and Popkin, *Chief of Staff,* 173-75. Also see John Osborne, *White House Watch: The Ford Years* (Washington, D.C.: New Republic Books, 1977), xxii-xiv, 210-15.

45. William D. Carey, "Presidential Staffing in the Sixties and Seventies," *Public Administration Review* 29 (September-October 1969): 454. The President's Task Force on Government Organization wanted to see Califano's role formalized and strengthened. In what became known as the Heineman report, issued in the summer of 1967, the task force recommended that Johnson "must inform Cabinet subordinates that he expects them to meet upon the call of the Director [of the newly proposed Office of Program Coordination]; that he expects major matters of interdepartmental program coordination to be settled in the forum provided by the Director; and that, when agency heads remain unable to compose agreement, he expects agreement to emerge and to 'stick' along lines prescribed by the Director" (Stephen Hess, *Organizing the Presidency,* rev. ed. [Washington, D.C.: Brookings, 1988], 99).

46. Peter Jacobson, quoted in Emmette S. Redford and Richard T. McCulley, *White House Operations: The Johnson Presidency* (Austin: University of Texas Press, 1986), 65.

47. Nathan, *Administrative Presidency,* 36.

48. Robert B. Semple, Jr., "Nixon's Inner Circle Meets," *New York Times Magazine,* August 3, 1969, 58. Evans and Novak, *Nixon in the White House,* 50. John Ehrlichman, *Witness to Power: The Nixon Years* (New York: Simon and Schuster, 1982), 89. Also see *New York Times,* December 3, 1972, 14.

49. Semple, "Nixon's Inner Circle Meets," 58.

50. E. E. Schattschneider, *The Semisovereign People: A Realist's View of Democracy in America* (1960; reprint, Hinsdale, Ill.: Dryden, 1975), 40.

51. These points are well made in Kernell, "Creed and Reality," 219-21.

52. *New York Times,* February 6, 1958, 18, emphasis added. "When you have worked as close to a man for as many years as Sherm has worked with the President," noted an administration official, "you get to know automatically what the boss's attitude or reaction will be to almost any ordinary affair" (Cabell Phillips, "Adams Role Crucial in Eisenhower Setup," *New York Times,* June 22, 1958, IV:7).

53. Haldeman, *Ends of Power,* 51, emphasis added.

54. Juan Williams, "John Sununu, The White House Chief of Gaffe," *Washington Post Weekly,* December 2-8, 1991, 22, emphasis added.

55. Dom Bonafede, "The Emergence of Eizenstat," *National Journal,* June 4, 1977, 865.

56. Anderson, *President's Men,* 352.

57. Kernell and Popkin, *Chief of Staff,* 89.

58. Cheney's preference for a low profile was evident in his decision to decline Ford's offer of cabinet rank. Cheney turned it down, according to an associate, because "he wanted to be a nuts and bolts operator and felt to do that he had to keep a

low profile" (*New York Times,* May 24, 1976, 18). In interviews, Cheney tended to downplay his role. See, for example, *National Journal,* March 20, 1976, 377.

59. Cheney averaged a little more than three entries a month in the *New York Times* index in his fourteen-month tenure as chief of staff, a figure that is on the low end for contemporary chiefs of staff. During the last twenty years only Kenneth Duberstein (1.0), Jack Watson (2.7), Samuel Skinner (2.9), and Jim Baker (3.0) have had lower public profiles, as measured by this indicator. Cheney's public profile appears to have been substantially lower than John Sununu (4.2), Hamilton Jordan (4.8), Howard Baker (4.8), Donald Rumsfeld (5.9), and Don Regan (7.8).

60. See, for example, *New York Times,* August 18, 1976, 1, 22.

61. *New York Times,* April 23, 1982, A20.

62. When Reagan had surgery for removal of a polyp in July 1985, Regan found that "avoiding television appearances and keeping contacts with the press to a minimum" could not keep him out of the news. "In obedience to the First Lady's wishes," Regan recalls, "I was the only one besides herself who was seeing the President. *Because he is news incarnate, that made me news"* (Regan, *For the Record,* 20; emphasis added).

63. Cheney quoted in Kernell and Popkin, *Chief of Staff,* 89. Similarly, Buchanan writes that "the [media] exposure [of chiefs of staff] has increased dramatically during the Reagan administration" (quoted in Bruce Buchanan, "Constrained Diversity; The Organizational Demands of the Presidency," in James P. Pfiffner, ed., *The Managerial Presidency* [Pacific Grove, Calif.: Brooks/Cole, 1991], 94).

64. During Adams's sixty-nine-month tenure, he averaged 7.8 entries a month in the *New York Times* index. From the time of Adams's resignation in 1958 until 1973, the chief of staff (or "first among equals" where, as in Kennedy and Johnson's times, there was no chief of staff) averaged only 1.8 entries a month. From 1973 until the end of Reagan's term in 1988, the chief of staff averaged 5.9 entries a month in the *Times.* These numbers were calculated by the author from the *Times* index, using names and tenures of chiefs of staff and "first among equals" provided in Dennis J. Donoghue, "A Comparison of Republican and Democratic Chiefs of Staff from President Eisenhower through President Clinton" (Paper prepared for the Western Political Science Association Meetings, Anaheim, Calif., March 18–20, 1993).

65. Louis W. Koenig, *The Invisible Presidency* (New York: Rinehart, 1960), 340. Columnist James Reston wrote that for five years Adams had "played the role of the 'anonymous man' in the White House" ("The Adams Onslaught," *New York Times,* January 22, 1958, 1). The *New York Times* described Adams as "a man who has made himself virtually invisible to press and public while in the White House" (September 23, 1958, 18).

66. The conventional portrait of Adams as a man obsessed with secrecy and oblivious to public relations is defied by the fact that it was Adams who was largely responsible for inviting journalist Robert J. Donovan into the White House to do a sympathetic behind-the-scenes look at the Eisenhower administration. Adams, by his own admission, was "Donovan's guide and main source of information" (Adams, *Firsthand Report,* 29; also see *New York Times,* July 1, 1956, IV:7). Donovan's book appeared shortly before the 1956 election as *Eisenhower: The Inside Story* (New York: Harper and Row, 1956).

67. In the Eisenhower administration, only John Foster Dulles, Richard Nixon, Charlie Wilson, Ezra Taft Benson, and Herbert Brownell were more prominent than Adams.

68. Of all subsequent chiefs of staff, only Al Haig (15.8) has a higher monthly average of entries in the *New York Times* index. Adams's visibility, as measured by this

indicator, is comparable to the visibility of Reagan's outspoken chief of staff Don Regan (7.8).

69. Kernell and Popkin, *Chief of Staff*, 87–88.

70. Among the many public forums Adams addressed during his almost six years in the White House were a two-day conference of Republican women in Washington, D.C., a luncheon session closing the 44th annual convention of the Association of National Advertisers, the fourth annual American Forest Congress, a Republican National Committee luncheon, the American Paper and Pulp convention, the 100th anniversary luncheon of the National Association of Cotton Manufacturers, a meeting of the Citizens for Eisenhower Congressional Committee, a luncheon session of the 20th annual international distribution congress of National Sales Executives, Connecticut's "Salute to Eisenhower" dinner, a luncheon at the annual meeting of the National Advertising Council, the Republican National convention, the 102nd annual meeting of the National Textile Association, a conference of the Smaller Business Association, the fiftieth anniversary dinner of the American Jewish Committee, a dinner at a Republican regional conference in Trenton, a region-wide finance meeting of the Republican National Committee delivered to Southern Republican leaders in Chattanooga, a $100-a-plate fund-raiser at the Cow Palace given by the San Francisco Republican Finance Committee, a luncheon meeting of the Republican Forum in Chicago, a nationally broadcast speech to six hundred Missouri Republicans at a $100-a-plate fund-raising dinner, the Minnesota United Republican dinner, Dartmouth College alumni dinner, as well as commencement exercises at St. Lawrence University, Bates College, Centre College in Danville, Ky., the University of Maine, and Holderness secondary school. See *New York Times,* April 24, 1953; September 24, 1953; October 31, 1953; February 7, 1954; February 19, 1954; May 21, 1954; June 1, 1954; June 10, 1955; January 21, 1956; April 4, 1956; August 22, 1956; September 28, 1956; October 3, 1956; April 14, 1957; May 25, 1957; October 3, 1957; October 15, 1957; November 19, 1957; December 10, 1957; January 21, 1958; February 6, 1958; June 8, 1953; June 14, 1954; June 3, 1957; June 10, 1957; and June 9, 1958.

71. See especially *New York Times,* February 19, 1954, 1; November 19, 1957, 26; February 6, 1958, 1.

72. See *New York Times,* February 24, 1953, 31; October 22, 1954, 4; October 17, 1955, 4, 2; October 19, 1955, 1; February 9, 1955, 12; April 12, 1955, 17; July 21, 1955, 13; January 15, 1956, 69; January 16, 1956, 12; January 29, 1956, 52; April 17, 1956, 2; April 22, 1956, 10; August 15, 1956, 8; December 14, 1956, 24; February 2, 1957, 17; April 8, 1957, 17.

73. *New York Times,* July 14, 1954, 22. Also see March 31, 1953; February 17, 1956, 4; September 21, 1956, 33; June 22, 1957, 1; September 10, 1957, 24; October 22, 1957.

74. Nixon, quoted in Haldeman, *Ends of Power,* 111.

75. Cannon, *President Reagan,* 176; also see 80. Donald Regan agrees that Reagan "dislikes confrontations more than any man I have ever known" (Regan, *For the Record,* 98).

76. Hedley Donovan, *Roosevelt to Reagan: A Reporter's Encounters with Nine Presidents* (New York: Perennial, 1987), 140.

77. William Safire, *Before the Fall: An Inside View of the Pre-Watergate White House* (Garden City, N.Y.: Doubleday, 1975), 467. In a similar vein, Henry Kissinger writes that Nixon "disliked and dreaded . . . face-to-face confrontations" (*White House Years* [Boston: Little, Brown, 1979], 48; also see 45).

78. W. B. Smith, quoted by Richard Nixon in *The Memoirs of Richard Nixon* (New York: Grosset and Dunlap, 1978), 198.

79. Deaver, *Behind the Scenes,* 135.

80. Ibid.; also see 224.

81. Cannon, *President Reagan,* 584-85.

82. *New York Times,* January 10, 1985, 20.

83. Haldeman, quoted in Jebb Stuart Magruder, *An American Life: One Man's Road to Watergate* (New York: Atheneum, 1974), 58.

84. Pfiffner, "Staff versus the Cabinet," 670.

85. Kernell and Popkin, *Chief of Staff,* 190-91.

86. Martin Anderson, *Revolution* (New York: Harcourt, 1988), 289. Don Regan, too, remarked on Reagan's "baffling reluctance to give orders, or even guidance, to his close subordinates" (Regan, *For the Record,* 425, from paperback version, quoted in Witherspoon, *Within These Walls,* 142).

87. Terrel H. Bell, *The Thirteenth Man: A Reagan Cabinet Memoir* (New York: Free Press, 1988), 39.

88. Bruce Buchanan, *The Citizen's Presidency: Standards of Choice and Judgment* (Washington, D.C.: Congressional Quarterly, 1987), 135 n5.

89. Alexander M. Haig, Jr., *Caveat: Realism, Reagan, and Foreign Policy* (New York: Macmillan, 1984), 82, 86; also see 76, 85, 148-50. Also see Cannon, *President Reagan,* 150, 195, 201.

90. Ehrlichman, *Witness to Power,* 283.

91. Kissinger, *White House Years,* 1419, 141, 819, 1409.

92. Haldeman, *Ends of Power,* 58. Shortly after Nixon's reelection, the *New York Times* described Haldeman as "the *transmitter* of Mr. Nixon's orders" (December 3, 1972, 14; emphasis added).

93. *New York Times,* February 8, 1972, 1. That it was a ruse is confirmed by Haldeman, who says, "I made the statement that I was told to make" (Kernell and Popkin, *Chief of Staff,* 89). Also see Safire, *Before the Fall,* 291.

94. *New York Times,* February 8, 1972, 12.

95. Ibid., 13.

96. Ibid., February 9, 1972, 38.

97. James Reston, "The Haldeman Case," *New York Times,* February 9, 1972.

98. Ibid., February 8, 1972.

99. Ibid., February 10, 1972, 20.

100. Ibid., 10.

101. Ibid., September 22, 1972, 43, emphasis added.

102. Ibid., February 11, 1972.

103. Ibid., February 17, 1972.

104. Rose, *Postmodern President,* 181.

105. Joel Haremann, "The Cabinet Band—Trying to Follow Carter's Baton," *National Journal,* July 16, 1977, 1109.

106. Kernell and Popkin, *Chief of Staff,* 173.

107. *New York Times,* February 19, 1954, 1.

108. Ibid., January 21, 1958, 1, 19. Koenig, *Invisible Presidency,* 387.

109. *New York Times,* February 8, 1972, 1.

110. Koenig, *Invisible Presidency,* 341. *New York Times,* February 7, 1954, 56.

111. Stephen E. Ambrose, *Eisenhower: The President* (New York: Simon and Schuster, 1984), 151. Also see Koenig, *Invisible Presidency,* 355-56.

112. On the disenchantment with Adams among congressional Republicans, see Barry Goldwater, Oral History-21, COHP, EL, June 15, 1967, 33; Leonard Hall, Oral History-478, EL, 38; Parmet, *Eisenhower and the American Crusades,* 182; Gray, *Eighteen Acres under Glass,* 41-42. *New York Times,* July 7, 1953, 21; Febru-

236 NOTES TO PAGES 114-16

ary 19, 1954, 17; November 27, 1957, 13. *U.S. News & World Report,* July 17, 1953, 67, 70; November 5, 1954, 57–58.

113. Tip O'Neill with William Novak, *Man of the House* (New York: Random House, 1987), 311.

114. Joseph A. Califano, Jr., *Governing America: An Insider's Report from the White House and the Cabinet* (New York: Simon and Schuster, 1981), 148, 411.

115. Cheney was reported to be "almost universally well-liked by members of the White House staff" (*New York Times,* May 24, 1976, 18).

116. *National Journal,* June 19, 1976, 868; July 31, 1976, 1084.

117. Osborne, *White House Watch,* xxiv–xxv.

118. Ibid., xxv.

119. *New York Times,* May 24, 1976, 18.

120. Kernell and Popkin, *Chief of Staff,* 178–79.

121. *New York Times,* May 11, 1990, II:6.

122. Ibid., December 12, 1990, II:12. Dole insists it was a slip of the tongue.

123. *Washington Post Weekly,* December 17–23, 1990, 6.

124. Ibid., December 24–30, 1990, 13. Six months later, however, Gingrich was quoted as saying about Sununu: "You have an extremely smart, energetic, tough assistant taking all the heat and delivering all the bad news. . . . A guy who's willing to throw himself between you and your opponents everyday. It's unbelievably valuable" (*New York Times,* June 26, 1991, 13). A similar judgment of Sununu's value was offered by Democrat Tony Coelho: "If you didn't have Sununu there, some people in the Cabinet would be running around doing their own thing. You need to have a tough guy who makes things work. A president like George Bush needs John Sununu" (*Washington Post Weekly,* December 17–23, 1990, 7).

125. *New York Times,* September 13, 1989, 18.

126. *Washington Post Weekly,* December 17–23, 1990, 7. Also see *New York Times,* October 29, 1990, 14.

127. *National Journal,* April 27, 1991, 1006.

128. See, e.g., Sununu, quoted in *New York Times,* December 12, 1990, II:12.

129. See *New York Times,* September 23, 1958, 19; June 15, 1958, 1, 42; June 16, 1958, 18; June 19, 1958, 1, 21; June 20, 1958, 1, 14; June 21, 1958, 1, 8; June 22, 1958, 1, 50; June 30, 1958, 1; August 14, 1958, 14; September 10, 1958, 1; September 11, 1958, 1; September 12, 1958, 17. Also see Medved, *Shadow Presidents,* 254, 256.

130. Felix Belair, "For Adams It's Business as Usual," *New York Times,* July 27, 1958, IV:6.

131. *National Journal,* May 11, 1991, 1129.

132. The same point is made in another context in Kernell, "Creed and Reality," 220.

133. *New York Times,* December 22, 1986, 16.

134. Ibid., November 30, 1986, 24.

135. Ibid., December 1, 1986, 10; December 11, 1986, 23.

136. Regan, *For the Record,* 47–48, 378.

137. Even before Eisenhower's first heart attack, Adams's power was reported to be "almost unlimited" (*U.S. News & World Report,* November 5, 1954, 57). According to one noted columnist, "Until [the Goldfine] scandal broke, Mr. Adams' authority to act for the President at the White House was absolute. . . . Mr. Adams' slightest wish became a command for persons of Cabinet rank and below who feared his wrath if they did not comply" (W. H. Lawrence, "'Adams Must Go' Mood Revived By Elections," *New York Times,* September 14, 1958, IV:9).

138. John Sununu has been identified as "the White House chief of everything"

(*New York Times,* January 5, 1991, 21) and "the driving force in domestic policy in the White House" ("Domestic Priority No. 1: Reelection," *Washington Post Weekly,* January 28–February 3, 1991, 4.

139. Rose, *Postmodern President,* 182.

140. Buchanan, "Constrained Diversity," 96.

141. H. R. Haldeman, "The Nixon White House and Presidency," in Kenneth W. Thompson, ed., *The Nixon Presidency: Twenty-Two Intimate Perspectives of Richard M. Nixon* (Lanham, Md.: University Press of America, 1987), 87.

142. Regan, *For the Record,* 336.

143. Bernard Weinraub, "Regan Taking Control of President's Schedule," *New York Times,* May 21, 1985, 23.

144. Bernard Weinraub, "How Donald Regan Runs the White House," *New York Times Magazine,* January 5, 1986, 32. Larry Speakes, *Speaking Out: The Reagan Presidency from inside the White House* (New York: Scribners, 1988), 73.

145. Speakes, *Speaking Out,* 73–74.

146. *New York Times,* December 5, 1985, 14.

147. Weinraub, "How Donald Regan Runs the White House," 52. Only after the Iran-contra revelations did Regan attempt to downplay his control over the White House: "Does the bank president," he asked, "know whether a teller in the bank is fiddling around with the books?" (*New York Times,* March 1, 1987, 12).

148. *New York Times,* July 15, 1985, 11.

149. Ibid.

150. Ibid., December 5, 1985, 14.

151. Weinraub, "How Donald Regan Runs the White House," 52.

152. *New York Times,* December 2, 1986, 35.

153. *New York Times,* December 11, 1986, 23.

154. Ibid. Also see Dick Kirschten, "Around the White House Bunker," *National Journal,* December 6, 1986, 2950.

155. Gerald Ford, *Time to Heal* (New York: Harper and Row, 1979), 147.

156. Kernell and Popkin, *Chief of Staff,* 73–74. Hess, *Organizing the Presidency,* 132–33.

157. Ford, *Time to Heal,* 186. Witherspoon, *Within These Walls,* 106–7. Osborne, *White House Watch,* 199.

158. Hess, *Organizing the Presidency,* 142, 146. Witherspoon, *Within These Walls,* 120.

159. Witherspoon, *Within These Walls,* 114.

160. Ibid., 129.

161. Ibid., 121. Patterson, *Ring of Power,* 302. Watson reports sending Carter similar signals in Kernell and Popkin, *Chief of Staff,* 70–71. Also see Witherspoon, *Within These Walls,* 122–23, and Dom Bonafede, "The New Model Year," *National Journal,* November 26, 1977, 1859.

162. Witherspoon, *Within These Walls,* 128–29. Gerald M. Boyd, "Dept. of Big Frogs and Mighty Ponds," *New York Times,* January 22, 1985, 16. Also see Kernell and Popkin, *Chief of Staff,* 71–73, and Pfiffner "White House Staff versus the Cabinet," 671.

163. Eizenstat, quoted in Witherspoon, *Within These Walls,* 129.

164. Richard Neustadt, "Does the White House Need a Strong Chief of Staff?" in Pfiffner, *Managerial Presidency,* 29. Also see Neustadt's "confession" in Kernell and Popkin, *Chief of Staff,* 142–43. Neustadt does not, however, endorse a chief of staff in the mold of Regan, Adams, and Haldeman. Rather, he prefers the chief of staff to be "part of a circle . . . of three or four key, virtually coequal top advisors" (Neustadt, "Does the White House Need a Strong Chief of Staff?" 30).

165. Medved, *Shadow Presidents,* 352. Samuel Popkin, "The Art of Managing the White House," in Kernell and Popkin, *Chief of Staff,* 10. Popkin's conclusion reflects a rough consensus reached by former top presidential aides who spoke about their experiences at a U.C. San Diego conference. A transcript of that discussion makes up the main text of *Chief of Staff.* Also see Roger B. Porter, "Advising the President," *PS: Political Science & Politics* 19 (Fall 1986): 867-69; and Pfiffner, "White House Staff versus the Cabinet," esp. 684-85. Dissents can be found in Buchanan, "Constrained Diversity," esp. 96-104; and Campbell, "The 'Let's Deal' Presidency," 217.

166. This is the model recommended by James Pfiffner, "The President's Chief of Staff: Lessons Learned," *Presidential Studies Quarterly* 23 (Winter 1993): 77-102.

167. In assuming the role of chief of staff, Kennedy followed not only his own inclinations but the advice of several counselors, including Clark Clifford, who advised the president-elect that "a vigorous President in the Democratic tradition of the Presidency will probably find it best to act as his own chief of staff," and Richard Neustadt, who told Kennedy that "if you follow my advice . . . you would be your own 'chief of staff.' *You* would oversee, coordinate, and interfere with virtually everything your staff was doing" (Clifford, Memorandum on Transition, November 9, 1960, quoted in Pfiffner, "White House Staff versus the Cabinet," 668; and Neustadt, Memorandum on Staffing the President-Elect, October 30, 1960, reprinted in Pfiffner, *Managerial Presidency,* 21).

168. Stephen Hess gave president-elect Carter the same advice that "a president need not have a chief of staff—he can divide the duties—but he should not be his own chief of staff" (*Organizing the Presidency,* xi).

CHAPTER 7. LIMITS OF THE LIGHTNING ROD

1. Richmond *Times-Dispatch,* October 24, 1957, 16.
2. See, for example, the Richmond *News Leader,* October 24, 1957, 12; *Arkansas Democrat,* October 25, 1957, 14; and *Mobile Register,* October 24, 1957, 8.
3. Richmond *Times-Dispatch,* October 24, 1957, 13.
4. *Mobile Register,* October 24, 1957, 1, 10. Not everyone, however, was persuaded that Brownell's successor, William P. Rogers, would be an improvement. The *Greenville Piedmont,* while sharing the belief that Eisenhower's decision to send troops into Little Rock "was dictated by Brownell's advice," also took note that "behind Brownell stood Rogers as his first assistant." They concluded that "Brownell is gone in name only. His policies remain in his successor. The South can take no comfort in that" ("Brownell Still with Us," October 26, 1957). Similarly, the *Jackson Daily News,* while allowing that Brownell had "engineered the President into that ill-fated decision," advised its readers to "hold up on the cheering" until we see "whether Rogers is a Brownell prototype" ("Hold up on the Shouting," October 24, 1957, 10).
5. *Mobile Register,* October 24, 1957, 1.
6. *New York Times,* November 18, 1957, 19. Also see Orval Faubus, Oral History-181, August 18, 1971, COHP, EL, 45-46.
7. Herbert Brownell with John P. Burke, *Advising Ike: The Memoirs of Attorney General Herbert Brownell* (Lawrence: University Press of Kansas, 1993), 297. Also see Herbert Brownell, "From Campaigning to Governance," in Kenneth W. Thomp-

son, ed., *The Eisenhower Presidency* (Lanham, Md.: University Press of America, 1984), 168.

8. Brownell, *Advising Ike,* 287. Also see Fred I. Greenstein, *The Hidden-Hand Presidency: Eisenhower as Leader* (New York: Basic Books, 1982), 179. Brownell explains that this was a view "I also came to appreciate and share" (*Advising Ike,* 287).

9. Brownell, *Advising Ike,* 287-88, 297.

10. Diary entry for July 24, 1953, in Robert H. Ferrell, ed., *The Eisenhower Diaries* (New York: Norton, 1981), 246-47.

11. Byrnes to Eisenhower, November 20, 1953, Name Series, AWF, EL.

12. Eisenhower to Byrnes, December 1, 1953, Name Series, AWF, EL, emphasis added. Eisenhower was not being particularly duplicitous here. As Brownell acknowledges in his memoirs: "In my discussion with the president . . . I knew I would not be persuasive if I made the argument [to accept the court's invitation] on [the basis of supporting civil rights]. Instead, I took a position that might resonate more favorably with Eisenhower's deep commitment to the importance of constitutional and professional duty—thus I told him that since I was an 'officer of the court' as a practicing attorney, it would be most difficult for me to reject the invitation to advise the Court. I also knew that Eisenhower would generally defer to my advice and trust my opinions on matters of the law and the legal process, an area in which he did not have extensive knowledge and experience, so I emphasized that the relationship between the Supreme Court and the Justice Department . . . would be strained if we refused the invitation" (*Advising Ike,* 190; also see 193, 215).

13. Eisenhower to Byrnes, December 1, 1953, Name Series, AWF, EL. In view of this correspondence, Byrnes's reaction to Little Rock is instructive. Although one of Eisenhower's most vocal backers in 1952, Byrnes was one of a multitude of southern politicians who immediately spoke out to condemn the administration's decision to send troops into Little Rock. While harshly criticizing the administration's decision, Byrnes still insisted that he had "complete confidence in the integrity of President Eisenhower," whom he characterized as "a man of good intentions." He accounted for the president's decision to send troops into Little Rock as the result of having "followed the advice of Attorney General Brownell, who had demonstrated a willingness to sacrifice everything to win the votes of certain minority groups in doubtful states." While unable to mask his disappointment with Eisenhower—he was "glad," he told his audience, that "I did not vote for him in 1956"—for having "blindly followed" the attorney general's advice, Byrnes reserved his fiercest barbs for "the master strategist," Herbert Brownell (*New York Times,* September 27, 1957, 12). That Byrnes placed the lion's share of the blame for the administration's actions on Attorney General Brownell rather than on the president seems to be a tribute to Eisenhower's ability to persuade Byrnes, through written correspondence and personal conversation, that his sympathies lay with southern whites and that it was Brownell and his associates at the Justice Department who were primarily responsible for administration actions in the area of civil rights.

14. News Conference, March 17, 1957, *Public Papers of the Presidents: Dwight D. Eisenhower, 1953-1961,* 8 vols. (Washington, D.C.: U.S. Government Printing Office 1960-1961), 176.

15. News Conference, May 15, 1957, *Public Papers,* 357.

16. Ibid., July 3, 1957, *Public Papers,* 521.

17. Eisenhower had acted in much the same manner when confronted with press inquiries in November 1953 about Justice Department charges that Harry Dexter White, a Treasury Department aide who had died in 1946, had provided information to the Soviet Union and that President Truman had done nothing about it despite warnings from the FBI that White was a spy. Asked by reporters whether it was

proper, given that a grand jury had found insufficient evidence to prosecute, for the attorney general to characterize White as a spy, Eisenhower replied that "I am not either a judge nor am I an accomplished lawyer. . . . You are asking me to answer questions [when] . . . the Attorney General is here to answer it himself. Let him answer it." Pressed as to whether he could say when Brownell would offer proof of the charges he had made, the president replied, "Of course I can't. I just told you that he has got to handle this case in his own way." Claiming that he did not have the information to make a judgment on the validity of the accusations, he informed the reporters that he had told Brownell "to follow your own conscience as to your duty" (News Conference, November 11, 1953, *Public Papers,* 763-65).

18. According to George Edwards's calculations, Eisenhower's approval rating in the South averaged 66.5 percent with a high of 68 percent (1955) and a low of 65 percent (1954). The average gap between approval for Eisenhower among southerners and nonsoutherners during the first term averaged 4 percent, with a high of 7 percent (1956) and a low of 1 percent (1954). See George C. Edwards III with Alec Gallup, *Presidential Approval: A Sourcebook* (Baltimore, Md.: Johns Hopkins University Press, 1990), 155. For the purposes of the Gallup poll, "the South" consists of Alabama, Arkansas, Florida, Georgia, Kentucky, Louisiana, Mississippi, North Carolina, Oklahoma, South Carolina, Tennessee, Texas, and Virginia.

19. Eisenhower seems also to have privately signaled his disagreement with *Brown* to some influential southerners. In a confidential letter to Virginia senator Willis Robertson, Virginius Dabney, editor of the Richmond *Times-Dispatch,* claims that "President Eisenhower told me that he 'tried to stop' the Warren decision in 1954, and 'went just as far as I thought I properly could, but it didn't have any effect'" (Dabney to Robertson, July 12, 1963, Dabney Papers, University of Virginia Library). Also see James W. Ely, Jr., *The Crisis of Conservative Virginia: The Byrd Organization and the Politics of Massive Resistance* (Knoxville: University of Tennessee Press, 1976), 105-6. Also see Stephen E. Ambrose, *Eisenhower: The President* (New York: Simon and Schuster, 1984), 408.

20. News Conference, May 19, 1954, *Public Papers,* 491-92.

21. Telephone Call, August 19, 1956, Ann Whitman Diary Series, AWF, EL.

22. Herbert S. Parmet, *Eisenhower and the American Crusades* (New York: Macmillan, 1972), 462. See also Eisenhower's telephone conversation with Ovetta Culp Hobby, March 21, 1956, Ann Whitman Diary Series, AWF, EL.

23. Although one should be careful not to read too much into any one poll (particularly since in a Gallup poll, of 1,500 respondents the number of southern whites in the sample is usually close to 300), the Gallup survey conducted in the middle of July, which shows Eisenhower's approval rating rebounding substantially from the last poll conducted at the end of June and first two days of July, does seem to indicate that Eisenhower's efforts to distance himself from the civil rights bill at his July 3 news conference may have had some positive effect on southern audiences. The subsequent poll, taken between August 8 and 13, shows a sharp fall again in Eisenhower's approval rating among southern whites. Three events would seem to be key to this decline. First, a presidential press conference at the end of July in which Eisenhower publicly and unambiguously opposed the trial-by-jury amendment favored by southern senators; second, a public statement issued by Eisenhower on August 2 that firmly condemned the Senate's passage of the jury-trial amendment for weakening the nation's commitment to civil rights; and third, Senate passage of the civil rights bill (with the jury-trial amendment intact) on August 7. In pointing to the importance of Eisenhower's July 3 and July 31 press conferences and his August 2 statement, I am not suggesting that the southern public hung on Eisenhower's every word, only that southern elites did. Southern newspapers that before the end of July

had held back from criticizing Eisenhower directly now saw the president as personally implicated in the civil rights bill. This elite discourse, in turn, shaped the way the public evaluated Eisenhower's performance.

24. Richmond *Times-Dispatch,* May 19, 1957, D2; June 22, 1957, 8.

25. Ibid., July 30, 1957, 14; August 3, 1957, 6; August 6, 1957, 10.

26. *Mobile Register,* March 12, 1957, 4; April 10, 1957, 4; April 17, 1957, 4.

27. Ibid., June 8, 1957, 4; June 9, 1957, 6; June 26, 1957, 4. Eisenhower evidently didn't think much of the speech either. He told a close friend, Swede Hazlett, that "I am just about to take off for Williamsburg where I am to address the Conference of Governors. I have a very banal and colorless talk to deliver. While it expresses an obvious truth—that governors ought to concern themselves more with retaining states' responsibilities if they are to retain states' rights—this subject has been so often discussed that I feel like I am giving a lecture on the virtues of sunlight" (June 24, 1957, in Robert Griffith, ed., *Ike's Letters to a Friend, 1941-1958* [Lawrence: University Press of Kansas, 1984], 181).

28. See, e.g., the *Mobile Register* editorials of July 9, 16, 20, and 30, which criticize the bill as "indefensible," "detestable," and "iniquitous," without ever mentioning Eisenhower's support for the bill.

29. Ibid., September 6, 1957, 6.

30. Minnich to Brundage, July 23, 1957, Legislative Leaders Series, AWF, EL. Michael S. Mayer, "Eisenhower's Conditional Crusade: The Eisenhower Administration and Civil Rights, 1953-1957" (Ph.D. dissertation, Princeton University, 1984), 445.

31. News Conference, July 31, 1957, *Public Papers,* 573.

32. Richmond *Times-Dispatch,* August 17, 1957, 6. The *Times-Dispatch* observed that Eisenhower's "popularity has become negative—an absence of hostility."

33. In the four Gallup polls conducted between the end of June and the end of August (see Table 7.1), the average disapproval rating among southern whites was 25.5 percent, only a 2.5 percent rise over the 23 percent disapproval rating Eisenhower received in April. Those with no opinion, on the other hand, rose from 14 percent in April to an average of 22 percent in the same four summer polls.

34. Ibid., September 25, 1957, 1.

35. *New York Times,* September 27, 1957, 1.

36. On September 22, Faubus told reporters: "I have no criticism whatever of the President in this matter; he has shown great patience and understanding in one of the most difficult problems facing this nation." But, he added, "some of those in the palace guard have agitated the situation and caused trouble. They were motivated politically." Asked to name some of the "palace guard," Faubus replied, "Mr. Brownell for one; he was rather adamant and it was his Justice Department that came into the case improperly, we thought" (*New York Times,* September 23, 1957, 14). After Eisenhower had sent troops into Little Rock, Faubus delivered a speech, which opened by accusing "the Justice Department, under Herbert Brownell" of "cleverly concealed plans . . . for the military occupation of Arkansas." He again assailed "the President's 'palace guard' " and insisted that "all we have ever asked for is a little time, and patience and understanding, as so often expressed by the President himself, in solving the problem" (*Mobile Register,* September 27, 1957, 9).

37. Richmond *Times-Dispatch,* September 29, 1957, 1.

38. Ibid., September 28, 1957, 8; September 29, 1957, D2; October 1, 1957, 14; October 3, 1957, 16.

39. *Mobile Register,* September 25, 1957, 4.

40. Ibid., September 26, 1957, 4. Brownell's account of the southern reaction to Little Rock is misleading. Brownell writes, "I became a major target in the storm of

protest. The segregationist press in the South was particularly vitriolic in its personal attacks upon me—an easier target than the popular Eisenhower" (*Advising Ike,* 213). After Little Rock, though, Eisenhower was not popular in the South and the "segregationist press" had absolutely no hesitation about criticizing the president personally.

41. *Mobile Register,* September 28, 1957, 6; October 1, 1957, 6. The same tendency to link Eisenhower with his advisers can be seen in a letter to the Richmond *Times-Dispatch,* criticizing "the national Republican leadership personified by President Eisenhower, Vice President Nixon, Attorney General Brownell, and general flunky and office boy Sherman Adams" for bringing "about a latter day reconstruction in the South as part of its vitriolic 'hate-the-South' campaign" (October 3, 1957, 16).

42. E. Frederic Morrow, *Black Man in the White House* (New York: Coward-McCann, 1963), 167–68. Dwight D. Eisenhower, *Waging Peace: 1956–1961* (Garden City, N.Y.: Doubleday, 1965), 160. Mayer, "Eisenhower's Conditional Crusade," 461–62. Ambrose, *Eisenhower,* 412.

43. Statement by the president on the civil rights bill, August 2, 1957, *Public Papers,* 587.

44. Cabinet Meeting, August 2, 1957, Cabinet Series, Office of the Staff Secretary, EL.

45. *Public Papers,* 176, 357, 521; quotation at 521. The dates of the news conferences were March 7, March 27, and May 15.

46. Richmond *Times-Dispatch,* July 9, 1957, 1, 11.

47. Ibid., July 10, 1957, 1, 12.

48. Ibid., July 10, 1957, 1; July 13, 1957, 7.

49. Ibid., July 10, 1957, 1; July 11, 1957, 9; July 13, 1957, 7; July 17, 1957, 12.

50. In his memoirs, Brownell admits that "Eisenhower's reluctance to associate himself with difficult policy decisions sometimes made it a little harder for [cabinet members] to do [their] jobs. I was, for example, a bit too vulnerable politically than I would have preferred to be in the Harry Dexter White affair and in the political battles over the Civil Rights Act of 1957." But Brownell goes on to add that, "I also understood [that] . . . had Eisenhower been more aggressive and forward in identifying himself with controversial policies, he might have weakened his ability to strike a bargain later down the road, and, especially, he might have compromised one of the high cards he could play in partisan battles: appearing to be above the political fray" (*Advising Ike,* 301).

51. See, for example, "Eisenhower's 'Stand' Aids Southerners," in Richmond *Times-Dispatch,* July 7, 1957, 5.

52. The costs and benefits of Eisenhower's blame-avoidance strategy are carefully and intelligently weighed in Greenstein, *Hidden-Hand Presidency,* especially in the final two chapters.

53. Richard E. Neustadt, *Presidential Power* (New York: John Wiley, 1980), 16.

54. Ibid., 17.

55. After meeting with Eisenhower, Texas Governor Allan Shivers came away with a similar impression that the president "was leaving it to Brownell and the others. He didn't know the legal ramifications" (Oral History-238, December 23, 1969, COHP, EL, 49). The view that Eisenhower was not well informed and/or had been misled by his advisers was shared by many other players in the Little Rock affair. See, for example, R. A. Lile, Oral History-219, August 19, 1971, COHP, EL, 25; William J. Smith, Oral History-240, August 20, 1971, COHP, EL, 29.

56. Faubus, Oral History-181, COHP, EL, 41–45, 51.

57. After Eisenhower met with Senator Richard Russell on July 10, 1957, to dis-

cuss the civil rights bill, Ann Whitman reported that "he is not at all unsympathetic to the position people like Senator Russell take; far more ready than I, for instance, to entertain their views" (July 10, 1957, Ann Whitman Diary Series, AWF, EL).
58. Faubus, Oral History-181, 72.
59. Greenstein, *Hidden-Hand Presidency*.
60. Even Brownell found that "at times I was left a bit in the dark about his true feelings" (*Advising Ike*, 301).
61. Telephone Calls, July 3, 1957, DDE Diary Series, AWF, EL. Also see Prepress Conference Notes, July 3, 1957, DDE Diary Series, AWF, EL. In the same vein, Eisenhower confided to Swede Hazlett that "some of the language used in the attempt to translate my basic purposes into legislative provisions has probably been too broad" (July 22, 1957, in *Ike's Letters to a Friend*, 187).
62. Cabinet Meeting, March 9, 1956, Cabinet Series, Office of the Staff Secretary, EL.
63. See, for example, his March 14, 1956, press conference in which Eisenhower stated that "we must be understanding of other people's deep emotions" (*Public Papers*, 304).
64. Memorandum for the attorney general, n.d., Cabinet Series, AWF, EL.
65. Cabinet Meeting, March 23, 1956, Cabinet Series, Office of the Staff Secretary, EL.
66. The argument that Folsom presented in the cabinet meeting is more fully spelled out in a letter written to Brownell, March 19, 1956, Gerald D. Morgan papers, EL. On Eisenhower's hope that a bipartisan commission would act as a "buffer," see James C. Duram, *A Moderate among Extremists: Dwight D. Eisenhower and the School Desegregation Crisis* (Chicago: Nelson-Hall, 1981), 131. At a meeting with legislative leaders earlier in the week Eisenhower had concluded that we should "stay away from controversy while [the] commission inquire[s]" (March 20, 1956, Legislative Meeting Series, OF, EL).
67. Cabinet Meeting, March 23, 1956, Cabinet Series, Office of the Staff Secretary, EL. Also see Legislative Leadership Meeting, April 17, 1956, DDE Diary Series, EL.
68. Memorandum from Gerald D. Morgan to Ann Whitman, March 24, 1956, DDE Diary Series, AWF, EL.
69. Personal correspondence with Brownell, June 9, 1988.
70. Eisenhower's willingness to defer to trusted cabinet members is perhaps sometimes underestimated by revisionists overanxious to demonstrate that Eisenhower was "in charge." So, for example, Fred Greenstein and Robert Wright write, "This is not to say that he didn't rely on advisers, but it is to say that he didn't defer to them" ("Reagan . . . Another Ike?" *Public Opinion* 3 [December/January 1981]: 55).
71. J. W. Anderson, *Eisenhower, Brownell, and the Congress* (N.p.: University of Alabama Press, 1963), 122, 43, and passim. These charges are repeated in, among other places, James L. Sundquist, *Politics and Policy: The Eisenhower, Kennedy, and Johnson Years* (Washington, D.C.: Brookings, 1968), 226-29; and Richard Alan Schlundt, "Civil Rights Policies in the Eisenhower Years" (Ph.D. Dissertation, Rice University, 1973), esp. 197. Both authors rely on Anderson's interpretation.
72. William Bragg Ewald, Jr., *Eisenhower the President: Crucial Days, 1951-1960* (Englewood Cliffs, N.J.: Prentice-Hall, 1981), 204.
73. On Eisenhower's "unbounded" admiration for Brownell, see Stephen A. Ambrose, *Nixon: The Triumph of a Politician, 1962-1972* (New York: Simon and Schuster, 1989), 274. Also see Greenstein, *Hidden-Hand Presidency*, 85-87.
74. See Michael S. Mayer, "With Much Deliberation and Some Speed: Eisenhower and the *Brown* Decision," *Journal of Southern History* 52 (February 1986):

43-76, esp. 59-60. In a telephone conversation with Brownell, Eisenhower explained that he felt torn "between the compulsion of duty on one side, and his firm conviction, on the other, that because of the Supreme Court's ruling, the whole issue had been set back badly" (Telephone Calls, August 19, 1956, Ann Whitman Diary Series, AWF, EL).

75. Press Conference, July 17, 1957, *Public Papers*, 547. Also see Eisenhower, *Waging Peace*, 156. Brownell reports that Eisenhower "had a very deep emotional feeling that the right to vote was absolutely fundamental to establish equal rights of citizenship" (Herbert Brownell, Oral History-157, COHP, EL, 214). Martin Luther King, Jr., echoed Eisenhower's view: "Give us the ballot," he told a Washington audience, "and we will no longer have to worry the Federal government about our basic rights" (Mayer, "Eisenhower's Conditional Crusade," 412-13).

76. Legislative Leadership Meeting, August 6, 1957, Legislative Meeting Series, Office of the Staff Secretary, EL.

77. "In the interests of gradual education and progress," he informed a friend, "I had no objection to the elimination of Section III" (Eisenhower to R. W. Woodruff, August 6, 1957, Name Series, AWF, EL).

78. Cabinet Meeting, August 2, 1957, Cabinet Series, Office of the Staff Secretary, EL. Sherman Adams described Eisenhower as "bitterly disappointed" by the passage of the jury-trial amendment. (*Firsthand Report* [New York: Harper and Brothers, 1961], 342).

79. Statement by the president on the civil rights bill, August 2, 1957, *Public Papers*, 587. At his next press conference, Eisenhower reiterated his belief that the jury-trial amendment "would be most damaging to the entire Federal judiciary" (News Conference, August 7, 1957, *Public Papers*, 601).

80. Prepress Conference Briefing, April 17, 1957, DDE Diary Series, AWF, EL.

81. See Eisenhower to Richard Russell, September 27, 1957, Administration Series, AWF, EL.

82. The same tradeoff is evident in the battle over the Bricker amendment. Duane Tananbaum has shown that Eisenhower's behind-the-scenes maneuverings against the amendment during 1953 allowed him to maintain cordial relations with Senator Bricker and made Brownell and Dulles the target of Bricker's wrath, but also allowed the conflict to drag on for much longer than it would have had Eisenhower taken a strong, public stand from the outset. Ensuring defeat of the measure required that Eisenhower take a firm public stand against the measure, which he finally did in January 1954. Having declared his unambiguous opposition to the amendment, Eisenhower became, for the first time, a direct target for Bricker's public attacks (*The Bricker Amendment Controversy: A Test of Eisenhower's Political Leadership* [Ithaca, N.Y.: Cornell University Press, 1987], esp. 78-79, 137-38, 190, 217-18).

83. *Advising Ike*, 218; also see 217.

84. Brownell recounts the development of the idea of section three entirely in the first person: "I initially concentrated almost exclusively on voting rights. . . . Then I began thinking about all the equal-protection matters that might come up during my testimony before Congress, and I decided that a more ambitious bill was necessary. So I created on my own, almost out of whole cloth, a set of proposals that would give the attorney general power to enforce civil rights; these proposals would become the controversial but important section three of the eventual bill" (*Advising Ike*, 218). Brownell also concedes that Eisenhower "was at times [disturbed about what I was doing], especially in civil rights" (301).

85. Administration actions in these areas are described in Maxwell Rabb, Oral History-265, October 16, 1970, COHP, EL; and Mayer, "Eisenhower's Conditional Crusade," esp. 495-501.

86. Neustadt, *Presidential Power,* 8.

CHAPTER 8. BLAME AVOIDANCE AND POLITICAL ACCOUNTABILITY

1. A number of scholars, with their eyes on the substantial successes of statistical methods of analysis in the fields of voting behavior and congressional studies, have urged practitioners in the field to look for "statistical patterns in the presidency." Gary King and Lyn Ragsdale, for instance, write that "presidential research is at a stage analogous to that at which the discipline of economics found itself in the 1950s and the study of the U.S. Congress found itself in the 1960s" (Gary King and Lyn Ragsdale, *The Elusive Executive: Discovering Statistical Patterns in the Presidency* [Washington, D.C.: Congressional Quarterly Press, 1988], 484). The implication is that presidential studies can reach the dizzy heights achieved by these fields of study through emulating their usage of statistical techniques.

It is to be expected that fields that have had less success in explanation and prediction will look for guidance to those fields that have been more successful. But a method appropriate to one field of study may prove inappropriate in another. One thinks, for instance, of the checkered history of importing biological concepts of function and natural selection into the social sciences. I find it difficult to share King and Ragsdale's optimism about the future of presidential studies, because the success of statistical analysis rests largely upon having a large number of units, such as votes or survey responses, that are amenable to numerical quantification. In some areas—the relationship between presidential popularity and the state of the economy being a notable example—the statistical method promises to be fruitful. In other areas, such as the relationship between leadership styles and presidential success, there is considerably less we can hope to achieve from statistical techniques. My reasons are elaborated in "What Can 19th Century Presidents Teach Us about the Twentieth Century Presidency," delivered at the 1990 Annual Meeting of the American Political Science Association, San Francisco, Calif., September 1990.

2. As Nelson W. Polsby has recently written, pundits and politicians' loyalties are to their conclusions rather than their premises. It is political scientists, Polsby reminds us, who are paid to "think about the premises, and . . . whether or not they are well founded" ("Where Do You Get Your Ideas?" *PS: Political Science & Politics* 26 [March 1993]: 86).

3. The same political motives are often at work in reverse when opponents label an adviser a liability to the president. Critics who portrayed Ezra Taft Benson as a liability to Eisenhower, for example, were interested in persuading the president to dump an adviser whom they believed to be hostile to their objectives and, in the case of farm-state congressmen, an obstacle to their chances for reelection. That they tagged Benson a liability to the president may in fact be evidence that the secretary was serving as a lightning rod—if, as seems to be the case, they believed that without Benson the president's policies would have been significantly different.

4. Buchanan had said, "With the vote on *contra* aid, the Democratic Party will reveal whether it stands with Ronald Reagan and the resistance—or Daniel Ortega and the communists" (John Anthony Maltese, *Spin Control: The White House Office of Communications and the Management of Presidential News* [Chapel Hill: University of North Carolina Press, 1992], 208).

5. Bernard Weinraub, "Eating Lightning Bolts and Liking the Taste," *New York Times,* March 25, 1986, A28.

6. See Phil Duncan, "Quayle: The Right Man for the Right Job," *Congressional Quarterly Weekly Report,* June 23, 1990, 2014, and Lee Atwater's comments in the *New York Times,* December 29, 1989, A16.

7. Steven R. Weisman, "Reagan Dissipates Heat by Delegating Authority," *New York Times,* October 11, 1981, V:4.

8. Lou Cannon, *President Reagan: The Role of a Lifetime* (New York: Simon and Schuster, 1991), 168–69.

9. See Rochelle L. Stanfield, "Tilting on Development," *National Journal,* February 7, 1987, 313–18.

10. Bert A. Rockman, "The Modern Presidency and Theories of Accountability: Old Wine *and* Old Bottles," *Congress and the Presidency* 13 (Autumn 1986): 143.

11. See George C. Edwards III, *Presidential Influence in Congress* (San Francisco: W. H. Freeman, 1980), chap. 4; Douglas Rivers and Nancy L. Rose, "Passing the President's Program: Public Opinion and Presidential Influence in Congress," *American Journal of Political Science* 29 (May 1985): 183–96; and George C. Edwards III, *At the Margins: Presidential Leadership of Congress* (New Haven, Conn.: Yale University Press, 1989), esp. chapters 6–8.

12. Robert A. Dahl, *Who Governs?: Democracy and Power in an American City* (New Haven, Conn.: Yale University Press, 1961), 305.

13. Richard E. Neustadt, *Presidential Power and the Modern Presidents: The Politics of Leadership from Roosevelt to Reagan* (New York: Free Press, 1990), 80, 82.

14. See Seymour Martin Lipset, "The Significance of the 1992 Election," *P.S.: Political Science and Politics* 26 (March 1993): 7–16.

15. McNeil-Lehrer News Hour, March 10, 1989.

16. Haynes Johnson, *In the Absence of Power* (New York: Viking, 1980), 168. In the same vein, Nelson W. Polsby has argued that "in time, Mr. Carter's natural allies despaired of cooperating with him, as did leaders of many of the interest groups—especially labor unions—who were natural allies of a Democratic President. All these negative attitudes drifted downward to the general public and sooner or later began to be reflected in low scores for the President in public opinion surveys measuring general confidence in the way he was doing his job" (Nelson W. Polsby, *Congress and the Presidency,* 4th ed. [Englewood Cliffs, N.J.: Prentice-Hall, 1986], 65).

17. Richard A. Brody, *Assessing the President: The Media, Elite Opinion, and Public Support* (Stanford, Calif.: Stanford University Press, 1991). Also see John R. Zaller, *The Nature and Origins of Mass Opinion* (Cambridge: Cambridge University Press, 1992).

18. Samuel Kernell, *Going Public: New Strategies of Presidential Leadership,* 2d ed. (Washington, D.C.: Congressional Quarterly, 1993), 194, 196.

19. A further difficulty with Kernell's argument is that it fails to explain why models of presidential popularity based largely on economic numbers do least well for President Eisenhower (see Samuel Kernell's own "Explaining Presidential Popularity," *American Political Science Review* 72 [June 1978]: 518; as well as Charles W. Ostrom, Jr., and Dennis M. Simon, "Promise and Performance: A Dynamic Model of Presidential Popularity," *American Political Science Review* 79 [June 1985]: 351). If Kernell's formulation were correct one would expect to find that models built upon objective economic indicators would do most well for a president like Eisenhower and would do least well for a more recent president like Reagan. But in fact we find the reverse. Reagan's popularity can be much more precisely modeled using basic economic indicators than can Eisenhower's. This suggests that, if anything, elite cues and media portrayals may have been more important for Eisenhower's popularity than for Reagan's.

20. My discussion here draws on Eric R. A. N. Smith, *The Unchanging American Voter* (Berkeley: University of California Press, 1989), 159–60. A study that surveyed "all available questions" measuring political knowledge asked between 1947 and 1962 found that whereas in the first eight years there was an average of eleven such questions a year, in the last four years that average had dropped to one question a year. The study cited is Hazel G. Erskine, "The Polls: Textbook Knowledge," *Public Opinion Quarterly* 27 (1963): 133–41.

21. Smith, *Unchanging American Voter*, 163–69. Also see Stephen Bennett, "Trends in Americans' Political Information, 1967–1987," *American Politics Quarterly* 17 (October 1989): 422–35; and Michael X. Delli Carpini and Scott Keeter, "Stability and Change in the U.S. Public's Knowledge of Politics," *Public Opinion Quarterly* 55 (Winter 1991): 583–612.

22. Why has a transformation in the public's information levels about politics not resulted from the undeniable transformation in the volume of information transmitted? Part of the explanation may lie in the nature of television. Studies have consistently found that while reading a newspaper has a substantial impact on people's knowledge of politics, television has little or no effect (Smith, *Unchanging American Voter*, 186). People's ability to recall what they have seen on network news broadcasts is often quite limited (see W. Russell Neuman, "Patterns of Recall among Television News Viewers," *Public Opinion Quarterly* 40 [Spring 1976]: 115–23). To the extent that people have become more reliant on television for their news (Roper Organization, *Trends in Attitudes toward Television and Other Media: A Twenty-Four Year Review* [New York: Television Information Office, 1983], but also see the useful cautionary remarks in W. Russell Neuman, *The Paradox of Mass Politics: Knowledge and Opinion in the American Electorate* [Cambridge, Mass.: Harvard University Press, 1986], 139–45), they may actually be learning less about Washington political relations. They may, as Kernell claims, be exposed to more messages about the president than ever before, but the increase in the number of messages may be offset by a decrease in the informational content of those messages.

Moreover, though the total amount of information available about Washington may have increased, that does not mean that people are utilizing this increased information. As Eric Smith concludes, looking at data spanning from 1956 to 1976, "Total media use did not change. . . . Instead there was a change in the mix of media that people used to follow politics" (*Unchanging American Voter*, 184–85). The cable communications explosion of the 1980s has meant people can watch news twenty-four hours a day and can follow congressional floor debates and committee hearings almost around the clock. But the growth of cable also means people have more opportunities to watch movies, music videos, sitcoms, and sports. As W. Russell Neuman points out, the net result of more viewing options will be that "the proportion of news viewing will actually go down" (*Paradox of Mass Politics*, 139).

Several scholars have suggested that declining political interest may be the culprit behind the absence of improvement, despite increasing education levels, in public awareness of political relations in Washington (Bennett, "Trends in Americans' Political Information"; Bennett, "Know-nothings Revisited: The Meaning of Political Ignorance Today," *Social Science Quarterly* 69 [June 1988]: 476–90; Neuman, *Paradox of Mass Politics;* and Carpini and Keeter, "U.S. Public's Knowledge of Politics," 607). In 1987, 23 percent of the public said they were very interested in "politics and national affairs," and 34 percent said they were not at all or only slightly interested in politics. In contrast, in 1967, 35 percent described themselves as very interested, and only 27 percent said they were not at all or only slightly interested. Lack of interest, Stephen Earl Bennett explains, "reduces motivation to take in and retain political information" ("Trends in Americans' Political Information," 433).

23. 1986 National Election Study, cited in Bennett, "Trends in Americans' Political Information," 423.

24. Neustadt, *Presidential Power and the Modern Presidents*, 74.

25. AIPO-594, January 24-29, 1958. AIPO-598, April 16-21, 1958.

26. A 1957 Gallup poll found only 35 percent of respondents able to recall the name of their congressman. Surveys conducted by Michigan's Survey Research Center before the midterm elections of 1958, 1966, 1970, and 1974 found that the percentage of people who could recall the name of the congressional incumbent never exceeded 44 percent. See Thomas E. Mann, *Unsafe at any Margin: Interpreting Congressional Elections* (Washington, D.C.: American Enterprise Institute, 1978), 27.

27. 1986 National Election Study. Data graciously provided by Stephen Earl Bennett. In a Gallup poll taken in the summer of 1985, 24 percent were able to correctly identify Weinberger from a photograph shown to them (June 22-July 13, 1985).

28. Survey no. 561, March 8-13, 1956, *The Gallup Poll: Public Opinion, 1935-1971*, 3 vols. (New York: Random House, 1972), 2:1410.

29. AIP0-593, January 2-7, 1958. Also see AIPO-561, March 8-13, 1956. Interestingly, the approval rates were roughly equal among farmers and the general public (29 and 28 percent respectively). The difference lay in the disapproval rates, which reached 48 percent among farmers compared with only 29 percent among the general public.

30. Farmers were much more likely to have an opinion about the administration's price-support policies. Asked in 1954 whether they were "satisfied or dissatisfied with the way the Republican Administration is handling the problem of farm prices and farm price supports," 21 percent of farmers expressed no opinion as opposed to 39 percent of urban residents (Survey no. 535, August 5-10, 1954, *Gallup Poll*, 2:1267). Repeating the question again in 1955, Gallup found that 35 percent of nonfarmers had no opinion, as compared with only 14 percent of farmers (Survey no. 557, December 8-13, 1955, *Gallup Poll*, 2:1392).

31. This according to Jack Bell, at the time Senate correspondent and chief political reporter for the Associated Press (Bell, Oral History-167, COHP, EL, 15).

32. In the first months of the Clinton administration, Jerry Lewis, Republican representative from California, advised his fellow Republicans not to "take the president on personally" (Kenneth J. Cooper and Kevin Merida, "Republicans Strategize to Get Their Message Out," *Washington Post National Weekly Edition*, March 8-14, 1993, 15). And Republican strategist Ed Rollins counseled Republicans to "just hold [Clinton's] coat. . . . Wish him well for the good of the country. And the moment he falters, be prepared to put the kick in his side on the way down" (David Van Drehle, "In the Big Game of Politics, Clinton is a Winner—So Far," *Washington Post National Weekly Edition*, April 5-11, 1993, 14).

33. The social psychological literature on blame attribution is vast. See, for example, Kelly G. Shaver, *The Attribution of Blame: Causality, Responsibility, and Blameworthiness* (New York: Springer-Verlag, 1985); and Kathleen M. McGraw, "Managing Blame: An Experimental Test of the Effects of Political Accounts," *American Political Science Review* 85 (December 1991): 1133-57.

34. Gallup, August 3-6, 1973. Similarly, 28 percent said they had never heard of John Ehrlichman.

35. *Los Angeles Times*, January 3-7, 1982.

36. Yankelovich, Skelly, and White, April 30-May 2, 1985.

37. AIPO-593, January 2-7, 1958. In Benson's case, 55 percent of the general public (compared with about 75 percent of farmers) and in Dulles's case close to two-

thirds of the public had an opinion about the president as well as the secretary in question. These data are more fully reported in Chapters 2 and 5.

38. Shanto Iyengar and Donald R. Kinder's *News That Matters* (Chicago: University of Chicago Press, 1987) is a model of the type of research that needs to be done in this area.

39. Emmette S. Redford and Richard T. McCulley, *White House Operations: The Johnson Presidency* (Austin: University of Texas Press, 1986), 145.

40. Richard L. Schott and Dagmar S. Hamilton, *People, Positions, and Power: The Political Appointments of Lyndon Johnson* (Chicago: University of Chicago Press, 1983), 49. Johnson's self-protective instincts are evident too in his extensive efforts to distance himself from the Federal Communications Commission (FCC) (the Johnson family had a considerable financial interest in communications). White House aide Ernest Goldstein recalls getting a "very distinct impression" from Johnson that he was to make judgments on matters concerning the FCC in such a manner that Johnson "would be completely insulated and divorced from it" (Redford and McCulley, *White House Operations,* 146). Also see James E. Anderson, "Presidential Management of the Bureaucracy and the Johnson Presidency: A Preliminary Exploration," *Congress and the Presidency* 11 (Autumn 1984): 154.

41. Johnson to LBJ, February 9, 1967, cited in Larry Berman, "Johnson and the White House Staff," in Robert A. Divine, *Exploring the Johnson Years* (Austin: University of Texas Press, 1981), 208. Also see Bob Hardesty to Robert Kintner, December 20, 1966, cited in ibid., 191, 208.

42. Polsby, *Congress and the Presidency,* 39. Hugh Sidey also stresses Johnson's "insistence on being credited with having spawned every idea which came out of his White House" (*A Very Personal Presidency: Lyndon Johnson in the White House* [New York: Atheneum, 1968], 254).

43. Thomas E. Cronin, among others, underestimates this incompatibility when he advises presidents to "claim credit when things go right and decentralize blame" (*The State of the Presidency,* 2d ed. [Boston: Little, Brown, 1980], 112).

44. Rowland Evans and Robert Novak, *Lyndon B. Johnson: The Exercise of Power* (New York: Signet, 1966), 473. Eisenhower, in contrast, often seemed uncomfortable being the center of public attention. Eisenhower, recalls Emmet John Hughes, was "averse . . . to solitary appearances requiring . . . people 'just to look at my face' " and much preferred public appearances in which he (literally) shared the stage with other members of his administration (*The Ordeal of Power: A Political Memoir of the Eisenhower Years* [New York: Atheneum, 1963], 258).

45. Nixon, particularly as his term wore on, also expressed dissatisfaction about being upstaged by other members of his administration. After the 1972 election, for instance, Nixon decided to take control of intergovernmental affairs away from Agnew, reasoning that "he'll just take the gravy and leave the President all the negatives and the problems" (John Ehrlichman, *Witness to Power: The Nixon Years* [New York: Simon and Schuster, 1982], 142). On Nixon's resentment of Kissinger's positive press, see ibid., 247; Henry Kissinger, *The White House Years* (Boston: Little, Brown, 1979), 918, 1408-10, 1424, 1455; Henry Kissinger, *Years of Upheaval* (Boston: Little, Brown, 1982), 770-71; and Barry M. Goldwater with Jack Casserly, *Goldwater* (New York: Doubleday, 1988), 270. Nelson Polsby contrasts Nixon's first cabinet, which was a "reasonably visible group," with his subsequent appointments, who were increasingly "people of no independent public standing" ("Presidential Cabinet-Making: Lessons for the Political System," *Political Science Quarterly* 93 [Spring 1978]: 15-16).

46. David Halberstam, "The Very Expensive Education of McGeorge Bundy," *Harpers,* July 1969, 36. Several years later Bundy told a group of *Time* editors, "The

worst thing you could do with Lyndon Johnson was to go public with something, which with Lyndon Johnson meant anyone but himself" (ibid.). Cited in Polsby, *Congress and the Presidency,* 232 n97.

47. Thomas J. Schoenbaum, *Waging Peace and War: Dean Rusk in the Truman, Kennedy, and Johnson Years* (New York: Simon and Schuster, 1988), 443.

48. Califano to the president, December 6, 1968, quoted in Berman, "Johnson and the White House Staff," 191. Also see Sidey, *Personal Presidency,* 252-53.

49. Milton S. Eisenhower, *The President is Calling* (Garden City, N.Y.: Doubleday, 1974), 273. Also see Milton S. Eisenhower, "Portrait of a Brother," in Kenneth W. Thompson, ed., *The Eisenhower Presidency* (Lanham, Md.: University Press of America, 1984), 9.

50. Don Paarlberg, Oral History-52, January 17, 1968, COHP, EL, 27. Paarlberg worked as economic adviser to Benson in the Department of Agriculture until 1957 and then moved over to the White House to become the president's economic adviser (replacing Gabriel Hauge). Carl McCardle, assistant secretary of state for public affairs from 1953 to 1957, confirms that "once a decision was made, [Eisenhower] let others announce it" (Oral History-116, August 29, 1967, COHP, EL, 4).

51. Henry Cabot Lodge, *As It Was: An Inside View of Politics and Power in the '50s and '60s* (New York: Norton, 1976), 121. Also see Paarlberg, Oral History-52, 65. This is not a particularly original or exceptional idea in politics. Tip O'Neill quotes Sam Rayburn as saying, "There is no limit to the amount of good you can accomplish if you're willing to let somebody else take the credit" (*Man of the House* [New York: Random House, 1987], 150), and a sign on President Reagan's desk in the Oval Office read, "There is no limit to what a man can do or where he can go if he doesn't mind who gets the credit" (Cannon, *Role of a Lifetime,* 186).

52. Reagan's grasp of this truth was perhaps informed by his past career as a movie actor. John Sears, Reagan's one-time campaign manager, explained, "A lot of people in political and corporate life feel that delegating is an admission that there's something they can't do. But actors are surrounded by people with real authority—directors, producers, scriptwriters, cameramen, lighting engineers, and so on. Yet their authority doesn't detract from the actor's role. *The star is the star. And if the show's a hit, he gets the credit*" (Ann Reilly Dowd, "What Managers Can Learn from Manager Reagan," *Fortune,* September 15, 1986, 35; emphasis added). Sears's interpretation is more persuasive than Cannon's view that the sign on Reagan's desk referred to in the previous note reflected the fact that Reagan "did not consider himself a politician and really didn't mind who got the credit" (Cannon, *Role of a Lifetime,* 186).

53. The debate between the "Exposure school" and the "Containment school" within the administration is documented in Evans and Novak, *Exercise of Power,* especially 438, 523. Also see Kathleen J. Turner, *Lyndon Johnson's Dual War: Vietnam and the Press* (Chicago: University of Chicago Press, 1985).

54. Doris Kearns, *Lyndon Johnson and the American Dream* (New York: Harper and Row, 1976), 253, emphasis added.

55. Anderson, "Presidential Management of the Bureaucracy," 148. Agriculture Secretary Orville Freeman attested that he "felt the strong hand of the President in administrative detail, in economy, in government and a lot of things" (quoted in Schott and Hamilton, *People, Positions, and Power,* 56). In a similar vein, a middle-level bureaucrat told Stewart Alsop, "I know it's just my imagination but I have the feeling that the President is always just behind me, breathing down my neck" (Stewart Alsop, "The Johnsonization of Washington," *Saturday Evening Post,* February 26, 1966, 20).

56. The degree of discretion granted a cabinet member varied, of course, depend-

ing on the president's knowledge of a policy area and his trust in the subordinate. At one extreme was Attorney General Brownell, who benefited from Eisenhower's trust as well as the president's limited knowledge of legal matters. At the other end of the continuum was Defense Secretary Charles Wilson, who often found himself on a short leash both because of Eisenhower's low opinion of Wilson's judgment and because of the president's extensive experience in the area of national defense. See Fred I. Greenstein, *The Hidden-Hand Presidency: Eisenhower as Leader* (New York: Basic Books, 1982), 83–86.

57. Sherman Adams, *Firsthand Report* (New York: Harper and Brothers, 1961), 59, 78.

58. Herbert S. Parmet, *Eisenhower and the American Crusades* (New York: Macmillan, 1972), 317. Also see Robert H. Ferrell, ed., *The Diary of James C. Hagerty: Eisenhower in Mid-Course, 1954–1955* (Bloomington: Indiana University Press, 1983), 193 (diary entry for February 15, 1955).

59. Richard Nixon often seemed unwilling to accept this trade-off. As John Ehrlichman explains, "Whenever discretion was granted to the Secretaries they failed to do things the way Richard Nixon wanted them done. Since Nixon was the one who had to go back to the people after four years, to explain why things had gone as they did, he reacted to their 'failures' by retaining almost all of the discretion" (*Witness to Power,* 112).

60. Even Jimmy Carter seems to have recognized the value of lightning rods. See Jimmy Carter, *Keeping Faith: Memoirs of a President* (New York: Bantam, 1982), 54; Zbigniew Brzezinski, *Power and Principle: Memoirs of the National Security Adviser, 1977–1981* (New York: Farrar, 1983), 41, 98, 524; and Joseph A. Califano, Jr., *Governing America: An Insider's Report from the White House and the Cabinet* (New York: Simon and Schuster, 1981), 190. Shortly after Carter took office, Hamilton Jordan told reporters that "the problem is too many presidents have tried to deal with all of the problems of the country from the White House. The first line of offense or defense is the Cabinet. That's where the problems should be dealt with, in the department and agencies. You can't do it all from the White House" (Dom Bonafede, "No One Tries to Roll over Jordan in the White House," *National Journal,* April 16, 1977, 584).

61. This characteristic of Eisenhower is accented in a recent biography by Piers Brendon. Eisenhower, Brendon writes, "was a palimpsest of conflicting views on which the latest impression was the clearest" (*Ike: His Life and Times* [New York: Harper and Row, 1986], 13). Brendon closes his book with two lines from Dryden's "Absalom and Achitophel":

A man so various that he seem'd to be
Not one, but all mankind's epitome.

The couplet would be more fitting if it did not continue:

Stiff in opinions, always in the wrong;
Was everything by starts, and nothing long;
But in the course of one revolving moon
Was chemist, fiddler, statesman, and buffoon.

62. Survey no. 547, May 12–17, 1955, *Gallup Poll,* 2:1340.

63. Hughes, *Ordeal of Power,* 105, 344; also see 147.

64. Ibid., 173.

65. E. Frederic Morrow, Oral History-92, January 31, 1968, COHP, EL. In a later interview, Morrow revealed that he "had a relationship with [Eisenhower] that was . . . just a beautiful thing. The problem was that most of his close friends were from the deep South." Eisenhower explained to Morrow that his earlier opposition to racial integration in the army had been because he had unwittingly followed the advice

of staff officers with a "southern exposure" (Oral History-376, February 23, 1977, EL, 17-19). Also see E. Frederic Morrow, *Black Man in the White House* (New York: Coward-McCann, 1963).

66. See Richard Ellis and Aaron Wildavsky, *Dilemmas of Presidential Leadership: From Washington through Lincoln* (New Brunswick, N.J.: Transaction Publishers, 1989), 193-97.

67. According to Larry Speakes, the phrase was coined by James Watt (Speakes, *Speaking Out: The Reagan Presidency from inside the White House* [New York: Scribners, 1988], 84).

68. Richard Rose, *The Postmodern President: The White House Meets the World* (Chatham, N.J.: Chatham House, 1988). Also see Ryan J. Barilleaux, *The Post-Modern Presidency: The Office after Ronald Reagan* (New York: Praeger, 1988). Although I am skeptical of the utility of the concept of a postmodern presidency, I have found Rose's ideas, particularly on "Keeping out of Trouble" (178-83), extremely helpful and largely compatible with my own views. A compelling critique of the postmodern presidency idea can be found in Michael Nelson, "Is There a Postmodern Presidency?" *Congress & the Presidency* 16 (Autumn 1989): 155-62.

69. This is not to suggest that these environmental conditions are entirely outside of a president's control. Neither expectations nor polarization are set in stone. Elite polarization is in part a product of the policies that a president pursues. Arguably, for instance, Reagan contributed to the greater polarization of the 1980s (see Martin P. Wattenberg, "The Reagan Polarization Phenomenon and the Continuing Downward Slide in Presidential Candidate Popularity," *American Politics Quarterly* 14 [July 1986]: 219-45), just as Eisenhower's middle-of-the-road policies probably helped dampen polarization in the 1950s, especially in foreign policy (Edwards, *At the Margins,* 66-67). Similarly, part of politics is altering expectations about who is responsible for what. A president's behavior can play a significant role in shaping the expectations that people harbor about presidential responsibility. By claiming credit for everything that happens in government, a president runs the risk of expanding those policy areas for which the public—mass or elite—holds him accountable. By the same token, a president may (within limits) be able to redefine expectations of presidential involvement and control downward. Bruce Buchanan suggests, for instance, that "Reagan's distancing taught the public and the media to expect less of him and more of his underlings" (Bruce Buchanan, *The Citizen's Presidency* [Washington, D.C.: Congressional Quarterly, 1987], 128). But though presidents may succeed in educating citizens to lower their expectations or in lowering the extent of polarization in society, presidents can only expect to alter these forces at the margins; much of it must be taken as a given.

70. Greenstein, *Hidden-Hand Presidency,* 231. Also useful is Richard E. Neustadt and Ernest R. May's reminder that the notion that the Truman and Eisenhower period was characterized by a lack of conflict in foreign policy is "almost pure fantasy." "The years from 1945 to 1960 saw bitter, partisan, and utterly consensus-free debate about the 'loss' of China, the long-term stationing of troops in Europe, the limiting of warfare in Korea, and whether a new war ought to be risked for Dien Bien Phu or Quemoy and the Matsus. Democrats blamed Eisenhower for what happened in Latin America, whether it was dictatorships replacing democracies or, as in Cuba, Communists replacing dictators. Over recognizing Israel in 1948 and the Suez affair of 1956 there was also little accord" (*Thinking in Time: The Uses of History for Decision-Makers* [New York: Free Press, 1986], 258-59).

71. Edwards, *At the Margins,* 59-63. A "key vote," as selected by Congressional Quarterly, "is one or more of the following: a matter of major controversy, a test of presidential or political power, and a decision of potentially great impact on the na-

tion and on lives of Americans" (23). The other measure used in Table 8.1, non-unanimous support, includes all votes on which the winning side numbered less than 80 percent of those who voted (21–22).

72. Two important caveats need to be mentioned here. First, Eisenhower's more "liberal" foreign policies (see Richard Fleisher and Jon R. Bond, "Are There Two Presidencies? Yes, But only for Republicans," in Steven A. Shull, ed., *The Two Presidencies: A Quarter Century Assessment* [Chicago: Nelson-Hall Publishers, 1991], 132) must get a substantial share of the credit for this low level of polarization. Had Robert Taft gained the presidency in 1952, foreign-policy polarization would no doubt have been substantially higher. Second, by ending with Reagan the data may overstate the secular increase in polarization. With the end of the cold war, there are indications that some of the ingrained left-right alignments in foreign policy may have broken down, e.g., whether to intervene in Bosnia.

73. Herbert McClosky, Paul J. Hoffmann, and Rosemary O'Hara, "Issue Conflict and Consensus among Party Leaders and Followers," *American Political Science Review* 54 (June 1960): 410.

74. Ibid., 411–12.

75. Warren E. Miller and M. Kent Jennings report that their finding of "large absolute differences" on issues between the convention delegates "are in accord with a number of previous findings, dating back to the 1956 convention delegates" (*Parties in Transition: A Longitudinal Study of Party Elites and Party Supporters* [New York: Russell Sage Foundation, 1986], 163, 164 n2). Also see Jeanne Kirkpatrick, "Representation in the American National Conventions: The Case of 1972," *British Journal of Political Science* 5 (July 1975): esp. 286–95.

76. No scholarship that I am aware of has systematically compared the extent of issue polarization among 1956 convention delegates and more recent convention delegates. The best systematic study we have that speaks to the question of changes in polarization over time among convention delegates is the work of Warren E. Miller and M. Kent Jennings, but it is limited to change since 1972. In *Parties in Transition,* Miller and Jennings compare convention delegates from 1972, 1976, and 1980 and find evidence of a "widening gulf between the parties during the 1970s" (161). "Party elites always diverge in their opinion cultures," Miller and Jennings concede, "but the gap opened up between 1972 and 1980 was truly remarkable" (176), a conclusion based not on changes in issue positions but rather on changes in attitudes toward groups such as union leaders, blacks, business interests, the women's liberation movement, conservatives, and liberals. In a follow-up study comparing 1980 and 1984 convention delegates, Miller documents that "the first four years of the Reagan presidency produced a visible extension of the ideological polarization of the parties that had taken place during the later 1970s" (*Without Consent: Mass-Elite Linkages in Presidential Politics* [Lexington: University Press of Kentucky, 1988], 16).

77. This 1984 data is from the Center for Political Studies and is reported in Nelson W. Polsby and Aaron Wildavsky, *Presidential Elections: Contemporary Strategies of American Electoral Politics,* 8th ed. (New York: Free Press, 1991), 149.

78. McClosky et al., "Issue Conflict and Consensus," 408–9.

79. I have omitted the other questions about policy preferences reported by Polsby and Wildavsky in Table 3.6 (*Presidential Elections,* 148) because these other questions did not share the same basic structure (increase/decrease/remain as is) as the McClosky questions.

80. Moreover, most of the issues have changed and the wording of the questions is not exactly the same. Three issues (though not the exact questions) are the same. Each of the three issues—federal aid to education, social security, and foreign aid— that were asked about in both the 1956 and 1984 surveys showed evidence of increas-

ing polarization, although in the case of social security and foreign aid these increases were slight and in the case of foreign aid neither survey showed much in the way of polarization (all sides favor reducing it). In reporting the 1984 data, Polsby and Wildavsky write that "even social security, which for years was uncontested between the parties . . . reveals large differences" (*Presidential Elections,* 147). The 1956 data would seem to suggest, however, that social security was far from uncontested in the 1950s.

81. Other studies, using different data bases, give further support to the thesis that the parties were more polarized in the 1980s than they used to be, although authors differ over whether this change is best described as "a modest, but significant, increase in interparty issue distance" (John A. Clark, John M. Bruce, John H. Kessel, and William G. Jacoby, "I'd Rather Switch than Fight: Lifelong Democrats and Converts to Republicanism among Campaign Activists," *American Journal of Political Science* 35 [August 1991]: 594) or whether these changes are better described as "fundamental" (Aaron Wildavsky, "Are American Political Parties Pretty Much the Same as They Used to Be in the 1950s, Only a Little Different, or Are They Radically Different? A Review Essay," *Journal of Policy History* 4 [1992]: 228). Wildavsky relies heavily on the dramatic evidence of change between 1978 and 1988 presented in Lynda W. Powell, "Changes in Liberalism-Conservatism in the U.S. House of Representatives, 1978–1988" (Paper prepared for the 1991 Annual Meeting of the American Political Science Association, Washington, D.C., August 29–September 1, 1991).

82. Polsby and Wildavsky, *Presidential Elections,* 158.

83. McClosky et al., "Issue Conflict and Consensus," 412. The difference between the Democratic and Republican "support ratios" among the mass public was .15 for level of farm price supports, .12 for government regulation of business, .10 for taxes on large incomes, and less than .10 for every other issue.

84. On Bush's admiration for Eisenhower, see *New York Times,* January 21, 1989, A9. That Bush tried to emulate Eisenhower's style is not to say that he succeeded. If Eisenhower was often more engaged than he appeared, Bush was often less engaged than he seemed. His hyperactive personality seemed to indicate a "hands-on" method of operating, but Bush's lack of patience for complex policy issues often meant he was anything but hands-on. His often frenetic energy level left many observers predicting trouble for Bush from the outset. "If Reagan was Teflon, Bush is a cast-iron skillet," said one friend. "It will take a week of soaking to get that egg out" (*New York Times,* January 21, 1989, A9). And Jonathan Alter wrote that "Bush's brand of activism has its more prosaic political hazards as well. One of the cruel ironies of modern governance is that engaged, accountable presidents tend to be more vulnerable to criticism than detached, aloof ones, as the contrasting experiences of Jimmy Carter and Ronald Reagan show" ("Bush Reaches Out," *Newsweek,* January 30, 1989, 24).

85. Duane M. Oldfield and Aaron Wildavsky, "Reconsidering the Two Presidencies," in Steven A. Shull, ed., *The Two Presidencies: A Quarter Century Assessment* (Chicago: Nelson-Hall, 1991), 184–86.

86. Greenstein, *Hidden-Hand Presidency,* 239.

87. Thomas B. Edsall, "It's a Tough Job but Someone's Got to Try It," *Washington Post National Weekly Edition,* November 19–25, 1990. This is a book review of Richard Neustadt's *Presidential Power and the Modern Presidents.*

88. Polsby and Wildavsky, *Presidential Elections,* 183. Powell, "Changes in Liberalism-Conservatism," 4.

89. During the 1992 campaign Bill Clinton seemed to have a clear sense of where

he wanted to take the Democratic party but seemed to lose sight of this vision in his first months in office.

90. Lincoln, though often cloaking his positions in ambiguity, never lost sight of his chief objectives—winning the war, ending slavery, and transforming the fledgling Republican party into the dominant party in the nation.

91. Bush's average approval score was kindly provided to me by George Edwards. Approval scores for Reagan, Eisenhower, and Kennedy are from Edwards, *Presidential Approval*, 156.

92. Reagan's reputation as a "Teflon president," who by "a strange kind of alchemy" avoided responsibility for his administration's actions (Jane Mayer and Doyle McManus, *Landslide: The Unmaking of the President, 1984-1988* [Boston: Houghton Mifflin, 1988], 12-13), is greatly exaggerated. Reagan's average approval for his eight years (52 percent) is not overwhelmingly better than the average approval scores of Nixon (48 percent), Ford (47 percent), and Carter (47 percent), and is significantly lower than the average approval scores of Kennedy (71 percent), Eisenhower (65 percent), Bush (61 percent), and Johnson (56 percent) (Edwards, *Presidential Approval*, 156, 175). And as D. Roderic Kiewiet and Douglas Rivers show, Reagan's popularity closely mirrored the state of the economy throughout his first term ("The Economic Basis of Reagan's Appeal," in John E. Chubb and Paul E. Peterson, eds., *The New Direction in American Politics* [Washington, D.C.: Brookings, 1985], 69-90).

Reagan's extraordinary likability as a person is also greatly exaggerated. It is true that many more people liked Reagan as a person than approved of his performance. On the average, the difference between approval of Reagan as a person and approval of his performance as president was 21 percentage points. But much the same discrepancy between evaluation of the person and the job performance was true of Carter. In a July 1978 poll, for instance, Carter's approval rating lagged at 39 percent while 76 percent felt he was a "likeable person." According to Edwards, Reagan was actually among "the least well-liked presidents of the past three decades" (Edwards, *Presidential Approval*, 131-32; also see George C. Edwards III, "Comparing Chief Executives," *Public Opinion* [June/July 1985]: 51).

93. Thomas E. Cronin, *The State of the Presidency* (Boston: Little, Brown, 1980). Godfrey Hodgson, *All Things to All Men: The False Promise of the American Presidency from Franklin D. Roosevelt to Ronald Reagan* (New York: Touchstone, 1980). George C. Edwards III, *The Public Presidency: The Pursuit of Popular Support* (New York: St. Martin's, 1983). Theodore Lowi, *The Personal President: Power Invested, Promise Unfulfilled* (Ithaca, N.Y.: Cornell University Press, 1985). Richard W. Waterman, ed., *The Presidency Reconsidered* (Itasca, Ill.: F. E. Peacock Publishers, 1993).

94. Arvind Raichur and Richard W. Waterman, "The Presidency, the Public, and the Expectations Gap," in Waterman, *Presidency Reconsidered*, 1-21.

95. Terry M. Moe, "The Politicized Presidency," in John E. Chubb and Paul E. Peterson, eds., *The New Direction in American Politics* (Washington, D.C.: Brookings, 1985), 235-71.

96. A 1979 Gallup poll found 73 percent of the public agreeing that the public's expectations of the president are higher than in the past (Edwards, *Public Presidency*, 191).

97. Jagdish Bhagwati, "Rough Trade," *New Republic*, May 31, 1993, 36.

98. In a recent essay, Robert DiClerico writes that "the public's expectations of presidential leadership are high and appear to be growing" ("The Role of Media in Heightened Expectations and Diminished Leadership Capacity," in Waterman, *Presidency Reconsidered*, 119). DiClerico, however, offers no evidence that public expec-

tations "appear to be growing," only a footnote referring to George Edwards's *Public Presidency*. On the cited page of Edwards's volume, one finds repeated the claim that "the public's expectations of the president's public and private behavior, his style of leadership, and his policy performance are high and appear to be climbing" (*Public Presidency*, 188). But while Edwards's discussion makes excellent use of a specially commissioned 1979 Gallup poll designed to tap public expectations of presidential performance, Edwards provides no evidence that speaks to the question of change over time. DiClerico does make use of indirect evidence drawn from analyses of media coverage of the presidency, but the evidence from these studies is much less conclusive than DiClerico suggests. See the Appendix for a discussion of this evidence.

99. Stephen J. Wayne, "Expectations of the President," in Doris A. Graber, ed., *The President and the Public* (Philadelphia: Institute for the Study of Human Issues, 1982), 18.

100. Wayne, "Expectations of the President," 19. The 1968 poll results were first reported in Glenn R. Parker, "Political Beliefs about the Structure of Government: Congress and the Presidency," Sage Professional Papers in American Politics, vol. 2, no. 04-018 (Beverly Hills, Calif.: Sage Publications, 1974), 18. The numbers for the 1968 poll represent an average of the three policy domains.

101. Wayne, "Expectations of the President," 20. The 1979 survey was conducted by Gallup in the fall of that year.

102. See Howard Schuman and Stanley Presser, *Questions and Answers in Attitude Surveys: Experimentation on Question Form, Wording, and Context* (New York: Academic Press, 1981). Also see George F. Bishop, Robert W. Oldenick, and Alfred J. Tuchfarber, "Change in the Structure of American Political Attitudes: The Nagging Question of Question Wording," *American Journal of Political Science* 22 (May 1978): 250-69.

103. Roberta S. Sigel, "Image of the American Presidency: Part II of an Exploration into Popular Views of Presidential Power," in Aaron Wildavsky, ed., *The Presidency* (Boston: Little, Brown, 1969), 296-309. The exact question wording was, "Now, which of the two statements comes closest to your own ideas: 'The President is an inspired leader; he has ideas of his own how to help the country. He should be able to make the people and Congress work along with him.' Or 'It is up to the people through their Congressman to find solutions to the problems of the day. The President should stick to carrying out what the people and Congress have decided.'" Sigel found 51.5 percent preferring the first statement and 40 percent preferring the second statement (299-300, 302).

104. Parker, "Political Beliefs about the Structure of Government," 18.

105. Gary C. Jacobson, *The Electoral Origins of Divided Government: Competition in U.S. House Elections, 1946-1988* (Boulder, Colo.: Westview Press, 1990), 118. Interestingly, too, a poll conducted at the beginning of 1986 showed that 59 percent thought Congress would "make better decisions about what to do to reduce the federal deficit" than Reagan would. Only 29 percent felt Reagan would do better. Asked whether they thought the budget would be balanced within five years, 77 percent said no. Moreover, of those who felt it would not be balanced in the next five years, 45 percent felt that such a failure would be Congress's fault and only 19 percent said it would be the president's fault. Twenty-six percent said the president and Congress would be jointly responsible for such a failure.

106. Hazel Erskine, "The Polls: Presidential Power," *Public Opinion Quarterly* 37 (Fall 1973): 493.

107. Richard E. Neustadt, *Presidential Power: The Politics of Leadership* (New York: John Wiley, 1960), 7.

108. Louis Brownlow, "What We Expect the President to Do," reprinted in Wildavsky, ed., *The Presidency,* 35.

109. Seymour Martin Lipset and William Schneider, *The Confidence Gap,* rev. ed. (Baltimore: Johns Hopkins University Press, 1987).

110. See Michael Baruch Grossman and Martha Joynt Kumar, *Portraying the President: The White House and the Media* (Baltimore: Johns Hopkins University Press, 1981), 265; Kernell, *Going Public,* 78; Fred Smoller, *The Six O'Clock Presidency: A Theory of Presidential Press Relations in the Age of Television* (New York: Praeger, 1990), esp. 45-49; Aaron Wildavsky, "The Media's American Egalitarians," in Aaron Wildavsky, *The Rise of Radical Egalitarianism* (Washington, D.C.: American University Press, 1991); DiClerico, "Role of Media in Heightened Expectations"; and Michael J. Robinson and Margaret A. Sheehan, *Over the Wire and on TV: CBS and UPI in Campaign '80* (New York: Russell Sage, 1983), 203-4.

111. Truman's average approval score of 44 percent is followed by Ford (47 percent), Carter (47 percent), Nixon (48 percent), Reagan (52 percent), Johnson (56 percent), Bush (61 percent), Eisenhower (65 percent), and Kennedy (71 percent). Approval scores for Eisenhower through Reagan are taken from Edwards, *Presidential Approval,* 156. Bush's average approval score was provided by George Edwards. Truman's average approval score is calculated from approval scores compiled in King and Ragsdale, *Elusive Executive,* 293-94, 295. Because so many fewer approval questions were asked in Truman's first term (13) than in his second term (29), I have averaged the sum of the first (52 percent) and second term averages (36 percent) in arriving at Truman's average approval score. The Eisenhower through Bush approval scores are an average of every opinion question asked by Gallup for each of these presidents.

112. Arthur Schlesinger, Jr., "After the Imperial Presidency," in *The Cycles of American History* (Boston: Houghton Mifflin, 1986), 288.

113. Walter Shapiro, columnist for *Esquire,* terms this Washington's "willful, cosmic amnesia." Washington, Shapiro says, "is a city where if you can remember the Kennedy administration you are thought to embrace the whole sweep of human history" (David Von Drehle, "Today's Special: Illegal Nannies," *Washington Post National Weekly Edition,* February 15-21, 1993, 12).

114. The same basic choice, under different labels, is identified by Bert Rockman as the choice between Greenstein's "strategy of risk aversion" and Neustadt's "strategy of risk-taking" (Rockman, "Modern Presidency," 150). Elsewhere, Rockman distinguishes between a style of leadership that emphasizes "articulating direction" and another that emphasizes "the calculation of minimum loss" ("The Leadership Style of George Bush," in Colin Campbell and Bert A. Rockman, *The Bush Presidency: First Appraisals* [Chatham, N.J.: Chatham House, 1991], 1). Similarly, Paul J. Quirk distinguishes between the "self-reliant presidency" and "the minimalist presidency" ("Presidential Competence," in Michael Nelson, ed., *The Presidency and the Political System,* 3d ed. [Washington, D.C.: Congressional Quarterly Press, 1990], 166).

115. Chief among these, as Greenstein acknowledges, is that Eisenhower's style is "not suited to effecting major political change" (*Hidden-Hand Presidency,* 230).

116. Thomas E. Cronin, *The State of the Presidency,* 2d ed. (Boston: Little, Brown, 1980), 282ff.

117. Stephen Hess, *The Washington Reporters* (Washington, D.C.: Brookings, 1981), 107-8.

118. Premodern treasury secretaries did more often fill such a role. On Alexander Hamilton and Salmon Chase as lightning rods for Presidents Washington and Lin-

coln respectively, see Ellis and Wildavsky, *Dilemmas of Presidential Leadership*, 43, 184.

119. *New York Times*, December 11, 1992, A16.

120. A few scholars have praised this trend toward greater centralization as enhancing the institutional capacities of presidents and enhancing bureaucratic responsiveness to electoral preferences (Moe, "Politicized Presidency," esp. 268, 271); more scholars have bemoaned it for overburdening an already overburdened president and undermining the institutional integrity and independence of executive agencies and departments (Lowi, *Personal President;* Stephen Hess, *Organizing the Presidency* [Washington, D.C.: Brookings, 1976]).

121. Some will argue that democratic government demands that the president, as the only elected executive official, make his preferences felt across and throughout the bureaucracy. There is something to this view, but it errs in assuming that the president has received an electoral mandate on every issue on which he has a preference. It is not just possible but inevitable that a president will get elected despite holding opinions on a range of issues that a majority disagrees with (see sources cited in Chapter 3, note 21). If presidential elections are not about the public endorsing specific policies, the case is strengthened for a more minimalist president who focuses on a few core preferences rather than a president who actively pursues his personal preferences across the entire range of governmental policies.

122. At a point when President Carter's approval score had fallen to 32 percent and his disapproval had reached 54 percent (King and Ragsdale, *Elusive Executive*, 304), Rosalynn Carter's approval score stayed up at 59 percent, while only 19 percent disapproved of her performance (*Gallup Opinion Index*, Report no. 170, September 1979, 6). An April 1987 poll found that 58 percent approved of Nancy Reagan's handling of her job, while only 23 percent disapproved (*Gallup Report*, no. 258, March 1987, 29); the same poll showed President Reagan with a 48 percent approval rating and a 43 percent disapproval rating (Edwards, *Presidential Approval*, 108). In August 1992, Barbara Bush had an 81 percent favorable (and 12 percent unfavorable) rating compared with a 50 percent favorable (and 47 percent unfavorable) rating for President Bush (*The Gallup Poll: Public Opinion 1992* [Wilmington, Del.: Scholarly Resources], 149).

123. In terms of the fourfold typology introduced in Chapter 1, presidential wives, when they are seen as politically relevant at all, are usually seen as assets, adding luster to the president's public standing. So, for example, a Harris press release reported that Betty Ford "is obviously well regarded by most of the public and must be viewed as an asset to the President" (Harris Survey press release, September 25, 1975). Similar comments were legion about Barbara Bush during the 1992 campaign. Ann McDaniel of *Newsweek*, to take but one example, wrote that "there is not much doubt that Bush is hoping that his wife's popularity will help his flagging image. She is, some would say, his only remaining asset" ("Barbara Bush: The Steel behind the Smile," *Newsweek*, June 22, 1992, 36).

124. Maureen Dowd, "Hillary Clinton's Debut Dashes Doubts on Clout," *New York Times*, February 8, 1993, C9.

125. See, for example, *The New Republic*, especially columns by Mickey Kaus and Fred Barnes.

126. Mickey Kaus, "Thinking of Hillary," *The New Republic*, February 15, 1993, 6.

127. Paul C. Light, *Vice-Presidential Power: Advice and Influence in the White House* (Baltimore: Johns Hopkins University Press, 1984), 258.

128. Only Dick Cheney and Jim Baker have gone on to have political careers after serving as chief of staff. And only Cheney has ever been elected to a political office

after serving as chief of staff. This is not surprising since not only do chiefs of staff make a lot of enemies, they are also often selected on the basis of their selflessness and lack of political ambitions.

129. On Eisenhower's desire for "selflessness" in a chief of staff, see Richard M. Nixon, *The Memoirs of Richard Nixon* (New York: Grosset and Dunlap, 1978), 198–99. Among the things President Reagan was reported to have liked about the idea of Regan as chief of staff "was that [Regan] had no further political ambitions and no personal agenda" (*New York Times,* January 11, 1985, 14).

130. Light, *Vice-Presidential Power,* 255.

131. Woodrow Wilson, *Congressional Government* (Cleveland: Meridan, 1956; originally published in 1885), 185–87. Also see Wilson, "The Study of Administration," *Political Science Quarterly* 56 (December 1941; originally published in 1887): 481–506, esp. 497–99. One could, with equal justice, trace the concern for concentrating power and responsibility in a single head to Alexander Hamilton's Federalist Paper no. 70. In it, Hamilton argued against "a multiplication of the Executive"—"either by vesting power in two or more magistrats of equal dignity and authority; or by vesting it ostensibly in one man, subject, in whole or in part, to the control and cooperation of others, in the capacity of counsellors to him"—on the grounds that "it tends to conceal faults and destroy responsibility." When the unity of the executive is destroyed, Hamilton maintained, "it often becomes impossible amidst mutual accusation, to determine on whom the blame or the punishment of a pernicious measure, or series of pernicious measures, ought really to fall. It is shifted from one to another with so much dexterity, and under such plausible appearances, that the public opinion is left in suspense about the real author" (*The Federalist* [New York: Modern Library, n.d.], 459). In contrast to Wilson, however, Hamilton argued that the system set up under the new Constitution *avoided* these faults.

132. "Toward a More Responsible Two-Party System: A Report of the Committee on Political Parties, American Political Science Association," *American Political Science Review* 44:3, pt. 2, Supplement (September 1950). Also see E. E. Schattschneider, *Party Government* (New York: Holt, Rinehart and Winston, 1942); James McGregor Burns, *The Deadlock of Democracy: Four-Party Politics in America* (Englewood Cliffs, N.J: Prentice-Hall, 1963); and Lloyd Cutler, "To Form a Government," *Foreign Affairs* 59 (Fall 1980): 126–43.

133. *The Hoover Commission Report* (New York: McGraw-Hill, 1949), 3–4, 21. An excellent account of the political context in which the commission's work was carried out can be found in Peri E. Arnold, "The First Hoover Commission and the Managerial Presidency," *Journal of Politics* 38 (February 1976): 46–70.

134. "When you stand up for what you believe in," Pat Buchanan explains, "you produce the politics of clarity" (Steven A. Holmes, "Mutineer Rocking the G.O.P. Boat: Patrick Joseph Buchanan," *New York Times,* February 19, 1992, A9).

135. See especially Pendleton Herring, *The Politics of Democracy* (New York: Norton, 1940); and idem., *Presidential Leadership* (New York: Rinehart, 1940).

136. Herring, *Presidential Leadership,* 112.

137. Pendleton Herring, "Executive-Leadership Responsibilities," *American Political Science Review* 38 (December 1944): 1160. Also see Herring, *Presidential Leadership,* 111.

138. Modern-day echoes of Herring's position can be found in Hess, *Organizing the Presidency,* esp. 10–11; and Richard Rose, "The President: A Chief but Not an Executive," *Presidential Studies Quarterly* 7 (Winter 1977): 6.

139. U.S. President's Committee on Administrative Management (Washington, D.C.: U.S. Government Printing Office, 1937), 37.

140. Herring, *Presidential Leadership,* 116–17.

141. Also see Herbert Agar, *The Price of Union* (Boston: Houghton Mifflin, 1950); and Austin Ranney and Willmoore Kendall, *Democracy and the American Party System* (New York: Harcourt, Brace, 1956).

142. Herring, *Politics of Democracy,* 108.

143. Ibid., 102. Woodrow Wilson, "Cabinet Government in the United States," cited in Jeffrey K. Tulis, *The Rhetorical Presidency* (Princeton, N.J.: Princeton University Press, 1987), 35. Also see Wilson, *Congressional Government,* 72-73.

144. Also relevant is Judith Shklar, "Let Us Not Be Hypocritical," *Daedalus* 108 (Summer 1979): 1-25.

145. Herring, *Presidential Leadership,* 111-12. Also see David B. Truman, *The Governmental Process: Political Interests and Public Opinion,* 2d ed. (New York: Knopf, 1971), 408.

146. This point is made in Nelson W. Polsby and Aaron Wildavsky, *Presidential Elections,* 6th ed. (New York: Charles Scribner's Sons, 1984), 265-66.

147. The phrase is used in Arthur M. Schlesinger, Jr., *A Thousand Days* (Boston: Houghton Mifflin, 1965), 724.

148. See the comments to this effect in Oldfield and Wildavsky, "Reconsidering the Two Presidencies," 190.

149. David Stockman, *The Triumph of Politics: Why the Reagan Revolution Failed* (New York: Harper and Row, 1986), 189.

150. On Eisenhower as a "leadership theorist," see Fred I. Greenstein, "Dwight D. Eisenhower: Leadership Theorist in the White House," in Fred I. Greenstein, ed., *Leadership in the Modern Presidency* (Cambridge, Mass.: Harvard University Press, 1988), 76-107.

151. See, e.g., Neustadt, *Presidential Power and the Modern Presidents,* 10.

152. Similar is Lowi's suggestion that "since building up the presidency has not met the problem of presidential capacity to govern, the time has come to consider building it down" (Lowi, *Personal President,* 208).

153. Grossman and Kumar, *Portraying the President,* 265.

154. Stephen Hess proposes that we redefine "the tasks of Presidents [as] those activities that they must perform and that cannot be performed by others. The corollary is that the many other tasks currently performed badly by presidents must be performed elsewhere." Presidents, Hess contends, "have made a serious mistake, starting with Roosevelt, in asserting that they are the chief managers of the federal government. . . . Rather than chief manager, the President is chief political officer of the United States. His major responsibility, in my judgment, is to . . . make a relatively small number of highly significant political decisions" (*Organizing the Presidency,* 10-11). Also see Aaron Wildavsky, "President Reagan as a Political Strategist," in Charles O. Jones, ed., *The Reagan Legacy: Promise and Performance* [Chatham, N.J.: Chatham House, 1988], 289-305.

APPENDIX

1. Elmer E. Cornwell, Jr., "Presidential News: The Expanding Public Image," reprinted in Aaron Wildavsky, ed., *The Presidency* (Boston: Little, Brown, 1969), 310, 311. Also see Alan P. Balutis, "Congress, the President and the Press," *Journalism Quarterly* 53 (Autumn 1976): 510.

2. Cornwell, "Presidential News," 318. Cornwell selected out six sample weeks in each of the years he studied.

3. Balutis also examined the *Buffalo Evening News* and here found evidence of an

increase in attention to presidential news, from an average of 327 column inches of front-page coverage in the years 1958–1960 to 496 column inches in 1961–1968 to 566 column inches in 1969–1973. These averages are calculated from Table 1 in Balutis, "Congress, the President and the Press," 511.

4. Coding procedures are explained in Cornwell, "Presidential News," 312–13; and Balutis, "Congress, the President and the Press," 510–11.

5. Stephen Hess, *The Washington Reporters* (Washington, D.C.: Brookings Institution, 1981), 98. Hess did find that the president appears in the headlines more often than the Congress, but he also found that of stories with neither Congress nor the president in the headlines, many more are about Congress.

6. Michael Baruch Grossman and Martha Joynt Kumar, *Portraying the President: The White House and the Media* (Baltimore: Johns Hopkins University Press, 1981). For this study, three coders read White House stories at fifteen-day intervals for a twenty-five-year period, from Eisenhower's inauguration through August 1978. They compiled 5,270 stories from the *New York Times* and 2,550 stories from *Time* magazine (254).

7. Samuel Kernell updated Grossman and Kumar's study through 1983 and found that for the *Times* Reagan's coverage was actually lower than Carter's and not significantly higher than Kennedy's. Only for *Time* magazine does Kernell's data show a relatively steady upward climb that continues into the Reagan era. Kernell altered the study somewhat by including only the second and third years of a president's first term in his analysis (*Going Public: New Strategies of Presidential Leadership* [Washington, D.C.: Congressional Quarterly, 1986], 180–81).

8. Nor, if we take Hess's comprehensive survey seriously, does it support the thesis that there is a massive imbalance in attention given to the presidency relative to Congress. Also see Susan Miller, "News Coverage of Congress: The Search for the Ultimate Spokesman," *Journalism Quarterly* 54 (Autumn 1977): 461.

9. Compare the above studies with Samuel Kernell and Gary C. Jacobson, "Congress and the Presidency as News in the Nineteenth Century," *Journal of Politics* 49 (November 1987): 1016–35.

10. Data gathered by Herbert Gans in a content analysis of *Newsweek* magazine for the years 1967, 1971, and 1975 indicated a progressive increase in the percentage of column inches in the magazine devoted to incumbent presidents (from 12 to 20 to 23 percent). Also suggestive but difficult to interpret was the finding that the percentage of column inches in the magazine devoted to members of the House and Senate dropped from 10 in 1968 and 12 in 1971 to 4 in 1975. Without more data points it is impossible to say whether 1975 is part of a trend or an atypical year. See Herbert J. Gans, *Deciding What's News* (New York: Pantheon, 1979), 10. *Newsweek* and *Time*'s concentration on the presidency is also confirmed by Bruce Miroff's finding from the mid-1970s that more than half to almost two-thirds of lead stories "dealt primarily with presidential activities" ("Monopolizing the Public Space: The President as a Problem for Democratic Politics," in Thomas E. Cronin, ed., *Rethinking the Presidency* [Boston: Little, Brown, 1982], 221).

11. This is a particular problem with John Orman's "Covering the American Presidency: Valenced Reporting in the Periodical Press, 1900–1982," *Presidential Studies Quarterly* 14 (Summer 1984): 382. Orman examined *The Reader's Guide to Periodical Literature* and found a steady and dramatic increase in the number of presidential stories over time. But without some measure of the ratio of presidential to congressional news, it is unclear how much of this increase is attributable either to an overall growth in attention to national news or to a proliferation of periodical magazines.

12. Robert E. Gilbert, "President versus Congress: The Struggle for Public Atten-

tion," *Congress and the Presidency* 16 (Autumn 1989): 86, 87. Michael J. Robinson and Margaret A. Sheehan found that close to 60 percent of all the lead stories on CBS network news during the 1980 campaign involved the presidency (*Over the Wire and on TV: CBS and UPI in Campaign '80* [New York: Russell Sage, 1983], 192).

13. Hess, *Washington Reporters,* 98. Hess analyzed all three networks for one week in 1978. Michael J. Robinson and Margaret A. Sheehan compared CBS network news with UPI in 1980 and found that as a percentage of all news stories CBS paid almost twice as much attention to the White House as did the wire service, although on stories not connected to the campaign the gap was considerably smaller (*Over the Wire and on TV,* 191-92). A discordant note is introduced by Herbert Gans, who compared CBS network news and *Newsweek* magazine for 1967 and found that television actually gave more coverage to members of Congress (17 percent of the 918 television stories about "known" leaders) than to the incumbent president (11 percent) whereas the news magazine gave slightly greater coverage to the incumbent president (12 percent of column inches about "knowns") than to members of Congress (10 percent). See Gans, *Deciding What's News,* 10.

14. Michael J. Robinson, "Three Faces of Congressional Media," in Thomas E. Mann and Norman J. Ornstein, eds., *The New Congress* (Washington, D.C.: American Enterprise Institute, 1983), 91 n37.

15. Ibid.

16. And few studies are likely to since the Television News Archives at Vanderbilt University, the data base that most scholars use, has film beginning in August 1968.

17. Polls conducted by the Roper organization show a steady increase in the public's reliance on television news, from 51 percent in 1959 to 65 percent in 1974. During the same time, newspapers have steadily declined as the public's primary news source, from 57 percent to 47 percent in 1974. The question Roper asks is, "First, I'd like to ask you where you usually get most of your news about what's going on in the world today—from the newspapers or radio or television or magazines or talking to other people or where?" Respondents were allowed to name more than one source. This and other relevant data are reported in Smith, *Changing American Voter,* 181.

18. W. Russell Neuman, *The Paradox of Mass Politics: Knowledge and Opinion in the American Electorate* (Cambridge, Mass.: Harvard University Press, 1986), 144-45.

19. Stephen Hess, *Live from Capitol Hill: Studies of Congress and the Media* (Washington, D.C.: Brookings Institution, 1991), 53, 140-41.

Index

Acheson, Dean, 63, 65, 66, 85, 98, 113, 215n61, 223n76; public approval of, 88–89, 174–75, 225n110; public awareness of, 74, 217n3; relationship with Truman, 89–92, 175, 225n114; Republican criticisms of, 84, 86–88, 221n43. *See also* Truman, Harry

Adams, Ansel, 42–43

Adams, Brock, 112

Adams, Sherman, 140, 159, 160, 177, 178, 199n77, 216n89, 237n164; attacks Democrats, 113; on Benson, 17, 31; characterized as lightning rod, 9; criticized for almost unlimited power, 95, 236n137; on Eisenhower, 66, 75–76, 198n51, 201n9, 244n78; as gatekeeper, 103–4, 114; and Goldfine affair, 115–16; relationship with Eisenhower, 106, 116, 232n52; Republican antipathy toward, 113–14, 115; on role as chief of staff, 101, 105, 229n5; visibility of, 107–8, 233nn64–68, 234n70. *See also* Eisenhower, Dwight David

Adviser: as asset, 7, 10, 258n123; as liability, 4, 7–8, 16, 36–47; as upstager, 7, 96–98, 174, 178–79, 228n162, 231n39, 249n45. *See also* Lightning rod

Agnew, Spiro, 56, 71, 249n45

Agriculture, Department of. *See* Benson, Ezra Taft

Albert, Carl, 155

Alcorn, Meade, 199n85

Allen, Richard, 104

Alsop, Stewart, 250n55

Ambrose, Stephen, 69, 74, 77, 114

Americans for Democratic Action, 58, 60

Anderson, Martin, 110, 202n17

Anderson, Patrick, 3, 192n12

Anderson, Robert, 69, 175, 216n89

Andresen, August, 30–31

Approval rating. *See* Presidential popularity; Public approval

Arens, Moshe, 45

Aswan Dam, 76, 79

Audubon Society, 38–39, 42, 205n61

Ayers, Eban, 223n68

Bacon, Francis, 1

Baker, Howard, 73, 233n59

Baker, James, 33–34, 50, 109, 258n128; as chief of staff, 104, 105; as lightning rod, 110–11, 153, 160; public awareness of, 154; Reagan's success attributed to, 231n39; visibility of, 12, 73, 107, 233n59; upstaging Bush, 7

Ball, George, 59

Balutis, Alan, 185–87, 260n3

Barkley, Alben, 55–56

Barnes, Fred, 209n106

Barrett, Laurence, 36

Bay of Pigs, 175

Bell, Jack, 248n31

Bell, Terrel, 8, 33, 110

Bennett, Stephen Earl, 247n22, 248n27

Bennett, William, 12, 73

Benson, Ezra Taft, 113, 116, 138, 159, 173, 178, 250n50; appointment of, 195n8; characterized as liability, 16, 195n10, 245n3; characterized as lightning rod, 16, 195n9; chastised by Eisenhower, 29–30, 199nn82,85; congressional criticisms of, 20–22, 28–29, 30–31, 197nn43,44, 199n77, 211n133; defended by Eisenhower, 25–26, 43, 200n89; differences with Eisenhower, 30–31; farmers' approval of, 17–19, 154,

263